Pope Francis

His Impact on and Relevance for the Church and Society

Pope Francis

His Impact on and Relevance for the Church and Society

Commemorating Five Years of His Papacy

Edited by
Kuruvilla Pandikattu SJ

 Jnana-Deepa Vidyapeeth

&

 Christian World Imprints™

© Jnana-Deepa Vidyapeeth, Pune

Individual Contributors and the Editor assert the moral right to be identified as Authors of the Articles included/published in this book.

First Published in 2018 by

Jnana-Deepa Vidyapeeth
Ramwadi, Nagar Road, **Pune-411014**
jdvoffice@jdv.edu.in
www.jdv.edu.in
Phone: +91 20 41036111

&

Christian World Imprints™
Christian Publishing & Books from India
H-12 Bali Nagar, **New Delhi-110015**
info@christianworldimprints.com
www.ChristianWorldImprints.com
Phone: +91 11 25465925

ISBN 13: 978-93-5148-277-2   ISBN 10: 93-5148-277-4

Cataloging in Publication Data--DK
  Courtesy: D.K. Agencies (P) Ltd. <docinfo@dkagencies.com>

Pope Francis : his impact on and relevance for the church & society : commemorating five years of his papacy / edited by Kuruvilla Pandikattu SJ.
    pages cm
    ISBN 9351482774
    ISBN 9789351482772
    1. Francis, Pope, 1936- --Influence. 2. Church and the world. 3. Christian leadership--Catholic Church.   I. Pandikattu, Kuruvila, editor. II. Jnana-Deepa Vidyapeeth, publisher.

  LCC BX1378.7.P67 2018 | DDC 262.13   23

Printed in India.

While this book is to celebrate five years of
Pope Francis life and message, I am gald to dedicate
this book to **Prof Dr Jacob Parappally MSFS,** well-known
theologian, who has completed 65 years of his life
with vigour, enthusiasm and hope. He radiates the
Gospel Joy by his life and teaching.
He has also helped me in the editing
of some articles of this book.

Contents

VIII. ENDURING IMPACT

Editorial

Pope Francis has become the conscience of the world. No wonder then, he is the most talked about person in the world today. Wherever he goes he draws a large crowd of people who recognize in him a spiritual leader who epitomizes in his life, and articulates in his words to a great extent, Jesus' vision of being a human in this world. He believes that human beings can experience the true meaning of human existence, and be joyful witnesses of the gospel values of love, justice, freedom, compassion, equality, reconciliation in a society that discriminates between humans on the basis of religion, class, caste, gender and nationality. He pleads with all people of good will to embrace a life of compassion and care for one another, and nature, trusting in a God who embraces everyone with infinite love and compassion.

The world recognizes Pope Francis as a man of God and a religious leader with great authority to inspire, challenge, and exhort everyone to live a life worthy of their human vocation, and to demand justice and fairness from governments and political leaders. Considering his advocacy for the poor, the marginalized, the refugee and the migrant, what impact has he on the Church? Certainly, his pastoral approach to vexing problems in the Church is recognized and appreciated by a majority of Church members. His encyclicals, apostolic letters and exhortations breathe a fresh air of pastoral concern, simplicity and intelligibility, that ordinary Christians and people of other religions easily comprehend. His universally acclaimed and widely discussed encyclical *Laudato Si'* is the best example of his clear and lucid articulation of the right relationship of humans with nature, and the responsibility each human being has in caring for the earth. In matters of faith and morals, Pope Francis seems to have adopted a style of articulating his teaching that use easily comprehensible theological terminologies, and avoid theological jargon in-so-far as possible. He is trying hard to liberate the Church from an ecclesiastical Nestorianism – a point of view that sees the Church dichotomized as an institution and as a spiritual reality. Simultaneouly, Pope Francis is also attempting to rescue the modern Church from an ecclesiastical Monophysitism which considers the Church only a spiritual reality.

The Second Vatican Council's openness of the Church to the modern world, and post-Vatican II struggles to make the Church relevant to that same world have found road-blocks as resistance from those who were alarmed with changes hardened. In fact, those who resist any reform are said to be those who directly benefit from the existing system that they desire to preserve. It is very clear that those who would resist any structural changes in the Vatican curia are probably not moved by any spiritual considerations, but by fear of their own loss of power. Those who resist liturgical reforms, ecumenical efforts toward unity in doctrinal and sacramental matters or inter-religious dialogue, are the very same who fear a loss of security and identity in exclusivism, arrogant absolutism, and static understandings of tradition. They resist maturing from their infantile faith to an adult faith. Those groups include priests, bishops and even cardinals who resist the intentions of Pope Francis to reform the Church as envisioned by the Vatican II Council. Resistance to reform is understandable as some are afraid to let go of a past Church in which they found security and certainty; despite the reality that this past Church no longer has significance.

Pope Francis' training in the school of Ignatian spirituality makes it very important for him to use discernment of the spirits in every decision that affects the universal life of the Church. The objective criteria of discernment are the Christological and ecclesiological congruity of decisions that affect whether and how Church members become more identified with Jesus Christ, and make Her grow in communion. While concerned about safe-guarding and teaching the living tradition of the Church, he exemplifies the human Jesus in his attitude, life-style and relationships. He recaptures and reaffirms the early Church's Christian identity as 'a community of believers with one heart and one soul' whose life-witness reveals that Jesus is still alive.

The overwhelmingly positive impact of Pope Francis on the Church's life is seen in his promotion of inclusivity, openness to dialogue with all humans of good will, compassionate pastoral approach to those who are marginalized within the Church and in society, and willingness to listen to all including those who oppose his views. The Holy Father has made clear that the Church is a true home for all who seek meaning in their lives. He has the courage and conviction to authoritatively speak to leaders of nations, reminding them of their duty to care for the poor, the needy, the refugee and migrant, and for nature. He walks the talk and makes the prophetic mission of Jesus alive - even to virulent critics of the Church who view it only as an institution with enormous power, riches and world-wide influence. Pope Francis reveals the human face of a Church in which one can discover the human face of Christ.

The present volume focuses on the life of Pope Francis and the impact of his papacy on both Church and world. No other global leadership is as frequently discussed as the papal leadership of Pope Francis. With him the world has been once again awakened to look at the Church positively as a community that promotes life and humanizing values.

Our first section is a historical overview. A profile of Pope Francis is first sketched, followed by an article discussing the impact of Pope Francis from reports of the global reception of Pope Francis and his views on the life and mission of the Church in the world of today. This is followed by a second article, which looks at the Pope's role as a "Supreme Bridge-Builder" in engaging other Christians and the larger world.

The next section reflects on his pastoral approach and draws mainly from *Amoris Laetitia*; the apostolic exhortation that has made great impact. These contributions highlight relevance and significant evolutionary changes in Pope Francis' moral and pastoral outlook, and relate how he challenges widespread attitudes that problems are solved by applying general rules or deriving undue conclusions from particular theological considerations in the absence of sufficient reflection and grounding. His "open ear and generous heart" come out forcefully in this exhortation.

The next four articles analyse his "bridge building" capacity and practice of reaching out to the modern world, laity, and religious. The paper, "Gazing at Our World with God's Eyes of Mercy: Pope Francis' Theological Vision" discusses the theological vision of Pope Francis. The author finds striking similarities with St. Francis of Assisi's love of poverty, enthusiasm to renew the Church, love for nature, and a willingness to dialogue with Muslims; it is Trinitarian both in its origin and end. The article "Embracing the Laity: The Vision of Pope Francis" describes a new vision for the Church, as projected by Pope Francis through signs and symbols, and words and actions, as expounded in his *Evangelii Gaudium*. Against the background of that vision, the laity's role is spelled out by a study of Francis' writings, interviews, homilies, messages, and discourses.

The fourth section, "Dialogue as Way of Life" features Pope Francis' dialogue with other religions and the sciences. It talks about the dialogical model of living and believing that is essential for the survival of contemporary humanity. Pope Francis has been at the forefront in dialogue with other religions and disciplines, including both social and natural sciences. The articles in this section discuss Pope Francis' involvement with the world of science to show how he is open to learn from the empirical disciplines and at the same time challenges science when it falls short of its commitment to the total welfare of humanity and nature. The paper also discusses some of the insights from his encyclical *Laudato Si,'* underscoring the need for responsiblity in protecting nature, and the urgent need for integrating Science and Faith.

The next section discusses another aspect very close to Pope Francis' heart: the poor, marginalised, refugees and ostracised. His concern for a just world order, free from exploitation and violence, clarifies his unambiguous stand for the poor.

This alone makes him a prophet for our times. One criticism, whether he has communist tendencies, is also addressed in the last chapter of this section. Here we show that far from communist leanings, Pope Francis is an ardent Christian, who tries to practice the primary Christian commitment to God and to our neighbour.

The three articles in the sixth section deal with his ecological concerns and are based on his earth-moving encyclical, *Laudato Si'*. The article, "The Trinitarian and Christological Dimensions of Ecology in *Laudato Si'*" explains how Pope Francis develops his theological vision on the essential relationship of humans with God and other humans and its implications for human's relationship with nature based on the Trinitarian and Christic experience of God. The following articles discuss the indirect influence of thinkers like Martin Buber, Martin Heidegger and Max Scheler on the encyclical *Laudato Si'* through Romano Guardini. The foundational philosophical vision of *Laudato Si'* is influenced by the critique of Martin Heidegger on Heidigger's "machinational" interpretation of beings that subjugates humans and commodifies nature, as well as his philosophical insights into a way of overcoming it.

Following the discussion of philosophical influences, we present a description of Francis' leadership style, which is life-affirming and merciful. "Pope Francis: Making a New History of Church Leadership" explains how Pope Francis' leadership is different from that of his predecessors and how it makes the Church credible in our times. By 'reading the signs of the times' his paradigm-shifting exercise of Papal ministry expresses the spirit and vision of the ecclesiology of Vatican II. One article also points out the significance of relationality in his understanding of leadership. The last article talks of Pope Francis as a game-changer, whose communitarian approach to leadership fosters a down-up method of decision making.

The final section talks about the 'why' and 'how' of his impact and focusses on his mass media attraction. Pope Francis' influence in both the Church and the world during his five-year period has been enormous. In the midst of numerous crises faced by the recent Church, God has raised up Pope Francis, a prophet for our times, to make the Church a credible witness to the compassionate love of God. His life-style and theological vision, his pastoral heart for those who feel abandoned by the Church because of its laws and regulations, his openness to all things human, and his challenge to the entire Church to make itself the home for the marginalized, make him an authentic Vicar of Christ. Pope Francis' ministers with a leadership and true authority that challenges and devalues all forms of power and power structures that enslave and dehumanize. His life is his mission and is the reflection of incredible witness to Jesus Christ and his Kingdom values. We believe that the Holy Father would agree that his impact is due primarily to his message. That clarion message of joy, peace, forgiveness and mercy, drawn deeply from Jesus' experience of a merciful God, is highly relevant for our times!

We have titled this book "Pope Francis: His Impact on and Relevance for the Church & Society," These sentiments form the basic persona and practice of Pope Francis: Compassion for the poor based on our experience of God, Commitment to God's people and His Kingdom, and Collaboration with ALL people of good will – from theist to atheist, from artist to scientist. It is our firm conviction that only by collectively committing ourselves to all people in compassion (or mercy) and collaborating with each other, can we make this world, "Our Common Home," a heaven on earth, a place of joy, an abode of hope and freedom!

Some of these articles have been adapted from the periodical, *Jnanadeepa: Pune Journal of Religious Studies* and we thank its editors for giving us permission to publish them in this volume. We are immensely grateful to the staff of Jnana-Deepa Vidyapeeth for their comments and suggestions for improving this volume. Some others who have helped me in bringing out this book are Prof Kurien Kunnumpuram SJ, Dr Don Frohlich, Ms Nirmala Chandy, Fr Biju Joseph, Fr Jacob Kulangara SJ and Fr Eric Cassel SJ, without whose helpful suggestions and meticulous corrections, this book would not have seen the day. I also remember my colleagues and students of both Jnana-Deepa Vidyapeeth and Papal Seminary, who have been a source of constant support and encouragement. Specially I acknowledge my indebtedness to Prof Selva Rathinam SJ, President of JDV; Rev Vincent Crasta SJ, Registrar, JDV; Fr Alex G SJ, Treasurer, JDV; Frs Jose Thayil SJ and Bhausaheb Sansare SJ, Rectors of Papal Seminary; and Fr Karunaidass, Minister of Papal Seminary, Pune.

I. HISTORICAL OVERVIEW

Chapter 1

Making of Pope Francis

Jacob Naluparayil MCBS
Smart Companion, Kochi, Kerala

Introduction

Jorge Mario Bergoglio was elected the 266th Pope of the Catholic Church on 13 March 2013, following the resignation of Pope Benedict XVI. Bergoglio has opted to be called Pope Francis, in honour of Saint Francis of Assisi. He is the first Jesuit Pope, the first from the Southern Hemisphere, and the first non-European Pope since Pope Gregory III, 1272 years earlier.

Pope Francis is God's unique gift to the Church, in our times. In order to understand the 'surprise' that he is, we need to look back at the past four and a half years of his pontificate and the tremendous impact he has made on the various facets of the Church and on the world. What was the situation in the Church just before Jorge Bergoglio assumed the Chair of Peter? The scene was marred with growing unrest against the priests accused of pedophilia, the Curia in the shadow of blame regarding homosexuality, and to crown it all, the Vatileaks, which challenged the Church's moral power, and created a feeling of 'fence eating the crop.' Thus the Argentinean Pope stepped in at a moment when the Church was feeling very low with a dwindling self-esteem, fragile and defenseless, her moral authority challenged from within and out. However, within a short span of about five years he has succeeded to conquer the hearts of many, not only among the Catholics or Christians but globally, arousing assurances of hope in all categories of people. Pope Francis' language has been one of mercy and forgiveness, joy and welcome. As a result, the table has been turned over. As of now, the whole world keeps tuned to the moral voice of Pope Francis, especially at the wake of each fresh issue that has global implications. He is perceived as a leader who courageously yet compassionately and wisely analyses and delves into the moral dilemmas and humanitarian problems across the world.

The basic reason for such an amazing paradigm shift in the life of the Church has been due to the unique personality of Pope Francis and its unusual expressions, his extra-ordinary administrative talent and watchfulness. That is why this article is intent on understanding the making of this person called Pope Francis.

The article is comprised of two parts. The first considers in brief, the life sketch of Jorge Mario Bergoglio, the native of Buenos Aires, who later became Pope Francis. The second part is an analysis. We explore the events and experiences that molded and formed Pope Francis, a leader of unprecedented courage and qualities. Thus, we concentrate on the 'making of Pope Francis', running through the significant turns and experiences in his life.

A Brief Life Sketch of Pope Francis

Jorge Mario Bergoglio was born in Buenos Aires, Argentina, on 17 December, 1936.[1] He was the eldest of the five children born to Mario José Bergoglio and Regina María Sívori. José was an Italian immigrant, employed as an accountant by the railways; his wife, a house-wife and a native of Buenos Aires belonged to a family of north Italian origin. In the sixth grade, Bergoglio attended Wilfrid Barón de los Santos Ángeles, a school run by the Salesians of Don Bosco, in Buenos Aires. He further attended the technical secondary school Escuela Nacional de Educación Técnica and graduated with a chemical technician's· diploma. He worked for a few years in the foods section at Hickethier-Bachmann Laboratory.[2] At the age of 21 he suffered from a life-threatening pneumonia and part of a lung was excised shortly afterwards, to do away with cysts.

1. Call to Priesthood

At first, Bergoglio entered the archdiocesan seminary, 'Immaculada Concepción,' in Villa Devoto, Buenos Aires City. Three years later, on 11 March 1958, he joined the Society of Jesus. At the conclusion of his novitiate on 12 March 1960, Bergoglio officially became a Jesuit, when he made the temporary religious profession of the vows.

During 1961-63, he studied Philosophy, graduating from the 'Colegio de San José' in San Miguel. From 1964 to 1965 he engaged a teacher of literature and psychology at The Immaculate Conception College in Santa Fé and in 1966 he taught the same subjects at the 'Colegio del Salvatore' in Buenos Aires. He studied Theology during the years 1967 to 70 graduating from the 'Colegio del San José'. He was ordained a priest on 13 December 1969, by the Archbishop Ramón José Castellano.

a. A Jesuit

Bergoglio completed his final stage of his spiritual formation as a Jesuit, the tertianship, at Alcalá de Henares, Spain during 1970-71, and took his perpetual vows in the Society of Jesus on 22 April 1973. Back in Argentina during 1971-72, he was appointed the novice master at 'Villa Barilari,' San Miguel and Professor at the Faculty of Theology of San Miguel.

He served as Provincial Superior of the Society of Jesus in Argentina from 31 July 1973 to 1979. After the completion of this term, in 1980, he was named the Rector of the Philosophical and Theological Faculty of 'San Miguel.' Before taking up this new appointment, he spent the first three months of 1980 in Dublin, Ireland, to learn English. He continued as Rector at 'San Miguel,' until 1986.[3]

He also spent few months at the Sankt Georgen Graduate School of Philosophy and Theology in Frankfurt, Germany, considering possible dissertation topics. In Germany he saw the painting of 'Mary Untier of Knots' in Augsburg and brought a copy of the painting to Argentina where it has become a popular Marian devotion. After three months of intense study in Germany, Bergoglio opted to return to Argentina, where he was assigned to teach at the seminary in Buenos Aires. In 1990, he was transferred to the Jesuit house in Cordova, 500 miles from Buenos Aires. In many timelines of Pope Francis' life, the years of 1990-1992 remain an unexplained gap.[4]

b. Bergoglio as a Bishop

Cardinal Antonio Quarracino, Archbishop of Buenos Aires, who recognized his real mettle, wanted him to be his close collaborator.[5] Thus on 20 May 1992, Bergoglio was named the auxiliary bishop of Buenos Aires. He chose his Episcopal motto as 'Miserando atque eligendo.' It has been drawn from the homily of Venerable Bede on Matthew 9:9-13: "…he saw him through the eyes of mercy and chose him."

On 3 June 1997, Bergoglio was further appointed Coadjutor Archbishop of Buenos Aires, with the right of automatic succession. In February 1998, he became the Archbishop of Buenos Aires, succeeding Antonio Quarracino. One of Bergoglio's major initiatives as Archbishop was to increase the Church's presence in the slums of Buenos Aires. Under his leadership, the number of priests assigned to work in the slums doubled. On 6 November 1998, he was named ordinary for the Eastern Catholics in Argentina who lacked a prelate of their own rite.

c. Cardinal Bergoglio and Pope Francis

Three years later, in February 2001, he was elevated as cardinal by Pope John Paul II. On 8 November 2005, Bergoglio was elected president of the Argentine Episcopal Conference for a three-year term (2005-08). He was reelected to another three-year term on 11 November 2008. While head of the Argentine Catholic Bishops' Conference, Bergoglio issued a collective apology for his Church's failure to protect the people from the *Junta* during the Dirty War. When he turned 75, in December 2011, Archbishop Bergoglio, as required by Canon Law, submitted his resignation to Pope Benedict XVI. But Divine Providence designed that Bergoglio be elected to the Chair of St. Peter succeeding Benedict XVI.

2. Making of Pope Francis

What exactly are the unique personality traits of Bergoglio, who is engaged to bring about such tangible transformation in the Church and the world scenario? How did the little Jorge transform into today's world acclaimed spiritual leader, Pope Francis? How can one decipher his journey of formation and transformation? One can guess beyond doubt that it was not just his life experiences, but more, his specific responses to them that shaped his life and personality. The modest attempt of this article is to decipher the key experiences and persons who contributed to the nurture of his unique personality.

a. "I am a Sinner"

Fr. Antonio Spadaro, in his first interview with Pope Francis on 19 Aug. 2013, put an abrupt question to Pope Francis, "Who is Jorge Mario Bergoglio?"[6] The reply came after a reflective silence: "I do not know what might be the most fitting description.... I am a sinner. This is the most accurate definition. It is not a figure of speech, a literary genre. I am a sinner...I am a sinner whom the Lord has looked upon."[7]

The Pope further said, "Yes, perhaps I can say that I am a bit astute, that I can adapt to circumstances, but it is also true that I am a bit naïve. Yes, but the best summary, the one that comes more from the inside and I feel most true is this is me, a sinner on whom the Lord has turned his gaze."[8]

When asked about his unique experience of God's mercy he said: "I don't have any particular memories of mercy as a young child. But I do as a young man."[9] It was on September 21, 1953. He was on his way to meet his girlfriend together with the Catholic Action and school friends to celebrate National Student's Day. As he was walking past the Basilica of St. Joseph, he felt an urge to go inside and he went in. Explaining this to Father Isasmendi, he said: "I looked, it was dark, it was a morning, may be 9.00 a.m. and I saw a priest walking, I don't know him, he wasn't one of the parish clergy. And he sits down in one of the confessionals... I don't quite know what happened next, I felt like someone grabbed me from inside and took me to the confessional. Obviously I told him my things, I confessed... but I don't know what happened... Right there I knew I had to be a priest; I was totally certain. Instead of going out with the others I went back home because I was overwhelmed."[10]

When Bergoglio was appointed bishop, he placed mercy of God at the heart of his motto. He explains it: "I always felt my motto, *Miserando atque Eligendo* [Having Mercy and Choosing Him], was very true for me." The motto is taken from the Homilies of Bede the Venerable, who writes in his comments on the Gospel story of the calling of Matthew: 'Jesus saw a publican, and since he looked at him with feelings of love and chose him, he said to him, 'Follow me.'" The Pope adds: "I think it is impossible to translate the Latin gerund 'miserando' both in Italian and Spanish. I like to translate it with another gerund that does not exist: 'misericordiando' ['mercy-ing']."[11]

His ministry as a bishop has always been one of constant remembrance and reflection of the great mercy of God he experienced in his life. He discloses some of his habits of recollecting God's mercy in his life: "...but when I had to come to Rome, I always stayed in (the neighborhood of) Via della Scrofa. From there, I often visited the Church of St. Louis of France, and I went there to contemplate the painting of 'The Calling of St. Matthew' by Caravaggio...That finger of Jesus, pointing at Matthew...that's me. I feel like him...like Matthew. It is the gesture of Matthew that strikes me: he holds on to his money as if to say, 'No, not me! No, this money is mine.' Here, this is me, a sinner on whom the Lord has turned his gaze. And this is what I said when they asked me if I would accept my election as pontiff." Then the Pope whispers in Latin: "I am a sinner, but I trust in the infinite mercy and patience of our Lord Jesus Christ, and I accept in a spirit of penance."[12]

We can guess for sure why the words and deeds of Pope Francis are mercy-laden. He is a man who always keeps alive his personal history of God's mercy on him. That is why he is capable of relating with merciful words and actions to every person who comes before him. That is why he could, without a moment's hesitation, draw closer to Vinicio Riva from Vicenza, who had a deformed and frightening face due to Neurofibromatosis, and embrace him warmly. As Pope he took the initiative to declare a special year of mercy and led it with his own examples of mercy to all categories of needy and distressed people. Yes, the intimate experience of divine mercy in his own life is the reason why he could enthrone mercy in the heart of Christian life, of ecclesial life.

b. Dark Night of the Soul

When Pope Francis was the Cardinal of Buenos Aires, a political leader who was forced to resign, came to visit him. He was seeking strength and comfort from the Cardinal to be able to face his loneliness and defeat. After a significant silence Bergoglio spoke to him: "Manuel, you've got to live your exile. I did. And afterward you'll be back. And when you do come back you will be more merciful, kinder, and you're going to want to serve your people more."[13]

While he gave this advice to this man, his mind must have been ruminating on his own experiences at Cordoba, during 1990-92. This was just before his becoming the Auxiliary bishop of Buenos Aires. He had completed his term as the Provincial of Argentinean Jesuit Province and had also served as rector for six years. He was just back from Germany after an aborted thesis plan. Many depict this period as the "dark night of his soul". We hardly know much about this period of his life in Cordoba.[14] After Bergoglio became the Pope, CNN Editor Daniel Burke undertook a journey to the Jesuit residence in Cordoba to meet and converse with the confreres of Bergoglio during the period of his life in 'darkness.'[15]

One of them, Brother Louis Rausch had this to say: "Bergoglio spent many hours in solitude. He understood that he had to remain silent and obedient because he was being punished... When he arrived in room no. 5 in Cordoba, Bergoglio was a priest without a portfolio...His official duty was to hear confessions, listening in his room for the buzz of the doorbell to tell him that some guilt-wracked soul wanted to unburden itself of sin... Occasionally, Bergoglio would say Mass, filling in for the head priest of the Iglesia de la Compania."[16]

Ricardo Spinacci was the housekeeper at the residencia, when Bergoglio lived there. Now he has reached his good old age. He describes his old friend as a creature of habit. "He began each day with the same chore, washing one of his two pairs of socks, and ate the same meal for lunch every day - vegetables and chicken. In the early morning hours, he prayed in the Jesuits' domestic chapel, alone with the bones of the Jesuit saints. He knew he was being punished. He prayed like a saint."[17]

Juan Carlos Scannone, an elderly Jesuit who has known Bergoglio since the 1950s said that casting him out to Cordoba was clearly a punishment and that he was truly suffering. "I saw it in his face. I could see he was going through a spiritual purification, a dark night."[18]

Javier Camara, a Catholic journalist who spoke to Bergoglio about this period said that Bergoglio was well aware of the 'darkness' of this period. He told Camara: "It was a time of purification. In darkness one can't see things clearly. So I prayed much, read a lot, wrote even more and lived my life. What I did in Cordoba had more to do with my inner life."[19]

Anyone can easily grasp the significance of this 'dark period' in the formation of the future Pope. Bergoglio was a person who handled the unpleasant experiences and the oppositions in his life with an attitude of prayerful and humble dependence on God. The antagonism towards him was the strongest in the Argentinean Jesuit Province, just after his term as the Provincial (1973-78) and rector (1980-86). His exile in Cordoba marked the climax of such opposition (1990-92). The state of his inner self in those 'dark' days had been transcribed in his writings of the time, which definitely held a mirror to his mind. One can conclude that the 'failures' and pains of his yonder days did have a significant role in his formation as today's Pope Francis.

c. Provincial and the Dirty War

At the backdrop of this dark period on could see is the time he was the Provincial of the Argentinean Jesuit Province. He was then a young Jesuit of 36. At that time Argentina was under the Military Regime of Jose Rafael Videla. Human rights violations and atrocities were rampant under the Videla regime. Anyone who dissented would disappear and about 30,000 people were reported missing during this period. Leftist Guerilla movements like the Montoneros (MPM) and the Marxist People's Revolutionary Army (ERP) fought against the Military rule.[20] Their policy was one of 'tit for tat' - fight violence with violence; fighting state terrorism with organized terrorism. These movements naturally had deep roots among the poor who were suffering in fear and distress.[21]

After the Vatican II with its thrust on renewal and openness to the world, Liberation Theology found a fertile soil in Argentina. These trends created at least two categories of people within the Church there. While one group silently supported the government, ignoring the pathetic state of the people, the other resorted to violence in order to free the people from the Army outrages.

The Jesuits at large stood for the cause of the people. Bergoglio kept a low profile, neither praising nor condoning the Military rule. As Provincial, his prime aim was to protect the priests under his care.[22] But the activities of two Jesuits in particular made his ministry very difficult. Inspired by the Liberation Theology, Franz Jalics and Orlando Yorio organized a 'base community' in a Buenos Aires barrio. Bergoglio allowed the priests to engage but warned them to be wary of the military.[23] Eventually as the situation turned risky for their life, they were asked to choose either the *barrio* or the Society of Jesus.[24] They preferred to choose the *barrio*. A few days later, the military arrested both of them and took them away. After two months they were left in a farmland, drugged and half naked.[25]

Bergoglio had to face a lot of criticism on account of the arrest and torture of these young priests. Yorio, for years, blamed the Provincial for their kidnapping, accusing him of leaving them unprotected, and even of pointing them out to the military. Instead, Jalics said he would not blame Bergoglio for his capture.[26]

Although this was a major issue during Bergolio's provincialship, what led him to Cordoba may not have only been this. The Jesuits in Buenos Aires had serious differences of opinion regarding his style of functioning and his priorities.[27] He has spoken about his style of performance at this time and the shortcomings he perceived in himself: "In my experience as a superior in the Society, to be honest, I have not always done the necessary consultation. And this was not a good thing. My style of government as a Jesuit at the beginning had many faults. That was a difficult time for the Society: an entire generation of Jesuits had disappeared. Because of this I found myself provincial when I was still very young. I was only 36 years old. That was crazy. I had to deal with difficult situations, and I made my decisions abruptly and by myself. Yes, but I must add one thing: when I entrust something to someone, I totally trust that person... But despite this, eventually people get tired of authoritarianism."[28]

One could not be more candid in acknowledging one's drawbacks as when he said, "My authoritarian and quick manner of making decisions led me to have serious problems and to be accused of being ultraconservative. I lived a time of great interior crisis when I was in Cordoba. It was my authoritarian way of making decisions that created problems."[29] Obviously, young Bergoglio, who as Provincial led the Argentinean Jesuits in a very critical historical period, learned some extremely hard lessons for life, from his own sufferings. It brought about solid changes in his life and behaviour. He said, "History and time has taught me many lessons. The Lord allowed me to grow in my administrative skills through my own sins and liabilities."[30] One can see how Bergoglio took life's lessons wisely and learnt from his mistakes with openness and humility - specific characteristics we see in him now as he goes through the many tensions of being a Pope in difficult times.

After the 'dark night' of Cordoba, we next see Bergofglio as the Auxiliary bishop of Buenos Aires. Later he was made the Archbishop. We can easily observe a U-turn in the style of his functioning in the new service. He was making a conscious effort to make decision-making more participative. He observes, "As Archbishop of Buenos Aires, I had a meeting with the six auxiliary bishops every two weeks, and several times a year with the council of priests. They asked questions and we opened the floor for discussion. This greatly helped me to make the best decisions."[31]

d. Dialogue, Discernment, Decentralisation

It was the person of Bergoglio who had been fashioned in the crucible of time, turmoil and grace, who stood as Pope Francis in the balcony of the St. Peter's Basilica, on 13 March, 2013, waving at the huge crowd gathered down square. After five days of his election as the Supreme Pontiff, he spoke to Cardinal Oscar Rodriguez about the formation of a consultative body to assist him in the new governance. Thus was formed a consultative body with eight cardinals. The number rose to nine when later Cardinal Pietro Parolin, the Secretary of State, was brought in. The first sitting of the consultants was in October 2013. Ever since, Francis has convened the body of consultants 20 times, the last being on 6-8 June, 2017.

Pope Francis is very committed to this consultative body and faithfully follows up every detail. His perception about the advisory group is significant: "The consultation group of eight cardinals, this 'outsider' advisory group, is not only my decision, but it is the result of the will of the cardinals, as it was expressed in the general congregations before the conclave. And I want to see that this is a real, not ceremonial consultation."[32] The shift from his old authoritarian style to the new consultative style is obvious. This consultative and decentralized style is yielding good results in his ministry as Pope.

In fact, decentralization of power in the Church is a dream in his mind, and is often explicated in his discourses about a participatory Church. He writes: "Like the ancient patriarchal Churches, Episcopal conferences are in a position 'to contribute in many and fruitful ways to the concrete realization of the collegial spirit'. Yet this desire has not been fully realized, since a juridical status of Episcopal conferences which would see them as subjects of specific attributions, including genuine doctrinal authority, has not yet been sufficiently elaborated. Excessive centralization, rather than proving helpful, complicates the Church's life and her missionary outreach."[33]

He has very clear vision about the National/Regional bishops' conferences and their specific role in the life of the Church. He specifies the orientation regarding the authority and mission of these Conferences as follows: "I would make it clear that not all discussions of doctrinal, moral or pastoral issues need to be settled by interventions of the magisterium. Unity of teaching and practice is certainly necessary in the Church, but this does not preclude various ways of interpreting some aspects of that teaching or drawing certain consequences from it... Each country or region, moreover, can seek solutions better suited to its culture and sensitive to its traditions and local needs."[34]

To peak it all, one can see that the utmost influence and motivation in his multifarious interventions, probably, is the Ignatian Spirituality. He seems to be rooted in it. To the question "Which aspect of Ignatian Spirituality does help you the most in the papal mission?" he responds with hardly any hesitation: "Discernment... It is one of the things that worked inside St. Ignatius. For him it is an instrument of struggle in order to know the Lord and follow him more closely."[35]

Pope Francis explains: "This discernment takes time. For example, many think that changes and reforms can take place in a short time. I believe that we always need time to lay the foundations for real, effective change. And this is the time of discernment... Discernment is always done in the presence of the Lord, looking at the signs, listening to the things that happen, the feeling of the people, especially the poor... Discernment in the Lord guides me in my way of governing."[36]

The Ignatian spirituality did play a definite role in the formation of this great spiritual leader. Not only during the period of 34 years from 1958 to 1992, but also, throughout his life and ministry, it was Jesuit formation and the spirituality of St. Ignatius, their Founder, that stood by him through thick and thin.[37]

e. Grandmother, Parents

On the occasion of the homily on a Palm Sunday, Francis drifted from the pre-prepared text and switched over to his spontaneous style: "My grandmother used to tell us children, 'A funeral shroud has no pockets!' As a child, I did not fully grasp the meaning of what she said. When I grew up I understood that a dead body does not need to carry a pocket full of things. Its journey is differently destined."[38] This is not the only occasion when Francis made references to his grandmother Rosa. It is obvious that she has had the greatest influence on young Bergoglio. Responding to a question, he said "...I feel a special devotion to my grandmother for all that she gave me in the first years of my life."[39]

Bergoglio recalled: "My strongest childhood memory is that of the life shared between my parents' house and my grandparents' house. The first part of my childhood, from the age of one, I spent with my grandmother." Rosa began taking care of Jorge after his brother Oscar was born, collecting him each morning and dropping him back in the afternoon.[40]

Again, it was his grandmother Rosa, who introduced him to Jesus and taught him to pray. She was a wonderful transmitter of faith. "On Good Friday she took her grandchildren to see the crucified Christ and told them how he was dead but would rise on Sunday."[41] When she was widowed and frail, Rosa was looked after by the Italian nuns in San Miguel. As she lay dying, Jorge kept vigil by her bed, holding her body until life left it. Sister Catalina, one of the sisters, recalls: "He told us: 'At this moment my grandmother is at the most important point of her existence. She is being judged by God... A few minutes later, he got up and left, as serene as ever."[42]

It was from her mother that Jorge learned a simple and thrifty life style. María Elena, sister of Bergoglio recalled: "We were poor, but with dignity... Mama succeeded in salvaging some article of clothing for us, even from our father's things: a ripped shirt or fraying pants got repaired and sewn up, became ours. May be the extreme frugality of my brother and mine comes from this."[43]

When Rubin and Ambrogetti asked about his culinary skills, Jorge said: "My mother became paralyzed after giving birth to her fifth child, although she recovered over time. But during that period, when we got home from school we'd find her seated, peeling potatoes, with all the other ingredients laid out. Then she'd tell us how to mix and cook them, because we didn't have any clue. 'Now put this in the pot and that in the pan...' she'd explain. That's how we learned to cook."[44]

Bergoglio recalls with great gratitude the positive influence his father had in his life: "I'm so grateful to my father for making me work. The work I did was one of the best things I've done in my life. In particular, in the laboratory I got to see the good and bad of all human endeavour."[45] It was when he finished elementary school, barely thirteen years old, his father asked him to take up a part-time job. Thus he started working in a hosiery factory, where his father worked for. For the first two years, he worked as a cleaner, and then he was shifted to administrative work. When he attended a technical school, he managed to find work in a laboratory, where he would work from 7a.m. to 1p.m. Thereafter he attended classes until 8 p.m.[46]

One of the three key women in his childhood was Sister Dolores Tortolo, a Mercy nun. She was the one who prepared him for his First Holy Communion at the age of eight. Later, when he was seriously sick as a young seminarian, she was there at his sick bed as a source of strength. As a priest and later archbishop, he used to visit her in the convent. When she died in 2006, he spent the whole night in prayer next to her body in the convent chapel.[47]

The childhood experiences and the persons whom he associated with in his younger years of life had tremendous influence in molding and forming Jorge Bergoglio: especially his grandmother Rosa, his parents and Sister Dolores.

Conclusion

Some say that the changes in the Church during the past four and a half years are more than what happened in last four centuries. While there has been absolutely no change in the dogmatic teachings of the Church, there has been a revolutionary change in her attitudes, approach and style. In spite of considerable resistance, such attitudinal and stylistic changes have evoked greater confidence, hope and enthusiasm in the ordinary believers. This shift has come about due to Pope Francis, his approach to the world, humanity and the environment.

As for everyone else, Bergoglio's life in the family and his childhood experiences definitely had a major share in his formation as a person. However, what made him the magnetic, charismatic, humble and trusting person he is today is his incomparable capacity to be open to his own experiences, to accept his failures and learn new lessons from them all. He was willing to 'walk humbly before his God' and to make desirable changes in his life, learning from the hard lessons, life taught him. Thus we have today Pope Francis, whose unparalleled brilliance and truth-based humility take him closer to humanity.

Endnotes

1   For an official life sketch of Pope Francis, see http://w2.vatican.va/content/francesco/en/biography/documents/papa-francesco-biografia-bergoglio.html

2   For details, see Austen ivereigh, *The Great Reformer: Francis and the Making of a Radical Pope,* Henry Holt and Company, New York, 2014, 33.

3   For a brief description on that period, see Paul Vallely, *Pope Francis: Untying the Knots,* Bloomsbury, 2013, last part of chapter 3. Also Ivereigh, *The Great Reformer,* 205-209.

4   http://w2.vatican.va/content/francesco/en/biography/documents/papa-francesco-biografia-bergoglio.html

5   The interview of Father Antonio spadaro S.J., the editor of the Jesuit Journal *Civilta Cattolica,* published under the title, "A Big Heart Open to God." It was a very significant an unprecedented papal interview and was simultaneously published in 15 Jesuit journals across the world. Cf. Ivereigh, *The Great Reformer,* 167-168. For the full text of the interview, see https://www.americamagazine.org/faith/2013/09/30/big-heart-open-god-interview-pope-francis.

6   https://www.americamagazine.org/faith/2013/09/30/big-heart-open-god-interview-pope-francis

7   https://www.americamagazine.org/faith/2013/09/30/big-heart-open-god-interview-pope-francis. See also Sergio Rubin - Franesca Ambrogetti, *Pope Francis: Conversations with Jorge Bergoglio: His Life in His Own Words*, Hodder & Stoughton, 2013, in Chapter 4.

8   Pope FRANCIS, *The Name of God is Mercy*, Random House, New York, 2016, 11.

9   Ivereigh, *The Great Reformer*, 35-36. https://www.americamagazine.org/faith/2013/09/30/big-heart-open-god-interview-pope-francis.

10   https://www.americamagazine.org/faith/2013/09/30/big-heart-open-god-interview-pope-francis. Pope Francis, *The Name of God is Mercy*, 11-12.

11   https://www.americamagazine.org/faith/2013/09/30/big-heart-open-god-interview-pope-francis. Ivereigh, *The Great Reformer*, 207.

12   IVEREIGH, *The Great Reformer*, 207.

13   For a brief description on that period, see VALLELY, *Pope Francis: Untying the Knots*, final part of chapter 3.

14   Daniel BURKE, *The Pope's Dark Night of the Soul*, See http://edition.cnn.com/interactive/2015/09/specials/pope-dark-night-of-the-soul/

15   http://edition.cnn.com/interactive/2015/09/specials/pope-dark-night-of-the-soul/

16   http://edition.cnn.com/interactive/2015/09/specials/pope-dark-night-of-the-soul/

17   http://edition.cnn.com/interactive/2015/09/specials/pope-dark-night-of-the-soul/; For a brief presentation of his life in Cordoba, see Ivereigh, *The Great Reformer*, 205-209.

18   http://edition.cnn.com/interactive/2015/09/specials/pope-dark-night-of-the-soul/

19   IVEREIGH, *The Great Reformer*, 98.

20   The political scenario of Argentina was more complex at that time. To have a summary description on that, see IVEREIGH, *The Great Reformer*, 96-99.

21   In his conversations with Rubin and Ambrogetti, Jorge Bergoglio opens his heart on this issue. See RUBIN-AMBROGETTI, *Pope Francis: Conversations,* Chapter 14.

22   On this see, IVEREIGH, *The Great Reformer*, 129-131, 151-164.

23   When asked on this, Jorge Bergoglio responds: "To answer that I must start by saying that they were planning to set up a religious congregation and they gave the first draft of the Rules to Monsignors Eduardo Pironio, Vicente Zazpe, and Mario José Serra. I still have the copy they gave me. The superior general of the Jesuits, who then was Father Pedro Arrupe, told them they had to choose between the community they were living in and the Company of Jesus, and ordered them to move to a different community. As they persisted in their project and the group broke up, they were asked to leave the Company. It was a long internal process that lasted more than a year. It was not a hasty decision of mine. When Yorio's resignation was accepted, along with that of Father Luis Dourrón, who was working with them. Jalics's couldn't be accepted, as he had taken the solemn vow; only the Pope could accede to the request - it was March 1976, the nineteenth, to be exact, that is five days before the government of Isabel Perón was overthrown. In view of the rumors of an imminent coup d'état, I told them to be very careful. I remember I offered them the chance to come and live in the Company's provincial house, in the interests of their safety." See RUBIN-AMBROGETTI, *Pope Francis: Conversations,* Chapter 14.

24   IVEREIGH, *The Great Reformer*, 161.

25   IVEREIGH, *The Great Reformer*, 164. To read the version of Pope Francis on this incident, see Rubin-Ambrogetti, *Pope Francis: Conversations,* Chapter 14.

26   To read more about the rift originated in the Jesuit province around the personality of Bergoglio, see IVEREIGH, *The Great Reformer*, 106-164. Vallely, *Pope Francis: Untyinng the Knots*, in Chapter 3: "The tension which was to grow between what developed into Bergogliano and anit-Bergogliano factions divided the province in two. There were two main areas of conflict. One was religious, the other political."

27   https://www.americamagazine.org/faith/2013/09/30/big-heart-open-god-interview-pope-francis

28   https://www.americamagazine.org/faith/2013/09/30/big-heart-open-god-interview-pope-francis.

29   https://www.americamagazine.org/faith/2013/09/30/big-heart-open-god-interview-pope-francis.

30   https://www.americamagazine.org/faith/2013/09/30/big-heart-open-god-interview-pope-francis.

31   https://www.americamagazine.org/faith/2013/09/30/big-heart-open-god-interview-pope-francis.

32   Pope FRANCIS, *Evangelii Gaudium (The Joy of the Gospel)*. Apostolic Exhortation, 2013, 32.

33   Pope FRANCIS, *Amoris Laetitia (The Joy of Love)*. Apostolic Exhortation, 2016, 3.

34   https://www.americamagazine.org/faith/2013/09/30/big-heart-open-god-interview-pope-francis. See also, Ivereigh, *The Great Reformer*, 170. Explaining 'discernment,' Pope Francis put it as "the Jesuit means of distinguishing good and bad spirits as the 'instrument of struggle in order to know the Lord and follow him more closely.' Discernment, he said, 'guides me in my way of governing."

35   https://www.americamagazine.org/faith/2013/09/30/big-heart-open-god-interview-pope-francis

36   To read more on this, see Alejandro Bermúdez, *Pope Francis: Our Brother, Our Friend. Personal Reflections about the Man who Became Pope*, Igantius, 2013.

37   http://www.catholicworldreport.com/2013/03/24/the-palm-sunday-homily-of-pope-francis/

38   RUBIN-AMBROGETTI, *Pope Francis: Conversations*, in Chapter 1.

39   IVEREIGH, *The Great Reformer*, 13. Rubin-Ambrogetti, *Pope Francis: Conversations,*in Chapter 1.

40   IVEREIGH, *The Great Reformer*, 14.

41   IVEREIGH, *The Great Reformer*, 16.

42   IVEREIGH, *The Great Reformer*, 17.

43   RUBIN-AMBROGETTI, *Pope Francis: Conversations*, in Chapter 1. Ivereigh, *The Great Reformer*, 25.

44   RUBIN-AMBROGETTI, *Pope Francis: Conversations*, Chapter 2.

45   RUBIN-AMBROGETTI, *Pope Francis: Conversations*, Chapter 2. See also, Ivereigh, *The Great Reformer*, 33.

46   IVEREIGH, *The Great Reformer*, 12.

47   IVEREIGH, *The Great Reformer*, 35-36 See also https://www.americamagazine.org/faith/2013/09/30/big-heart-open-god-interview-pope-francis.

Chapter 2

Pope Francis
Pontifex Maximus

Mathew Chandrankunnel CMI
Director, Ecumenical Christian Centre, Bangalore, Karnataka

Presence can change the history of humanity. Mahatma Gandhi, Martin Luther King, Nelson Mandela have changed the course of history through their magnificent presence in our times. Cultures and nations followed them because of their self-sacrificing presence, meaning giving presence. They were the new paradigms, new style of functioning, transforming the individual and the society at large just like a catalyst in a chemical reaction. At present Pope Francis is changing the course of history through his infectious smiling presence, attracting everybody with his simple humanistic approach, irrespective of whether s/he is religious or an atheist. His presence exhibits the power of presence; existence as message, transforming everyone in this planet in a positive way. His presence is magnificently visible as the greatest bridge builder, between nations, for example between the United States and Cuba, divided factions in Columbia, between the Orthodox Churches and the Catholic Church through the mediation of Patriarchs and esteemed Church leaders like His Holiness Patriarch Kyril in Havanna, Cuba, standing with the suffering Christians of Egypt and in communion with the Coptic Christians and Pope Tewadros, sharing the pain of the Armenians who were martyred during the World War I in Armenia, and visiting numerous countries where Christianity is a minority like Myanmar, Bangladesh, Sri Lanka, Bosnia-Herzegovina, Albania etc. The puritanical outlook towards the LGBT community was reformed by Pope Francis by asking the question, "Who am I to judge them"? Through the encyclical, *Laudato Si'* Pope Francis brought out the cry of the poor and the cry of nature to be listened to for the progress and sustainability of humanity and nature. It was similar to St. Augustine of the 4th century and St. Bonaventure of the 13th century being in dialogue with the culture, critically evaluating its foundations and rebooting its values and principles. Thus through his presence, Pope Francis is becoming a bridge builder, meaningfully bearing his title as Pontifex Maximus![1]

1. Diagnosis of Crisis by Husserl

Edmund Husserl, the founder of phenomenology, a mathematician turned psychologist-philosopher diagnosed in his last unfinished work "The Crisis of European Sciences and Transcendental Philosophy" the severe maladies that affected the European civilization.[2] In his description of the European culture, he found a crisis that affected not only the sciences but also of life itself. He was concerned about the situation and proposed ways and means of recovering from this crisis, the hopelessness and the meaninglessness that firmly gripped a fraction of humanity almost a century ago. In his analysis the crisis starts with Galileo and his founding of the Science in terms of studying the phenomena in terms of mathematics and practical experiments with the final goal of manipulating nature through the technological conversion of the scientific knowledge into gadgets that help in encountering the immediate environment of humanity.[3] In addition to Galileo, Husserl pinpointed two other thinkers of the modernity, namely Descartes for his dualistic division of reality and his dissection of the human person into *Res Cogitans* and *Res Extensa,* namely the division of reality into matter and spirit, body and mind. In the same way Kant divided reality into *noumena* and *phenomena* and came out with the proposal that pure reason could not reach out to the noumena and as a regulating mechanism, practical reason can attain knowledge about the noumenal, namely, God, the immortality of the soul and the totality of the world. This scientific analysis of Husserl was continued vigorously by the great thinkers of the twentieth century like Heidegger who advocated that the present day sciences are calculative instead of meditative and found that the malady is because of the oblivion of *Being* and made the clarion call for the recovery of the *Being.* Maurice Merleau Ponty, Emmanuel Levinas and scores of other phenomenologists continued the Husserlian analysis of the crisis and proposed methods of instilling hope and meaning into each individual human person and society in general to save humanity from this impending fall of gloom.

It must be seen that the development and progress of the West occurred due to the epistemological explosion brought about by the interpretation of the Christian faith employing the Aristotelian Philosophy by Thomas Aquinas. Greek philosophical categories could interpret the Christian faith through this integration. The capability of the human rationality in penetrating the regularities of nature was underlined by Aquinas. This acknowledgement of the power of human reason paved the way for the development of science in unravelling the mysteries of the universe. The Cartesian dualism enhanced the atomistic attitude that reinforced the development of science and technology. Kantian division of the Noumena and Phenomena and the rejection of the possibility of knowing the thing as such shifted the emphasis on to phenomena. Kant made a distinction between the religiously driven morality and the axiomatically driven ethics and enforced the categorical imperative as the underpinning ethical foundation rejecting the religious realm altogether. The Masters of suspicion, namely Nietzsche, Marx and Freud, catapulted the Kantian division and the rejection of the Noumena in an unprecedented way. Nietzsche rejected God altogether, and interpreted the Christian morality as slavish and proclaimed the death of God and projected the East and Zarathustra as a replacement. Marx promoted matter as the basis of life and value and proposed class struggle as the medium of progress. Freud brought in the libidinal energy as the driving force of human life and called for the expression of it explaining the suppression and inhibition of them would create neurosis and psychosis. In continuation of the trend and the apotheosis of matter, Husserl brought in the new method of phenomenology as a solution to the crisis. Unfortunately, the Kantian introduction of the phenomena and the apotheosis of the matter received an altogether impetus from this Husserlian phenomenological interpretation which is indeed taken up further by scientists and technocrats. Matter reigned supreme, market became the norm, science and technology created new oeuvre in reducing the spiritual and psychical into the physical degrading the dignity of the human person and throwing him or her into the dustbin of history. Richard Dawkins,[4] Stephen Hawking,[5] Daniel Dennet[6] and many others proposed that science and technology can explain everything and proposed that the Comtean climax of the human history has already arrived passing through the phases of the religious, metaphysical and the scientific culture.

2. Present-Day Crisis of Humanity

It is almost two decades since humanity has entered into the twenty first century. When Husserl wrote about the European crisis, science was galloping through the European continent by the scintillating discoveries of the theory of relativity, quantum mechanics and the epoch-making industrial revolution that changed the life and meaning of humanity at that time that catapulted the humanity towards unprecedented progress in every field. Today, science and technology are at the verge of transforming every human dream and wish into reality. Virtualand reality are enmeshed and it is difficult to distinguish between them because the real and the virtual are merging into a continuum without knowing where one ends and the other begins. Biomedical engineering creates transferrable body parts that are made out of stem cells; any cell can be made to switch on as stem cells with the infinite potential possibilities of transforming the body; harvesting body parts from face, heart, liver to uterus and implanting them into the live body of another is now possible except that of the brain; genes can be transferred from plants to animals to humans and vice versa; as an example, insulin producing cows in their milk is already a possibility, biologically modified cotton, fruits, meats etc are possible; brinjals almost the size of a pumpkin is possible by transferring genes; cloning and surrogate motherhood stretches the facticities of the human possibilities extending the existence into a wider horizon of unreality and eternity.[7] Biotechnology, Information Technology, Neurotechnology, Nano Technology are fusing the matter, life and consciousness into an inextricable intertwining continuum. Now cyborgs, updating of the memory through nanochips, biomodified microchips are all possibilities that create artificial intelligence transferring robots with almost human like behaviour. The developments and advancements in science and technology is all the more fabulous and one cannot imagine what they would bring in tomorrow. Migration to Mars, getting the resources from other planets, interplanetary travel and the journey to the interior of the body and mind are all possible today. Instead of writing and sending emails, people could send telepathic messages and instead of speaking to the audience, they could download the thoughts of a speaker and the teacher could scan the brain of a student for evaluating him or her. Science and technology are bringing dreams into realities today and what they will bring tomorrow is unimaginable.

Not only in the realm of thought but in the area of economics, politics and many other areas is the Western cultural edifice crumbling down. The melting down of the economy, the Boston Tea Party, the encroachment of the Wall Street are indices of the disillusion and crises of the Western cultural dynamics and the capitalist principles. Warren Buffet, Bill Gates and others are distributing their money for humanitarian causes which seem to be a stop gap mechanism to save capitalism. The collapse of the Soviet Union and Communism is another symbol of the failure of the systems and ideologies that were governing masses and cultures. Thus the Velvet Revolution, the riots in France, the Anna Hazare Movement and the Aam Admi Party in India, and the Arab Spring and the bloody counter revolution against the Muslim Brotherhood underscrope the criseshumanity isfacing today. Isms, systems are collapsing; idols like Marx, Lenin, Mao are crumbling; people and cultures are dissatisfied with the existing systems, rulers, styles and dynamics.

Thus, the unprecedented steam rolling of science and technology also brings in a storm of ethical and moral issues. It is all the more frightening that there is the crisis situation of not only of the Western Culture, but also of the Eastern Culture, the Arab Culture, the African Culture, the Asian Culture almost all cultures and humanity altogether; a crisis because of the erosion of truth, value, spirituality based on God and soul. It is indeed a crisis deeper than Husserl might have conceived of; it is a crisis of the soul which could not be rectified by the mere proposition of a newism like phenomenology or a new method of analysing reality through a discipline. The crisis which Husserl diagnosed and continued in terms of the categories proposed by other thinkers is an index of the importance of the deep rootedness of the crisis and the wide spreading of the crises engulfing not only Europe but the whole world and all cultures. Humanity altogether is at a loss how to find a solution for this crisis and it could only be resolved through new ways of thinking and acting.

3. The Culture of Death

In the twentieth century, Saint Pope John Paul II and Pope Benedict also analysed the cultural situation of today and termed the culture of the times as a "culture of death" that is prevailing and pervading over humanity. Death at the beginning, at the end, as abortion, euthanasia, freezing of human embryos which are potential human beings in the laboratories and fertility centres, manipulation of the stem cells derived from the abortion of embryos for further treatment, are all ethical questions that show the culture of death prevailing over the culture of life. The driving forces of this culture of death are science and technology, market forces, globalization etc. So now the crisis is not only belongs to Europe alone as denoted and diagnosed by Husserl, but spread widely and wildly to the very nook and corner of the globe. So is there any redemption from this looming large gloomy crisis with which we all are entangled?

4. Pope Francis: A Magnificent Presence

At this critical juncture, here comes a meaningful presence. It is the possibility of hospitality, invitation and smile that betrays transcendence. It is the embodiment of beingness, manifesting the unmanifest, visibilising the invisible and making it possible to encounter the mystery. It is a presence that through simple and meaningful gestures and actions initiates and effectively manifests a transformation in person and society. The visible presence effects the invisible transcendence and reminds once again of the necessity of the noumena in the individual and amidst society. The mere silent presence becomes an eloquent unstoppable movement. The presence touches the heart and soul of every individual and moves the masses brining in a new style of presence. This ordinary presence brings in the extraordinary, a decisive and infectious style that catches the attention of the world. It is the smiling presence of Pope Francis with a new style of being the ordinary, making an extraordinary effect on the consciousness of every individual and human society at large. The elderly, the middle-aged, adults, adolescents, men and women and the children, all are caught up in the presence of the Pope with his openness, heroic hospitality, ordinary words, dialogue and communion becoming an infectious movement, instilling the importance of the invisible and the immanence of the transcendence. Pope Francis brings together cultures, nations, communities and once again he holds as the moral authority whose power presides all over the world. I am happy to say that I am proud to be a

Catholic. Pope Francis is indeed a transforming transcendental consciousness, the presence of the manifoldness of meaning with significance.

His style is beingness, emphasizing the ordinary, simplicity, a hospitable presence. Just after his election, he stunned the universe, by bowing before them to get their blessing before he blessed them. Coming by bus with other brother cardinals, being in the queue to get back his stuff, paying from his own pockets rather than designating somebody to collect them, carrying his own bag for international travels, wearing an ordinary habit, sharing ordinary meals, speaking to their hearts, going to the streets, giving hope and love by hugging the depressed, faceless and horrible looking men, welcoming the sick, afflicted and the beggars just as if they were Presidents and Prime Ministers who were queuing up to meet him, being attracted both by the atheists and the theists altogether, by proclaiming that he does not believe in a Catholic God, that God is not reserved to any community orreligion and making aloud the proclamation of the Second Vatican Council, that as God's people every one is moving towards this ultimate destiny; these are the facts and experiences all unravelled before us, denoting the infectious style of Pope Francis. Nobody is threatened before his presence, even a boy sits on his throne and clings on to him with infinite confidence, a child writing on his grey hair filled head with its little finger is indeed an index of the hospitality it feels as if in the presence of its own mother. Pope Francis is not an intimidating presence but an an amazing grace selected and given by the Holy Spirit to renew and remould the world with a transcendental and luminal presence. His authority is a healing presence. I remember, when Bhartratna CNR Rao told me that he wanted to meet Pope Francis definitely because of seeing how he influences the masses with his mere presence and humble ways. It is not only the view of a scientist, but atheist, political leader, humanist, adult, child, elderly everyone is being attracted by him. Almost the same way, Prof. Dr. Anil Kulkarni, a world-renowned UN expert on climate change, also participated in the Conference organized by the Vatican Academy of Sciences and met Pope Francis, and informed me about the influence of his magnificent presence. His style and substance is the same, becoming a merciful, compassionate fatherly presence rather than an authoritative, dogmatic, assertive pontiff. As Augustine already observed, Pope Francis' task "in this life" therefore "consists in healing the eyes of the heart so that all may be able to see God."

Though he did not change the dogmatic position of the Church, he did not become judgmental by often quoting from them. Pope Francis described that we are just like in a war situation. Like in a field hospital, everyone is wounded. Therefore, there is no point in highlighting the pressure, cholesterol levels of the patients. What is important is providing healing to them. According to Pope Francis, the ministry of the Church is making the healing rather than emphasizing certain doctrinal positions and explaining axiological parameters. He showed it through baptizing the child of an unwed mother in the Sistine Chapel, calling people directly from his own phone, writing to them, interacting with them, inviting the household of the Pope for Mass, etc. Through such simple ordinary actions, he touched the hearts of the people. It generated a transformational leadership and transcendental consciousness. There are many who want to see that the Pope is a Pantocrator, Omnipotent Lord of the whole Universe. But seeing the simplicity of the Pope some could not digest and even kept harping that he should resign. The oft-repeated being with the Church acclaim *Centire cum Ecclesia* is selectively forgotten as if they could only be with the Church if their own projections of the Church are visible and practised. Pope Francis is indeed his name sake, following the footsteps of the Master, Jesus Christ, being with the people and in communion with the Father. He is an embodiment of love, compassion, mercy, friendliness though he acts with firmness, conviction and vision. The ideas of Vatican Council's openness towards humanity are glowing in his eyes; the joy of the Gospel is what he drives home into every individual's heart. The Encyclical "The Joy of the Gospel" has become the manifesto of Pope Francis' Pontificate. The challenges Pope Francis faces are numerous. The dwindling attendance in church in Europe and North America, hunger and persecution in the Middle East, Africa and Latin America, the scandals of the Church leaders as paedophilia, money laundering, etc., at the global level; moral issues like gay marriage, abortion and communion for the remarried and divorced Catholics, the increasing gap between the rich and the poor, are to be resolved sternly and calmly. Pope Francis attends to these challenges as opportunities. On February 14, 2017 he called engaged couples and addressed them. They enthusiastically welcomed him and, he in turn, advised them on the necessity of having the attitudes expressed in such ordinary words as 'please''thank you''sorry' etc. As Tony Augustine, a layman and catechism Principal of Ulsoor, Bangalore, where I was Parish Priest, said that though the advice of the Pope is tough to follow these principles, but it is a brilliant talisman for building a peaceful and complementary family, where the partners are expected to be respectful to towards each other in encountering everyday life affectionately. In short, Pope Francis has taken the aging institution of the Church which could have been drowning in the risk of irrelevancy, revitalized it through a series of meaningful symbolic gestures like kissing the face of a disfigured man or washing the feet of a Muslim woman, the image that resonates beyond the boundaries of the Catholic Church, into the hearts of people and reverberates as a movement of compassion, mercy and love. At a time when the limits of leadership are decaying cultures, here is a man with no army or weapons, but armed with his infectious smile, simplicity and generosity is renewing the Church, arousing hope and peace all over the world and stands as the light of the world and salt of the earth. So by bringing back the noumena, transcendence into the midst of the public space through his presence, that is rejected both by science and philosophy, Pope Francis could turn the tsunami of the cultural crisis deepened with the crisis of the soul. He is indeed a consciousness that influences the humanity, in its urge for transformation and transcendence. Being of a transformational, transcendental consciousness, Pope Francis can lead the crisis-driven humanity towards peace and harmony, to meaning and endless hope.

5. Pope Francis: Bridge Builder

From the very beginning of his papacy, Pope Francis showed a new touch of humility, humanity and endearment. Bowing his head before the assembled crowd at St. Peter's Square and his description of himself as a sinner, showed a new style, touching the heart of the common man.[8] In his first interview he accepted that in his leadership style as the Jesuit provincial in Argentina, he had problems and faults. He accepted that "it was my authoritarian way of making decisions that created problems". As he was aware of the authoritarianism, Pope Francis wanted to have a Synodal Church, a communion of Churches. The Secretary of the Congregation for Christian Unity Bishop Farrel confirms this.[9]

Pope Francis has in mind a reform both of the papacy and of the episcopate. So he holds: "Since I am called to put into practice what I ask of others, I too must think about a conversion of the Papacy. It is my duty, as the Bishop of Rome, to be open to suggestions which can help to make the exercise of my ministry more faithful to the meaning which Jesus Christ wished to give it and to the present needs of evangelization" (*Evangelii Gaudium* 32). Further, Pope Francis is convinced that, as he said at the commemoration of the fiftieth anniversary of the Synod of Bishops, on 17 October 2015, "in a Synodal Church, greater light can be shed on the exercise of the Petrine primacy. The Pope is not, by himself, above the Church; but within it as one of the baptized, and within the College of Bishops as a Bishop among Bishops, called at the same time — as Successor of Peter — to lead the Church of Rome which presides in charity over all the churches."

Bishop Farrel continued that the other Churches appreciated the welcome revolution Pope Francis brought into the Catholic Church and asked the question why were the ecumenical partners happy? Bishop Farrel continued that "They nourish high hopes that the work of reform he has undertaken in the Catholic Church will bring a decisive benefit to their communities too, and that their dialogue with the Catholic Church, renewed along the lines suggested by Pope Francis, will more and more become a joint search for the will of Christ, free from any preconceived self-sufficiency or self-reference." Pope Francis might have been convinced of his authoritarian rule as the Provincial of the Jesuits and how it misfired and that led to his motivation for collective decisions and gave freedom to air different views even in synods. In the encyclical Pope Francis observed that "The Second Vatican Council stated that, like the ancient Patriarchal Churches, Episcopal Conferences are in a position to contribute in many and fruitful ways to the concrete realization of the collegial spirit'. Yet this desire has not been fully realized, since the juridical status of Episcopal Conferences has not yet been sufficiently elaborated" (*Evangelii Gaudium* 32). Pope Francis' love and affection for the Orthodox Churches is also very remarkable. He expressed that "To give just one example, in the dialogue with our Orthodox brethren, we Catholics have a chance to learn something more about the meaning of Episcopal collegiality and their experience of synodality" (*Evangelii Gaudium* 246). That is the reason why Pope Francis took all the diplomatic efforts to meet the Patriarch Kyril of Moscow since the Russian Orthodox Church had a very difficult relationship with the Catholic Church. The generous gift of the relic of St. Nicholas to the Russian Orthodox Church made the relations between the Churches more cordial and mutually acceptable. When I was visiting Russia a decade ago, I felt the strong revulsion they felt towards the Catholic Church. When they hear that 'I am a Catholic', I remember a monk in a Monastery was running away exclaiming "Oh he is a Catholic". Pope Francis took new initiatives to break such old barriers and connect deeply with the Orthodox Churches. He visited the Armenian Church and prayed together and commemorated the centenary of the sad genocide of the Armenian Christians. He also visited Egypt and showed his compassion and support to the Ethiopian Church that was experiencing martyrdom due to the is activities. Three years ago, I had the opportunity to visit His Holiness Baselios Paulose II Catholicose of the Orthodox Church of India. As soon as I met him, he told me that 'we all should come together'. Then His Holiness explained that he received much affection and love from the Holy Father when he visited Rome. He narrated that experience. After the usual meetings and theological discussions, in an early morning before day break, Catholicose was waiting for his car to arrive so that he could take leave of the Vatican. Then he saw a figure in white coming towards him and, to his surprise, it was Pope Francis! He was coming to embrace him and to see him off! That gesture of love and warmth really touched Catholicose as he really expressed his affection and love towards me as a Catholic with the genuine interest of welcoming a fellow Christian. It was not the theological discussions nor the personal relationships but the warmth and affection that changed the whole attitude of Catholicose. Yes, I think Pope Francis is in this perspective, a great builder of bridges through his personal charm, approachability and genuine expression of communion.

Pope Francis participated in the Fifth Centenary of the Catholic-Lutheran Divide in Sweden on 31ˢᵗ October 2016 and signed the Joint Declaration that would pave "a new opportunity for a common path". Pope Francis prayed that "the Holy Spirit help us to rejoice in the gifts that have come to the Church through the Reformation, prepare us to repent for the dividing walls that we, and our forebears, have built, and equip us for common witness and service in the world." During the celebration Pope Francis emphasized that this new opportunity should help us to move from dissension and discord and move towards reconciliation and renewal. This anniversary is an "opportunity to mend a critical moment of our history by moving beyond the controversies and disagreements that have often prevented us from understanding one another," and this separation "has been an immense source of suffering and misunderstanding". On October 29, 2017 in Bangalore, the CSI, Catholic, Orthodox, Jacobite and Lutheran Churches came together in continuing the vision created by Church leaders to heal the wounds and search for a common path in St. Mark's Cathedral. The gesture of Pope Francis has thus reverberations all over the world. This commemoration of the Fifth Century was inaugurated by His Eminence George Cardinal Alenchery at St. Mark's Cathedral. For the first time a Catholic Church Cardinal was invited to preach there. Thus, Pope Francis' leadership in Ecumenism is paying dividends in bringing together the divided Churches to a communion of witnessing the love and compassion of Christ Jesus.

In the same way Pope Francis was instrumental in bringing together the Pentecostal believers and the Catholic Charismatic leaders. Pope Francis invited around 300 Pentecostal and evangelical leaders to Rome during the 50th Anniversary of the Catholic Charismatic renewal that was celebrated from 31 May to 4 June, 2017. "Catholics, Orthodox, Anglicans and mainline Protestants all come from the same tradition and historical experience of the church of the first millennium and more," that was what Bishop Farrell, the Secretary of the Congregation for Christian Unity observed. "Receptive Ecumenism" is what Bishop Farrel called these kinds of sharing and living together and experiencing the mutual gift. When the Italian Pentecostal leaders came together and met Pope Francis, he told them "unity is achieved through walking patiently together". When he met the Pentecostal leaders Pope Francis commented that he "felt in his heart" the need to undertake steps towards reconciliation, citing the examples of his meeting with the Waldensian Community or with the Russian Orthodox Patriarch Kirill. Unity is achieved step by step, through a patient and continuous journey together. Full unity, he said, will be achieved after "the Son of Man returns" but in the meantime, he stressed, Christians must pray, repent of their sins and walk together. Pope Francis' friend Pentecostal Pastor Traettino observed that "The election of Pope Francis clearly opened a new season, especially in relations with us" because "Pentecostals and Catholic Charismatic's have not always gotten along". Papal house hold preacher, Capuchin Father Raniero Cantalamessa, commented: "How many of the divisions among Christians have been due to the desire to make a name for ourselves or for our own church more than for God. A renewed outpouring of the Holy Spirit will not be possible without a collective movement of repentance on the part of all Christians." Thus, very effectively, Pope Francis is bringing together the left, right and the middle of the Christians into a communion with his presence, personal warmth, genuine interest and deep prayer life.

With the Jewish, Muslims, Hindus, Buddhists and even Atheists Pope Francis wants to build bridges so that humanity could come together in celebrating the compassion, love and warmth of Christ Jesus. As the Vicar of Christ, he is indeed the servant of the servants, governing the Church not through authority but through the simplicity, humility, humanity and openness of Christ Jesus. By writing the encyclical *Laudato Si* Pope Francis took up the care of our human habitat and the cry of nature and identified it with the cry of the poor. The world appreciated Pope Francis' gesture and actions and tried to emulate him as best as possible. He has given a new fresh outlook to the Catholic Church, continuing the tradition of Pope John XXIII and the Second Vatican Council, a Church that could be meaningful in the world. Pope Francis through his presence and his ability to build bridges with Churches, Nations, Religions, brings together the entire creation of God into a living community.

Endnotes

1   Pontifex Maximus from Latin literally means the "greatest pontiff" or "greatest bridge-builder," or "Supreme Pontiff." He was the high priest of the College of Pontiffs (Collegium Pontificum) in ancient Rome.

2   Edmund HUSSERL, *The Crisis of European Sciences and Transcendental Phenomenology: An Introduction to Phenomenological Philosophy*, Trans. by, David Carr, Northwestern University Studies in Phenomenology & Existential Philosophy, Illinois, 1970.

3   Mathew CHANDRANKUNNEL, *Ascent to Truth: The Physics, Philosophy and Religion of Galileo, Chavara Cancer Society Publication*, Thiruvananthapuram, 2011.

4   RICHARD DAWKINS, *Brief Candle in the Dark: My Life in Science*, Bantam Press, 2015. ------., *The God Delusion*, Bantam Press, 2006.

5   Stephen HAWKING, Leonard Mlodinow, *The Grand Design*, Bantam Books, 2010.

6   Daniel C. DENNET, *Breaking the Spell: Religion as a Natural Phenomenon*, Penguin, 2007. "Hawking, Dawkins and Science and Religion" *Sathydeepam*, January 11, 2012. "Hawking, Dawkins and Science and Religion", *Sathydeepam*, January 18, 2012.

7   "Biotechnology-Hope or Horror?" (65-84) *Dharma Deepika*, Chennai, June 2006.

8   Dhiya KURIAKOSE, "Pope Francis: 'I am a sinner whom the Lord has looked upon'" *The Guardian* Sept 19, 2013. See https://www.theguardian.com/world/2013/sep/19/pope-francis-highlights-interview-america

9   Bishop Brian FARRELL, "The Church as communion: A notion that still needs to flourish" Ecumenicall Lecture delivered at the Ecumenical Conference" organized by the Focolare Movement at Castelgoldalfoon 12th May, 2017. I had the opportunity to interact with Bishop Farrell and got more clarity on Pope Francis vision of the Church as communion.

II. PASTORAL APPROACH

Chapter 3

A Rediscovery of the Gospel and the Discipleship Enduring Impact of *Evangelii Gaudium*

Thomas Padiyath
Professor and Dean of Studies at Paurastya Vidyanikethan,
Changanacherry, Kerala

Introduction

British mathematician, scientist and philosopher Alfred North Whitehead (1861-1947) has made a statement: "The modern world has lost God and is seeking him" (RM 72).[1] He added further that "if the modern world is to find God, it must find him through love and not through fear, with the help of John and not of Paul" (RM 73). It is a re-discovering of the "Galilean origin of Christianity" as Whitehead claims (PR 343) and still it is a "rebound from dogmatic intolerance to the simplicity of religious truth" (RM 73). When I read Whitehead each time I am reminded of Pope Francis. Pope Francis has invited great applause as well as radical criticism; however, it is equally true to say that no one can ignore him. It is in this context I am persuaded to think of Pope Francis, Discipleship and New Evangelization. The reason is, the Pope has stirred a radical re-thinking of discipleship which I see as making possible an effective new evangelization.

1. The Call of the Council

The Second Vatican Council which aimed at the revival and revitalization of the Church, focused on both *aggiornamento* and *ressourcement*. The Council Fathers judiciously realized that no revival was possible without the rediscovery of the riches of the Church's faith and spiritual traditions, and a return to a Whiteheadian "Galilean origin of Christianity". This is what has impressed me about Pope Francis. He is inviting the Pastors of the Church to rediscover the heart of the discipleship of Jesus that is disclosed in the Gospels. The reason is, "As children of this age, though, all of us are in some way affected by the present globalized culture which, while offering us values and new possibilities, can also limit, condition and ultimately harm us. I am aware that we need to create spaces where pastoral workers can be helped and healed …" (EG 77).[2] Moreover, Pope Francis reminds Pastors that they (are), "Called to radiate light and communicate life, in the end they are caught up in things that generate only darkness and inner weariness, and slowly consume all zeal for the apostolate" (EG 83). Thus, the urgency of the time is a "pastoral and missionary conversion" as Pope Francis envisions.

One is called to read the prophetic call of the Council from the perspective that any renewal of the Church greatly depends on the renewal and training of its Pastors and ministers: "Animated by the spirit of Christ, this sacred synod is fully aware that the desired renewal of the whole Church depends to a great extent on the ministry of its priests" (OT 1; See also CD 16; PO 1, 12; PC 1, 18). It is also true today in the sense that what one wants to avoid in one's own life, as well as in the life of others, takes place in his/her own actual life; "The evils of our world – and those of the Church – … [become] excuses for diminishing our commitment and our fervor" (EG 84). For, "every period of history is marked by the presence of human weakness, self-absorption, complacency and selfishness … [and] concupiscence which preys upon us all. … So I propose that we pause to rediscover some of the reasons which can help us …" (EG 263). One must situate the clarion call of Pope Francis for a "pastoral and missionary conversion" in this context. The departure point of the new evangelization for Pope Francis, is the disciples themselves.

2. New Evangelization

New Evangelization is a concept that is very lively in the thought, life, and proclamation of the Church for the last four-five decades. Today it is a matter of lively discussion as it had been selected as the theme of the 13th ordinary General Assembly of the Synod of Bishops held in Rome from October 7-28, 2012. New evangelization can be understood as the Church's creative efforts to respond to the challenges faced by the Gospel and the Christian culture in the contemporary world.

It was Pope John Paul II who used the concept New Evangelization for the first time during his Apostolic Visit to Poland on June 9, 1979. However, the encyclical *Evangelii Nuntiandi* of Pope Paul VI can be considered as the forerunner of this concept. In this way one can rightly say that the visionary of the New Evangelization is Pope Paul VI and the Prophet and the Progenitor is

Pope John Paul II. Pope Benedict XVI is the one who popularized it.[3] And, now Pope Francis is the herald of New Evangelization, who gives it a new hermeneutics by his word and deed.

The "new evangelization" is applied to the Church's renewed efforts to meet the challenges that today's social and cultural milieu pose to Christianity. In facing these challenges, the Church does not surrender or retreat into herself, but undertakes a project to revitalize herself. It is the readiness and willingness to engage contemporary culture in spiritual activity "to reread the memory of faith and to undertake new responsibilities and generate new energies to joyously and convincingly proclaim the Gospel of Jesus Christ" (Lineamenta 5).

New evangelization is nothing but a New Way of "Being the Church" (Lineamenta 9). Moreover, it is understood as a Vision for the Church of Today and Tomorrow, and exhorts us "to rekindle in ourselves the impetus of the Church's beginnings and allow ourselves to be filled with the ardour of the apostolic preaching which followed Pentecost" (*Lineamenta* 24).

3. Pope Francis and Discipleship

Anyone who reads the post-synodal Apostolic Exhortation *Evangelii Gaudium* will distinguish three separate ideas: a) the call of the Second Vatican Council for the renewal of Priests and the Consecrated; b) the call of the Church for New Evangelization; and c) Pope Francis' radical thinking on the Discipleship.[45] For me, it is the first two points that motivated Pope Francis to focus on the third. In a radical re-thinking of discipleship, and within the context of the Synod on New Evangelization, Pope Francis deemed that the Church cannot engage in a fruitful new evangelization without a renewal and revitalization of its disciples. Hence, the Pope has called for a pastoral and missionary conversion on the part of priests and consecrated men and women.

4. The Imperative of Pastoral Conversion

Only in the context and light of the above can one read the hope expressed in *Evangelii Gaudium* that "all communities will devote the necessary effort to advancing along the path of a pastoral and missionary conversion which cannot leave things as they presently are" (EG 25). Quoting his own blessed predecessor Pope Paul VI, Pope Francis clarifies what is meant by pastoral conversion:

> The Church must look with penetrating eyes within herself, ponder the mystery of her own being... This vivid and lively self-awareness inevitably leads to a comparison between the ideal image of the Church as Christ envisaged her and loved her as his holy and spotless bride (cf. *Eph* 5:27), and the actual image which the Church presents to the world today... This is the source of the Church's heroic and impatient struggle for renewal: the struggle to correct those flaws introduced by her members which her own self-examination, mirroring her

exemplar, Christ, points out to her and condemns (EG 26; *Ecclesiam Suam* 9 -11).[5]

Moreover, the heart of this pastoral conversion is a self-renewal that is characterised by total fidelity to the Lord in the life of the entire Church. Therefore, it is basically an "ecclesial conversion" (EG 26) which consists of a "constant self-renewal" (EG 26). Citing the Council Fathers, Francis clarified further that "every renewal of the Church essentially consists in an increase of fidelity to her own calling… Christ summons the Church as she goes her pilgrim way… to that continual reformation of which she always has need, in so far as she is a human institution here on earth" (UR 6, cited in EG 26).[6] Thus, by pastoral conversion the Holy Father aims not only at the conversion of hearts, but also a conversion that includes all ecclesiastical institutions.

> I dream of a "missionary option", that is, a missionary impulse capable of transforming everything, so that the Church's customs, ways of doing things, times and schedules, language and structures can be suitably channelled for the evangelization of today's world rather than for her self-preservation. The renewal of structures demanded by pastoral conversion can only be understood in this light … (EG 27).

For example, the Holy Father writes of the parish: "The parish is not an outdated institution … . While certainly not the only institution which evangelizes, if the parish proves capable of self-renewal and constant adaptivity, it continues to be "the Church living in the midst of the homes of her sons and daughters" (EG 28).

Pope Francis envisions that only by a radical conversion of the "disciples" and institutions. can the Church engage in a fruitful new evangelization. This first condition is an encounter with Jesus because those who encounter Jesus and accepts his offer of salvation are "set free from sin, sorrow, inner emptiness and loneliness" (EG 1). It is this condition that makes for an effective pastoral life with the Joy of the Gospel. From here, one can formulate a **Decalogue** of Christian Discipleship from the writings of Pope Francis.

4.1 Discipleship is a Re-birth

Discipleship is a response to a loving call by God the Father (Rejoice 4). "It is about being reborn through vocation" (Rejoice 4).[7] Every vocation is an invitation to surrender oneself, what one has and one is, to the Lord in order to become a new creation. In the Pauline version "… if anyone is in Christ, he is a new creation …" (2 Cor 5, 17). The Lord said to Nicodemus: "Very truly I tell you, no one can see the kingdom of God unless they are born again … . "Very truly I tell you, no one can enter the kingdom of God unless they are born of water and the Spirit" (John 3, 3-5). For Pope Francis, discipleship is a re-birth. It is always an initiative of God. It "means continuously making an 'exodus' from yourselves in order to centre your life on Christ and on his Gospel..." (Rejoice 4). This rebirth "has a name and a face: the face of Jesus Christ. He teaches us to become holy. In the Gospel he shows us the way, the way of the Beatitudes ..." (Rejoice 5). That is why it is said that "Consecrated life is in fact a continuous call to follow Christ, and to be made like him" (Rejoice 5).

It is true of every disciple in the Old Testament as well as in the New Testament. They are invited to leave their kith and kin, whatever they have and in some cases are asked to abandon their own names (eg. Abraham and Paul). The pastoral and missionary conversion demands a rebirth; only then will one be able to produce fruits. It can be rightly said that primary goal of formation is this rebirth. As St Paul wrote, "it is no longer I who live, but it is Christ who lives in me" (Gal 2, 20).

4.2 Discipleship and Permanent Conversion

A discipleship worthy of its call demands a permanent conversion. Disciples themselves are "wounded healers," and the Apostles needed this healing (Lk 10, 35-45; Mt 20, 20-28). Pope Francis wishes to "create spaces where pastoral workers can be helped and healed" (EG 77), "places where faith itself in the crucified and risen Jesus is renewed, where the most profound questions and daily concerns are shared, where deeper discernment about our experiences and life itself is undertaken in the light of the Gospel, for the purpose of directing individual and social decisions towards the good and beautiful" (EG 77). It is in this sense that the Holy Father refers to the temptations of the pastoral workers.

a) Yes to the Challenge of a Missionary Spirituality

Today many pastors are subject to the temptation of "an inordinate concern for their personal freedom and relaxation" and ministry becomes "a mere appendage to their life, as if it were not part of their very identity". As a result, "spiritual life comes to be identified with a few religious exercises which can offer a certain comfort but which do not encourage encounter with others, engagement with the world or a passion for evangelization". In many this finally results in "a heightened individualism, a crisis of identity and a cooling of fervor" in spite of their good prayer life. For Pope Francis these "three evils ... fuel one another" (EG 78). Thus, even pastoral workers become prey to a "practical relativism" characterised by a life "consists in acting as if God did not exist, making decisions as if the poor did not exist, setting goals as if others did not exist, working as if people who have not received the Gospel did not exist" (EG 80). This further leads even they whom initially have "solid doctrinal and spiritual convictions" to an inordinate "attachment to financial security, or to a desire for power or human glory at all cost, rather than giving their lives to others in mission" (EG 80).

b) No to Selfishness and Spiritual Sloth

Today, pastors and ministers of the Church find themselves in a paradox: On the one hand we are living in a time "when we most need a missionary dynamism" and on the other, we see "some resist giving themselves over completely to mission and thus end up in a state of paralysis and acedia" (EG 81). The problem is not that no work, or an excess of work, is done, but rather "activity undertaken badly, without adequate motivation, without a spirituality which would permeate it and make it pleasurable". The outcome is, "work becomes more tiring than necessary, even leading at times to illness. Far from a content and happy tiredness, this is a tense, burdensome, dissatisfying and, in the end, unbearable fatigue" (EG 82). The Pope points out reasons for acedia one by one (EG 83). However, the biggest danger (quoting the words of Pope Benedict XVI) Pope Francis writes, gradually takes shape in "the gray pragmatism of the daily life of the Church, in which all appears to proceed normally, while in reality faith is wearing down and degenerating into small-mindedness" (EG 83). Thus the pastors of the Church develop a "tomb psychology" that gradually "transforms Christians into mummies in a museum". The result is that "disillusioned with reality, with the Church and with themselves, they experience a constant temptation to cling to a faint melancholy" (EG 83). People who are called to "radiate light and communicate life" are "caught up in things that generate only darkness and inner weariness, and slowly consume all zeal for the apostolate" (EG 83). Thus, the Holy Father earnestly wishes: "Let us not allow ourselves to be robbed of the joy of evangelization" (EG 83).

c) No to a Sterile Pessimism

Another major challenge confronted by Pastors is unproductive pessimism. The problem is that many fail to live the "Joy of the Gospel" which set them free "from sin, sorrow, inner emptiness and loneliness" (EG 1). Neither the evils that exist elsewhere, nor the evils in one's own mind, shall hinder pastoral efforts, but rather challenges should be taken up as opportunities: "The evils of our world – and those of the Church – must not be excuses for diminishing our commitment and our fervour. Let us look upon them as challenges which can help us to grow" (EG 84). Pope Francis recalls the prophetic words of St John XIII to substantiate his point: "In this modern age they can see nothing but prevarication and ruin … We feel that we must disagree with those prophets of doom who are always forecasting disaster, as though the end of the world were at hand" (EG 84). We need a pastoral and missionary conversion in order to overcome the call of the prophets of doom. Therefore, one has to rekindle the light of faith and "our faith is challenged to discern how wine can come from water and how wheat can grow in the midst of weeds" (EG 84).

Together with an unproductive pessimism one has to overcome the fear of a failed fruitful pastoral ministry amidst the manifold challenges. The Holy Father warns: "One of the more serious temptation which stifles boldness and zeal is a defeatism which turns us into querulous and disillusioned pessimists, "sourpusses" (EG 85). He further adds, "the evil spirit of defeatism is brother to the temptation to separate, before its time, the wheat from the weeds; it is the fruit of an anxious and self-centred lack of trust" (EG 85). Today there are places where "spiritual "desertification"' has evidently taken place and attempts are made to build up societies "without God or to eliminate their Christian roots" (EG 85). On the other hand, "there are innumerable signs, often expressed implicitly or negatively, of the thirst for God, for the ultimate meaning of life" (EG 85). Therefore, today's imperative is for disciples to rediscover "the joy of believing" in the desert where we rediscover the value of faith. "In the desert people of faith are needed" who, "are called to be living sources of water from which others can drink" (EG 85). For this, no disciples should allow themselves to be robbed of hope! Only "a committed missionary knows the joy of being a spring which spills over and refreshes others" (EG 272). Christian faith is essentially hope but, "if we allow doubts and fears to dampen our courage, instead of being creative we will remain comfortable and make no progress whatsoever. In this case we will not take an active part in historical processes, but become mere onlookers as the Church gradually stagnates" (EG 129). Therefore, "let us not allow ourselves to be robbed of hope" (EG 86)!

d) No to Spiritual Worldliness

Today pastors and ministers of the Church are victims of a two-fold secularization. On the one hand, for many, often the Gospel does not become the norm of life. This is what is meant by the secularization of the priestly and consecrated life. On the other hand, as Pope Francis states, many are subjected to a "spiritual worldliness", that is the second kind of secularization. A disciple is called by the Word to follow the life of Jesus radically. We have no other norm than the Gospel of Jesus Christ and the Christ of the Gospel. In this context it is proper to recall what the Church reminds priests and the consecrated during the Ordination and Religious Profession: may the Christ of the Gospel be the source of strength and Light for you and let the Gospel of Jesus be the norm for your life. "A true missionary, who never ceases to be a disciple, knows that Jesus walks with him, speaks to him, breathes with him, works with him. He senses Jesus alive with him in the midst of the missionary enterprise" (EG 266). Jesus Christ is the ultimate norm for a disciple. Pope Francis is categorical in his vision:

> ... it is not the same thing to have known Jesus as not to have known him, not the same thing to walk with him as to walk blindly, not the same thing to hear his word as not to know it, and not the same thing to contemplate him, to worship him, to find our peace in him, as not to. It is not the same thing to try to build the world with his Gospel as to try to do so by our own lights (EG 266).

Today's Disciples of Jesus are victims of secularization because they find themselves in a world which is very much led by principles of consumerism. Pope Francis characteristically draws out the nature of secularization: "The great danger in today's world, pervaded as it is by consumerism, is the desolation and anguish born of a complacent yet covetous heart, the feverish pursuit of frivolous pleasures, and a blunted conscience. ... Many fall prey to it, and end up resentful, angry and listless" (EG 2).

In *Evangelii Gaudium* Pope Francis is concerned largely with Spiritual Worldliness. For him, spiritual worldliness often "hides behind the appearance of piety and even love for the Church". And it "consists in seeking not the Lord's glory but human glory and personal well-being. ... It is a subtle way of seeking one's "own interests, not those of Jesus Christ" (EG 93). Moreover, because it is "based on carefully cultivated appearances, it is not always linked to outward sin; from without, everything appears as it should be. But if it were to seep into the Church, 'it would be infinitely more disastrous than any other worldliness which is simply moral'" (EG 93). Pope Francis refers to two attitudes or conditions that fuel spiritual worldliness. One is "gnosticism, a purely subjective faith whose only interest is a certain experience or a set of ideas and bits of information which are meant to console and enlighten, but which ultimately keep one imprisoned in his or her own thoughts and feelings", and the other is "the self-absorbed promethean neopelagianism of those who ultimately trust only in their own powers and feel superior to others because they observe certain rules or remain intransigently faithful to a particular Catholic style from the past" (EG 94).[8] St Paul reminds Timothy of this spiritual worldliness (2 Tim 3,5). For Pope Francis it is "a tremendous corruption disguised as a good" (EG 97). If God is to heal his "disciple" from this spiritual worldliness "with superficial spiritual and pastoral trappings", one has to breath in "the pure air of the Holy Spirit who frees us from self-centredness cloaked in an outward religiosity bereft of God" (EG 97).

As part of 'pastoral and missionary conversion', Pope Francis adds the following: No, to warring among ourselves (98-101). Yes, to the new relationships brought by Christ (87-92). Yes, to the challenge of a missionary spirituality (78-80). No, to an Excessive clericalism (102). If pastors do not heed this invitation, "the edifice of the Church's moral teaching risks becoming a house of cards" and the "message will run the risk of losing its freshness and will cease to have 'the fragrance of the Gospel'" (EG 39).

4.3 Heart of Discipleship is Faithfulness Not Success

A unique and distinctive characteristic feature of Jesus' disciple is faithfulness. Without exception all of the magisterial teachings highlight it. For example, the Post-Synodal Apostolic Exhortation *Vita Consecrata* states that "what is required of each individual is *not success, but commitment to faithfulness.*[9] What must be avoided at all costs is the actual breakdown of the consecrated life, a collapse which is not measured by a decrease in numbers but by a failure to cling steadfastly to the Lord and to personal vocation and mission" (VC 63). For Pope Francis "to accept this teaching means to renew our existence in accordance with the Gospel …" (Rejoice 1).

The identity of the disciple is nothing other than the identity of the Master himself. So our Church teaches us that 'the seal on the foreheads of the disciples is Christ, and he is the seal on your hearts: on the forehead because you always profess him; on the heart because you always love him; he is the seal on your arms because you are always working for him (Rejoice 5). What is the identity that the Master manifested in his words and deeds? The Apostle reminds us that 'the one who called you is faithful' (I Thes 5, 24). Pope Francis puts it this way: "In calling you, God says to you: 'You are important to me, I love you, I am counting on you'" (Rejoice 4). Therefore, faithfulness should be the identification mark of a disciple. Moreover, for Pope Francis, the JOY of the GOSPEL is "a faithful 'yes'" (Rejoice 6). So it is stated that "anyone who has met the Lord and follows him faithfully is a messenger of the joy of the Spirit" (Rejoice 6). And, what the disciple lacks the most is faithfulness itself. So the disciples are reminded again and again that "we are experiencing a crisis of fidelity, understood as a conscious adherence to a call that is a pathway, a journey from its mysterious beginnings to its mysterious end" (Rejoice 6). A faithful discipleship has different aspects: faithfulness to God, to others, to oneself and faithfulness to the Church. Therefore, faithfulness is characterised as "the awareness of a love that points us towards the "Thou" of God and towards every other person, in a constant and dynamic way when we experience within ourselves the life of the Risen One" (Rejoice 6). Thus, faithful discipleship itself is understood as "grace and love in action; it is the practice of sacrificial charity" (Rejoice 6). One of the goals of the celebration of the Year of the Consecrated and Year for the priests was nothing other than to invigorate and renew this faithfulness in one's own life. Therefore, it is asked to each one of us: "Is Jesus really our first and only love, as we promised he would be when we professed our vows?" (Witnesses of Joy 2)[10] The Year of Consecrated Life challenged us to examine our fidelity to the mission entrusted to us (Witnesses of Joy 2). Faithfulness is indispensable in the life of the disciple.

4.4 Discipleship: Transformation from Individual to Person

Another characteristic of pastoral and missionary conversion in the disciple is a transformation of self-understanding. For Pope Francis, "individualism of our postmodern and globalized era favours a lifestyle which weakens the development and stability of personal relationships and distorts family bonds" (EG 67). A disciple with the JOY of the Gospel never understands himself as an individual who is often closed and content within himself. He understands himself as a person who is 'other' oriented and communitarian. When the individual does have vertical and horizontal relationships, with God and with fellow human beings, a person realizes that it is the vertical relation with God and horizontal relation with fellow human beings that gives meaning for existence. That is why Pope Francis states: "indeed, those who enjoy life most are those who leave security on the shore and become excited by the mission of communicating life to others. ... she is simply pointing to the source of authentic personal fulfilment. For 'here we discover a profound law of reality: that life is attained and matures in the measure that it is offered up in order to give life to others'" (EG 10). Pope Francis writes that "we become fully human when we become more than human, when we let God bring us beyond ourselves in order to attain the fullest truth of our being" (EG 8). For Pope Francis one of the effects of Pentecost was that "the Spirit made the apostles go forth from themselves and turned them into heralds of God's wondrous deeds, capable of speaking to each person in his or her own language" (EG 259). This is what the disciples are invited to do: to be for others.

It is in this context one has to re-read the statement in *Vita Consecrata* that " ... the subject of formation is the individual at every stage of life, the object of formation is the whole person, called to seek and love God "with all one's heart, and with all one's soul, and with all one's might, and one's neighbour as oneself" (VC 71). This is also the reason why the two fundamental laws become equally important. In other words, in and through formation one has to grow from an individual to person. Here 'person' has to be understood as an 'integral subject' whose life is characterized by "a sound interior life, without divisions or contradictions." The reason is, it is the "whole person, with all that he is and all that he possesses, who will be at the Lord's service ..." (RF 92).[11]

4.5 Disciples in the Footsteps of the Good Shepherd

Disciples are invited to search for the lost sheep following the Good Shepherd (LK 15, 1-7). It is a call of Pope Francis: "In fidelity to the example of the Master, it is vitally important for the Church today to go forth and preach the Gospel to all: to all places, on all occasions, without hesitation, reluctance or fear" (EG 23). This is also the reason why he tells us that "missionary outreach is *paradigmatic for all the Church's activity*" (EG 15). Therefore, the pastors and ministers of the Church "cannot passively and calmly wait in our church buildings"; but rather we are called to move "from a pastoral ministry of mere conservation to a decidedly missionary pastoral ministry" (EG 15) that sets out in search of lost sheep.

The encounter with Jesus "does not lead to shutting oneself in but to opening oneself" (Rejoice 10). That is Why Pope Francis reminds us that "the ghost to fight against is the image of religious life understood as an escape and consolation in face of an 'external' difficult and complex world" (Rejoice 10). Therefore, he urges us to "leave the nest" (Rejoice 10) of our comfort zones (Rejoice 10) "in these days when fragmentation justifies widespread sterile individualism and when the weakness of relationships breaks up and ruins the care of the human person ..." (Rejoice 9). Men and women disciples need a "new aspiration for holiness, which is unthinkable without a jolt of renewed passion for the Gospel at the service of the Kingdom" (NWNW 10).[12] To conclude, I would quote Pope Francis:

> ... the Church must accompany with attention and care the weakest of her children, who show signs of a wounded and troubled love, by restoring in them hope and confidence, like the beacon of a lighthouse in a port or a torch carried among the people to enlighten those who have lost their way or who are in the midst of a storm. Let us not forget that the Church's task is often like that of a field hospital (*Amoris Laetitia* 291).[13]

4.6 Administrators Versus Dispensers of Divine Mercy

Institutionalization is deeply rooted in the ecclesial life of today. Numerous temporal concerns have reduced pastors to the level of mere administrators. That is why the Church reminds pastors that "it seems as though consecrated life is almost completely wrapped up in managing the day-to-day or in mere surviving. ... the risk is that one may get completely wrapped up in containing problems rather than imagining paths" (NWNW 8). The goal of consecrated life is not to "maintain itself in a permanent state" but to "maintain the permanence of evangelical conversion" (NWNW 40). Therefore, Pope Francis admonishes: "Let us think of the damage done to the people of God by men and women of the Church who are careerists, climbers, who use the people and the Church ... as a spring board for their own ends and personal ambitions. These people do the Church great harm" (NWNW 44). Pope Francis is unambiguous in warning the Church: "More than by fear of going astray, my hope is that we will be moved by the fear of remaining shut up within structures which give us a false sense of security, within rules which make us harsh judges, within habits which make us feel safe ..." (EG 49).

A pastoral and missionary conversion demands a radical shift in the self-understanding of disciples. The Pastors of the Church must be "bringing God's embrace" to the people because "people today certainly need words, but most of all they need us to bear witness to the mercy and tenderness of the Lord which warms the heart, rekindles hope, and attracts people towards the good" (Rejoice 8). One is reminded that ministry in the Church "is to bring to the men and women of our time the consolation of God, to bear witness to his mercy" (Rejoice 8).[14] That is why the Holy Father reminds priests with a motherly heart: "the confessional must not be a torture chamber but rather an encounter with the Lord's mercy which spurs us on to do our best" (EG 44). Thus, the Church must be a mother with an open heart; "a Church which "goes forth" is a Church whose doors are open" (EG 46). Today the Church discloses her motherly love in and through her ministers. Pope Francis urges:

... when a priest is not a father to his community, when a sister is not a mother to all those with whom she works, he or she becomes sad. This is the problem. For this reason I say to you: the root of sadness in pastoral life is precisely in the absence of fatherhood or motherhood that comes from living this consecration unsatisfactorily, which on the contrary should lead us to fertility (Rejoice 10).

Lastly, no disciple "closes itself off, never retreats into its own security, never opts for rigidity and defensiveness. ... it always does what good it can, even if in the process, its shoes get soiled by the mud of the street" (EG 45). Disciples are dispensers of divine mercy and should be like "the father of the prodigal son" (EG 46) and "the Church is called to be the house of the Father, with doors always wide open" (EG 47). This is the pastoral and missionary conversion that Pope Francis has called for.

4.7 Discipleship and the Divine Discontent

The life of a disciple should also be characterised by a divine discontent, for s/he is called to grow into the perfection of the heavenly Father (Mt 5, 48). What should rightly disturb a disciple who enjoys the JOY of pastoral conversion is that, "so many of our brothers and sisters are living without the strength, light and consolation born of friendship with Jesus Christ, without a community of faith to support them, without meaning and a goal in life" (EG 49). Therefore what Pope Francis proposes to the disciples is a divine discontent, a "*restless searching*" similar to that of Augustine of Hippo because a 'restlessness in his heart brought him to a personal encounter with Christ ... . This is an ongoing search. ... The *restlessness of seeking the truth*, of seeking God, ... restlessness to know him ever better and to come out of himself to make others know him. It was precisely the restlessness of love" (Rejoice 5).

Only a restlessness of this sort can lead one to a spirit-filled evangelization, because "no words of encouragement will be enough unless the fire of the Holy Spirit burns in our hearts" (EG 261). This is the reason why the Holy Father desires to begin a new chapter of evangelization; in fact, a new evangelization "full of fervour, joy, generosity, courage, boundless love and attraction" (EG 261). For the Church grows not by proselytizing, but "by attraction" (EG 15). For a fruitful evangelization we need both prayer and work: *ora et labora*.[15] On the one hand, we need to pray because "without prayer all our activity risks being fruitless and our message empty" (EG 259; 262); and on the other, "mystical notions without a solid social and missionary outreach are of no help to evangelization, nor are dissertations or social or pastoral practices which lack a spirituality which can change hearts" (EG 262). That is why it is all the more vital that "evangelizers who proclaim the good news [must do it] not only with words, but above all by a life transfigured by God's presence" (EG 259). Then, the "religious should be men and women able to wake the world up" (Rejoice 1). One has to evangelize himself in the sense that if seek to "advance in the spiritual life, then, we must constantly be missionaries. The work of evangelization enriches the mind and the heart; it opens up spiritual horizons; it makes us more and more sensitive to the workings of the Holy Spirit, and it takes us beyond our limited spiritual constructs" (EG 272). In other words, the prayer of the Lord has to be materialized in the life of every disciple: "For them I sanctify myself, that they too may be truly sanctified" (John 17, 19).

4.8 Discipleship and Self-Criticism

Pope Francis has chosen for himself 'a road less travelled'! He categorically states:

> The Church must look with penetrating eyes within herself, ponder the mystery of her own being... This vivid and lively self-awareness inevitably leads to a comparison between the ideal image of the Church as Christ envisaged her and loved her as his holy and spotless bride (cf. *Eph* 5:27), and the actual image which the Church presents to the world today... This is the source of the Church's heroic and impatient struggle for renewal: the struggle to correct those flaws introduced by her members which her own self-examination, mirroring her exemplar, Christ, points out to her and condemns (EG 26).

Today what the Church in general, and the disciples in particular, lack is healthy self criticism. The invitation is for a better self-understanding in view of renewal. What Socrates said Millennia ago is ever relevant: 'an unexamined life is not worth living'. As the distance between the ideal image and the actual image increases, crises also increase. This logic is applicable to both individuals and institutions. The Church, as the chief agent of evangelization, "ought to let others be constantly evangelizing" her (EG 121). Priests as pastors are invited to accompany the sheep in their spiritual journey, but as disciples of the Lord "ought to grow in awareness that he himself is continually in need of being evangelized" (PDV 26). That is why it is all the more important "to remove our sandals before the sacred ground of the other" (EG 169). For, "the Church does not evangelize unless she constantly lets herself be evangelized" (EG 174). In order to be a "committed missionary [who] knows the joy of being a spring which spills over and refreshes others" (EG 272), one must undergo the pastoral conversion of which Pope Francis speaks. A life that ignores this demand for pastoral conversion, the Holy Father reminds us, "is nothing less than slow suicide" (EG 272). In order to keep our missionary fervour alive one needs firm trust in the Holy Spirit, and to nourish this trust one needs to "invoke the Spirit constantly" (EG 280).

4.9 Discipleship and Ministry of Listening

Today pastoral ministry demands accompaniment. Only then "ordained ministers and other pastoral workers can make present the fragrance of Christ's closeness and his personal gaze" (EG 169) to others. Therefore, mother Church wants "to initiate everyone – priests, religious and laity – into this 'art of accompaniment'" (EG 169). One condition for fruitful accompaniment is the willingness to listen to others. That is why the Holy Father suggests that pastors must "practice the art of listening" (EG 171). The art of listening is

> ... an openness of heart which makes possible that closeness without which genuine spiritual encounter cannot occur. Listening helps us to find the right gesture and word which shows that we are more than simply bystanders. Only through such respectful and compassionate listening can we enter on the paths of true growth and awaken a yearning for the Christian ideal: the desire to respond fully to God's love and to bring to fruition what he has sown in our lives (EG 171).

In order to make a good homily Pope Francis exhorts pastors to be good listeners, because a "preacher must know the heart of his community" (EG 137). Our Lord himself is the model *par excellence*, because Jesus himself was a good listener (LK 2, 46). "The preacher also needs to keep his ear to the people and to discover what it is that the faithful need to hear. A preacher has to contemplate the word, but he also has to contemplate his people" (EG 154). Another condition for a fruitful ministry is listening for the Lord. One who does not hear the Lord in prayer and meditation on the Word of God cannot be good listener. That is why the Church teaches that if one "does not take time to hear God's word with an open heart, if he does not allow it to touch his life, to challenge him, to impel him, and if he does not devote time to pray with that word, then he will indeed be a false prophet, a fraud, a shallow impostor" (EG 151). For fullfilling and productive community life, as well as for the proper exercise of authority, skill in the art of listening is a must. Hence, the Magisterium teaches that "discussion among brothers and sisters and the listening of individual people becomes an essential place for the evangelical service of authority" (NWNW 41). Moreover, the consecrated are invited to "live the *mysticism of encounter*, which entails 'the ability to hear, to listen to other people; the ability to seek together ways and means'" (Witnesses of Joy I, 2).

4.10 A Disciple's 'No' to a Complacent Attitude

A serious enemy of pastoral and missionary conversion is a complacent mind and attitude. In a complacent mind the "evangelical fervour is replaced by the empty pleasure of complacency and self-indulgence" (EG 95). A complacent mind is comrade of the spiritual worldliness, as we discussed above. The reason is because in a person motivated by 'spiritual worldliness' the "mark of Christ, incarnate, crucified and risen, is not present" (EG 95). Conversely, in some people

> ... this spiritual worldliness lurks behind a fascination with social and political gain, or pride in their ability to manage practical affairs,

or an obsession with programmes of self-help and self-realization. It can also translate into a concern to be seen, into a social life full of appearances, meetings, dinners and receptions. It can also lead to a business mentality, caught up with management, statistics, plans and evaluations whose principal beneficiary is not God's people but the Church as an institution (EG 95).

A complacent attitude manifests itself in "some people nowadays [who] console themselves by saying that things are not as easy as they used to be". We should remain aware that "every period of history is marked by the presence of human weakness, self-absorption, complacency and selfishness, to say nothing of the concupiscence which preys upon us all" (EG 263). Therefore, no disciple shall sit idle. On the other hand, s/he has to realize that "I am a mission on this earth; that is the reason why I am here in this world. We have to regard ourselves as sealed, even branded, by this mission of bringing light, blessing, enlivening, raising up, healing and freeing" (EG 273). A pastoral ministry immersed in the JOY of the Gospel, and with a "missionary key, seeks to abandon the complacent attitude that says: "We have always done it this way" (EG 33). That is why the Holy Father invites "everyone to be bold and creative in this task of rethinking the goals, structures, style and methods of evangelization in their respective communities" (EG 33). It certainly seems appropriate to quote Michelangelo (1475-1564), who said centuries ago: "the greatest danger for most of us lies not in setting our aim too high and falling short; but in setting our aim too low and achieving our mark."

Conclusion

Pope Francis chaellenges Christian discipleship by word and deed. The Apostolic Exhortation *Evangelii Gaudium, Magna Carta* of his pastoral vision for the renewal of the Church, says something to all of us; to the hierarchy, to priests and consecrated men & women, to theologians, to the lay faithful, and to youth and children. It is a document rich in content and filled with pastoral love. Here, heart speaks to the heart. Above all it is an invitation to Disciples of Jesus for a pastoral conversion. In light of the basic demands of pastoral conversion, today's Church asks disciples to take some time to "to look at what is going on inside the *wineskins* of our consecrated life. It is a matter of determining the quality of the *new wine* and the *best wine*, and not about placing blame or accusing" (NWNW 9). It has been observed that "authentic and long lasting changes are never automatic" (NWNW 3). The call of the Holy Father, and the efforts of the Church, for a personal and committed self-renewal is an opportune occasion to revise the identity, lifestyle and ecclesial mission of discipleship.

Endnotes

1   Alfred North WHITEHEAD, *Religion in the Making* [1926]. New York: World Publishing, 1960. Herewith abbreviated as RM.

2   Pope FRANCIS, *Evangelii Gaudium*, Apostolic Exhortation, 2013. Herewith abbreviated as EG.

3   New Evangelization is a radical option for the Person of Jesus Christ. In this regard, the words of Pope John Paul II to the Church in Europe are particularly indicative and concise: "…an urgent need [has arisen] for a 'new evangelization', in the awareness that 'Europe today must not simply appeal to its former Christian heritage: it needs to be able to decide about its future in conformity with the person and message of Jesus Christ'" (*Lineamenta* 5). *Lineamenta* for 2012 Synod on the New Evangelization.

4   Though *Evangelii Gaudium* is meant for all Christians it does speak particularly to the disciples of Jesus. As the Second Vatican Council Fathers rightly observed no renewal is possible without the renewal of the priests and the Consecrated. Hence, Pope Francis is also making a radical appeal to the priests and the Consecrated in his Post-Synodal Apostolic Exhortation for a "pastoral and Missionary Conversion" in view of the new evangelization.

5   Pope PAUL VI, *Ecclesiam Suam,* Encyclical, 1964.

6   *Unitatitis Redintegratio*, Second Vatican Council Decree on Ecumenism, 1964.

7   *Rejoice,* A letter to consecrated men and women, A message from the teachings of Pope Francis, Congregation for the Institutes of Consecrated Life and Societies of Apostolic Life, 2014. Herewith abbreviated as Rejoice.

8   One cannot discuss here all the details because of the limited scope of this article, however Pope Francis clarifies further the dangers of spiritual worldliness *Evangelii Gaudium* Nos. 95-97.

9   *Vita Consecrata*, Post-Synodal Apostolic Exhortation, 1996. Herewith abbreviated as VC.

10   Pope Francis, *Witnesses of Joy*, Apostolic Letter to all Consecrated People, 2014.

11   *Ratio Fundamentalis Institutionis Sacerdotalis, The Gift Priestly Vocation, Congregation for the Clergy*, 2016. Hereafter abbreviated as RF.

12   *New Wine in New Wineskins, Guidelines*, Congregation for the Institutes of Consecrated Life and Societies of Apostolic Life, 2016. Herewith abbreviated as NWNW.

13   Pope FRANCIS, *Amoris Laetitia*, Apostolic Exhortation, 2016.

14   We have sufficiently dealt with this topic during the Year of Mercy. Hence it does not need further explanation.

15   "Spirit-filled evangelizers are evangelizers who pray and work" (EG 262). We should pray earnestly: "If we do not feel an intense desire to share this love, we need to pray insistently that he will once more touch our hearts. We need to implore his grace daily, asking him to open our cold hearts and shake up our lukewarm and superficial existence" (EG 264).

Chapter 4

Pope Francis on Catholic Bioethics
The Impact and Significance

Jery Njaliath
Asst. Director, Lisie Hospital, Ernakulam, Kerala

Before presenting the impact of Pope Francis on Catholic Bioethics, it is important to outline the contribution of personalism to Catholic bioethics. It is this personalist approach in bioethics that gave the Catholic bioethics its spine to defend rationally the Church's stance in the secular world. Treatment of this topic becomes more important in this article because personalism provides the continuity for Pope Francis' approach towards bioethics even when a clear discontinuity is evident in the way he does bioethics. Thus in the first section, I shall introduce the role of personalism in the Catholic bioethics and in the second, the impact of Pope Francis on Catholic bioethics.

1. Catholic Bioethics

Catholic Bioethics is personalist bioethics. Personalism is a "philosophy, a way of looking at reality, based on an understanding of what it means to be a person. Generally speaking, personalism holds that persons, that is to say, humans, are the center of moral reflection and indeed of morality."[1] It is extremely important to define the personalism followed by Catholic bioethics. This is because there are at least "a dozen Personalist doctrines, which at times have nothing more in common than the word 'person.'"[2] Williams, based on Armando Rigobello's observations, suggests two types of Personalisms: Personalism in a strict sense and Personalism in a broader sense. The strict Personalism, according to him, draws extensively from existentialism making it to become an autonomous metaphysics. Whereas the broader Personalism rests on a metaphysical foundation and it is this ontological thrust that justifies the person (not the person who justifies the metaphysics as in existential Personalism). Thomistic Personalism falls into this second category and this avoids the subjective drift to which other Personalisms are prone.[3] This Thomistic personalism that skews too much to the objective aspect of human being is further polished by Wojtyla to balance with the subjective aspect of human being. Aquinas understands person as in the Boethius definition, "the person is an individual substance of a rational nature." Thus for Aquinas, the rational nature constitutes the essence of person. Consciousness is something like a derivative of rationality. This thesis was rejected by Descartes and later by Kant and this position was reiterated by existentialists. For them, the essence of person is the consciousness and self-consciousness and body is a kind of mechanistic adjunct to the person. Person for them is merely a certain property of lived experiences and can be distinguished by means of those experiences, for they are conscious and self conscious experiences. Thus for them there is nothing objective in relation to person. What Wojtyla tried to do is to bridge this gap between the subjectivity in personalism of existentialists and the objectivity of personalism of Aquinas. He accepts the weakness in Aquinas' understanding of human person when he writes: "thus St. Thomas gives us an excellent view of the objective existence and activity of the person, but it would be difficult to speak in his view of the lived experiences of the person."[4] Even though Wojtyla does not share the modern view that the person is consciousness, he shares the modern interest in consciousness and self-consciousness. Wojtyla used phenomenology[5] as a means to explore the objective nature of human consciousness. This led to the formulation of a personalism that avoids the extremes of objectivity and subjectivity.

This personalism bases its view of person as a rational individual substance, the foundation of objectivity and universality, with her own self-consciousness, the foundation of subjectivity and existentialities. It is through her self-conscious free acts of self-giving she actualizes her nature. This personalism speaks about the intellect and free will. It also speaks about experiential aspect of human person as well. It sees each person as unique even when each person shares the objectivity/universality coming from human nature. The recognition of the presence of her own human nature in the other calls her to respect the dignity of the other in her intrinsic dignity. This attention to dignity calls each person to uphold her own intrinsic dignity and the dignity of others through responsible actions. This takes place in a community of persons where the rule of life is self gift. Second Vatican Council and later Pope John Paul II spread the theory of personalism based on the above mentioned understanding of person.

Personalism in Catholic understanding does not restrict only to the objective understanding of person by Aquinas. Catholic personalist thought continues to build on the objective base laid by Aquinas. While acknowledging the objective properties of the person that form the natural basis of his unique dignity, Catholic personalism goes beyond the objective analysis to complement it with a subjective, experiential reading of the person. With Aquinas as a point of departure and permanent reference point, Catholic personalism offers a specific contribution to Thomas's doctrine on the person, which facilitates the passage from Thomas's anthropology to personalist ethics.

Cardinal Sgreccia, who pioneered Catholic bioethics, took the orientation provided by John Paul II and Vatican Council II in developing a personlist bioethics. Sgreccia and other Catholic bioethicists chose this theory for the following three reasons. One, the shift that took place in the Catholic theology and magisterium with Vatican Council II was towards personalist approach. The Compendium of the Social Doctrine of the Church explicitly states: "The immediate purpose of the Church's social doctrine is to propose the principles and values that can sustain a society worthy of the human person."[6] In very simple terms one could say that "the Church has shifted from an emphasis on God the father as lawgiver who has written his will into the laws of nature, to an emphasis on Christ as our model of perfection and human dignity as the grounding of morality."[7] Even though a shift in emphasis is there to see from natural law to person, this personalist theory is in line with natural law[8] and is compatible with the traditional teachings of the Church. Thus no post-Vatican Council II research that looks for Catholic identity in any aspects of human reality can go forward setting aside the personalist approach. Two, personalism is proposed as the response to dehumanizing trends came from collectivism and individualism in the 19th century.[9] Collectivism was spurred by idealism of Hegel and later took lines of communism proposed by Marx and nationalist socialism spurred by Nietzsche. In this intellectual environment, man came to be seen as a mere phenomenal being, easily assimilated into the collectives of the family, the community, and the state. He was a product of external forces, an insignificant piece in cosmic puzzle, without dignity, freedom or responsibility. Along the rise of Hegelian determinisms, came another form of dehumanization of the individual. The individual is everything. In its first impression, it could be seen as opposite to the Darwinian determinism. But it resembles closely Darwin's survival of the fittest than Christian understanding of the inviolable dignity and worth of human person. Liberalism based on individualism took the real inspiration from Hobbe's concept of man as a-social and instinctively hostile to other individuals. Personalism was a reaction to determinism, materialism, evolutionism, liberalism and idealism by seeking to rescue the human person from absorption into larger, determining forces while at the same time recognizing his inter-personal nature offsetting the liberalist idea of individualism. Personalists like Maritain, Scheler, Mounier, and Buber stressed "the inviolable dignity of the individual person and at the same time his social nature and vocation to communion."[10] An ethical system if not built around this understanding of person shall lead to the Nazi type dehumanization. Three, this is a normative ethical theory that is intelligible for reason-seeking man of today, even to an atheist.[11] Even though this personalism is profoundly theological,[12] it is also very much reason oriented. This connection at once with the theology and public is expressed by Brady in the following terms: "Personalism is deeply theological but outwardly very public. As described in the above paragraphs, it is expressed in universal and objective terms. Yet personalism recognizes the mystery of human nature and that persons are not static by nature. Reality, including the reality of persons, is dynamic and indeed evolutionary. Personalism, then, is at once grounded on theological ideas and open to non-theological understandings of the human condition. Personalism takes into account the data of the sciences as well as the experiences of communities. At any given time, our understanding may be limited, and so it must remain open to other sources of reflection on the human condition."[13]

Personalism helps to define bioethical dilemmas in terms appealing to all religions and even to atheists but without explicitly using the terms of revelation. Roman Catholic priest and moral theologian Charles Curran suggests that Catholic theological tradition has always insisted on the basic goodness of the human and has seen divine mediated in and through the human. He also notes that this personalist understanding leads us to believe that "what Catholics are obliged to do in this world is at the very best not that much different from what all others are called to do."[14] Personalist understanding gives thrust to the thinking that by the very fact of their personhood, every individual is a moral agent to determine course of her action but with responsibility. In this sense a Catholic bioethics can be defined in personalist terms as a method of analysis of life issues demonstrating the greatest respect for human dignity with a view to humanize[15] the area of concern. Thus in a pluralist context like India where many non-Catholics live, a neutral language to discuss and articulate Catholic identity instead of using an explicit Catholic language is a good strategy. As we have already noted in the beginning, personalism is in complete harmony with Church teachings and revelation even if it does not use these terms explicitly.

2. Pope Francis and Catholic Bioethics

Catholic personalism is committed to the human dignity of every human being from the moment of her conception to the death. Every ethical discourse starts from this commitment and commitment to the human dignity of every human being is the cornerstone of Catholic bioethics. Pope Francis is a personalist to the core. His concerns for poor, marginalised, refugees and voiceless is based on this basic principle of personlism, that is commitment to human dignity. As a principle, this is the same concern he extends to the bioethical discourses. Thus as far as the principles are concerned, there is no discontinuity in Pope Francis' approach in bioethical matters since Second Vatican Council. His personalist approach in dealing with human realities is evident when he writes with the words of John Paul II, "human beings are ends in themselves and never a means of resolving other problems. Once this conviction disappears, so do solid and lasting foundations for the defence of human rights, which would always be subject to the passing whims of the powers that be. Reason alone is sufficient to recognize the inviolable value of each single human life, but if we also look at the issue from the standpoint of faith, "every violation of the personal dignity of the human being cries out in vengeance to God and is an offence against the creator of the individual."[16] He is continuing the same principles of personalism in analysing human problems in the realm of life, politics and economics as his predecessors after Second Vatican Council.

But what is different in Pope Francis regarding bioethics is his tone. To understand his approach towards bioethics, one must look how frequent and firmer he is in matters regarding politics, economics and social issues compared to bioethical issues. In bioethical matters, even though he is quite firm in the basic principle that is personalist idea of human dignity, he immediately acknowledges his incompetency in dealing complicated issues and engage in a 'who am I to judge' attitude and a dialogical approach. But in social and political concerns, he looks to be quite firm, judgemental and confrontational. The frequency with which Pope Francis deals with bioethical issues is also an indicator of what priority he gives to bioethics in his pastoral plan. His statements on bioethical issues are few and brief when compared to other Popes and also when compared to the overall attention he has paid to the morality in politics, economics and social realities.

He has quite frankly said that he is not interested to present bioethical discourses as the face of the Catholic church of today. This is a sweeping change in Catholic Church's approach. Regarding Catholic bioethics, the papacy of John Paul II was the spring time and lots of bioethics faculties and schools were started in catholic universities. During his time, personalist bioethics responded to every issue in detail and effectively as well. Catholic bioethical discourses actually contributed immensely to the cultural wars in the west during the times of Pope John Paul II and then during the papacy of Benedict XVI as well. But one of the first statements of Pope Francis set the tone of his approach to Catholic bioethics: "Pastoral ministry in a missionary style is not obsessed with the disjointed transmission of a multitude of doctrines to be insistently imposed."[17] For him the face of the Church must be mercy and all other aspects including bioethics must be situated in it. He has keenly observed what happened in the past. The Catholic church, notwithstanding, doing mainly the acts of mercy, was noted not for that, but for the cultural wars she engaged. This is what he has in mind when he says, "In today's world of instant communication and occasionally biased media coverage, the message we preach runs a greater risk of being distorted or reduced to some of its secondary aspects. In this way certain issues which are part of the Church's moral teaching are taken out of the context which gives them their meaning. The biggest problem is when the message we preach then seems identified with those secondary aspects which, important as they are, do not in and of themselves convey the heart of Christ's message. We need to be realistic and not assume that our audience understands the full background to what we are saying, or is capable of relating what we say to the very heart of the Gospel which gives it meaning, beauty and attractiveness."[18]

His strategy is to minimize the normative character of bioethics and put it in the context of mercy. This looks to be a fine and effortless thing for today's audience. But this is an arduous task. One of the strong points of personalist bioethics is its emphasis on the responsibility of the person to do good and to humanize the personhood. But an exaggerated emphasis on mercy might undercut this responsibility and lead into universalism. It undercuts the motivation to work for the coming of Jesus' Kingdom, which is one of the objectives behind developing Catholic bioethics. Another problem with this approach of giving lesser attention is that faithful will have a thinking that bioethics is not important and slowly without much noise bioethical concerns will be sidelined in the Church teachings.[19] Someone may criticise Pope Francis saying that he uses this strategy of giving lesser attention to bioethical issues in order to change subtly the doctrines regarding the safeguarding of life of the weak without explicitly stating the change. Such a criticism has merits as well. Cherry states that "shifts in the tone of discourse can also lead to foundational changes. An entirely new framework for Roman Catholic bioethics may be taking shape through Francis' subtle but significant change in tone and focus. In many quarters, for example, Pope Francis' shift in emphasis and his failure consistently to reiterate and underscore traditional condemnations of abortion, artificial insemination, homosexual acts, and assisted suicide, have already been taken as a tacit affirmation of a subtle but significant change in Roman Catholic bioethics."[20] But at the same time a keen observer will be able to note that such a change is only in the tone and emphasis. This indicates that even if the Pope who succeeds Francis gives more emphasis to bioethical issues, there shall not be the problem of discontinuity. That is the beauty with which Pope Francis deals with this issue. He does not change anything at the level of principles. He changes only the tone and emphasis which if a new pope wants to bring back can easily do so without the problem of discontinuity. In today's world, Pope Francis believes that a change in tone and emphasis is needed if his pastoral objectives are to be tasted success. He does not want his message of mercy to be blocked by the wall built on pure doctrines.

Conclusion

In Pope Francis, one can observe both continuity and discontinuity in the way Catholic church is doing her bioethics. The basic principles shall remain firm. But the approach will take a different route. Catholic bioethics now onward shall be more pastoral. The struggle Catholic bioethicists shall encounter is how to reconcile between personal responsibility on which the personalist bioethics of Catholic Church is built and unending mercy that might undercut this responsibility.

Endnotes

1   B.V. Brady, *Essential Catholic Social Thought*, Orbis Books, New York 2008, 33; Williams offers another definition of personalism: "The title "personalism" embraces any school of thought or intellectual movement that focuses on the reality of the person (human, angelic, divine) and on his unique dignity, insisting on the radical distinction between persons and all other beings (non-persons). As a philosophical school, personalism draws its foundations from human reason and experience." (T.D. Williams, "What is Thomistic Personalism?", *Alpha Omega* 2 (2004), 164); For Warren, "Personalism puts primacy on the ethical or moral realm. In dealing with economic issues, for example, personalist morality and what we owe to others takes precedence to questions of utility. In political contexts, persons and their life worlds take precedence over systems or structures. Personalism is thus an attempt, in an age of increasing depersonalization, to defend both the concept and the reality of persons. If there is consensus among personalists concerning the primacy and importance of the person, there is no dogma or unified doctrine that further constitutes a personalist ideology. Although, the majority of personalists have been theists, there is no unified theology, or even a requirement that to be a personalist one must believe in God. There are no agreements about methods or definitions; indeed, even the definition of "personhood" remains an open question. But because personalism opens up the middle ground between individualism and collectivism its contribution can no longer be ignored." (R.C. Warren, "Putting the Person Back into Human Resource Management", *Business & Professional Ethics Journal* 19 (2000), 193).

2   J. Maritain, *The Person and the Common Good*, University of Notre Dame Press, Notre Dame 1985, 12-13.

3   T.D. Williams, "What is Thomistic Personalism?", *Alpha Omega* 2 (2004), 165-166.

4   K. Wojtyla, Person and Community, quoted in J.E. Smith, "Natural Law and Personalism in Veritatis Splendor", *International Catholic University*, in https://icucourses.com/pages/002-03-personalism-and-natural-law.

5   "Phenomenology helps to disentangle the intricacies of human experience and leads us up to the fundamental questions which properly belong to the realm of metaphysics. Metaphysics, for its part, helps phenomenology not to get lost in the mazes of its interpretations. Metaphysics allows us to see, in a certain sense, the fundamental frame and the skeleton of experience while phenomenology shows us the tendons and muscles supported by this skeleton. Together they constitute the living body of philosophical experience." (R. Buttiglione, "The Political Praxis of Karol Wojtyla and St Thomas Aquinas", *John Paul II Forum in YouTube,* in https://www.youtube.com/watch?v=Yv_QSW0cUR8; 32.10).

6   Pontifical Council For justice and peace, *Compendium of the Social Doctrine of the Church* (2005), in http://www.vatican.va/roman_curia/pontifical_councils/justpeace/documents/rc_pc_justpeace_doc_20060526_compendio-dott-soc_en.html, 580.

7   J.E. Smith, "Natural Law and Personalism in Veritatis Splendor", *International Catholic University*, in https://icucourses.com/pages/002-03-personalism-and-natural-law.

8   It is true that emphasis is different in natural law and personlism. But they are compatible. The personlism we follow is a personalism informed both by natural law and phenomenology. Tarasiewicz notes that even though all over the world Karol Wojtyla passes for a phenomenologist rather than a Thomist, the truth of the fact is that for him phenomenology was not essential, but rather a supplemental means of doing philosophy, that he was a metaphysician who reached for phenomenology to gain a fuller grasp of man.

(P. Tarasiewicz, "The Common Sense Personalism of St. John Paul (Karol Wojtyla)", *Studia Gilsoniana* 3 (2014), 627.); "What I claim here is that the metaphysical view of man was regarded by Wojtyla as necessary, but insufficient. His Aristotelian Thomistic formation found its enrichment in phenomenological method, which was employed "merely in order to explore human interiority, including consciousness and self-consciousness."" (P. Tarasiewicz, "The Common Sense Personalism of St. John Paul (Karol Wojtyla)", *Studia Gilsoniana* 3 (2014), 628).

9 R.C. Warren, "Putting the Person Back into Human Resource Management", *Business & Professional Ethics Journal* 19 (2000), 182.

10 T.D. Williams, "What is Thomistic Personalism?", *Alpha Omega* 2 (2004), 168-169.

11 In the postmodern age, man is against the grand normative ethical theories. In postmodernism the capacity of these theories to explain everything is questioned. The lack of a sound normative ethical theory to explain the objectives and programmes of any organization will eventually lead to its annihilation. Frame writes about postmodern churches: "left-leaning, cause-driven, liberal Protestant churches that lack doctrinal rigor and are preoccupied with promotion of social justice and cultural inclusion will be the first to go." (T. Frame, *Losing My Religion. Unbelief in Australia,* University of New South Wales Press, Sydney 2009, 299). Personalism with its thrust for objectivity of human nature and interest in subjectivity of human person provides a solid rail for the trains to reach safely the destination.

12 Catholic personalism is based on three fundamental theological ideas namely, creation, the incarnation and the final end of humanity (B.V. Brady, *Essential Catholic Social Thought*, Orbis Books, New York 2008, 34).

13 B.V. Brady, *Essential Catholic Social Thought*, Orbis Books, New York 2008, 35.

14 C.E. Curran, "The Catholic Identity of Catholic Institutions", *Theological Studies* 58 (1997), 92.

15 "Today there is talk of the "humanization of medicine," but distinct or, if you will, complementary concepts are found within this term. Some use it to underscore the intersubjective relationship between the patient and health care personnel in the face of technological encroachment or hospital standardization. For others it means the introduction of humanities, particularly psychology, into medical school curricula. Yet the most profound meaning of this appeal, which in a way sums up the preceding aspects, consists in recognizing the personal dignity of every human subject, beginning, as will be shown, at the moment of his conception and continuing until the moment of death. This recognition is also accompanied by an awareness of human spirituality and immortality." (E. Sgreccia, *Personalist Bioethics. Foundations and Applications,* The National Catholic Bioethics Centre, Philadelphia 2012, 105).

16 JOHN PAUL II, Post-Synodal Apostolic Exhortation Christifideles Laici. 30 December 1980. See Francis, *Evangelii Gaudium* (2013), in http://w2.vatican.va/content/francesco/en/apost_exhortations/documents/papa-francesco_esortazione-ap_20131124_evangelii-gaudium.html, 213.

17 Francis, *Evangelii Gaudium* (2013), in http://w2.vatican.va/content/francesco/en/apost_exhortations/documents/papa-francesco_esortazione-ap_20131124_evangelii-gaudium.html, 35.

18 Francis, *Evangelii Gaudium* (2013), in http://w2.vatican.va/content/francesco/en/apost_exhortations/documents/papa-francesco_esortazione-ap_20131124_evangelii-gaudium.html, 34.

19 Cfr. H. T. Engelhardt Jr, "A New Theological Framework for Roman Catholic Bioethics: Pope Francis Makes a Significant Change in the Moral Framework for Bioethics", *Christian*

Bioethics 21 (2015), 130-134; M. J. CHERRY, "Pope Francis, Weak Theology, and the Subtle Transformation of Roman Catholic Bioethics", *Christian Bioethics* 21 (2015), 84-88.

20   M. J. CHERRY, "Pope Francis, Weak Theology, and the Subtle Transformation of Roman Catholic Bioethics", *Christian Bioethics* 21 (2015), 86.

Chapter 5

The Era of Pope Francis: Break or Beginning?
Pastoral Care of the Divorced and Remarried with an Open Ear and a Generous Heart

J. Charles Davis

Humboldt Research Fellow, Albert Ludwig University of Freiburg, Germany

Introduction

Pope Francis speaks a clear language understandable to everyone even outside the Church. He uses expressive metaphors instead of traditional speech patterns. For example, "the Church is not a tollhouse; it is the house of the Father, where there is a place for everyone, with all their problems."[1] His message of mercy found resonance worldwide in a short time and went straight into the hearts of those who are considered irregular or disorderly. His impact is huge in lives of many ordinary as well as influential personalities. Pope Francis speaks the language of a heart. His words and actions simply inspire people.

The carefree voice of the Pope has however shaken some heads and made surprises inside the Church. Pope Francis has become a challenging and remarkable person globally. No other papal document has been so much discussed as his post-synodal Exhortation *Amoris Laetitia* (AL) – *the Joy of Love*.[2] Some critique his phrases to be vague and non-doctrinal and four cardinals raised doubts and sought clarifications on certain points in *Amoris Laetitia*. Unwillingness and stubbornness of certain conservatives not to understand the pastoral concern of the Pope can be compared to a willful ignorance "ignoranta affectata" and behind regret and allegation of unclear phrasing of Pope Francis lies a refusal to understand his call for a paradigm shift and reflects lack of openness to accept new pastoral solutions.[3]

In fact, Pope Francis does not break any doctrinal Catholic teaching. He cites John Paul II and Benedict XVI many times signifying the unbroken continuity in apostolic teachings. When we read *amoris laetitia* in contrast to *Familiaris Consortio* (1981) or the *Catechism of the Catholic Church* (1992), there are however significant differences in perspective with regard to sexuality and love, marriage and family. Very clearly, Pope Francis has switched from an objective moral teaching grounded on static metaphysics of essence to a gospel oriented practical theology characterized by relevance for a larger life.

1. The Message of Pastoral Mercy

1. The message of the gospel is the logic of Pope Francis marked by love, mercy and compassion. His heart is filled with the message of pastoral mercy. He proclaims a gospel of integration and not condemnation: "No one can be condemned for ever, because that is not the logic of the Gospel" (AL 297). The religion is for salvation of people and not for condemning them, hence the Church should not condemn but embrace the sinners. He says, "The logic of integration is the key to their pastoral care" (AL 299). His words are simple, sharp and to the point and out of his own lived-experience. He is often criticized for statements without doctrinal credentials, but one must well notice that his emphasis is not on doctrines or norms but humans. His message is clear that sabbath is for humans and not otherwise. He has not altered any doctrine, but only wants the Church to move from dogmatic rigidity to pastoral discernment. He wants the Church to be active in the pastoral care of the faithful and not remain a watchdog of norms. Doctrines and norms are applicable in normal conditions. In conflict situations, he suggests that we go back to the root message of the gospel for pastoral discernment. His teachings of love, mercy and compassion is vividly seen in his own life and he comes across as a loving, merciful and compassionate face of God.

2. The papacy of Francis is marked by openness and humility. He is open to and humble to learn from the local Church. He says that "not all discussions of doctrinal, moral or pastoral issues need to be settled by interventions of the magisterium. Unity of teaching and practice is certainly necessary in the Church, but this does not preclude various ways of interpreting some aspects of that teaching or drawing certain consequences from it [...]. Each country or region, moreover, can seek solutions better suited to its culture and sensitive to its traditions and local needs" (AL 3). He has given a new direction in application and implementation of Church's general norms in particular situations. Pastoral solutions and exceptions need not affect standard norms and should not become scandalous either. According to

Marquard, "Hermeneutics is the art to find out from a text which is not in it?"[4] We need to interpret a text and find something more from it, such as a general norm, for its implementation in many complex contexts. However, interpretations do not go against the spirit of the whole text. A general principle must be interpreted according to situations for applications in various cultures. It does not mean relativization or weakening of normative credentials. Hermeneutics helps to interpret the general norms for respective situations.

3. Pope Francis presents a positive account of doctrines on marriage and family with the most important aspects of unity, indissolubility, sacramentality, fidelity, openness for life in continuity with Vatican II (*Gaudium et Spes*), Pope Paul VI (*Humanae Vitae*), John Paul II (*Familiaris Consortio*) and Benedict XVI. (*Deus Caritas est*). Not even an iota of apostolic teachings of his predecessors has been changed by Pope Francis. He has changed nothing in core teachings, yet he changed everything through the message of mercy. Not only his message is of inclusion and integration, but his very method is inductive. Amoris laetitia is actually an inductive summary of the results of the preceding XIV ordinary 2014 and III extraordinary 2015 synodal explorations (*Relatio Synodi und Relatio finalis*) on family. Pope Francis wants to be inductive and is sceptic of a deductive method in application of general rules in particular pastoral situations or deriving undue general conclusions from particular theological considerations (AL 2). Pope Francis warns against the stereotyped ideal families ignoring real situations and difficulties. Cardinal Kasper says that the moral ideal is an optimum yet is unreachable by many that we may often have to choose the lesser evil. There is no black and white but only different nuances and shadings in pastoral situations.[5] Rightly so, the Pope says, "we have been called to form consciences, not to replace them." (AL 37) It means that we need to form consciences of people in the light of the moral norms and not replace them with moral norms, laws and rules. While stressing the need for education of the faithful in marriage and family, sexuality and love, Pope Francis promotes respect for personal conscience of the concerned persons to deal with conflict issues, such as, communion to the divorced and remarried, artificial contraception and same sex partnerships. Failures and difficulties in following the ideals do neither make these persons automatically objective offenders against the teachings of the Church nor do they lose human dignity due to the "irregular situations" in which there are in.

4. Mercy is the hallmark of Pope Francis who does not want to abandon even one sinner, as he says, "Jesus himself is the shepherd of the hundred, not just of the ninety-nine. He loves them all" (AL 309). In the variety of situations affecting families "the Church is commissioned to proclaim the mercy of God, the beating heart of the Gospel, which in its own way

must penetrate the mind and heart of every person. The Bride of Christ must pattern her behaviour after the Son of God who goes out to everyone without exception."[6] Therefore, the Church should not lack mercy in her preaching and her witness, because "the Church is not a tollhouse; it is the house of the Father, where there is a place for everyone, with all their problems" (AL 310).[7] Therefore, Pope Francis wants the Church to *avoid* a cold bureaucratic morality in dealing with more sensitive issues and *adopt* a pastoral discernment filled with merciful love to understand, forgive, accompany, hope and above all integrate the concerned persons (AL 312). The Church must be a welcoming home for everyone who believes in Christ.

2. From a Legal Morality to a Virtue Morality: Dealing with Frailty: Accompanying-Discerning-Integrating

5.   An Apostolic Exhortation of a Pope has a formal and binding character, so also *Amoris Laetitia*. There lies a sound theological position behind this pastoral document. There is however a paradigm shift in *Amoris Laetitia*, which does not replace the previous teaching. Cardinal Kasper confirms that "*Amoris Laetitia* does not change an iota of the teaching of the Church, yet it changes everything." The Cardinal says that the Church with Pope Francis is gradually moving away from a "legal morality" toward a "virtue morality."[8] Thomas distinguishes between the speculative and practical reason. The speculative reason deduces conclusions logically from the principles strictly. In the practical world, it is not possible. At the practical level, objective norms are always incomplete, since they never can take account of all specific circumstances. Thus, the application cannot happen through logical deduction but means of the virtue of prudence. It is the *rechta ratio agibilium* according to the reason for the act (*Summa Theologiae* I/II q. 57 a.4). Prudence is root, measure, guiding and mother of all virtues (*Summa Theologiae* I/II q. 57 a. 6). Prudence uses the good, a goal approved by reason, to apply in the concrete situations (*Summa Theologiae* II/II q. 47 a. 2-6). Prudence does not establish norms out of situations. It does not make norms, but assumes the norm and applies in the concrete situation. Prudence will say what the norm here and now means. It applies with responsibility in the light of the norm to the actual reality of the situation. Prudence is actually based on love, which inspires and moves prudence. Thus, prudence is the root and characterising form of all virtues.[9] Every Catholic is bound to follow what the Pope says in *Amoris Laetitia*, in which he promotes a positive and realistic understanding of love, sexuality, marriage and family. He begins his Exhortation with these words: "The joy of love experienced by families is also the joy of the Church" (AL 1). Again, he reaffirms his address at the meeting of families in Santiago de Cuba, "families are not a problem;

they are first and foremost an opportunity" (AL 7) and gives respect to the genuine words of the local Bishops of Chile who stated that "the perfect families proposed by deceptive consumerist propaganda do not exist... Consumerist propaganda presents a fantasy that has nothing to do with the reality which must daily be faced by the heads of families" (AL 135).[10] In a very positive appreciation of love in families, Pope Francis says that erotic love should not considered simply as a permissible evil or a burden to be tolerated for the good of the family. Erotic love is a gift from God that enriches the relationship of the spouses. Cardinal Kasper praises the realistic, open and relaxed way of dealing with sexuality and eroticism: "With a grain of salt, we can say that *Amoris Laetitia* distances itself from a predominantly negative Augustinian view of sexuality and turns toward the Thomistic view on affirming creation."[11] Through *Amoris Laetitia*, Pope Francis reinstated the positive aspect of erotic love in marital relationships. This will have an impact in the Church's teaching on sexual morals.

6. Marriage is a fulfilment in grace and not a lifelong burden. Marriage is such a fragile thing in the modern world that couples need constant support and encouragement. Relationships do sometimes break down, despite all good will of the couples and good preparation before marriages. The reasons can vary from personal self-doubt or shattered plans to economic woes. At times, hurt is so deep that couples are not able to stay together. A durational separation is ideal and can make room for healing, but circumstances lead some to get divorced from their relationships completely and among them some remarry after the civil divorce. Divorce is not permitted in the Church. The Church has objections to divorce of sacramental unions of an indissoluble nature as well as to a remarriage of divorced couples whose previous bond is still existing without annulment. Thus, the Church considers them to be in objective negation of Church's teaching and denies communion to those divorcees. Civil remarriage contradicts the visible symbol of the sacrament of marriage, but *Amoris Laetitia* does not stop at categorical exclusion from the sacraments. Pope Francis says that we cannot guide broken family sufficiently "simply by stressing doctrinal, bioethical and moral issues, without encouraging openness to grace" (AL 37). Many of the divorcees may not be subjectively culpable in the grave situations of break-down in marital partnerships. Children of those failing relationships are most affected. Thus, we need to address here two issues: pastoral care to those children and failing couples, and communion to the divorced and civilly married. Pope Francis has given pastoral solutions to both aspects in *Amoris Laetitia*. However, he holds the sacramental teaching of the Church that the indissolubility of marriage is part and parcel of the Church's indispensable set of beliefs inherited from Christ himself.

7.   Pope Francis is absolutely within the tradition when he makes concession of forgiveness to sinners. The Old Testament tradition writes off debts during the jubilee years. The New Testament goes after the one sheep leaving the ninety-nine and welcomes the prodigal son. That is the sense of integration and the logic of the gospel (AL 297). In complex irregular situations, we cannot apply norms geometrically, but the unconditional love and mercy of God would justify integration of those who are in serious sin but have earnest desire to return to God. The church should thus "avoid judgements which do not take into account the complexity of various situations" and "to be attentive, by necessity, to how people experience distress because of their condition" (AL 79, 296).[12] Therefore, Pope Francis asks the divorced and civilly married to use "internal forum" of pastors whom he suggests the three aspects of "accompanying, discerning and integrating" as guiding principle. Those affected should not feel excommunicated from church but as living members able to experience her as a mother who welcomes them always (AL 299). Here, the existing canon law (915 or 916 CIC/1983)[13] is not violated, since *Amoris Laetitia* does not offer a general rule of automatic mechanism to admit all divorced and civilly remarried to the sacraments. Nor do canons 915 and 916, or any canon of CIC 1983 exclusively mention the divorced and remarried or prohibition on reception of the Eucharist by them. With *Amoris Laetitia*, as Cardinal Kasper comments, remarried divorcees are now no more punished with automatic excommunication but instead are invited to participate as living members of Church life in ecclesiastical, liturgical, pastoral, educational, and institutional services (AL 299). The term "excommunication" is not even once mentioned in *Amoris Laetitia*. The position of Pope Francis is similar to the concessional position of John Paul II who gave permission to the remarried divorcees to receive Communion, if they lived as brother and sister though sexual abstinence. John Paul II had clarified that, "There is in fact a difference between those who have sincerely tried to save their first marriage and have been unjustly abandoned, and those who through their own grave fault have destroyed a canonically valid marriage. Finally, there are those who have entered into a second union for the sake of the children's upbringing, and who are sometimes subjectively certain in conscience that their previous and irreparably destroyed marriage had never been valid" (*Familiaris Consortio* 84). Yet, John Paul II continued the status quo of the general ban on receiving communion by the divorced and remarried based on Sacred Scripture and on the fact that their state and condition of life objectively contradict that union of love between Christ and the Church which is signified and effected by the Eucharist (*Familiaris Consortio* 84). Pope Benedict XVI maintained the position of his predecessor and suggested that the remarried Catholics following a divorce should make a spiritual communion. However, Pope Francis has now

permitted communion to the divorced and remarried couples after pastoral discernment of individual cases.

8. *The Catechism of the Catholic Church* (n. 2352) mentions that "imputability and responsibility for an action can be diminished or even nullified by ignorance, inadvertence, duress, fear, habit, inordinate attachments, and other psychological or social factors" (AL 302). Therefore, an objective contradiction need not lead to the culpability of the person. Therefore, the Pope confirms the statement of the synod fathers: "Therefore, while upholding a general rule, it is necessary to recognize that responsibility with respect to certain actions or decisions is not the same in all cases. Pastoral discernment, while taking into account a person's properly formed conscience, must take responsibility for these situations. Even the consequences of actions taken are not necessarily the same in all cases" (AL 302).[14] The traditional approach differentiates the material from the formal dimension in relation to the gravity of the sin. The material dimension refers to the objective facts of the case and the formal depends on the disposition of the acting subject. A serious offense, which is contrary to a basic standard, is not a grave sin subjectively because there are limitations in knowledge, will or freedom of the acting subject. The objective facts are not enough to judge an act to be sinful. *Amoris Laetitia* takes this differentiation between formal and material dimension seriously and considers mitigating conditions or limitations to evaluate the individual situations of the people (AL 301-303, 305, 308). Thus, *Amoris Laetitia* accepts the differentiation between objective and subjective situations made by the Pontifical Council for Legislative Texts and not the opinion of the c. 915 (CIC 1983) that a serious sin in the objective sense is a sufficient reason for the exclusion.[15] In addition, the logic of mercy and compassion (the logic of the Gospel) assumes the responsibility for inclusion. *Amoris Laetitia* underscores: "No one can be condemned for ever, because that is not the logic of the Gospel!" (AL 297).

9. According to the magisterial teaching, the remarried divorcees find themselves in a situation that objectively contravenes God's law (CCC 1650) and a remarried spouse is then in a situation of public and permanent adultery (CCC 2384). In contrast, *Amoris Laetitia* opts for a differencing and respecting views. It distinguishes not only between the objective situation and the subjective condition of a sinner, but also acknowledges the grace of God effective in these situations as well as takes into consideration the subjective life on love and loyalty. Situations, that do not fully comply with a moral norm or a moral ideal, need not be subjectively culpable. Thus, *Amoris Laetitia* describes that the corresponding life no longer is simply a contradiction to the ideal of sacramental marriage. Hence, "it is can no longer simply be said that all those in any "irregular" situation are living in a state of mortal sin and are deprived of sanctifying grace" (AL 301). Those affected

must anyway make an assessment themselves in their conscience. This position is given a high priority and strengthened in *Amoris Laetitia* without relativism or subjectivism. The emphasis on the value of conscience does also correspond to the importance on formation of personal conscience and its competence. The spiritual and pastoral accompaniment serves, similar to the process of discernment, the formation of conscience that one may become aware of one's situation before God and correspond to the best of one's own will even in situations that may not (quite) correspond to a norm or an ideal. Thereby, *Amoris Laetitia* does not question the fruitfulness of "the ideal of marriage, marked by a commitment to exclusivity and stability" (AL 34). The document demands clarification and differentiation of the specific situation of a civil remarriage after divorce characterized as a permanent and public adultery (CCC 2384) . In the light of the new perspective initiated by Pope Francis, we may need to revise or at least formulate the numbers 1650 and 2384 of the Catechism of the Catholic Church precisely and differently following *Amoris Laetitia.*[16]

10.   Pope Francis has clearly introduced a paradigm shift in *Amoris Laetitia* with extraordinary permissions in individual cases to receive the Eucharist following a responsible personal and pastoral discernment. As Cardinal Kasper and Eberhard Schockenhoff explain, extraordinary permissions, as granted by Pope Francis in individual cases, do not abolish the objective contradiction of the ongoing bond of marriage of the first sacramental marriage and the second civil marriage.[17] In this way, Pope Francis does not break the norm, but much more brings an alternative solution to the existing problem. He relies on the Thomistic teaching that the circumstances must be taken into consideration in applying a norm to evaluate an act. Following Aristotelian tradition, Aquinas says that a human act is good or bad depending on the final goal - *telos* at which all human actions aim. According to the teaching of Thomas Aquinas (+1274) and Alphonse Liguori (+1787), a judgement on the moral quality of a human act as crime or sin is not reliable exclusively from *forum externum* and its external object. To a free, responsible and moral act of humans belong much more the intention of the actors and circumstances than mere object of the act. That is why, it is not possible to make a judgment on an act without taking into consideration of the will of the person in his conscience and of the pastoral assessment of the life situation in *forum internum*. In our context, it might mean that some of the divorced and remarried are subjectively convinced in their conscience that their previous marriage was really invalid. Thus, according to the new perspective of Pope Francis following the Thomistic tradition, pastors need an open ear and a generous heart to listen to those affected and make right distinction of each individual situation. Thus, it is no longer possible to claim that all who live in any so-called irregular situation are in a state of mortal

sin and lost the sanctifying grace (AL 301). The new position eliminates the condition under which the sanction of exclusion from the sacraments of the Church to such situations was considered the only possible response. Pope Francis has thus shown a new way that pastoral discernment is an alternative solution to permit reconciled persons in irregular situations to receive the Eucharist following the sacrament of confession, penance and reconciliation. If the Church attends prudently to the competence of the conscience of her believers and differentiates the respective life situations carefully, she cannot automatically judge every irregular situation to be an objective state of mortal sin that could separate God permanently. Careful pastoral discernment can help to detect whether the bond of the first marriage was really valid or a fiction, thereby can help for a speedy annulment and successive nuptial blessing of the existing civil marriage.

3. Concluding Remarks: The Mercy of God and the Way of Love

The teaching of moral theology should not fail to incorporate the pastoral considerations of gratuitous offer of God's love, although concern must be shown for the integrity of the Church's moral teaching. In support of his view, the International Theological Commission confirms that "natural law could not be presented as an already established set of rules that impose themselves a priori on the moral subject; rather, it is a source of objective inspiration for the deeply personal process of making decisions."[18] The synodal Fathers regretted that "rather than offering the healing power of grace and the light of the Gospel message, some would "indoctrinate" that message, turning it into "dead stones to be hurled at others" (AL 49).[19] Thus, Pope Francis critiques the rigidity of pastors that "we put so many conditions on mercy that we empty it of its concrete meaning and real significance. That is the worst way of watering down the Gospel" (AL 311). Pastors must rather make room for God's unconditional love in pastoral activity with an open heart and a generous heart especially to those living on the outermost fringes of society[20] (AL 312). With these distinctive words, Pope Francis says that the logic of exclusion and condemnation should no longer determine the path of the Church. Pastors must invite everyone to continue the journey on the way of love in which they recognize a possible response to the call of God in their consciences (cf. AL 303). Further, the Pope warns that "a pastor cannot feel that it is enough simply to apply moral laws to those living in "irregular" situations, as if they were stones to throw at people's lives" 305). The force of the language of Pope Francis with deep compassion of the message of mercy reveals that he will leave a spiritual legacy which will have a telling impact on the understanding of sexuality, marriage and family in days to come. It is a great beginning of renewal and revival for the Catholic Church to be a compassionate mother. With an open ear to the concerns of the synod's reflections, the Pope says that "there is no stereotype of the ideal family, but rather a challenging mosaic made up of many different realities, with all their joys, hopes and problems. The situations that concern us are challenges. We should not be trapped into wasting our energy in doleful laments, but rather seek new forms of missionary creativity" (Al 57). Today, the pastoral effort to strengthen marriages in order to prevent their breakdown is much more important than the pastoral care of failures (AL 307). The salvation of souls, as the final canon CIC 1752 states, must always be the supreme law of the Church.

Endnotes

1   Pope FRANCIS, Apostolic Exhortation *Evangelii Gaudium* (24 November 2013) 47: AAS 105 (2013), 1040.

2   Pope FRANCIS, Post-Synodal Apostolic Exhortation *Amoris Laetitia* (Vatican: Libreria Editrice Vaticana, 19 March 2016): AAS CVIII (2016) N. 4. pp. 311-443.

3   Eberhard SCHOCKENHOFF, "Traditionsbruch oder notwendige Weiterbildung?: Zwei Lesarten des Nachsynodalen Schreibens Amoris Laetitia," *Stimmen der Zeit* 3 (2017) 147-158: 147. See Bernhard Häring, *Das Gesetz Christi: Moraltheologie dargestellt für Priester und Laien*, Vol. 1 (Freiburg: Wewel, 1963), 153, 172.

4   Odo MARQUARD, "Frage nach der Frage, auf die die Hermeneutik eine Antwort ist," in: Odo Marquard, Abschied vom Prinzipiellen (Stuttgart: Philosophische Studien, 1981), 117-146, 117.

5   Walter KASPER, "Amoris Laetitia: Ein Bruch oder Abbruch? Eine Nachlese," *Stimmen der Zeit* 11 (2016), 723-732, 725.

6   Bull *Misericordiae Vultus* (11 April 2015), 12: AAS 107 (2015): 407.

7   Apostolic Exhortation *Evangelii Gaudium* (24 November 2013), 47: AAS 105 (2013), 1040.

8   KASPER, "Amoris Laetitia: Ein Bruch oder Abbruch?," 725-26.

9   KASPER, "Amoris Laetitia: Ein Bruch oder Abbruch?," 726.

10   Chilean Bishops' Conference, *La vida y la familia: regalos de Dios para cada uno de nosotros* (21 July 2014).

11   KASPER, Amoris Laetitia: Ein Bruch oder Abbruch?, 725. "Cum grano salis kann man sagen: "Amoris laetitia" nimmt Abstand von einer vorwiegend negativen, augustinischen Sicht der Sexualität und wendet sich der schöpfungsbejahenden thomistischen Sicht zu."

12   *Relatio Finalis* 2015, 51.

13   Can. 915: Those who have been excommunicated or interdicted after the imposition or declaration of the penalty and others obstinately persevering in manifest grave sin are not to be admitted to holy communion. Can. 916: A person who is conscious of grave sin is not to celebrate Mass or receive the body of the Lord without previous sacramental confession unless there is a grave reason and there is no opportunity to confess; in this case the person is to remember the obligation to make an act of perfect contrition which includes the resolution of confessing as soon as possible.

14   *Relatio Finalis* 2015, 85.

15   Eva-Maria FABER and Martin M. LINTNER, "Theologische Entwicklungen in Amoris laetitia hinsichtlich der Frage der wiederverheirateten Geschiedenen," in: Stephan Goertz and Caroline Witting (eds.), *Amoris laetitia – Wendepunkt für die Moraltheologie?* (Freiburg: Herder, 2016), 279-320, 288f.

16   FABER and LINTNER, 315-6.

17   KASPER, "Amoris Laetitia: Ein Bruch oder Abbruch?," 729-31; Schockenhoff, "Traditionsbruch oder notwendige Weiterbildung?," 150-51.

18   International Theological Commission, *In Search of a Universal Ethic: A New Look at Natural Law* (2009), 59.

19   Concluding Address of the Fourteenth Ordinary General Assembly of the Synod of Bishops (24 October 2015): *L'Osservatore Romano*, 26-27 October 2015, p. 13.

20   *Misericordiae Vultus* (11 April 2015), 15: AAS 107 (2015), 409.

Chapter 6

Pope Francis' Moral and Pastoral Approach in *Amoris Laetitia*

George Therukaattil MCBS
Prof and Head (Emeritus), Department of Christian Studies,
University of Mysore, Mysore, Karnataka

Introduction

In the introductory paragraphs of the post-synodal Apostolic Exhortation on Love and Family, *Amoris Laetitia,* Pope Francis plainly sets out his moral and pastoral approach.[1] He asks the Church to meet people where they are - to accept them in the concrete circumstances and complexities of their lives. He pleads the Church to respect people's consciences and their discernment in moral decisions and underscores the importance of considering norms and mitigating circumstances in pastoral discernment.

The Apostolic Exhortation is mainly a document that reflects on family life and encourages family persons in their struggle to be faithful to the Lord. But it is also the Pope's reminder that the Church should avoid simply judging people and imposing rules on them without considering their struggles. The goal of the Exhortation is to help families—in fact, everyone—experience being touched by an unmerited, unconditional, gratuitous mercy of God and know that they are welcome in the Church.

In the introduction of the Exhortation itself Pope Francis makes it clear that although unity of teaching and practice is certainly necessary for the Church, it does not preclude various ways of interpreting some aspects of that teaching or drawing certain consequences from it. Each country or region, moreover, can seek solutions better suited to its culture and sensitive to its traditions and local needs.[2] In his address at the end of the Synod of the 2015, he also drew attention to different contexts where what is lawful in one place is deemed outside the law in another. "What seems normal for a bishop on one continent is considered strange and almost scandalous – almost! – for a bishop from another; what is considered a violation of a right in one society is an evident and inviolable rule in another; what for some is freedom of conscience is for others simply confusion."[3]

Stating this, the Pope referred to declarations of his predecessors, included the contributions of Synods on the family held in 2014 and 2015 and also quoted a number of declarations of bishops' conferences of various countries for references.[4] Using insights from the Synod of Bishops on the Family and from Bishops' Conferences from around the world, Pope Francis affirms Church teaching on family life and marriage and strongly emphasizes the role of personal conscience and pastoral discernment, urging the Church to appreciate the context of people's lives when helping them make good decisions"[5]

Though much of AL incorporated "the propositions voted upon by the Bishops at both 2014 and 2015 Synods as much as possible, as we see from the abundant references he makes to them in the footnotes of AL,"[6] Pope Francis calls his pastoral and moral approach as something new with regard to the pastoral practice in the way pastoral care is to be extended as help and encouragement to those in difficult marital situations or in irregular unions and to families in their daily commitments and challenges.[7] The Pope asks for a compassionate pastoral concern to such persons since they continue to be members of the Church and brothers and sisters of God's household. In addition he encourages everyone to be a sign of mercy and closeness wherever family life remains imperfect or lacks peace and joy.[8] In addition to these, the introductory section of *Amoris Laetitia's* significant account and vision of conscience and communal discernment (including more input and collaboration from the laity) on moral matters that is consistent with the exhortation's pastoral practice mentioned above. Further, Pope Francis' call in his *Evangelii Gaudium* for "a Church which is bruised, hurting and dirty because it has been out on the streets," suggest that the moral and pastoral practice of the Church should be more attentive to the realities and complexities of life in the concrete rather than in the abstract.[9] "The result is a challenging reappraisal that expects moral theologians to promote a genuine culture of discernment in the church."[10]

Details of Pope Francis' new moral and pastoral approach can be seen especially in Chapters Six and Eight of *Amoris Laetitia*. In Chapter Six, one can see the Pope's pastoral perspectives (AL199-258) and in Chapter Eight, he writes about the need of accompanying, discerning and integrating weakness (AL 291-312).

1. Pastoral Perspectives

In the Chapter Six, Pope Francis treats various pastoral perspectives that are aimed at forming solid and fruitful families according to God's plan. Stating about the pastoral perspectives, the Pope affirms that it is not enough to present a set of moral rules, but present values that are clearly needed today.... In practice is to be determined, he writes, not by "a new set of general rules, canonical in nature and applicable to all cases," but by "a responsible personal and pastoral discernment of particular cases."[11]

Thus, in family planning, though the decisions should be reached in dialogue and respect for the other and considerations proceeding from *Humanae Vitae* and *Familiaris Consortio* are in place as also the role of a formed conscience as taught by *Gaudium et Spes* (n. 50),[12] people undergoing a crisis in their married life or people in difficult or critical situations do not seek pastoral assistance, since they do not find in them, a sympathetic, realistic and 'individual-case-by-case-concerned' approach.[13] This follows from Pope's Francis' different approach from that of *Familiaris consortio* of John Paul II and *Humanae Vitae* off Paul VI:"... the final report does not follow John Paul II in going further and repeating like him, Paul VI's insistence that "each and every marriage act must remain Prone to the transmission of life."[14]

Further, *The Final Report* spells out "generative responsibility" in a way that echoes but without citing an examination of conscience for married people proposed in 1977.[15] It put three questions to married couples: "In agreement with my spouse, have I given a clear and Conscientious answer to the problem of birth control? Have I prevented a conception for egotistic motives? Have I brought a life into the world without a sense of responsibility? These questions tested the loving and responsible decision of the two spouses. But nothing was asked about the methods used to prevent what they together judge would be an "irresponsible" pregnancy. Such a decision was left to their conscientious agreement.[16] Pope Francis spends a whole chapter on married love being made fruitful through responsible parenthood.[17] In the name of "Natural Law", while Pope Paul VI's *Huamanae vitae* based its opposition to contraception on a largely biological "Physicalist," moral viewpoint, *Familiaris Consortio* in John Paul II's theology of body states that sexuality is "an interpersonal language wherein the other is taken seriously in his or her sacred and inviolable dignity", Pope Francis does not follow their "Natural Law" approach. Pope Francis takes as his starting point the actual experience of married life – an approach that resembles the experiential method that Vat II adopted in *Gaudium et Spes*.

Pope Francis is nothing if not realistic about "current realities" that confront and condition married and family life today.[18] Care and respect need to be shown for those suffering, especially the poor, from unjustly endured separation, divorce or abandonment, or those maltreated by a husband or wife to interrupt their life together. Those, who are divorced and have entered into new unions, must also be made to feel as part of the Church.[19] Mixed marriages, with disparity of cults, need special pastoral care since those marriages provide occasions for inter-religious dialogue.[20] While those with homosexual orientation are to be shown pastoral concern, homosexual marriages have no grounds to be seen as analogous to God's plan for marriages and the family.[21] All these persons remain, the Pope insists "part of the ecclesial community," and "should be made to feel part" of it, and should be encouraged to participate in the life of the community."[22] This requires that the whole Church, and not just her official pastors, become open to discerning a great variety of irregular situations and ready to "help each person [In such irregular situations] find his or her proper way of participating in the ecclesial community."[23]

Regarding the norms of sexual morality, Pope Francis certainly sees the need for a humane and ethical analysis of the state of sexual intimacy, personal commitment, erotic longing, and gender rights and encourages the young people to be sexually responsible, especially since the mature use of contraceptives could avoid a later choice about abortion. He solves this dilemma with the so-called pastoral solution, which allows us to quietly defy Vatican dogma, when the situation seemed to call for it. In the confessional booth or in the Parish priest's parlour, the parish priest could encourage his parishioners to decide for themselves, by helping them to examine their own consciences, whether the doctrine of the Church applied to them in their particular circumstance. (*Gaudium et Spes* of Second Vatican Council, taking up the theme of responsible parenthood, had said, "The parents themselves, and no one else, should ultimately make this judgment in the sight of God.")

"Who am I to judge?" With those five words, in reply to a reporter's question about the status of gay priests in the Church, Pope Francis stepped away from the disapproving tone, the explicit moralizing typical of Popes and bishops. The phenomenon of same sex orientation cannot simply be dismissed as an aberration of individuals. The biological and social causes that are alleged to be behind this have to be seriously looked into. If the persons concerned are sexually differently oriented from birth or due to social upbringing and if they are not to be blamed for this, what does the Great Mystery expect us to do? Even if they have personally contributed to this and are not able to get out of it what do we do with them? What provisions have we made for the transgender, who may be a microscopic minority, but are still people created in God's image?[24] What are we to say to voices of science that say sexual orientation is neither a personal choice nor a matter of social conditioning but rests in the deepest ontological make-up of the individual and thus forms part of the mystery of human nature which is good?[25]

Pope Francis elaborated his thinking about homosexuals in an interview.[26] Pope Benedict had defended the "dignity" of all peoples, including homosexuals, but called homosexual acts "an intrinsic moral evil." Saying that "the inclination itself must be seen as an objective disorder," he barred the admission of gay men to seminaries, even if they were celibate, and denounced the idea of gay marriage. Pope Francis has not altered the impossibility of gay marriage in the Church, but his tone is very different. "A person once asked me, in a provocative manner, if I approved of homosexuality," he said. "I replied with another question: 'Tell me: when God looks at a gay person, does he endorse the existence of this person with love, or reject and condemn this person?' We must always consider the person."[27]

Pope Francis makes quite clear his two central convictions. On the one hand, he insists that the Church must continue to propose the full ideal of marriage and clearly express her objective teaching. The integrity of the Church's moral teaching requires nothing less than that. On the other hand, to those who press for a more rigorous pastoral care which leaves no room for confusion, the pope responds that if we put so many conditions on [God's] mercy that we empty it of its concrete meaning and real significance, we will be indulging in the worst way of watering down the Gospel.[28]

Repeatedly, Pope Francis argues that the Church's purpose was more to proclaim God's merciful love for all people than to condemn sinners for having fallen short of ideal, especially those having to do with gender and sexual orientation. His break from his immediate predecessors—John Paul II, and Benedict XVI, is less ideological than intuitive, an inclusive vision of the Church centred on an identification with the poor. From this vision, theological and organizational innovations can follow.

Pope John Paul II and Pope Benedict XVI used the Catholic tradition as a bulwark against the triple threat of liberalism, relativism, and secularism. But Pope Francis views the Church as a field hospital after a battle.[29] "The thing the Church needs most today is the ability to heal wounds and to warm the hearts of the faithful," he said. "It is useless to ask a seriously injured person if he has high cholesterol and about the level of his blood sugars! You have to heal his wounds. Then we can talk about everything else. Heal the wounds."[30]

Pope Francis violated a set code of Catholic ethical and philosophical discourse when, in an open letter to the prominent Italian journalist and atheist Eugenio Scalfari, in September, he wrote, "I would not speak about 'absolute' truths, even for believers … Truth is a relationship. As such, each one of us receives the truth and expresses it from within, that is to say, according to one's own circumstances, culture, and situation in life." When Spadaro asked Francis about "the great changes in society, as well as the way human beings are reinterpreting themselves," Francis got up to retrieve his well-thumbed breviary. He read from a fifth-century saint's writings on the laws governing progress: "Even the dogma of the Christian religion must proceed from these laws. It progresses, solidifying with years, growing over time." Then Francis commented, "So we grow in the understanding of the truth. . . . There are ecclesiastical rules and precepts that were once effective, but now they have lost value or meaning. The view of the Church's teaching as a monolith to defend without nuance or different understanding is wrong."[31]

Pope Francis has not overthrown the traditional teachings of the Church, as many Catholics had either hoped or feared that he would, in this post-Synod exhortation. Instead he has sought to carve out ample room for a flexible pastoral interpretation of those teachings, encouraging pastors to help couples apply general moral principles to their specific circumstances.

2. Accompanying, Discerning and Integrating Weakness

The eighth chapter of Pope Francis' Exhortation is an invitation to mercy and responsible personal and pastoral discernment in situations that do not fully match what the Lord proposes. Pope Francis begins the eighth Chapter on irregular situations by saying, "The way of the Church is not to condemn anyone for ever; it is to pour out the balm of God's mercy on all those who ask for it with a sincere heart...No one can be condemned for ever, because that is not the logic of the Gospel!"[32] Pope Francis goes on to talk about accompanying and integrating into the life of the Church the baptized who are divorced and civilly remarried.

According to me, the eighth Chapter of *Amoris Laetitia* is very sensitive. It is an invitation to mercy and pastoral discernment in particular cases, one which would recognize that, since 'the degree of responsibility is not equal in all cases;' the consequences or effects of a rule need not necessarily always be the same.[33] Pope Francis' emphasis on mercy towards the divorced and remarried does not only mean that those people will more freely partake of Communion. It also means that the doctrine of the indissolubility of marriage, however much it is still held up as an ideal, will not grip the moral imagination of the Church as it once did.[34] Such a progression has already occurred in Catholic attitudes about contraception. Once the vast majority of the faithful took for granted their right and duty to weigh situation against principle—and decided, mostly, that the principle did not apply—it was only a matter of time before the hierarchy itself did the same. That is the significance of Pope Francis' own conclusion, offered in February on his flight back from Mexico, that the Zika-virus pandemic requires a change in the Church's policies on contraception. In that drastic situation, the principle of "*Humanae Vitae*" simply does not apply. As has happened before, the private forum had become public. Official Church teaching on birth control may never change, but its meaning will never be the same. Moral discernment belongs to the people.

In addressing the fragile, complex or irregular situations, Pope Francis emphasizes three important fundamental tasks in Church's pastoral praxis: guiding or accompanying, discerning and integrating weakness. Here the Pope himself identifies as the core of his message. Pope Francis shows his true character as a pastor: encouraging, guiding, questioning, cajoling, sympathizing, instructing, helping readers to gain a deeper appreciation for the Church's understanding of sacramental marriage. He upholds the ideal of Christian marriage, recognizes that no fallen human lives up to that ideal, and offers the support of the Church to all those who are willing to continue the lifelong struggle to grow in love.

Moreover, the Pope recognizes, and clearly states, that the Christian understanding of marriage is the only reliable antidote to a host of ills that plague contemporary society, especially in the West. Particularly in the second chapter of *Amoris Laetitia*, he rightly insists that at a time when marital breakdown has reached epidemic proportions, Catholics must not allow themselves to be deterred from delivering the message that our society needs to hear—even while he recognizes that the message is unpopular, and those who proclaim it may face mounting hostility. It is a matter accompanying those who have breached the marriage bond; he compares the Church's task to that of a field hospital. (AL 291). It is a matter of reaching to everyone, of needing to help each person find his/her proper way of participating in the ecclesial community, and thus to experience being touched by an unmerited, unconditional and gratuitous mercy of God.[35]

Quoting the synod Fathers, Pope Francis states that the Church does not disregard the constructive elements in those situations which do not yet or no longer correspond to her teaching on marriage, which is a sacrament that unites a man and wife and grants them the grace to become a 'domestic church' and a leaven of new life for society.[36] Marriage unions that are *de facto* irregular are to be dealt with as Jesus dealt with the Samaritan woman, with mercy and reinstatement. Pope Francis here follows the 'law of gradualness' in pastoral care as proposed by John Paul II.[37] "In making his call in *Amoris laetitia* to practice a responsible discernment of particular cases – a discernment which involves not only the couples themselves but also their bishop, parish priest, and/or other spiritual guides – the pope appeals at length to passages from Thomas Aquinas, *Familiaris Consortio,* the Catechism of the Catholic Church, the International Theological Commission, and other sources. They all provide help towards discerning, on an individual basis, appropriate access to the sacraments of reconciliation and Eucharist for the divorced and civilly remarried (AL 300-312). The key theological argument for accepting such an access comes from ancient Christian teaching about forgiving, healing and nourishing power of the Eucharist."[38] Pope Francis never says in so many words that "in some, justifiable circumstances, those in a second marriage may receive the sacrament of reconciliation and Eucharist." To say that would clash with his refusal, in the light of "the immense variety of concrete circumstances," to produce "a new set of general rules."[39] He would need to spell out those circumstances and produce detailed legislation that took account of reasons for the collapse of the first marriage, length of time since the second marriage was civilly contracted, the number of children involved, and so forth. He leaves such "discernment" to the local authorities.[40]

3. Pastoral Discernment

As far as pastoral discernment with regard to "irregular" situations is concerned the Pope states: "There is a need 'to avoid judgements which do not take into account the complexity of various situations' and to be 'attentive, by necessity to how people experience distress because of their condition."[41] The pastoral solution of Pope Francis lies in this realm of "particular situations," where, as the Pope insists, "constant love" *must prevail over judgmentalism*. Every situation and mitigating factors or circumstances may be different, and so a subtle pastoral and moral discernment is required to see how general principles apply to it. For centuries, the assumption of the Catholic hierarchy was that lay people were not capable of such discernment, but, with Francis, that is no longer true. "The Joy of Love" is directly addressed to the laity, who is encouraged to pursue conscientious moral discernment by consulting not only pastors but one another. The married people know the ins and outs of married life better than unmarried people.

What Pope Francis proposes about discerning and mercifully helping those in "irregular" married situations invites us to remember past changes in church teaching and practice and open to new ones. Any list of such developments and even reversals (which do not encompass the essentials of faith professed in the Creed) concern, for instance, what happened to official teaching about slavery, torture, death penalty, religious freedom, sharing prayer with other Christians and with followers of other faiths (*communicatio in sacris),* and the anointing of the sick.... Pope Francis has done something similar, albeit not identical, by opening the door for the divorced and civilly remarried, after due discernment and in appropriate circumstances, to receive the sacrament of reconciliation and Eucharist.[42]

The change that Pope Francis has wrought on the Catholic imagination is one that moral theologians never imagined would come from a Pope. So Pope Francis says: "I understand those who prefer a more rigorous pastoral care which leaves no room for confusion."But Pope Francis' approach is different. He "sincerely believes that Jesus wants a Church attentive to the goodness which the Holy Spirit sows in the midst of human weakness." The point, of course, is that the Church, too, is marked by human weakness, as this halting progress toward reform so clearly shows. But here, again, the goodness is what counts. Pope Francis is inviting the Church to leave behind the tidy moralism of the pulpit and the sacristy in order to do "what good she can, even if in the process, her shoes get soiled by the mud of the street."[43] He has taken to heart the significant warning of Jesus, "It is not those who are well who need the physician, but those who are sick" (Lk 5:31). He obviously hopes that others who minister in the Church—bishops, priests, moral theologians, confessors and pastoral counsellors—will follow Jesus' example. Pope Francis cites the 2014 Synod, saying, "the Church must accompany with attention and care the weakest of her children, who show signs of a wounded and troubled love, by restoring in them hope and confidence". To this extent the synod was a success as the entire community of the Church was "directly or indirectly involved in the discerning and decision-making process, listening and dialoguing and trying to understand the different viewpoints emerging from diverse cultures and contexts, challenging and being challenged, being faithful to the tradition and being open to the challenges of the present day self-understanding of humans, discovering the limitations of yesterday's solutions for today's problems, searching for what the Spirit is saying to the Church today."[44]

4. Conscience

Admitting the tension between gospel's high ideal for family life and the inevitable imperfections of reality, and hence called to live in the 'already' but 'not yet' tension, the Exhortation seeks to help all families, including those in so-called "irregular" situations by emphasizing the primary responsibility of conscience for the moral life, indicating that the crux of the moral life is discernment in one's particular context. Pope Francis' Exhortation significantly develops a new vision of conscience and moral discernment that empowers the faithful to attend to the voice of God echoing in their depths on all moral matters. What the Pope has offered us is what James Bretzke would call a 'thick description' of what formed and informed conscience in the concrete.[45] "Although Bretzke connects this assertion to *Amoris Laetitia's* suggestions for a married couple's decisions about "responsible parenthood," the place where the primacy of conscience is most apparent in the Exhortation's consideration is in the possibilities for including divorced and remarried Catholics more fully in the life of the Church. After citing the traditional teaching that concrete factors can influence subjective culpability for the agent who commits an objectively illicit act, Pope Francis explains that the "individual conscience needs to be better incorporated into Church's praxis in certain situations which do not objectively embody our understanding of marriage."[46] This is why Pope Francis proposes an "examination of conscience" to help divorced and re-married Catholics to determine their subjective culpability for the end of their previous marriage and their immediate responsibilities to their new partner.[47]

Pope Francis' vision of conscience and the process of its examination establish the basis for his widely quoted assertion of "development of doctrine,"[48] which admits the possibility of readmission to the Eucharist for divorced and remarried Catholics, albeit on a case-by-case basis. It is in this context we should read *Amoris Laetitia's* hotly debated passage: "... it is possible that in an objective situation of sin–which may not be subjectively culpable or fully such – a person can be living in God's grace, can grow in the life of grace and charity, while receiving the Church's help to this end."[49] The footnote adds, "In certain cases, this can include the help of the sacraments," and includes explicit references to confession and the Eucharist.[50] This statement and its oblique, accompanying foot note make it clear enough that an individual may have committed an objectively sinful action and yet he/she may not be completely morally responsible on a subjective level. This is in complete agreement with the traditional Catholic understanding of sin.[51] "Thus it is not surprising that *Amoris Laetitia* turns to the *Catechism of the Catholic Church* when listing "mitigating factors and situations" (AL 301) that diminish, and in some cases remove, subjective culpability for an objectively sinful act (AL 302)."[52] Also, Pope Francis follows here the traditional teaching on conscience that the evil done as a result of invincible ignorance or a non–culpable error of judgement may not be imputable to the agent. Only that Pope Francis is incorporating this consideration on conscience into the question of sacramental inclusion of divorced and remarried Catholics.

Incorporation of these considerations on conscience takes on new significance. Pope Francis' discussion on conscience is not simply a restatement of traditional teaching on the effects of an erroneous conscience on moral culpability. Exhortation's other comments on conscience reveals that something 'more' is going on for a genuine reassessment on the role of conscience. In the first sentence in paragraph 303 of *Amoris Laetitia* indicates a development: "Yet conscience can do more than recognize that a given situation does not objectively correspond to the overall demands of the Gospel." The reference here is to the aspect of conscience that judges an agent's actions, either during the process of deliberation that precedes an action or as part of a moral analysis that occurs after the fact.[53] This judgement, in keeping with Thomas Aquinas' definition of conscience as "knowledge applied to an individual case,"[54] determines whether or not an individual's course of action aligns with the more general moral norm that would typically govern similar situations. "The way Pope Francis describes the operation in this sentence in *Amoris Laetitia* sounds specifically like operation of a guilty conscience when it recognizes *ex post facto*, a disconnect between one's action and the proper moral order."[55] The well-known moral theologian John Mahoney attests to this aspect of conscience in the experience of many Catholics approaching the confessional, where a guilty conscience has historically been the focal point of conversation between penitent and priest.[56]

So, although the notion of conscience as *judgement* was a consistent element in the traditional moral teaching, it is not, as *Amoris Laetitia* proposes, an adequate, sufficient description of conscience. Conscience can do 'more'; it "can also recognize with sincerity and honesty what for now is the most generous response which can be given to God, and come to see with a certain moral security that it is what God himself is asking amid the concrete complexity of one's limits, while not yet fully the objective ideal."[57] This description of conscience is not an 'act' or juridical conception, but a more personalist account that resonates with the dynamic understanding of conscience found in the writings of contemporary moral theologians.[58]

This is also consistent with the famous definition of *Gaudium et Spes*: Conscience is the most secret core and sanctuary of a man where he is alone with

God, Whose voice echoes in his depths.[59] Pope Francis presupposes this definition when he writes that conscience is indeed the place of encounter with the divine, wherein God directly speaks to the soul and illuminates the correct path in the midst of conflicting demands and moral obligations.[60] This is a significant advance and progress over the magisterial understanding of conscience suggesting another step in the process of 'development' of the tradition.[61] Though this definition of conscience is contested,[62] nevertheless it provides the basis for a clearer understanding of what it means to claim that conscience can do more than judge. The surrounding paragraphs in *Amoris Laetitia* connect it to the larger issue of moral discernment.[63] This shows that the personalist understanding of conscience in *Amoris Laetitia* of Pope Francis is a facet of personal moral discernment, and not just an identifier of rules to apply.[64]

5. Moral Discernment

Moral discernment as *Amoris Laetitia* presents demands careful moral adjudication of an individual in his/her situation in all its complexity. Pope Francis asserting what Aquinas says that general norms will fail as we descend more and more into details. Basing on this teaching of Aquinas, the Pope writes: "It is true that general rules set forth a good which can never be disregarded or neglected, but in their formulation they cannot provide absolutely for all particular situations. At the same time, it must be said that, precisely for that reason, what is part of a practical discernment in particular circumstances, cannot be elevated to the level of a rule."[65] Thus, Pope Francis writes in the Exhortation that the moral life of Christian "is not defined by simple rules in black and white but incarnated richly in shades of gray."[66] And so, a Christian is not called to a set of rules but, rather, to a *relationship* with God. He/she is called to "find possible ways of responding to God and growing in the midst of limits."[67] The Pope thus re-evaluates Christian moral life in decidedly personalist terms and calls for a process of moral discernment, 'what for now is the most generous response which can be given to God' by an individual in his/her particular situation in all its complexities. Pastors, therefore, need to help people not simply follow rules, but to practice "moral discernment," which implies prayerful decision making before God.

Moral discernment as proposed by Pope Francis does not abrogate the need for moral norms and principles, nor does it lead to relativism. "Instead, this conception of the moral life as an ongoing relationship with God presumes the clear identification of an absolute and unchanging ideal."[68] This moral discernment, according to the Pope, is a dynamic and ongoing process which must remain ever open to new stages of growth and to new decisions which can enable the ideal to be more fully realized.[69] Thus, the main task of a Christian is to discern the demands of God in the midst of his/her complex relationships and relationships, rather than mere applying of the rules to the particular situation. What the Pope wants to emphasize here is that Church must find ways "to make room for the consciences of the faithful, who very often responds as best they can to the Gospel amid their limitations, and are capable of carrying out their own discernment in complex situations."[70]

This is not to downplay the objective ideal which is to be clearly and persuasively presented to critique one's actions, and to show ways of living that expressly contradict the ideal and to reinforce the value of seeking the ideal in the first place. The Pope says that holding on to doctrine, principle, norms and ideal should not be in their letter, but in their spirit; "not ideas but people; not formulae but the gratuitous of God's love and forgiveness."[71] Having said that, the Pope speaks about the desired relativism of the law, warning against two specific temptations to which Jesus' followers are susceptible. He refers to the first of these as a "spirituality of illusion," whereby we walk alongside Jesus, but avoid being bothered with the problems of others. "A faith that does not know how to root itself in the life of people remains arid and, rather than oases, creates other deserts."Jesus turned the law upside down… the law of Sabbath, breaking it for humans…. against ritual purity. He said that it was not what goes inside but what comes from the mouth that defiles.[72]

The Pope thus challenged those who find false security in the laws and regulations which are good in themselves but not good enough to channelize God-experience to the people who are certain that the God revealed in Jesus Christ is compassion itself. According to him, the Church should not relativize the demands of the Gospel but at the same time she should not absolutize her laws so that she disfigures the Compassionate face of God revealed in Jesus Christ. Basing his arguments upon the evidence of real people and not on depersonalized abstractions, the Pope was following Jesus, for whom what mattered was people and their needs; everything else was relative.[73]

Rather than looking to real problems of real people as divorced/remarried and homosexuals, the 'self-righteous' who oppose them deal with abstractions. The Church needs to meet with people where they are, not where they wish them to be. The mercy for which they yearn is not one of pity but of comprehension of the truth of *who* and *how* they are.

Thus, Pope Francis is against a rigid dogmatism that attempts to answer every possible question with sweeping pronouncements; rather he says that we 'must leave room for the Lord' which means accepting uncertainty at times. In fact, *Amoris Laetita* outlines moral life more in terms of a process of moral discernment amidst doubt and uncertainty. "If God is understood to be as mysterious and infinite as the Christian tradition proclaims, and if conscience – the place where this infinite mystery speaks to the human heart on a personal level – is the true arbiter of moral discernment, then there must be some place for surprise and for new development along the way."[74]

Addressing the question of contingency in moral life will rightly require statements of certain kind of absolute norms. But what *Amoris Laetitia* states is only that absolute norms and prohibitions should not be the focus in moral life. The Exhortation's emphasis on conscience that the chief locus of moral reflection is not the general but the particular, indicates that majority of moral decisions will take place in an area where absolutes do not directly apply. Moral absolutes do not admit contingency and uncertainty. So, in moral questions that admit variety, uncertainty and doubt, moral absolutes are of no help for moral discernment. Hence, the number of moral absolutes must be as few as possible and only as a last resort. Also, the determination of absolute norms should involve community and communal insights and a *process* of moral and pastoral discernment.[75]

Given this modified relationship between absolute norms and personal moral discernment in particular contextual complexities, "*Amoris Laetitia* places greater weight on individual consciences and adds substantial responsibility to the process of discernment."[76] This is the challenge of moral discernment that calls for serious, communal deliberations about the normative ideals of Christian moral life and the variety and flexibility in specificity that may be permitted in relation to those ideals.[77]

6. Culture of Moral Discernment

Amoris Laetitia's discussion of conscience and discernment offers resources for a concrete vision of moral life that aims at the creation of a culture of moral discernment in the Church. By shifting the focal point of morality from rules for judging to a personal relationship with God, the document places greater weight on individual conscience and adds substantial responsibility to the process of moral discernment. When emphasis is laid on discernment of conscience in particular cases, there is the possibility of error in moral matters. One could either make the wrong decision about the legitimacy of difference in interpretation or mistakenly identify the wrong norm. "Faith in the guidance of the Holy Spirit can help to ameliorate fears of error,...but this still does not eliminate the possibility of error because misinterpretation and self-deception are still possible."[78] For protection against this possibility of error, traditionally, the Catholic Church had relied on the Magisterium to provide assurance against error, asserting that the Holy Spirit protects the institutional church from falling into error. But we see that in history the possibility of error even as magisterial teachings are reversed on certain moral matters.

In the face of this, a culture of communal discernment becomes all the more important. Besides, epistemic humility in moral matters demands that we converse, especially those with whom one might disagree. This would offer a valuable opportunity to re-examine one's moral conclusions. In fact Aquinas proposed this sort of solution to the issue of error in 'contingent particular cases' asserting that when matters are considered by several with greater clarity, since what one takes note of escapes the notice of another.[79] Even Aristotle's classical resource of the virtue of prudence for the determination of right conduct[80] in particular situations must be 'taught by others' if it is going to develop properly.[81] All these show that *Amoris Laetitia*'s insight of a culture of communal discernment is the only right response and necessary check against the danger of error in moral judgement. In addition, such a culture would provide a degree of accountability, which is essential because, again, according to *Amoris Laetitia*, if "discernment is dynamic; it must remain ever open to new stages of growth and to new decisions which can enable the ideal to be more fully realized."[82]

One possible objection to communal discernment could be that in communal conversations about the process of responding to God in a way that departs from the ideal may seem to invite other people's conscience to make decisions that an individual should make for himself/herself. To this objection *Amoris Laetitia* in line with traditional moral theology states that conscience is to be *formed* in conversation with the community of faith and its dictates are properly developed with a genuine concern for the social implications of personal actions.[83] "Incorporating communal discernment into the conscience's process of reflection and judgements therefore ensures that conscience functions responsibly while also combating the risks of errors.[84]

Unfortunately traditional moral theology more readily proposed a prophetic approach that concentrated on 'safety' and certainty rather than nuance. But *Amoris Laetitia* proposes a pilgrim perspective that acknowledges the eschatological not yet alongside the prophetic already. When facing ethical decisions in their pilgrim lives on earth, the faithful discover that there not many resources or common language for them in the Church to adjudicate those decisions, nor explain the processes behind their decisions so that their moral choices have to be made alone. Here what is needed in the Church is the creation of a culture of communal moral discernment. "If the Catholic Church had an authentic culture of moral discernment, then the faithful would have a tool kit of resources to help them sort through the contingencies and complexities that make decisions of conscience so intimately particular. Catholics would then be prepared for the type of nuanced discernment that *Amoris Letitita* suggests is at the heart of the Christian moral life."[85] The faithful will have then a shared resource "so that they would be able to discuss openly the means of discernment used in a particular decision of conscience and others would be able to reflect on that process and contribute to it in a way that might mitigate the potential for error."[86]

On the discussion of conscience and discernment Pope Francis admitted that one could discern in conscience "with sincerity and honesty what for now is the most generous response which can be given to God... while not yet fully the objective ideal."[87] Here there is the greater risk of error because the distance from the ideal can be easily coloured by self-deception. Then again, the presence of a culture of moral discernment can be a help to the faithful.

For all these reasons, the pursuit and goal of creating a culture of moral discernment that *Amoris Letitita* proposes is appropriate. This goal cannot remain as a mere abstraction, if we are to respond to Pope Francis' invitation to change the role of conscience in our lives. So, we propose a few suggestions for the creation of a culture of moral discernment:

First, moral theology should rescind from questions about absolute moral norms and avoid the production of rules. "A space for rules, not just absolute, is still consistent with Pope Francis' stated emphasis on individual conscience, for he has insisted that the need to attend to consciences in difficult cases 'in no way detracts from the importance of formulae – they are necessary – or from the importance of laws and divine commandments.'"[88] *Second*, moral theology should define the role and meaning of the ideal in the Christian moral life. If moral life is to be recast in terms of ideals and growth as *Amoris Laetitia* has propsed, "Church will need a clearer sense of how one is supposed to respond to ideal in good conscience."[89] And when the faithful face conflicting situations, where they have no alternative option, they may make use of 'the principle of lesser evil' which many contemporary moral theologians propose – tolerating an action that falls short of the ideal emphasizing the virtuous role of regret in the pilgrim life of the faithful. "With this stance and its practical application, moral theologians will be able to incorporate *Amoris Laetitia's* emphasis on the primacy of conscience in a way that preserves the function and value of the ideal as a genuine guide in the moral life."[90] *Third*, more importance is to be given to ethical question that arise in people's ordinary lives. This has already arisen with today's virtue ethics with its emphasis on virtue as a question in every part of the lives of the faithful. This is a direct corollary of the commitment to a culture of moral discernment because the process of discerning is a practice, like all practices, is strengthened and refined with repeated application.[91] This will encourage the faithful to examine the moral importance of their everyday decisions so that they will cultivate the practice of communal moral discernment.

By embracing this goal and task of creating a culture of moral discernment, moral theology will respond to the invitation of Pope Francis to form consciences of the faithful. This will adequately honour the dignity of conscience, which, as the voice of God echoing in the depths of the human heart, deserves the high esteem that a culture of moral discernment affords.

Conclusion

In fine, Pope Francis' Apostolic Exhortation *Amoris Laetitia* is profound reflection on the mission of families to embrace God's vision for marriage and on how the Church can offer healing for those who are struggling in their journey of faith. It is a pastoral triumph. It asks the Church to meet people where they are, to consider and take into account families and individuals in all their complexity of various situations, to respect their consciences when it comes to moral decisions. It offers rich resources for the creation of a culture of dynamic moral discernment to practise 'discernment' that implies prayerful decision making.[92]

When we evaluate Pope Francis' pastoral and moral approach in *Amoris Laetitia*, we can say that he "has treaded the sound and sane middle path (*via media*) in applying Church doctrine to present day realities. It has not changed the doctrine but applied that doctrine to pastoral realities using the traditional Catholic moral concepts/principles of the Church...has highlighted and brought back some of the basic, common sense gospel doctrines... such as 'no one can be condemned for ever, because that is not the logic of the Gospel' (AL, No:297); we cannot think everything to be black or/and white (AL, No:305)."[93] And though baseless criticisms and allegations have been hurled at it even by the ecclesiastics of the highest rank in *Amoris Laetitia's* efforts to link doctrine to pastoral needs, "in the last analysis, a conscientious Christian cannot forget that all doctrines are for persons and not persons for doctrines as their Master so prophetically taught them long ago (Mk.2:27)."[94]

Pope Francis' pastoral and moral approach in *Amoris Laetitia* is not strictly *revolutionary*, it is certainly *evolutionary*. It does prod this pilgrim church, which has been sitting in wayside for 35 years, forward. With this Exhortation, Pope Francis continues to shift the structure of authority in the Church. His repeated message is: Don't look to Rome and rule books for all the answers. ("Not all discussions of doctrinal, moral or pastoral issues need to be settled by interventions of the magisterium.") Find answers that fit your tradition and your local situation. ("Each country or region, moreover, can seek solutions better suited to its culture and sensitive to its traditions and local needs.") Trust yourselves. ("The Spirit guides us towards the entire truth.") Francis is again calling *for an adult Church.*

Overall, Pope Francis' moral and pastoral approach in *Amoris Laetitia* is one of understanding, compassion and accompaniment. It is no different from that of Jesus whose Vicar, he is on earth. Jesus proposed a demanding ideal "but never failed to show compassion and closeness to the frailty of individuals like the Samaritan woman or the woman taken in adultery."[95] The details of his moral and approach, as we have seen in the Exhortation, derives from his vision of a pastoral and merciful Church, "the fertile Mother and Teacher, who is not afraid to roll up her sleeves to pour oil and wine on people's wound; who doesn't see humanity as a house of glass to judge or categorize people. This is the Church, One, Holy, Catholic, Apostolic, and composed of sinners, needful of God's mercy... It is the Church that is not afraid to eat and drink with prostitutes and publicans. The Church that has doors wide open to receive the needy, the penitent and not only the just or those who believe they are perfect! The Church that is not ashamed of the fallen brother and pretends not see him, but on the contrary feels involved and almost obliged to lift him up and encourage him to take up the journey again and accompany him toward a definitive encounter with her Spouse, in the heavenly Jerusalem."[96] All this comes from the Pope's vision of a pastoral and merciful Church that encourages everyone to experience the "joy of love."[97]

Such a compassionate pastoral concern to those in difficult and struggling situations may not solve all moral problems, but Pope Francis with his Apostolic Exhortation *Amoris Laetitia* has heralded a new moral and pastoral vision, approach and praxis in the Church that certainly would witness to a God who loves unconditionally and whose mercy has no limits.[98] But such an approach would certainly move the entire discipline of moral theology out of the confines of a static approach to a dynamic one to grapple with conflict situations and moral dilemmas in our life, because it is open to and dialogue with the concrete human situations and historicity.

In conclusion, Pope Francis' moral approach and "logic of pastoral mercy" of listening with sensitivity and compassion confirms the phenomenological and existential reflection on our existence and the Scriptural understanding of moral life as responding to the unbounded and unconditional mercy God in the many, complex happenings of our existence rather than adhering to a pre-determined pattern. It shows that we are not only responsible in the sense that we are answerable for our actions but also and pre-eminently in the sense that we are persons who respond in a conscientious way to the demands laid upon us by God and our fellowmen and the world in concrete situations. It deciphers a lifestyle for us based on the compassionate love and Praxis of Jesus and offers us a fresh vision of Gospel values and principles. It provides a kind of "framework within which we can make moral judgments as compassionate and responsible persons so that our lives becomes best possible mediations of the Gospel values to the temporal realities and relations and guides us in establishing a pattern of moral life as authentic disciples of Jesus."[99]

Endnotes

1   *Amoris Laetitia* (hereafter AL) AL 3.

2   *Ibid.*

3   Pope Francis' Address at the end of the Synod of Bishops 2015.

4   Episcopal conferences of Spain, Korea, Argentina, Mexico, Columbia, Chile, Australia, Latin American and Caribbean Bishops, Italy and Kenya.

5   AL 199.

6   Vimal TIRIMANNA, "Two Critical Questions Frequently Asked About *Amoris Laetitia*" in *VJTR*, 80, 2016, pp. 919-920.

7   AL 4.

8   AL 5.

9   AL 3.

10   Conor M. KELLY, "The Role of the Moral Theologian in the Church: A Proposal in Light of *Amoris Laetitia*" in *Theological Studies*, 2016, Vol. 77 (4), p. 923.

11   AL 201.

12   AL 222.

13   AL 234.

14   Gerald O'COLLINS, "The joy of love (*Amoris Laetitia*): The Papal Exhortation in its Context" in *Theological studies*, vol. 77, no. 4 December 2016, p. 912.

15   Final Report (hereafter FR) no. 63.

16   Gerald O'COLLINS, *Art.cit.,* p. 912.

17   AL 165-198.

18   AL 31-57.

19   AL 242-3.

20   AL 248.

21   AL 251.

22   AL 243, 246.

23   AL 297.

24   George THERUKAATTIL, "Desired Norms v/s Absolute Norms" in *Light of Truth,* December 1-15, 2015, p. 11.

25   From the Statement of Indian Theological Association of 2015.

26   Interview with Antonio Spadaro, S.J., of the Jesuit journal La Civiltà Cattolica, in August, 2013 (later published in English in the magazine America).

27   Interview with *America Magazine*, Sept. 30, 2013.

28   Gerald O'COLLINS, *op.cit.,* p. 920, cf. AL 307-311.

29   AL 291.

30   The Pope Francis Interview: "A New Balance" for the Church in *The New Yorker*, Sept. 19, 2013.

31   Gerald O'COLLINS, *Art.cit.,* p. 920.

32   AL 291.

33   AL 300.

34   George THERUKAATTIL, "Post-Synodal Apostolic Exhortation Amoris Laetitia" in *Light of Truth,* May 1-15, p. 11.

35   AL 297.

36   AL 292.

37   *Familiaris Consortio*, n. 34. This is not a 'gradualness of law' but gradualness in the prudential exercises of free acts on the part of subjects who are not in a position to understand, appreciate or fully carry out the objective of the law.

38   Gerald O'COLLINS, *Art.cit.,* p. 919.

39   AL 300.

40   EG 16.

41   AL 296.

42   Gerald O'COLLINS, *Art.cit.,* p. 920.

43   Interview with Pope Francis by La Croix by Guillaume Gubet and Sebastien Maillard, Vatican city December 26, 2016.

44   George THERUKAATTIL, "Desired Norms v/s Absolute Norms" in *Light of Truth,* December 1-15, 2015, p. 11.

45   James T. BRETZKE, "In Good Conscience," in *America*, April 8, 2016.

46   AL 303.

47   AL 300.

48   Gerald O'CONNELL, "Pope Francis' Exhortation on the Family an 'Organic Development of Doctrine'," *America*, April 8, 2016.

49   AL 305.

50   Al 305, no. 351.

51   Thomas AQUINAS, *Summa Theologiae*, I-II, q 88, a 2, c.

52   Conor M. Kelly, "The Role of the Moral Theologian in the Church: A Proposal in Light of *Amoris Laetitia*" in *Theological Studies*, 2016, Vol. 77 (4), p. 925.

53   Timothy O'CONNELL, "An Understanding of Conscience," in *Conscience: Readings in Moral Theology No.14*, ed. Charles E. Curran, New York: Paulist 2004, pp. 25-38.

54   Thomas AQUINAS, *Summa Theologiae*. ST1, q 79, a 13, c.

55   Conor M. KELLY, *Art.cit.*, pp. 926-927.

56   John MAHONY, *The Making of Moral Theology: A Study of Roman Catholic Tradition*, Oxford: Clarendon, 1987, pp. 30-31.

57   AL 303.

58   James KEENAN, "To follow and Form Over Time: A Phenomenology of Conscience" in *Conscience and Catholicism: Rights and Responsibilities, Institutional Response*s, ed. David D DeCosse, Maryknoll, N.Y.: Orbis, 2015, pp. 1-15.

59   GS, no. 16.

60   AL 303.

61   Conor M. KELLY, *Art.cit.*, pp. 927-928.

62   Edward PENTIN, "Moral Theology and *Amoris Letitia*: Some Expert Assessments," in *National Catholic Register*, April, 22, 2016.

63   Al 304-306.

64   Conor M. KELLY, *Art.cit.*, p. 928.

65   AL 304.

66   AL 305.

67   AL 305.

68   Conor M. KELLY, *Art.cit.*, p. 929.

69   AL 303.

70   AL 37.

71   Pope FRANCIS, "Conclusion of the Synod of Bishops, Address of His Holiness Pope Francis" (Synod on Family, Rome, October 24, 2015).

72   George THERUKAATTIL, "Desired Norms v/s Absolute Norms" in *Light of Truth*, December 1-15, 2015, p. 11.

73   *Ibid.*

74   Conor M. KELLY, *Art.cit.*, p. 931.

75   *Ibid.*, p. 932 Emphasis mine.

76   *Ibid.*, p. 933.

77   *Ibid.*

78   Conor M. KELLY, *Art.cit.*, p. 941.

79   *ST* I-II, q 14, a 3, c.

80   ARISTOTLE *Nichomachean Ethics*, 1140a24-1141b23.

81   Daniel J DALY, "The Relationship of Virtues and Norms in *Summa Theologiae*," in *The Heythrop Journal* 51, 2010, pp. 221-223.

82   AL 303.

83   AL 37, 303, 304, cfr also, Bernard Haering, *Free and Faithful in Christ*, Vol. I, New York: Seabury, 1978. pp. 265-270.

84   Conor M. KELLY, *op.cit.,* p. 943.

85   *Ibid.,* p. 944.

86   *Ibid.*

87   AL 303.

88   Pope FRANCIS, "Conclusion of the Synod of Bishops" quoted by Conor M. Kelly, *op.cit.,* p. 945.

89   Conor M. KELLY, *op.cit.,* p. 946.

90   Ibid, p. 947.

91   *Ibid.*

92   George THERUKAATTIL, "Post-Synodal Apostolic Exhortation Amoris Laetitia" in *Light of Truth,* May 1-15, p. 11.

93   Vimal TIRIMANNA, "Two Critical Questions Frequently Asked About *Amoris Laetitia*" in *VJTR,* 80, 2016, pp. 941-942.

94   Ibid. p. 943.

95   AL 38.

96   From Pope's Concluding Speech of the Synod on Family quoted in *Smart Companion India,* November 2014, p. 12.

97   George THERUKAATTIL, "Post-Synodal Apostolic Exhortation *Amoris Laetitia*" in *Light of Truth,* May 1-15, p. 11.

98   Errol D' LIMA, "Compassionate Pastoral Concern For Those In Difficult Marital Situations" in *VJTR,* 80, 2016, p. 915.

99   George THERUKAATTIL, *Compassionate Love-Ethics, Vol. I Fundamental Moral Theology,* Kochi: Karunikan Books, 2014, p. 52.

III. BUILDING BRIDGES

Chapter 7

Gazing at Our World with God's Eyes of Mercy
Pope Francis' Theological Vision

Francis Gonsalves SJ
Jnana-Deepa Vidyapeeth, Pune, Maharashtra

Introduction

In the short span of the first four years of his papacy, Pope Francis has made a profound and lasting impact not only on Christians, but also on our world's citizens, at large. Many might not agree with everything that the pope says and does;[1] yet, few will contest the fact that he has voiced radical and revolutionary opinions on the world stage, loud and clear. Whether he is addressing world bodies like the UN General Assembly, the US Congress or eminent global leaders and religionists, Pope Francis does not mince words. He astutely addresses problems, analyzes issues, builds bridges, critiques evil in all its avatars and maps pathways for making this world a better place. In all his endeavours there is a refreshing newness and a Spirit-powered dynamism that makes people yearn to follow what he says; and even more, to do what he does. Indeed, Pope Francis 'walks the talk', so to say. That is why people listen and learn from him.

This article examines the wellsprings of Pope Francis' life to provide a framework for understanding his theological vision. To achieve this end, while drawing inspiration mainly from Pope Francis' writings, it will also tap relevant fragments from the pope's personal life, pastoral praxis, Jesuit training, daily homilies and the witness of his works, which often preach even louder than his words. Before entering into details of what I hold to be Pope Francis' theological vision, I provide a framework—which could be called a 'Peter Paradigm'—that could help us to comprehend his theological vision.

1. A 'Peter Paradigm' Integrating Identity, Community and Mission

Simon Peter is considered as the 'First Pope' of Christian history. His life could be a model for church leaders who desire to follow Jesus faithfully and lead his flock fruitfully. In a engaging encounter with his apostles (Mt 16:13-20), Jesus gives Simon, son of Jonah, a new identity, entrusts him with a community and commissions him on a mission. In identifying Jesus as the Christ, God's Anointed One, Jesus gives Simon an identity as *Petros* (Greek) or *Cepha* (Hebrew), the Rock, entrusting him with shepherding a Christic/Messianic community, commissioning him for the ministry of reconciliation.

The Bible positively uses 'rock' for no one else except God. David sings: "The Lord is my rock, my fortress, my deliverer; my God, my rock, in whom I take refuge" (2 Sam 22:2-4). On the one hand, the psalms have rich references to God as Rock (18:2; 31:3; 62:2; 78:35; 95:1, etc.), for in God the Israelites experience safety and security; but, on the other, if people seek security in creatures rather than in their Creator, then God can become "a rock one stumbles over—a trap and a snare for the inhabitants of Jerusalem" (Isa 8:14-15). After being identified as the 'Christ/Messiah' Jesus renames Simon as *Petros* or *Cepha*, i.e., Rock, thereby giving him a positive identity as one who will be the cornerstone for his new community, the church. Sadly, soon after Simon is renamed and given a leadership role in the church, he becomes a stumbling block to Jesus' journey towards Jerusalem. Here, Jesus sternly reprimands him with the negative nuance attached to *Petros*: "Get behind me, Satan! You are a *stumbling block* to me..." (Mt 16:23). By placing obstacles in Jesus' pathway to his passion and death, Peter seemingly partners Satan who tempts Jesus at the start of his ministry (Mt 4:1-11). Nonetheless, later, a repentant and renewed Peter will use both, the positive and negative nuances of rock imagery in his writings to describe Christ and the new Christic community.[2]

It is beyond the scope of this article to enter into Biblical details of these passages. Suffice it to say that the awareness of one's identity leads to conception and construction of a particular community, and consequent involvement in mission. Community, identity and mission, therefore, are interlinked and interpenetrate to mutually influence each other. Put in theological terms one can say that a *Christology/theological anthropology* (i.e., 'who' one understands oneself to be vis-à-vis 'who' one understands Christ to be) influences one's *ecclesiology* (one's concept of church/community), and determines one's *missiology* ('what' one's mission is). We will examine the life and the mission of Pope Francis within this framework of Community, Identity and Mission.

2. Interrogating the Identity of Pope Francis

After the 2013 papal conclave, Cardinal Jorge Mario Bergoglio's assuming the name 'Francis'—after St. Francis of Assisi—coming after 23 Johns, 16 Benedicts, 14 Clements, 6 Pauls and 2 John Paul's is strikingly singular, selective and suggestive. Among other virtues, Francis of Assisi is universally loved even today, because he: (a) embraced poverty with unprecedented ardour, (b) sought relentlessly to renew the church of his times when he heard a voice from a crucifix at San Damiano saying, "Go and repair my house which is falling into ruin!"[3] (c) loved nature and all living creatures as his sisters and brothers, and, (d) journeyed to Egypt to meet a Muslim sultan and can, by extension, be regarded as a pioneer in what today we call interfaith dialogue.[4] These four traits can be seen in large measure in the life and mission of Pope Francis.

The personal poverty of Pope Francis can be perceived in his lifestyle already when he was a pastor in a poor parish in Buenos Aires, Argentina. He would travel by public transport or walk around frequently to visit the poorest of poor in his parish. Interestingly, soon after being elected as pope, he refused the pompous paraphernalia of the papacy—cape of fur, gold ring and cross, new shoes, special papal vehicle, etc., and travelled together with fellow cardinals to his residence, queuing up to pay his bills.

Pope Francis treasures poverty not because poverty is good in itself [it is not!]; but, since, in the poor and the sick, one meets God. In one of his homilies, he said, "To encounter the living God it is necessary to tenderly kiss Jesus' wounds in our hungry, poor, sick and incarcerated brothers and sisters."[5] He added, "The path to our encounter with Jesus-God are his wounds. There is no other."[6] According to Pope Francis, all Christians derive their identity from the poor Christ. In his Lenten Reflection for the year 2014, he wrote: "In imitation of our Master, we Christians are called to confront the poverty of our brothers and sisters, to touch it, to make it our own and to take practical steps to alleviate it."[7]

Pope Francis is humble and self-effacing to the core. In one of his first interviews after being elected pope, he openly confessed, "I am a sinner, but I trust in the infinite mercy and patience of our Lord Jesus Christ."[8] This has led him to stress not only his need for God's mercy, but also to create much-needed awareness that all of us, Christians, are sinners in need of God's mercy. This 'stamp of sinfulness', so to say, and need for God's mercy, will run throughout the papacy of Francis since the theme of mercy figures prominently in his papal motto: "*miserando atque eligendo*," literally meaning, "by having mercy, by choosing him."[9] This motto was not something he cleverly crafted on being elected pope; but it was already his catch-line during his tenure as bishop.

Among many outstanding virtues that characterize Pope Francis, we highlight but three, which we have hinted at. First, Pope Francis is a 'poor pastor' in the image and likeness of God's Poor Son, Jesus. Second, Pope Francis is deeply humble and aware of his own sinfulness against the light of God's overwhelming mercy. Third, Pope Francis "*experiences* the love of the Most Holy Trinity" with his eyes fixed on "the most merciful gaze of Jesus."[10] By experiencing and identifying Jesus as 'The Merciful One' Francis, in turn, sees himself as a disciple of Jesus and a 'chosen one' for a Trinity-given mission of mercy. This tripod seems to be the bedrock upon which Pope Francis builds community (church and world), and maps out the church's mission in our times and places.

3. Pope Francis' Conception of a Poor and Open Church

In his dual dynamic of: (a) identifying Christ as the poor, humble, merciful Son of God, and, (b) identifying himself as a Francis-of-Assisi type apostle of the 'good news' of this same Christ, Pope Francis provides pointers of 'what' this church-body ought to be and 'who' ought to be its prime organs and privileged beneficiaries. A few days after being elected pope, in a BBC interview, Francis spoke of his dreams to have "a poor church for the poor."[11] This theme finds initial mention in *Lumen Fidei*, his first encyclical released in July 2013. Pope Francis writes:[12]

Nor does the light of faith make us forget the sufferings of this world. How many men and women of faith have found mediators of light in those who suffer! So, it was with Saint Francis of Assisi and the leper, or with Blessed Mother Teresa of Calcutta and her poor. They understood the mystery at work in them.... To those who suffer, God does not provide arguments which explain everything; rather, his response is that of an accompanying presence, a history of goodness which touches every story of suffering and opens up a ray of light.

Mention of the poor and the image of a poor church features more forcefully in *Evangelii Gaudium*, Pope Francis' November 2013 Apostolic Exhortation on the 'Proclamation of the Gospel in Today's World'. Notably, he does not see the poor as mere beneficiaries of Christian charity, but as subjects who have taught him valuable lessons about Christian joy. He writes, "I can say that the most beautiful and natural expressions of joy which I have seen in my life were in poor people who had little to hold on to."[13] It is to these that all Christians and the church must "go forth from our own comfort zone in order to reach all the 'peripheries' in need of the light of the Gospel."[14]

Francis wants a *poor church* to go the *peripheries* not as a macho conquistador but as a loving mother nursing sick, wounded children, even if it means apparent defilement:[15]

I prefer a Church which is bruised, hurting and dirty because it has been out on the streets, rather than a Church which is unhealthy from being confined and from clinging to its own security. I do not want a Church concerned with being at the centre and then ends by being caught up in a web of obsessions and procedures. If something should rightly disturb us and trouble our consciences, it is the fact that so many of our brothers and sisters are living without the strength, light and consolation born of friendship with Jesus Christ, without a community of faith to support them, without meaning and a goal in life

The church that goes forth to love and serve the poor, needy, sick, suffering, peripheral peoples, etc., must comprise of joyful evangelizers, not mournful "sourpusses" and "disillusioned pessimists"[16] obsessed with "a business mentality, caught up with management, statistics, plans and evaluations whose principal beneficiary is not God's people but the Church as an institution."[17] Pope Francis prays: "God save us from a worldly Church with superficial spiritual and pastoral trappings! This stifling worldliness can only be healed by breathing in the pure air of the Holy Spirit who frees us from self-centredness cloaked in an outward religiosity bereft of God."[18] Thus, we see him pleading for a church nourished with a deep spirituality rather than depending on human intelligence and competence to accomplish God's will.

Being in the echelons of ecclesial power, concomitant with his episcopal and cardinal engagements, Pope Francis wisely seeks to turn the church's pyramidal hierarchy topsy-turvy by what seems to be a three-pronged strategy aimed at greater equality and wider participation: First, in ironic 'Christmas wishes' to members of the Vatican Curia, he enumerated 15 'ailments' that paralyze church functioning. His diagnosing of these ills as *Martha-ism*, Spiritual Alzheimer's, Existential Schizophrenia, Exhibitionism, Funereal Face, etc., conveyed an unequivocal message that the messy Vatican bureaucracy needed trimming and cleansing.[19] Second, while being rightly critical of a rigid, legalistic and Roma-centric Vatican Curia, a month after his election to the papacy, Pope Francis appointed a 'Council of Cardinals' with 8 members from all the continents to advise him on church matters, worldwide. Third, to offset the grave dangers of clericalism and to restore to the lay faithful their rightful roles and responsibilities in the church, he organized two 'Synods of the Family', the outcome of which was his Post-Synodal Apostolic Exhortation '*Amoris Laetitia*' on love in the family on March 19, 2016.

While constantly speaking about the important and indispensable role of the 'domestic church', the family, in fostering the peace and prosperity of church and world, Pope Francis once again echoes a clear 'option for the poor' (i.e., the economically poor as well as unwed mothers and single-parent families), for whom he pleads that: "In such difficult situations of need, the Church must be particularly concerned to offer understanding, comfort and acceptance, rather than imposing straightaway a set of rules that only lead people to feel judged and abandoned by the very Mother called to show them God's mercy."[20] In this regard, should one think of Pope Francis as just another social worker striving to solve socio-political and economic problems of families, one must note the many times that his visions for family, church and global community are solidly based on his contemplation of the Holy Family of Nazareth and the Triune God. He writes:"Every family should look to the icon of the Holy Family of Nazareth."[21]

Moreover: "In the human family, gathered by Christ, 'the image and likeness' of the Most Holy Trinity (cf. Gen 1:26) has been restored, the mystery from which all true love flows. Through the Church, marriage and the family receive the grace of the Holy Spirit from Christ, in order to bear witness to the Gospel of God's love."[22]

By desiring an 'open church' with open doors and windows, Pope Francis combats all forms of '*Churchianity*', clericalism, legalism and sterile institutionalization, while endorsing a '*Regnocentrism*': a focus on ushering in God's Reign—that 'Kingdom of God' which Jesus lived and died for. This inclusive ecclesial endeavour comes with consciousness of our own sinfulness and limitations, coupled with an unfaltering faith that the Triune God directs our history. This also makes us humbly aware of the 'already' and the 'not-yet'. In a climactic conclusion to *Amoris Laetitia*, Pope Francis writes:[23]

No family drops down from heaven perfectly formed; families need constantly to grow and mature in the ability to love. This is a never-ending vocation born of the full communion of the Trinity, the profound unity between Christ and his Church, the loving community which is the Holy Family of Nazareth, and the pure fraternity existing among the saints of heaven. Our contemplation of the fulfilment which we have yet to attain also allows us to see in proper perspective the historical journey which we make as families, and in this way to stop demanding of our interpersonal relationships a perfection, a purity of intentions and a consistency which we will only encounter in the Kingdom to come.

Rooted in our kenotic Christic identity and in the Triune God's revealed intent for the blossoming of God's Reign with the church as its seed, servant and sacrament, Pope Francis draws designs for mission—not as some triumphalist conquest of church-planting to the ends of the earth, but as a collaborative '*com-mission*'—sowing the seeds and inviting peoples of goodwill to co-operate *with* God in establishing God's Reign, today.

4. Pope Francis' Vision for Mission: I, You, and We on Divine '*Com*-mission'

Just as Pope Francis' vision of family, church and world overflow from his own identity and the identity that he imputes to Christ, so does his vision of mission depend on his conception of the poor and open church. Indeed, though theoretically and theologically distinct, the triptych of community-identity-mission is inseparable since each influences the other two, and, in turn, is moulded by the other two. Nitpicking on which comes first: community? identity? mission? is like haranguing about which comes first: chicken or egg? One should rather see Pope Francis' mission mapping as a series of concentric circles beginning with 'I', then overflowing to 'You' [singular and plural], and culminating with a 'We' (embracing church, society, world and cosmos).

"*I am* a mission on this earth" is one of the finest and most cryptic of lines penned by Pope Francis.[24] This pithy phrase is sandwiched between two others, i.e., "My mission of being in the heart of the people is not just a part of my life or a badge I can take off; it is not an 'extra' or just another moment in life. Instead, it is something I cannot uproot from my being without destroying my very self"; and: "We have to regard ourselves as sealed, even branded, by this mission of bringing light, blessing, enlivening, raising up, healing and freeing." We normally think of mission at the level of 'doing'. By contrast, Francis situates mission at the level of '*being*'. Mission *is* my DNA, my deepest identity. Mission is "*in* my heart" and unfailingly leads me "*in* the heart of people." I must confess that I have not been able to fully comprehend the depth-height-width-breadth of this statement no matter how much I've tried. It always takes me to the 'beyond', the 'more'; or, what, as a Jesuit, my namesake, Pope Francis, and I, would call the '*magis*'.

I might, at best, sound presumptuous, or, at worst, be woefully wrong, by suggesting that the 'Francis' that our pope sought to emulate was, yes, *consciously* Francis of Assisi, but *unconsciously* also Spanish Jesuit Francis Xavier. Doesn't one see and sense that in his persistence on poor pastors, going forth, [from] open churches, [to] crucified peoples, [for] peripheral missions, Pope Francis is also revealing his inner '*Jesuitness*' animated by the glowing example of Jesuit saints like Francis Xavier? To substantiate my claim, I can only mention Chris Lowney's book "Pope Francis: Why He Leads the Way He Leads" that unearths the Jesuit wellsprings from which Pope Francis draws inspiration.[25] Be that as it may, the 'discernment' woven into Pope Francis' missionary style is indubitably part of the Jesuit legacy.[26] He writes: "It is not advisable for the Pope to take the place of local Bishops in the *discernment* of every issue which arises in their territory. In this sense, I am conscious of the need to promote a sound 'decentralization.'"[27] Also, "The kingdom, already present and growing in our midst, engages us at every level of our being and reminds us of the principle of *discernment* which Pope Paul VI applied to true development: it must be directed to 'all men and the whole man.'"[28]

Through prayer and discernment, the "I" must venture out to find some suitable "You" (individuals and groups of people of goodwill) to cooperate in the divine *com*-mission. I purposefully break up the word 'commission' into '*com*-mission', referring to a 'mission *with*' [God] since Pope Francis is always and everywhere mindful that God is the Alpha and Omega of all our missionary stirrings and strivings. The church, therefore, does not work for God in isolation, but partners all peoples who can also be seen as 'missionaries'. Thus, in part IV entitled 'Social Dialogue as a Contribution to Peace' of the larger chapter 4 of *Evangelii Gaudium* entitled: 'The Social Dimension of Evangelization', Pope Francis goes beyond the confines of church to call upon all peoples of goodwill to dialogue and cooperate with each other to construct a more just and peaceful world for all.[29] This style of first making an appeal to Christians, and then amplifying his appeal to all people of goodwill, is conspicuously evident in what can be considered the most distinctive encyclical of Pope Francis: *Laudato Si'* on the care for our common home. Here, in chapter V entitled, 'Lines of Approach and Action', Pope Francis draws up an integral, extra-ecclesial and global plan for tackling the massive ecological problems of our day.[30] Ultimately, are not 'You' and 'I' inseparably bound together as a global, familial 'We'—all God's children irrespective of manmade divisions of creed, colour, class, culture, caste and country?

Community, for Pope Francis, does not only mean a community of human beings, but, like his patron, Francis of Assisi, refers to all God's creatures in our cosmic 'common home'. Hence, he denounces as 'sin' our abuses of nature. He writes: "Nor can we overlook the social degeneration brought about by *sin*, as, for example, when human beings tyrannize nature, selfishly and even brutally ravaging it. This leads to the desertification of the earth (cf. Gen 3:17-19) and those social and economic imbalances denounced by the prophets, beginning with Elijah (cf. 1 Kg 21) and culminating in Jesus' own words against injustice (cf. Lk 12:13; 16:1-31)."[31] This sin must be purged by joint action of human effort and God's grace. Recently, Pope Francis gave a surprising TED talk on the theme: '*The Future 'You'—Why the Only Future Worth Building Includes Everyone,*'[32] wherein he says that the future of each and every one of us is interlinked and interdependent. Therefore, each and every one of us is responsible for ensuring a better future, and building a better world. He says, "I ... and you... and you ... and you ... become a 'We' to begin a 'revolution of tenderness' that can transform the world."

Conclusion

Having examined the three pillars—community, identity, mission—upon which Pope Francis' theological vision is built, one might summarize it as an integral and 'circular' theology born in the Triune God and finding its fulfillment in the same Triune God. The story of Simon Peter gives us a clue that, first, it is God who identifies and calls everyone personally and uniquely. Then, it is also God who assembles and anoints those whom God calls and consecrates. Finally, the calling and consecrating in church-community is for a '*com*-mission' to carry back everything '*with* God' and to God at the end of times when God will be "all in all" (1 Cor 15:28). Thus, we can summarize Pope Francis' theological vision in one line: 'Gazing with God and Going Back to God'.

Endnotes

1   Recently, an Indian, Catholic priest in Italy said in a homily: "In four years Pope Francis has only been bad for the church." See http://www.ucanindia.in/news/indian-priest-criticizes-pope-people-walk-out-of-mass-in-italy/34576/daily. Interestingly, the congregation walked out in protest!

2   See, for instance, 1 Pet 2:4-8, which reads as follows: "So as you come to him, a living *stone* rejected by men but chosen and priceless in God's sight, you yourselves, as living *stones*, are

built up as a spiritual house…. For it says in scripture, 'Look, I lay in Zion a *stone*, a chosen and priceless *cornerstone*, and whoever believes in him will never be put to shame.' …. So you who believe see his value, but for those who do not believe, the *stone* that the builders rejected has become the *cornerstone*, and a *stumbling-stone* and a *rock* to trip over." Italics added.

3   John V. TAYLOR, "Telling the Stories – The Story of St. Francis," in *Joy in All Things*, ed. D. Kirkpatrick et al. (Norwich: Canterbury Press, 2002), 6.

4   See Michael F. CUSATO, "From Damietta to La Verna: The Impact on Francis of His Experience in Egypt," in "Daring to Embrace the Other—Franciscans and Muslims in Dialogue," *Spirit and Life* 2 (2008): 81-112.

5   See his homily on http://www.news.va/en/news/pope-francis-encounter-the-living-god-through-christ on the feast of St. Thomas on July 3, 2013. Web-link accessed on May 11, 2017.

6   Ibid.

7   https://w2.vatican.va/content/francesco/en/messages/lent/documents/papafrancesco_2013122_messaggio-quaresima2014.html.

8   See Stephen BULLIVANT, "'I am a Sinner': The Deep Humility of Pope Francis," in *America* (September 25, 2013). Accessible at http://www.americamagazine.org/issue/%E2%80%98i-am-sinner%E2%80%99.

9   See Vatican Radio's web-link http://www.news.va/en/news/pope-francis-miserando-atque-eligendo of March 22, 2013. This finds mention in no. 8 of *Misericordiae Vultus*, Pope Francis' Bull of Indiction of the Extraordinary Jubilee of Mercy, 2015.

10 See *Misericordiae Vultus*, nn.6-9, for God's infinite attributes of mercy and compassion. Quote from n.8.

11 See BBC Internet-TV news of March 16, 2013, entitled "Pope Francis wants 'poor Church for the poor'" on website http://www.bbc.com/news/world-europe-21812545.

12 *Lumen Fidei*, n.57.

13 *Evangelii Gaudium*, n.7.

14 *Evangelii Gaudium*, n.20.

15 *Evangelii Gaudium*, n.49. See also nn.46-48 for the image of church as mother, forgiving father, etc.

16 *Evangelii Gaudium*, n.85.

17 *Evangelii Gaudium*, n.95.

18 *Evangelii Gaudium*, n.97.

19 See Abby OHLHEISER, "The 15 Ailments of the Vatican Curia, according to Pope Francis," in *The Washington Post* (Dec. 22, 2014); at https://www.washingtonpost.com/news/world/wp/2014/12/22/the15-ailments-of-the-vatican-curia-according-to-pope-francis/?utm_term=.1b46edca94ab.

20 See *Amoris Laetitia*: Post-Synodal Apostolic Exhortation on love in the family (March 19, 2016), n.49.

21 *Amoris Laetitia*, n.30.

22 *Amoris Laetitia*, n.71. See also nn.11,63, for this same Trinitarian vision, the foundation of family life.

23 *Amoris Laetitia*, n.325.

24 *Evangelii Gaudium*, n.273.

25   I write this article in an adivasi mission-station, Dadwada, south Gujarat, with no access to books but only the materials saved in my laptop. This explains the non-availability of details for this book.

26   Pope Francis mentions 'discernment' in his writings many times. For instance, in *Evangelii Gaudium,* nn. 16, 30, 33, 43, 50, 64, 77, 133, 154, 166 & 181, with regard to church and mission; and in *Amoris Laetitia,* nn. 6, 37, 77, 79, 242, 243, 249, 293, 297, 298, 300, 301, 303, 304, 305 & 312, with regard to marriage and family life.

27   *Evangelii Gaudium*, n.16. Italics added.

28   *Evangelii Gaudium*, n.181.

29   In this section of *Evangelii Gaudium* Pope Francis discusses the possibilities dialogue between faith, reason and science [nn.242-243], ecumenical dialogue [nn.244-246], relations with Judaism [nn.247-249], interreligious dialogue [nn.250-254], and, social dialogue in a context of religious freedom [nn.255-258]

30   In this section of *Laudato Si'*, Pope Francis deals with: (1) dialogue on the environment in the international community [nn.164-175], (2) dialogue for new national and local policies [nn.176-181], (3) dialogue and transparency in decision-making [nn.182-188], (4) politics and economy in dialogue for human fulfilment [nn.189-197], and (5) religions in dialogue with science [nn.198-201].

31   *Amoris Laetitia,* n.26.

32   This talk is accessible on 'You Tube' with the same title.

Chapter 8

The Pilgrim Church Building Bridges with the Modern World

Antony D'Cruz J. O. Praem
Pressath, Germany

Introduction

From the human point of view every theological investigation seeks to understand the mystery of God in relation to human persons. "Seeking" is an important function in theologizing, and creativity and insight are affirmed as necessary ingredients. Although revelation in theologizing is complete with Jesus Christ,[1] the human understanding of it is not.[2] For instance, in *Dei Verbum*, a principal document of Vatican II that deals with the fullness of revelation in Jesus Christ, there is no expression of "Christ's universal presence among human beings. But the text is such as to leave the field open for ongoing theological investigations and for the debate that to this day has not come to an end."[3]

Following the same line of thought, the nature and style of Pope Francis' teaching and functioning give the impression that he seeks to remain within this framework of "seeking." His definition of God as Merciful Father, and his favourite scripture passage "*'The Lord, a God merciful and gracious, slow to anger, and abounding in steadfast love and faithfulness'*" (Ex. 34:6),[4] are examples of this fact. The Pope's attitude is, therefore, "who am I to judge;" i.e., while he refuses to draw a line to human understanding of God's unfathomable love, he opens the vistas of eschatological provisionality,[5] that need to guide the Church in her mission. Neither is his understanding of ecclesiology an ecclesio-centrism of triumphalism, but rather of a poor church that is on a journey.

Here we seek to understand some emerging ecclesiological thrusts which are found in the Pope's teaching. We shall see that these thrusts are in line with conciliar teachings,[6] namely, the Church as a pilgrim, which reforms itself; the Church's identity as revealing that she is the People of God; the way to ecumenism as the way of Jesus, and religious life as the pillar of ecclesial expression.

1. Pilgrim Church, *Semper reformanda est*

Pope Francis, in his Apostolic Exhortation *Evangelii Gaudium* (henceforth EG), begins the very first chapter with the mission command of Jesus, "Go therefore and make disciples of all nations..." (Mt 28:19), and concludes with his own words: "Let us go forth, then, let us go forth to offer everyone the life of Jesus Christ" (EG 49). These highlight the pilgrim Church as missionary by her very nature (AG 2). The Church *understands* herself as a pilgrim church (AG 2) who finds her origin in Christ who made her as Sacrament of Salvation. J. Moltmann very aptly expresses this:

> The church's first word is not 'church' but Christ. The church's final word is not "church" but the glory of the Father and the Son in the Spirit of liberty. Because of this the church, as Ambrose said, is like the moon, which has no light of its own or for itself. If it is the true church, the light that is reflected on its face is the light of Christ, which reflects the glory of God, and it shines on the face of the church for the people who are seeking their way to freedom in the darkness.[7]

Moltmann's words highlight the eschatological provisionality, abundantly attested to by scripture, that affects or should affect everything in the Church's life.[8] The number of councils from the time of the New Testament (Act 15) to the Gregorian Reform of the eleventh century, to Vatican II in our time, prove that the Church has always exhibited herself in need of update. One passage in the Decree on Ecumenism of Vatican II speaks explicitly, though very guardedly, saying that this ecclesial reform touches not only on personal, but also on institutional reform:

As an institution of men here on earth that goes her pilgrim way, Christ summons the Church to continual reformation. Therefore, if the influence of events or of the times has led to deficiencies of conduct, Church discipline, or even the formulation of doctrine (which must be carefully distinguished from the deposit itself of faith), all should be appropriately rectified at the proper moment (*Unitatis Redintegratio* 6).

Vatican II's concept of pilgrim church has implications for self-understanding in the Church. Vatican II didn't say "a church of pilgrims;" rather, it said we're a pilgrim church. The Church *herself* is on the way. In *Lumen Gentium* (henceforth LG) Vatican II claims that the church "will not achieve its perfection until the end of history" (LG 48). The implication of such an affirmation is that the church is not perfect. If the church is not perfect, then there is need for change and reform.

Vatican II highlights an implicit ecclesiology wherein Jesus Christ is properly identified as the founder of the Church (cf. LG 1-4). The Church's self-reformation is possible as long as she continues to maintain the original intention and will of Jesus and the Kingdom of God (cf. LG 5).[9] Vatican II envisions two distinctive features of the Church. Firstly, the Church as a *congregatio fidelium*, is the sacrament of God, and as a pilgrim church, is *ecclesia semper reformanda*.[10] Pope Francis' decision to set up an eight-member Council of Cardinals to advise him on the government of the universal Church and plan the reform of the Roman Curia reflects this mindset of Vatican II. In fact, Pope Francis in his address to the Curia states that malicious resistance to Vatican reform is inspired by the devil:

> There are ... cases of *malicious resistance*, which spring up in misguided minds and come to the fore when the devil inspires ill intentions (often cloaked in sheep's clothing). This last kind of resistance hides behind words of self-justification and, often, accusation; it takes refuge in traditions, appearances, formalities, in the familiar, or else in a desire to make everything personal, failing to distinguish between the act, the actor, and the action.[11]

Thus, the papacy of Pope Francis is not only concerned with the question of *why* the Church should proclaim Christ, i.e., the missionary nature of the Church, but also *how* the Church should proclaim Christ. He teaches that:

> The Church's mission, then, is not to spread a religious ideology, much less to propose a lofty ethical teaching. Many movements throughout the world inspire high ideals or ways to live a meaningful life. Through the mission of the Church, Jesus Christ himself continues to evangelize and act; her mission thus makes present in history the *kairos*, the favourable time of salvation.[12]

Pope Francis then prefers "a Church which is bruised, hurting and dirty because it has been out on the streets, rather than a Church which is unhealthy from being confined and from clinging to its own security. I do not want a Church concerned with being at the centre and which then ends by being caught up in a web of obsessions and procedures" (EG 49).

2. The Church *of the People*

Against this background of the pilgrim Church, we appreciate the Pope's own ecclesial vision: "The image of the church I like is that of the holy, faithful people of God."[13] It is argued that Pope Francis' theological vision of the Church as the People of God progresses from his predecessor's theological vision of the Church, namely, the Church's *Communio* to the people's ecclesiology.

2.1 *Communio*: Prominent Teaching in the Pre-Papacy of Pope Francis

John Paul II in his Apostolic Exhortation teaches that "The ecclesiology of communion is a central and fundamental concept in the conciliar documents. *Koinonia*—communion, finding its source in Sacred Scripture, was a concept held in great honour in the early Church and in the Oriental Churches, and this teaching endures to the present day" (*Christifideles laici* 19).

The papacy of Benedict XVI reflected his earlier vision and as conciliar theologian wrote that communion "can serve as a synthesis of the essential element of conciliar theology."[14] As the head of the Congregation of Doctrine of Faith (CDF), he also asserted that "the concept of *communion* (*koinonia*), which appears with a certain prominence in the texts of the Second Vatican Council, is very suitable for expressing the core of the Mystery of the Church, and can certainly be key for the renewal of Catholic ecclesiology."[15]

Pope Benedict's *communion* springs from the theology of the Church as the mystical body of Christ (cf. 1 Cor. 12:27). The Church remains ever new because, through the work of the Holy Spirit, the mystery of the incarnation remains present in the Church. Therefore, the Church is not an idea, but the experience of Christ existing in her. Christ exists in the members not only in a spiritual way because he exists with others, with the permanent Community that continues through the ages. Consequently, she has a communal orientation. "It [the Church] does not exist in someplace; rather, we ourselves are it. Of course, no one can say, 'I am the Church,' but each one can say and must say, 'We are the Church.'"[16] Against this background we also need to read his Eucharistic ecclesiology. For him the Church is the celebration of the Eucharist: the fullness of the Church is found in the Eucharist because sharing in the Eucharist breaks down the divisive walls of our subjectivity, gathering us into a deep communion with Christ and with each other. Thus, the Church and Eucharist do not simply stand side by side; they are one and the same.[17]

Pope Francis therefore follows the teaching of his predecessor John Paul II, who taught that there exists an inherent relationship between the Eucharist and the concept of *Communio*: "the Eucharist, as the supreme sacramental manifestation of communion in the Church, demands to be celebrated in a context where the outward bonds of communion are also intact" (*Ecclesia de Eucharistia* 38). In *Deus Caritas Est,* Benedict XVI repeated this theme and taught that Christ in the Eucharist summons all Christians to communion: "I cannot possess Jesus Christ just for myself; I can belong to him only in union with all those who have become, or who will become his own. Communion draws me out of myself towards him, and thus towards unity with all Christians" (14). Therefore, Benedict XVI taught that "the unity of ecclesial communion is concretely manifested in the Christian communities and is renewed at the celebration of the Eucharist, which unites them and differentiates them in the particular Churches...(cf. LG 23)" (*Sacramentum caritatis* 15).

2.2 People of God as the Concrete Reality of *Communio*

The ecclesiologies of Francis' predecessors affirm the inner dynamism of the Church as communion: "She is certainly a mystery rooted in the Trinity." However, Pope Francis also highlights the historical reality of the Church as the People of God: "yet she exists concretely in history as a people of pilgrims and evangelizers, transcending any institutional expression, however necessary" (EG 111).

"People of God" is the principle paradigm of the Church in Vatican II's teachings (LG 9-17). When Vatican II taught about the Church as the People of God, it wanted to accentuate the basic equality of all the members in the Church; thus the chapter on the People of God is placed before chapters concerned with the functional differences in the Church. Secondly, the concept People of God brings to mind the paradigm of the Church as pilgrim. This Church is a poor church: "How I would like a church that is poor and for the poor."[18]

Pope Francis sought to highlight this equality of the People of God on the very day of his election as pope, when he appeared before the faithful gathered at St. Peter's Square. He broke tradition when he said:

I would like to give the blessing, but first I want to ask you a favor. Before the bishop blesses the people, I ask that you would pray to the Lord to bless me— the prayer of the people for their Bishop. Let us say this prayer—your prayer for me

As a result, he was not only envisaging his style of ministry, but also regards the ministerial priesthood in the Church in terms of service and humility. He asked the Priests to: "be shepherds, with the 'odour of the sheep,' make it real, as shepherds among your flock, fishers of men."[19] The "smell of Sheep" (EG 16)[20] is a favourite expression of Pope Francis, who accentuates the need for ministry of the Church to enter into a deeper and more profound solidarity with the world. Thus, he seems to show that he has no interest in a neo-cultic theology of priesthood, or any neo-clericalism. Francis has attempted to exemplify his teaching by his symbolic actions, namely his celebration of the Holy Thursday Mass of the Last Supper at a prison, where he washed the feet of 12 inmates; and his invitations of the homeless to the Sistine Chapel, the Vatican Museum, and to dine with them. Also appreciated is his sense of simplicity in his papal attire.

2.3 From the Structure to the Life of the Church

A basic characteristic of the pilgrim Church is that she is poised between the "already" of the resurrection of Jesus and the "not yet" of his parousia. She is a community that is "living and partly living" the life of the Spirit (to change the image of the allusion). She is a pilgrim people that must go always further towards her fulfilment. According to Avery Dulles, the image of "People of God" interpreted in the light of the concept of sacrament[21] will enable us to rid ourselves of ecclesial *monophysitism*, and to understand the Church as the sacrament of salvation. Dulles explains:

The First letter of Peter, relying on Exodus, depicts the Church as a sacred people, a royal priesthood, set aside for worship, praise and *testimony* before all nations (1 Pt 2:9; cf. Ex 19:6). In the fourth Servant Song of Isaiah, the people of God is seen as the "light of the nations (*Lumen Gentium*)" (Is 42:6). Understood in this way, the People of God, like the Body of Christ, *is, in* Christ, the universal sacrament of salvation.[22] (italics mine)

Pope Francis conceives of the Church as the pilgrim community, and his writings and exhortations seek to distance him from ecclesial *monophysitism*. The church is constantly called to configure its image to that of Christ:"I do not want a Church concerned with being at the centre and which then ends by being caught up in a web of obsessions and procedures" (EG49). His vision of the Church is to "go forth to everyone without exception" (EG 48). Churches "with closed doors must never be called churches, they should be called museums!"[23] In such affirmations one can see the influence of non-European theologies. The Pope's concern can be formulated in terms that see the Church as a mystery and not merely a social reality (cf. Eph. 3:9). Nevertheless, as a historical reality, the Church is also the actualization of the mystery of Christ in humankind. Very particularly, as a social reality she reveals the love of God in the world in order to transform the whole creation. Therefore, he writes that "The Church has realized that the need to heed this plea is itself born of the liberating action of grace within each of us... The word 'solidarity' is a little worn and at times poorly understood, but it refers to something more than a few sporadic acts of generosity. It presumes the creation of a new mindset which thinks in terms of community and the priority of the life of all over the appropriation of goods by a few" (EG 188).

"God's heart has a special place for the poor, so much so, he himself became poor" (EG 197). Pope Francis "want[s] a Church which is poor and for the poor" (EG 198) because God has a heart for the poor and so must we. The option for the poor is "primarily a theological category which reflects the way God came into the world.", and he has taken up the concept in his encounter with Religious Superiors: "I am convinced of one thing: the great changes in history were realized when reality was seen not from the center but rather from the periphery. It is a hermeneutical question: reality is understood only if it is looked at from the periphery..."[24]

By affirming this fact, the Pope seems to distinguish between the structure of the Church and the life of the Church. He seems to affirm that his concern is more for the life of the Church, including, inevitably, the option for the poor, which assures the accomplishment of the Church's mission and the achievement of its purpose. For God, the Incarnation was an act of preferential option for the poor, and so Pope Francis says, "They have much to teach us. Not only do they share in the *sensus fidei*, but, in their difficulties, they know the suffering Christ. We need to let ourselves be evangelized by them" (EG 198). By introducing the concept *sensus fidei*, Pope Francis calls to mind the much discussed ideal of the "listening church" (*pie audit*) of Vatican II (DV 10). For Pope Francis, it means to acknowledge the *sensus fidei* of the Faithful and "thinking with the Church."[25] It means thinking with the whole Church and not only with the Hierarchy of the Church or with theologians. "The ideal of the 'listening Church' is to become a Church in dialogue."[26] The Pope affirms that if the dialogue is genuine, then "it is assisted by the Holy Spirit."[27] Pope Francis quoted the words of a humble, elderly woman he once met: "If the Lord did not forgive everything, the world would not exist;" and he commented with admiration: "that is the wisdom which the Holy Spirit gives."[28] Congar argues that the whole truth about salvation is grasped only in communion with all of the faithful because true faith does not exist without the fraternal communion of the faithful. The Holy Spirit who animates and guides the Church (cf. Jn. 15:26) operates within the mutual love of the faithful, as a Spirit of love and fraternal communion.[29]

For Pope Francis, such listening and dialogue is the foundation for "missionary aspiration to reach everyone" (EG 31). The idea of a "listening Church" is again taken up in his Bull of Induction for the Extraordinary Jubilee of Mercy: "And let us enter more deeply into the heart of the Gospel where the poor have a special experience of God's mercy" (*Misericordiae Vultus* 15) in order to reawaken the conscience that is often grown dull in the face of poverty. The Listening Church, which the Pope himself practices, can bring a multitude of changes in the way the Church's Curia and theological faculties function.

3. The Way of Jesus, the Way to Ecumenical Unity

In an interview with Antonio Spadaro SJ, Pope Francis stated, "In ecumenical relations it is important not only to know each other better, but also to recognize what the Spirit has sown in the other as a gift for us." He concluded by stating, "We must walk united with our differences: there is no other way to become one. This is the way of Jesus."[30]

Francis writes in EG: "How many wars take place within the people of God and in our different communities! ... Whom are we going to evangelize if this is the way we act?" (98-100). This is a sincere lamentation from a pope who thinks that if the Church wants to have an impact globally, then the Church should have unity.[31] Consequently, the Pope's preference is often for pastoral doctrine, which needs to be interpreted in relation to the core Christian kerygma; in light of the particular pastoral context. This commitment to pastoral doctrine was seen in his visit to the Lutheran Church of Christ in Rome in 2015.

On the question of an Evangelical Christian who is married to a Catholic, who expressed sorrow at "not being able to partake together in the Lord's Supper," Pope Francis spoke with astonishingly open words that can be heard from different perspectives. It was evident how the Pope appreciated this question as the personal decision of the individual Christian when he said, "Always refer to Baptism: 'One faith, one baptism, one Lord,' as Paul tells us, and take the outcome from there. I would never dare give permission to do this because I do not have the authority. One Baptism, one Lord, one faith. Speak with the Lord and go forward. I do not dare say more."[32] Certainly the Pope's affirmation has dogmatic repercussions for the Magisterium of the Church, and has caused quite a stir in Germany,[33] but it echoes his pastoral doctrine.[34]

Pope Francis' commitment to a pastoral doctrine echoes the vision of the Vatican II. The Decree on Ecumenism, *Unitatis redintegratio*, begins with the statement, "The restoration of unity among all Christians is one of the principal concerns of the Second Vatican Council." In the same breath it teaches that "Christ the Lord founded one Church and one Church only [and]…division openly [among Christians] contradicts the will of Christ, scandalizes the world, and damages the holy cause of preaching the Gospel to every creature" (1). In a similar vein, the Pope affirms that "in a Christian community, *division is one of the gravest sins*, because it makes it a sign not of God's work, but of the devil's work, who is by definition the one who separates, who destroys relationships, who insinuates prejudice."[35]

In an ecumenical comment, George M. Soares-Prabbhu wrote that the Christian mystery, namely the events in the confessional history (the *incarnation*, the *cross*, and the *resurrection*), unite Christians; but "mechanisms" or models like the two natures in one person of Chalcedon, which explain the mystery, separate Christians because they are tied to specifically conditioned worldviews.[36]

On the importance of Christian unity, Pope Francis inspiringly evokes the example of the Taizé community. According to him, many Orthodox, Catholic, and Protestant youth come together at the Taizé community "because they ignore the differences which still separate us; but because they are able to see beyond them, they are able to embrace what is essential and what already unites us."[37] In his address at the plenary session of the Congregation for the Doctrine of the Faith, Pope Francis distilled his understanding of doctrine in one sentence: "In reality, doctrine has the sole purpose of serving the life of the People of God and it seeks to assure our faith of a sure foundation."[40]

The question that the Church needs to pose is that of Paul to the Christians of Corinth: "Has Christ been divided?" (1 Cor. 1:13). Pope Francis prophetically taught in a similar context:

Of course, Christ was not divided. But we should recognize with sincerity and pain that our communities continue to live in division that is scandalous. Division among us Christians is a scandal. There is no other word: a scandal. "Each one of you," St Paul wrote, "says, 'I belong to Paul,' or 'I belong to Apollos,' or 'I belong to Cephas,' or 'I belong to Christ'" (1 Cor 1:12) … the name of Christ creates communion and unity, not division! He came to bring communion among us, not to divide us. Baptism and the Cross are central elements of the Christian discipleship which we share. Division, however, weakens the credibility and effectiveness of our work in evangelization and risks stripping the Cross of its power (cf. 1 Cor 1:17).[38]

The Pope who chose the name of St. Francis of Assisi wants the Church to be humble and selfless and to live according to the Beatitudes of the Gospel. Only in humility is a sincere dialogue between people possible to foster a common good.[39] He thus tries to back away from any Pre-Vatican triumphalism or Ecclesio-centrism and desires instead that the Church, as people of God, be the "little flock" following the humble Jesus. "The unity of all his disciples was the heartfelt prayer that Jesus Christ offered to the Father on the eve of his passion and death (cf. Jn 17:21). The fulfilment of this prayer is entrusted to God, but it also involves our docility and obedience to his will."[40] Thusly, to be united is essential to the nature and mission of the Church. Walter Kasper argues that, "the unity as an essential characteristic of the church is not a future, or much less an eschatological goal; the church is already the '*una sancta ecclesia*' (*UR*, 4; *UUS*, 11-14)."[41] Unity is the face of the Church as the herald of Good News, for it shows the effectiveness of that part of the Church that has appropriated Christ's saving work (Jn. 17:21).[42]

Vatican II teaches that "we are a pilgrim church," and "At the end of time it [the Church] will gloriously achieve completion..." (LG 2, also LG 9). Therefore, we know that the Church admits that she is not perfect. The Decree on Ecumenism makes some remarkable assertions about the history of divisions in the Church. For example, 11th-century division resulted in Orthodoxy, and together with the Protestant traditions in the 16th century, "often enough, men of both sides were to blame" (UR 3). The same Decree teaches that "Christ summons the Church to continual reformation as she sojourns here on earth. The Church is always in need of this, in so far as she is an institution of men here on earth" (UR 6).

4. Religious: Joy of the Church

"The joy of the gospel fills the hearts and lives of all who encounter Jesus;" thus begins the Pope's First Apostolic exhortation, and develops the theme of the proclamation of the Gospel in the contemporary world. The Gospel proclaims the joyous salvation given by the Risen Christ and says that the Christian mission is to announce this joy. Through religious vocation he believes, "We are called to know and show that God is able to fill our hearts to the brim with happiness."[43] Religious vocation in communities is a "different way of doing things, of acting, of living,"[44] and authentic joy has to be cultivated within the community in which a person is called to live, not elsewhere. He affirms, "Where there are religious, there is joy."[45]

I have elsewhere written that the "ecclesiality" of a religious community becomes *real* through the acknowledgment of its charism within a given context. It is not enough for a community merely to trace its historical patrimony or its glorious past. Often the rhetoric that enshrines the *patrimony* of monastic religious life has the upper hand over the voice of its prophetical relevance *today*.[46]

Pope Francis asserts that in today's polarized society, where people of different cultures have difficulty to get along and inequality abounds, consecrated persons "are called to offer a concrete model of community that, by acknowledging the dignity of each person and sharing our respective gifts, makes it possible to live as brothers and sisters."[47]

Nevertheless, he does not advocate that religious life is to be confined to the security of the four walls of the convent. "The fulfilment of the evangelical command 'Go to the whole world and proclaim the Gospel to every creature' (Mk 16:15) can be accomplished with this hermeneutical key shifted to the existential and geographical periphery. It is the most concrete way of imitating Jesus, who went toward all the peripheries."[48] He adds that, though it is risky, "The charism is not a bottle of distilled water. It needs to be lived energetically as well as reinterpreted culturally."[49]

Members of religious communities are called to know and show that God is able to fill our hearts to the brim with happiness; that we need not seek our happiness elsewhere; that the authentic fraternity found in our communities increases our joy; and that our total self-giving in service to the Church, to families and young people, to the elderly and the poor, brings us lifelong personal fulfilment.[50]

I want to say one word to you and this word is "joy." Wherever there are consecrated people, seminarians, men and women religious, young people, there is joy; there is always joy! It is the joy of freshness, the joy of following Jesus; the joy that the Holy Spirit gives us, not the joy of the world. There is joy! But— where is joy born?[51]

Pope Francis adds that true joy comes from the encounter with the one who has called him, and authentic witness to his Gospel brings joy in others. Therefore, true joy does not come from the seeming assurance of structure, which, though certainly necessary and important, should never obscure the one true joy God gives.

Conclusion

In his message to participants in the Second International Congress of Theology, Pope Francis told the participants that Catholic theology should be done in the stream of the Church's living Tradition:

Not infrequently we identify doctrine with the conservative, the retrograde; and, on the contrary, we think that pastoral care is an adaptation, a reduction, an accommodation. As if they had nothing to do with one another. Thus, we create a false opposition between the so-called "pastorally-minded" and the "academics", those on the side of the people and those on the side of doctrine. We create a false opposition between theology and pastoral care; between the believer's reflection and the believer's life; life, then, has no space for reflection and reflection finds no space in life.... One of the main contributions of the Second Vatican Council was precisely to seek a way to overcome the divorce between theology and pastoral care, between faith and life. I dare say that the Council has revolutionized to some extent the status of theology—the believer's way of doing and thinking.[52]

We have begun this article affirming that every theology works to continue to explore the mystery of God. While we remain loyal to the unique message of faith revealed in history, simultaneously we look forward to the realization of the message in order to answer the questions of each age.

The Church needs reform, and the Church has always tried to reform itself in order to be updated. All of its saints were, in their own way, reformers. Each council—or maybe we could say each papal encyclical—was a work of reform.[53] Vatican II taught that "every renewal of the Church essentially consists in an increase of fidelity to her own calling" (UR 6). Pope Francis in his own style is trying to reform the self-understanding of the Church. His teachings are shaped in such way so as to take up the project of Vatican II, and re-engage the Church with the world and move it forward. Thusly, Pope Francis affirms that "The church sometimes has locked itself up in small things, in small-minded rules. The most important thing is the first proclamation: *Jesus Christ has saved you.*"[54] This is the primary duty of the People of God, and these People of God are dynamic because they are constantly walking, "*Camminare:*"

Walking: the House of Jacob. "O house of Jacob, Come, let us walk in the light of the Lord." This is the first thing God said to Abraham: "Walk in my presence and be blameless." Walking: our life is a journey and when we stop, there is something wrong. Walking always, in the presence of the Lord, in the light of the Lord, seeking to live with that blamelessness, which God asks of Abraham, in his promise.[55]

This is the vision Pope Francis for the Church, a Church that is always looking forward to the future of the Lord. If the future is obviously something already fully present and actual, then there is nothing to hope for. Therefore, Pope Francis adds: "If one has the answers to all questions—that is proof that God is not with him. It means that he is a false prophet using religion for himself. The great leaders of the people of God, like Moses, have always left room for doubt. You must leave room for the Lord, not for our certainties; we must be humble."[56]

Looking towards the future with hope is at the heart of his theology. Therefore, he says that "God never ever tires of forgiving us."

Pope Francis shows that he has new vigour and confidence in guiding the Church, and in many ways, sets a new example for leading the Church. Nevertheless, as the always thoughtful Paul Baumann recently warned:

> Whatever people think Pope Francis is offering, he is no magician; he can't alter the course of secular history or bridge the church's deepening ideological divisions simply by asserting what in truth are the papacy's rather anaemic powers. In this light, the inordinate attention paid to the papacy, while perhaps good for business, is not good for the

church. Why not? Because it encourages the illusion that what ails the church can be cured by one man, especially by a new man. In truth, no pope possesses that kind of power, thank God.[57]

It is certainly true that Pope Francis' papacy has brought a promising influence on the life of the Church, however we can only pray that it remains to have a lasting impact on the Church's self-understanding!

Endnotes

1   J. Neuner wrote, "This finality [fullness of revelation], however does not mean that God has nothing to tell us anymore: We will continue to learn how this union with God has been reached in other religions, how it unfolded in other religions." See J. NEUNER, "Revelation and Faith," *Jeevadhara*, 31 (2001): 174.

2   G. O'COLLINS, S.J., has made a similar point. In one sense, Jesus Christ definitely embodies and transmits the fullness of revelation, but in another sense, he does not. The final vision of God is still to come, as St. John puts it: "...what we shall be has not yet been revealed..." (1 John 3:2). As Paul puts it: "for now we see in a mirror, dimly, but then we will see face to face..." (1 Cor. 13:12). See G. O'Collins, "Watch Your Language" (Review ofGavin Costa's *The Meeting of Religions and the Trinity*), *The Tablet* (November 2000): 1490.

3   J. WICKS, "The Fullness of Revelation in Christ: A Genetic Study the Doctrine of Dei Verbum and a Proposal for its Presentation Today," http://www.unigre.it/struttura_didattica/Teologia/specifico/tf_la_ pienezz.htm.

4   Pope FRANCIS, "General Audience," *Libreria Editrice Vaticana,*January 13, 2016, https://w2.vatican.va/content/francesco/en/audiences/2016/documents/papa-francesco_20160113_udienza-generale.html.

5   I borrow this concept from G. O'Collins, who argued that the eschatological provisionality abundantly attested to by scripture affects or should affect everything in the Church's life: worship, belief, standards of behaviour, and patterns of organisation. See O'Collins, "Did Apostolic Continuity ever Start? Origins of Apostolic Continuity in the New Testament," *Louvian Studies* 21 (1996): 149.

6   It has been affirmed that Pope Francis was elected on a reform mandate. Cf. John L. ALLEN Jr., ed., "The Risks of Pope Francis' Never-ending Vatican Reform," *Crux*, December 22, 2016, https://cruxnow.com/analysis/2016/12/22/risks-pope-franciss-never-ending-vatican-reform/.

7   J. MOLTMANN, *The Church in the Power of the Spirit. A Contribution to Messianic Ecclesiology* (Minneapolis: Fortress Press, 1993), 19.

8   As argued by O'COLLINS, "Apostolic Continuity," 149.

9   Cf. S. PIÉ-NINOT, "Church II: Jesus and the Church," in *Dictionary of Fundamental Theology,* ed. R. Fisichella and R. Latourelle (New York: Crossroad, 1994), 151-53.

10   Cf. S. PIÉ-NINOT, *La Teologia Fondamentale: Rendere ragione della speranza(1 Pt 3,15)*, trans. P. Crespi (Brescia: Queriniana, 2002), 459-60. *Ecclesia semper reformanda est* (Latin for "the church must always be reformed." This phrase implies that the church must continually re-examine itself in order to maintain its purity.

11   Pope FRANCIS, "Presentation of the Christmas Greetings to the Roman Curia," *Libreria Editrice Vaticana*, December 22, 2016, https://w2.vatican.va/content/francesco/en/speeches/2016/december/documents/papa-francesco_20161222_curia-romana.html#_ftnref18.

12 Pope FRANCIS, "Message of Pope Francis for World Mission Day 2017: Mission at the Heart of the Christian Faith," *Libreria Editrice Vaticana,* para. 3, https://w2.vatican.va/content/francesco/en/messages/missions/documents/papa-francesco_20170604_giornata-missionaria2017.html.

13 Pope FRANCIS, "A Big Heart Open to God," interview by Antonio Spadaro, SJ, *America,* September 30, 2013, print,http://americamagazine.org/pope-interview.

14 Joseph RATZINGER, "The Ecclesiology of the Constitution on the Church, Vatican II, 'Lumen Gentium,'" *L'Osservatore Romano,* September 19, 2001, http://www.ewtn.com/library/curia/cdfeccl.htm.

15 Joseph RATZINGER, "Letter to the Bishops of the Catholic Church on Some Aspects of the Church Understood as Communion," May 28, 1992, http://www.vatican.va/roman_curia/congregations/cfaith/documents/rc_con_cfaith_doc_28051992_communionis-notio_en.html.

16 Joseph RATZINGER, "The Ecclesiology of the Second Vatican Council," *Communio* 13(1986): 241.

17 His argument is based on 1 Corinthians 10:16-17, i.e., our becoming the one body of Christ by sharing in his body in the Eucharist. He argues that the Church is founded on the Eucharist: "The Church is the celebration of the Eucharist: The Eucharist is the Church; they do not simply stand side by side; they are one and the same." See Joseph RATZINGER, *Principles of Catholic Theology: Building Stones for a Fundamental Theology* (San Francisco: Ignatius Press, 1987), 53.

18 Pope FRANCIS, "Audience to Representatives of the Communications Media: Address of the Holy Father Pope Francis," *Libreria Editrice Vaticana,* March 16, 2013, https://w2.vatican.va/content/francesco/en/speeches/2013/march/documents/papa-francesco_20130316_rappresentanti-media.html.

19 Pope FRANCIS, "Chrism Mass Homily of Pope Francis," *Libreria Editrice Vaticana,* March 28, 2013, http://w2.vatican.va/content/francesco/en/homilies/2013/documents/papa-francesco_20130328_messa-crismale.html. The Pope repeated this again in his "Chrism Mass Homily of His Holiness Pope Francis," *Libreria Editrice Vaticana,* April 2, 2015, http://w2.vatican.va/content/francesco/en/homilies/2015/documents/papa-francesco_20150402_omelia-crisma.html.

20 See also Pope FRANCIS, "Address to a Group of Newly Appointed Bishops Taking Part in a Conference," *Libreria Editrice Vaticana,* September 19, 2013, https://w2.vatican.va/content/francesco/en/ speeches/2013/september/documents/papa-francesco_20130919_convegno-nuovi-vescovi.html.

21 According to Avery DULLES, Vatican II uses a broader sense of the term "sacrament" than the mere seven rites. Thus he says, "The broader use of the term 'sacrament', however, was common in the early Christian writers and pre-Scholastic medieval theologians who quite commonly called Christ the sacrament par excellence. In the Latin Bible, *sacramentum* was sometimes used to translate the term *mysterium,* though the two are not perfectly synonymous. 'Mystery' emphasizes the incomprehensibility of God's saving plan, whereas sacrament serves to bring out its visible or incarnational dimension." See Avery Dulles, "The Sacramental Ecclesiology of *Lumen Gentium,*" *Gregorianum* 86 (2005): 551.

22 DULLES, "Sacramental Ecclesiology," 554.

23 Pope FRANCIS, *Evangelii Gaudium,* November 24, 2013, https://w2.vatican.va/content/francesco/en/apost_exhortations/documents/papa-francesco_esortazione-ap_20131124_evangelii-gaudium.html.

24 Antonio SPADARO, SJ, "'Wake Up the World!' Conversation with Pope Francis About the Religious Life," *La Civiltà Cattolica*, 165 (2014): 3.

25 "And all the faithful, considered as a whole, are infallible in matters of belief, and the people display this *infallibilitas* in *credendo*, this infallibility in believing, through a supernatural sense of the faith of all the people walking together" (Pope Francis, "A Big Heart Open to God").

26 J.J. BURKHARD, "The *Sensus Fidelium*: Old Questions, New Challenges" CTSA Proceedings, June 11, 2015, https://ejournals.bc.edu/ojs/index.php/ctsa/article/.../8751/7969.

27 Pope FRANCIS, "A Big Heart Open to God."

28 Pope FRANCIS, "Angelus Address," March 17, 2013, in International Theological Commission, "*Sensus Fidei* in the Life of the Church," (2014), para. 2.

29 See Yves CONGAR, *True and False Reform in the Church* (Collegeville: Michael Glazier, 2011), 229-30.

30 Pope Francis, "A Big Heart Open to God."

31 He has made some spectacular ecumenical encounters; namely, in 2014, he celebrated an ecumenical service with Orthodox churches in the Holy Sepulchre Church in Jerusalem. In the same year he visited a Pentecostal community in Caserta. In June 2015 he became the first Pope to enter a Waldensian church. In 2015 he also visited the Lutheran Church of Christ in Rome and on February 12, 2016 he met Russian Orthodox Patriarch Kirill in Havana.

32 Pope FRANCIS, "Address of His Holiness Pope Francis: Visit to the Evangelical Lutheran Church of Rome," *Libreria Editrice Vaticana*, November 15, 2015, https://w2.vatican.va/content/francesco/en/speeches/2015/november/documents/papa-francesco_20151115_chiesa-evangelica-luterana.html.

33 P. METZGER, "Gewissen nicht Lehre," *Zeitzeichen* 17 (2016): 40–42.

34 There has been talk of footnote 351 of *Amoris Laetitia* being "dogmatically problematic" and endorsing communion for those who are divorced and remarried without an annulment. But in the text preceding this note Pope Francis observes that, while certain individuals may be objectively in sin, they may not be fully culpable. This is nothing new; the Church has long taught that mortal sin requires the presence of three criteria: grave matter, full knowledge, and freedom of the will (CCC 1857). One can read in the Pope's emphasis on pastoral doctrine that, though grave matter is always present in an irregular union, the other two criteria may not be. In *certain cases* (my emphasis), this can include the help of the sacraments. Hence, "I want to remind priests that the confessional must not be a torture chamber, but rather an encounter with the Lord's mercy." I would also point out that the Eucharist "is not a prize for the perfect, but a powerful medicine and nourishment for the weak." In other words, language surrounding footnote 351 does not at all describe people who "obstinately persevere in manifest grave sin, rather he speaks elsewhere (cf. §222) of the need for pastors to help couples develop a "fully formed conscience. See Scott Eric Alt, "*Amoris Laetitia*: Confused by Footnote 351? A Look at 329 Can Help," *Aleteia*, April 14, 2016, https://aleteia.org/2016/04/14/amoris-laetitia-confused-by-footnote-351-a-look-at-329-can-help/.

35 Pope FRANCIS, "General Audience," *Libreria Editrice Vaticana*, August 27, 2014, https://w2.vatican.va/content/francesco/en/audiences/2014/documents/papa-francesco_20140827_udienza-generale.html

36   See George M. SOARES-PRABHU, "The Jesus of Faith: A Christological Contribution to an Ecumenical Third World Spirituality," in *The Dharma of Jesus*, ed. Francis Xavier D'Sa (New York: Orbis Books, 2003) 85-86.

37   Pope FRANCIS, "Address of Pope Francis: Divine Liturgy," *Libreria Editrice Vaticana*, November 30, 2014, http://w2.vatican.va/content/francesco/en/homilies/2014/documents/papa-francesco_20141130_divina-liturgia-turchia.html.

38   Pope FRANCIS, "General Audience," *Libreria Editrice Vaticana*, January 22, 2014, http://w2.vatican.va/content/francesco/en/audiences/2014/documents/papa-francesco_20140122_udienza-generale.html.

39   Pope FRANCIS, "Address of the Holy Father: Meeting with the Participants in the Fifth Convention of the Italian Church," *Libreria Editrice Vaticana*, November 10, 2015, https://w2.vatican.va/content/francesco/en/speeches/2015/november/documents/papa-francesco_20151110_firenze-convegno-chiesa-italiana.html

40   Pope FRANCIS, "Address of His Holiness Pope Francis to the Delegation of the Ecumenical Patriarchate of Constantinople," *Libreria Editrice Vaticana*, June 27, 2017, https://w2.vatican.va/content/francesco/en/speeches/2017/june/documents/papa-francesco_20170627_delegazione-patriarcato-costantinopoli.html

41   Walter KASPER, "The Decree on Ecumenism—Read Anew After Forty Years," in *Searching for Christian Unity: 40 Years of Unitatis Redintegratio,* ed. Walter Kasper, (New York: New City Press, 2007), 22.

42   Cf. K. KUNNUMPURAM, *Towards a New Humanity. Reflections on the Church's Mission in India Today* (Mumbai: 2005), 235.

43   Pope FRANCIS, "Apostolic Letter of His Holiness Pope Francis to All Consecrated People on the Occasion of the Year of Consecrated Life," *Libreria Editrice Vaticana,* November 21, 2014, https://w2.vatican.va/content/francesco/en/apost_letters/documents/papa-francesco_lettera-ap_20141121_lettera-consacrati.html.

44   SPADARO, "Wake Up the World!" 3.

45   Pope FRANCIS, "To All Consecrated People."

46   Antony D'CRUZ, "The Role of Charisms in the Church Some Contemporary Considerations," *Vidyajyoti* 78 (2014): 583.

47   Pope FRANCIS, "Apostolic Letter Marking the Start of the Year of Consecrated Life," *Origins* 44, no. 29 (December 2014): 483.

48   SPADARO, "Wake Up the World!" 4.

49   Ibid.

50   Pope FRANCIS "To All Consecrated People."

51   Pope FRANCIS, "Address of Holy Father Francis: Meeting with Seminarians and Novices," *Libreria Editrice Vaticana*, July 6, 2013, https://w2.vatican.va/content/francesco/en/speeches/2013/july/documents/papa-francesco_20130706_incontro-seminaristi.html.

52   Pope FRANCIS, "Video Message of His Holiness Pope Francis to Participants in an International Theological Congress Held at the Pontifical Catholic University of Argentina," *Libreria Editrice Vaticana*, September 1-3, 2015, https://w2.vatican.va/content/francesco/en/messages/pont-messages/2015/documents/papa-francesco_20150903_videomessaggio-teologia-buenos-aires.html.

53   See CONGAR, *True and False Reform*, 19.

54   Pope FRANCIS, "A Big Heart Open to God".

55   Pope FRANCIS, "1st Homily: Missa pro Ecclesiae in the Sistine Chapel," *News.va*, March 14, 2013, http://www.news.va/en/news/pope-francis-1st-homily-full-text.

56   Pope FRANCIS, "A Big Heart Open to God."

57   Paul BAUMANN, "The Public Pope," *Slate*, March 11, 2014, http://www.slate.com/articles/news_and_politics/foreigners/2014/03/pope_francis_at_one_year_why_intense_focus_on_the_papacy_is_bad_for_the.html.

Chapter 9

Embracing the Laity
The Vision of Pope Francis

A. Pushparajan
Professor Emeritus, Kamaraj University, Madurai, Tamil Nadu

Introduction

Pope Francis has undoubtedly captured a unique position in the history of papacy. This can be indicated with reference to various counts. But for the purpose of this article it is sufficient to indicate some of those symbols that he sent out at the very beginning of his papacy to signify the new vision for the Church. And he has been consistently harping upon the important role of the laity. Once we grasp his radical vision of the Church then we can easily draw out his views on the role of laity in the 'new' Church that he has envisioned. Hence, in the first part of this article, an attempt is made to describe the new vision of the Church by Pope Francis. Against the background of that vision, Part 2 tries to bring out the specific role the laity can play.

1. The Radical Vision of the Church by Pope Francis

In this section a modest attempt is made to portray the changed vision of the Church as projected by Pope Francis. This is done at three levels. First by picking up some signals that he sent out already at the time of his election as the Pope. Then by recalling the brief intervention Cardinal Jorge Mario Bergoglio made just before the election. Thirdly by analysing the clear cut vision that he has enunciated in his first major document released by him as Pope: *Evangelii Gaudium*.

1.1 The Distinctive Signals of Pope-elect for his New Vision of the Church

No one can propose a vision of anything in vacuum. Nor does any vision mushroom from one's imagination purely, and all of a sudden. It is indeed an offshoot of the whole of the one's personality. Often enough it is the pile of perceptions and other experiences one has accumulated over the years as well as the ideals and goals of life one cherishes that contribute to emergence of a particular vision. It is the 'apperception'[1] of an individual that has a major say in the evolution of a vision. No doubt a particular occasion serves as a triggering point for spelling out the vision. But before articulating the vision in clear contours, one is bound to send out certain signals that indicate the salient features of his/her apperception. Hence, there is a need to take note of the unusual symbols one emits at one's critical point of life.

Viewed from this standpoint, it is quite interesting to recount some of the distinctive responses given by Cardinal Bergoglio immediately after the election as Pope. They are significant for understanding his unique convictions regarding Christ our Lord, the Church in general, and his own personal commitment in particular. It must be noted they were all spontaneous in the sense that they did not arise from deliberate attempts to do them in that way. In fact there was no time at all for the pope-elect to sit and to reflect upon what type of name one has to choose, which type of dress one wants, and which colour of the shoes one has to wear etc. Even then, if his gestures and postures, words and actions were unique, it only proves that the man was already filled with radical and revolutionary ideas and projections about the Church. They are all symbolic of the radical vision of the Church which he had been treasuring for quite some time and which he would clearly describe after assuming his office as Pope. It is significant to note that he hinted at it already during the pre-Conclave meeting. Let me mention some of the symbolic responses he gave just at the time of his election as a Pope.

On the fifth ballot, on 13 March 2013, when Cardinal Jorge Mario Bergoglio secured 77 votes, it was decisively clear in the conclave that he is now the Pope. But after reading out the final vote (90 out of the 115) the one in charge approaches him to get his consent with this question: "Do you accept your canonical election as Supreme Pontiff?" The expected response would normally be: "I accept". But his answer was: "Although I am a sinner, I accept it, trusting in the mercy and patience of God in suffering." It is a clear sign of his extraordinary humility and trust in the providential care of the Father.

The next question is: "What name do you take?" Swiftly he replies: "I will be called Francis". This name is quite unusual down the line. This was a clear indication that he would make a radical break with the past. No doubt his neighbour Cardinal in the conclave had whispered to him 'to think of the poor' which has inspired the new Pope to choose St. Francis of Assisi. But he had already described St. Francis of Assisi in his book of dialogue with Rabbi Abraham Skorka: "He brought to Christianity an entire new concept about poverty in the face of the luxury, ride and vanity of the civil and ecclesial powers of the time. He changed history."[2]

Then, the Cardinal is led to the sacristy of the Sistine Chapel to be presented with Papal dress. While changing his scarlet robes into white, he is offered red *mozzetta,* the short elbow-length vestment that covers the shoulders and is buttoned over the frontal breast, usually worn by the Roman pontiff. But quietly he declines the offer. Here the message is clear: "He doesn't like the trappings of monarchy that surrounded the papacy."[3]

Now he is presented with the gold-jewelled pectoral cross. However, as a sign of his preference for utter simplicity of life style, he reaches out for his old silver metal cross which he has been wearing since he became a bishop in Argentina. Next the boxes of red leather shoes of different sizes are shown to him so that he would choose among them his proper size. But he calmly looks down at his battered black shoes and says: "These are fine with me". Again it is clearly a break from the papal practice that goes back to the Byzantine era, when only three individuals were allowed to wear red footgear: the Emperor, the Empress and the Pope.

Meanwhile, the fellow-cardinals have lined up in the *Sala Clementina* to offer their congratulations and pledges to the new pontiff. In the traditional manner, the new pope was to sit on the papal throne. But, this pope is determined to drop the centuries-old symbol of the past in which the papacy saw itself as the equal of imperial power. He does not even stand on an elevated platform. But, on equal footing, he offers to greet them all one by one with a hug. When somebody insisted on bending to kiss his ring, he too bent to kiss the ring of the one who pays such a homage. It is definitely a symbol of his rejection of the past notion that Pope was the Prince in the pyramid model of autocratic feudal monarchy. It was a clear sign that he will recover the authentic concept of collegiality in which pope would be seen merely as the first among equals. In fact he addressed them as 'brother cardinals' rather than "Lord Cardinals'.

It is time now for the new Pope to appear on the balcony to bless the people *urbi et orbi* (city and the world). However he prefers to call himself as the Bishop of Rome to the people of his diocese. Besides, he speaks in Italian, the language of the people. He even begins with informal and intimate, for this momentous of occasions: *"Buona Sera"* (Good evening). He also initiates the crowd to pray for his predecessor with the prayers best known to them: "the Our Father, the Hail Mary and the Glory be". It is quite significant that he referred to his predecessor not as 'Pope Emeritus', but as the 'Emeritus Bishop of Rome'. Again it is important to note his utterance: "Now let's begin this journey, bishop and people, this journey of the Church of Rome, which is one that **presides in charity** over all the churches—a journey of brotherhood, love and trust among us." Here the phrase "presides in charity' is actually taken from the first century bishop Ignatius of Antioch, indicating a radical shift in the understanding of the Church: the community in which Pope is put back in the college, to **preside in love.**

While he was about to give the papal blessing, *urbi et orbi* (to the city and the world), he recognizes the extraordinary mutuality of the pope and the people: "Let us pray for one another. I will bless you, but I will ask you a favour, for your prayers to bless me as your bishop. Let's pray silently". It is remarkable that he could evoke a perfect silence even in such a big crowd of people counting more than a million in the piazza below. This is itself a clear manifestation of the power of spiritual aura of a great personality.

At the end of the blessing he tells them: "Brothers and sisters, I'll leave you. Thank you so much for the welcome. Pray for me. We'll see each other soon. Good night and sleep well". It is again a wonderful sign of the loving concern of a good shepherd with his sheep. After the dinner the Pope is guided to the black Mercedes. Yet, he chooses to travel in the minibus that took the cardinals to return to their residence. At the residence, over there, when all the cardinals had retired to their beds, he asks the officials whether an ordinary Italian car was available. When the driver was found, the Pope who styled himself as the bishop of Rome goes for a drive into streets of the city of Rome, watching the people amused from the inside of a small, unmarked car. A clear sign of the new Pope being really the pastor of the people.

On the following morning, he is off to the Basilica of Santa Maria Maggiore, in an ordinary car, not the papal limousine, to pray before an icon of the Virgin Mary, *Salus Populi Romani*, the Protectress of the Romans. The security officers try to close the basilica to the public, he waives them away telling them: "Leave them alone. I am a pilgrim too". Are they not extraordinary signs of revealing himself a true shepherd of the people, identifying with them?

On returning from the Basilica, the Pope-elect goes to collect his luggage at the hostel. There at the porter's desk he asks for a new bulb, because he remembers that bulb for the bedside lamp had blown. So it needs to be replaced. The surprised official gives him one. A short while later he comes down with his luggage, pays the bill, salutes everyone and returns to the Vatican, with a joy that 'the bulb had been changed'[4] This is truly asymbolism unparalleled in history except perhaps that of St. John XXIII. Just as the 'good pope' opened the window to indicate the need of letting fresh breeze into the 'ghetto minded' Church before Vat. II, so also the present pope by changing the fused bulb, signified that the present church, which he is going to preside and guide, is in need of glowing the light of Christ.

In sum, the very beginning of Francis' papacy, packed with symbolism of so many kinds, signposts a new vision for the Church, signalling "that things were going to be rather different from now on."[5] All the nine symbolic responses, put together, suggest a new vision of the Church, the head of which would be a humble pastor fully conscious of his frailties and wholly dependent on God's Providence, keeping the poor and the least in mind, entirely breaking away from the monarchical traces, totally collegial with the fellow bishops, and integrally related with the people at large, mutually praying for one another, even sharing in their popular religiosity, particularly devoted to Mother Mary and above all determined to change its blown bulb with the real light of Christ.

1.2 The New Vision Already Envisaged

Far beyond the symbolisms, Pope Francis had marked his uniqueness in respect of the vision for the Church in the brief intervention he made in the Cardinal's meeting two days before his election. In the pre-conclave period, *sede vacante,* the cardinals of the Church gathered in a series of meetings that are known 'general congregation of cardinals'. In order to prepare themselves for electing a worthy pope, each cardinal was supposed to make a brief intervention for five minutes. Those interventions were meant to shed light on the problems they feel need to be addressed in the Church and type of personality who could lead the Church appropriately.

The intervention by Cardinal Bergoglio lasted less than four minutes.[6] But it was so impressive that Cardinal Jaime Ortega, Archbishop of Havana, Cuba, asked him a copy of his speech. But the speech had been given off the cuff, just with the help of a few hints jotted in a chit of paper. Anyway that night he got a hand-written note from Cardinal Bergoglio, and circulated it as *aide memoir,* evidently hoping to influence his fellow cardinals. Later he also obtained Pope Francis' permission to share the small document, and to get it published too. It provides us with a valuable Preamble to his manifesto and a key to understand the vision of the Church which Cardinal Bergoglio had in mind. It reads as follows:[7]

1. Evangelizing pre-supposes a desire in the Church to **come out of herself**. The Church is called to come out of herself and to go **to the peripheries**, not only geographically, but also the existential peripheries: the mystery of sin, of pain, of injustice, of ignorance and indifference to religion, of intellectual currents, and of all misery.

2. When the Church does not come out of herself to evangelize, she **becomes self-referential and then gets sick.** (cf. the deformed woman of the Gospel (Lk. 13:10-17). The evils that, over time, happen in ecclesial institutions have their root in self-referentiality and a kind of theological narcissism. In Revelation, Jesus says that he is at the door and knocks (Rev. 3:20). Obviously, the text refers to his knocking from the outside in order to enter but I think about the times in which Jesus knocks from within so that we will let him come out. The self-referential Church keeps Jesus Christ within herself and **does not let him out.**

3. When the Church is self-referential, inadvertently, she believes she has her own light; she ceases to be the *mysterium lunae* (Latin, "mystery of the moon," i.e., **reflecting the light of Christ** the way the moon reflects the light of the sun) and gives way to that very serious evil, spiritual worldliness (which according to

de Lubac, is the worst evil that can befall the Church). It lives to give glory only to one another.

Put simply, there are two images of the Church: Church which evangelizes and comes out of herself, the *Dei Verbum religiose audiens et fidente proclamans* (Latin, "Hearing the word of God with reverence and proclaiming it with faith"); and the worldly Church, living within herself, of herself, for herself. This should shed light on the possible changes and reforms which must be done for the salvation of souls.

4. Thinking of the next pope: He must be a man who, from the contemplation and adoration of Jesus Christ, helps the Church to **go out to the existential peripheries** that helps her to be the fruitful mother, who gains life from "the sweet and comforting joy of evangelizing."

In short, the predicted vision of the Church that Cardinal Jorge Brogoglio had before becoming Pope, may be formulated thus:

As against 'the worldly Church' which is self-referential and self-glorifying, we should think of an 'evangelizing Church' which, by getting back authentically to the Master, should reflect the light of Christ, go to the existential peripheries and prove thereby to be a fruitful mother who gains life from joy of evangelizing. That alone will save her from continuing to be sick and deformed.

True to this vision Pope Francis showed in words and actions that he was resolute to bring about changes in a big way. To begin with, he decided not to move to the Apostolic Palace, but to remain in the Casa Santa Marta. This was indeed a powerful signal to the world indicating that his papacy was not to be in the path of monarchic tradition but that it was clearly a poor Church for the poor.[8] His appointment of the C9,[9] with commission to draw up a new apostolic constitution for the Vatican, incorporating the long awaited reform of the Roman curia was a further sign of his firmness to change the distorted image of the Church. It also indicated clearly that the new Pope's focus was more on a decentralized Church. Subsequently in many of the Interviews Pope was candid in his remarks about the present state of the Church and the lines of change he wanted to bring about. The most important of such Interview was the one he gave to his fellow Jesuit, Rev. Fr. Antonio Spadaro S.J., editor in chief of *La Civiltà Cattolica*, the Italian Jesuit journal, in August 2013. Moreover, the radical ideas he expressed in public during his visit to USA were so impressive that the media over there came out with such headlines as "The remarkable new vision Pope has for Catholic Church". There also he gave an interview to "*America Magazine*," in which he made it clear that the "Church must not be obsessed with issues related to gay marriage or contraceptives. He called for new balance. H even warned that "if the Catholic Church doesn't make changes, it could fall like a house of cards."[10]

Finally, with the release of his Apostolic Exhortation[11] which was indeed his manifesto, Pope Francis elaborated the details of his vision for the Church. It was ingenious of Pope Francis to have projected his own vision in and through the deliberations of the XIII Synod of Bishops[12] on the theme "The New Evangelization for the Transmission of the Christian Faith." Now it is necessary to glean some of the insights from it.

2. The Vision of the Church in *Evangelii Gaudium*

In pursuance of the vision prefigured in his intervention in the pre-conclave meeting, Pope Francis in his first major document, Apostolic Exhortation *Evangelii Gaudium (The Joy of the Gospel)*, elaborates that vision, chalking out even his agenda for Church reform and pastoral provisions. It engages the Church-world relationship in multiple constructive ways. It unveils Pope Francis' "blueprint for a de-centralized and more pastoral Church that is focused on the needs of those within and outside it rather than preoccupied with its own prestige."[13]

The document starts with a call for the Church to embrace the new evangelization with joy. In this connection it distinguishes between the real joy and pleasure. Moreover, it points out that there is a great danger in today's world in so far as it is suffering from various ills: "desolation and anguish, born of a complacent yet covetous heart, the feverish pursuit of frivolous pleasures, and a blunted conscience"*(EG 2)*. On the one hand it points out that today's world, pervaded by consumerism, suffers from the desolation and anguish born of a complacent yet covetous heart, the feverish pursuit of frivolous pleasures, and a blunted conscience, and is caught up in its own interests and concerns, with no place for others and the poor, with not much scope for hearing God's voice, or feeling the quiet joy of his love, and even the desire to do good fading away. This is a very real danger for believers too. Many fall prey to it, and end up resentful, angry and listless. Worse still, the very same situation prevails in the Church because she too has been self-complacent, self-glorifying and hierarchical, and giving way to such serious evils like spiritual worldliness (*EG* 93).

Precisely as an antidote to this dangerous image of the Church, the *Evangelii Gaudium* affirms that the real source of joy lies in a *determination toa renewed* personal encounter with Jesus Christ, or at least an openness to letting him encounter us unfailingly each day *(EG 3)*. The Lord never disappoints. Whenever we take a step towards Jesus, we come to realize that he is already there, waiting for us with open arms. Time and time again he bears us on his shoulders. He is always capable of restoring our joy, because he is risen. "The Gospel, radiant with the glory of Christ's cross, constantly invites us to rejoice"*(EG 5)*. Thus, it is only by returning to Jesus that the Church can really prove to be the *mysterium lunae* (mystery of the moon), i.e., reflecting the light of Christ just as the moon reflects the light of the sun).

This joy is not to be individualistic. "Life grows by being given away, and it weakens in isolation and comfort. In fact the law of reality is that "life is attained and matures in the measure that it is offered up for giving life to others"*(EG*

10). And, those who **enjoy life most** are those who leave security on the shore and become excited by the mission of communicating life to others. Moreover, "Goodness always tends to spread. Every **authentic experience** of truth and goodness seeks by its very nature to grow within us, and any person who has **experienced a profound liberation** becomes more **sensitive to the needs of others**" (EG 9). In other words, the Church needs to go in search of the "existential peripheries." Rightly therefore Pope Francis is rightly called the "Pope of the Peripheries."[14]

So too is his vision of the Church!, because in this Pope suggests way forward to the existing Church. By connecting the necessary reform to the task of evangelization, he says that "would recall the Church to its purpose and the source of its life."[15] He is clear that the wellsprings of the Church are to be found precisely in the existential peripheries. The term 'periphery', in the Latin American vocabulary, means "outskirts" or "margins." So by this phrase Pope Francis wants to convey that the Church must reach out to the poor, the suffering, and the oppressed. Within the Church, also, there are the existential peripheries, namely the laity, "God's holy people," including the women and young. That is why he calls for "a more incisive female presence" (EG 103) and opportunities for young Catholics to exercise greater leadership (EG 106). Even those who have been considered as the ostracized such as the gay people, divorcees and the so called "sinners" are included in the new vision of Church. Regarding access to the sacraments, the document says the doors of the sacraments should not be closed for "simply any reason". (They) are "not a prize for the perfect but a powerful medicine and nourishment for the weak," (EG 47). It is these peripheries who bring back the Church to its first mission—to offer them the Gospel of hope and redemption even before they ask for it, and, in so doing, to rekindle the joy and the passion that comes with the sharing of one's faith.

Francis' vision of the Church calls for a "sound decentralization" in the way the Church is run. The conciliar vision of the "collegial spirit" is to be visibly found, whereby local bishops would take a greater share in decision-making (EG 32). The universal head of the Church openly declaring: "It is not advisable for the Pope to take the place of local bishops in the discernment of every issue which arises in their territory" (EG 16).

Francis also called for greater cultural diversity within the Church (EG 117), which he said should be tied to "modes of expression which European nations developed at a particular moment of their history" (EG 118). Missionaries should not "impose a specific cultural form" when reaching new peoples with the Gospel.

In fact, the different ideas of Pope Francis' vision of the Church were all built on the image of the Church as 'People of God', already defined in Vat. II. It is not merely the clergy, bishops and religious that constitute the Church, but the whole people of God. To quote his own words he expressed in his Interview with Antonio Spadaro:

The image of the church I like is that of the faithful, holy people of God. This is the definition I often use, and then there is that image from the Second Vatican Council's 'Dogmatic Constitution on the Church' (No. 12). Belonging to a people has a strong theological value. In the history of salvation, God has saved a people. There is no full identity without belonging to a people. No one is saved alone, as an isolated individual, but God attracts us looking at the complex web of relationships that take place in the human community. God enters into this dynamic, this participation in the web of human relationships.[16]

Mission, therefore, never means to be self-complacent or self-boasting, neither to be dejected or discouraged, but **authentically experiencing** the joy of the risen Christ, and **spontaneously sharing** it with others, and deepening our enthusiasm and comforting joy of evangelizing, even when it is in tears that we must sow," and becoming "ministers of the Gospel whose lives **glow with fervour**, who have first received the joy of Christ" (EG 10).

In this connection Pope Francis urges Catholics to guard against two-fold dangers: on the one hand it may be a feeling of "defeatism which turns us into querulous and disillusioned pessimists, 'sourpusses' (EG 85)" and on the other hand it may be the feeling of superiority some people cherish "because they observe certain rules or remain intransigently faithful to a particular Catholic style from the past". Here the Pope points out that "a supposed soundness of doctrine or discipline leads one to a narcissistic and authoritarian elitism, whereby instead of evangelizing, one analyzes and classifies others, and instead of opening the door to grace, one exhausts his or her energies in inspecting and verifying,...In neither case is one really concerned about Jesus Christ or others ... It is impossible to think that a genuine evangelizing thrust could emerge from these adulterated forms of Christianity." (EG 94).

How fittingly does John Thavis[17] remark about the new-ness of the vision Pope Francis:" He's laying down some real markers about the kinds of reforms he expects to preside over, including greater decentralization, openness to diversity in the church, and a greater emphasis on the gospel message of salvation as opposed to church doctrines and rules."[18]

In sum, the vision of the Church by Pope Francis is determined to change the present image of deformed Church which is self-referent, self-complacent, self-glorifying and clerical-centered into an authentic spouse of the Master, concerned with recovering of the original Christ-experience and reflecting his light to the world, enthusiastic about sharing that joy with all, especially the existential peripheries, respecting decentralized structures, diversity of cultural forms so that she would be really a fruitful mother who gains life from joy of evangelizing Church.

3. The Unique Place of Laity in the New Vision

It is already implied in the inclusive vision of the Church, outlined above, that laity occupy a significant and irreplaceable role to play in the Church. From the very fact that Pope Francis envisions a Church to be reaching out to the 'existential peripheries' it is clear that the laity who have been treated as the lowest of the rung or the bottom of the pyramid will never be considered so in his vision. Apart from that implication, Francis has emphatically affirmed the specific, positive roles they need to play in the new vision. It is important to cull those aspects declared by the Pope on various occasions and presented them together.

First and foremost it is indeed remarkable that Pope Francis starts with a positive definition of laity in his *Evangelii Gaudium:* "Lay people are, put simply, the vast majority of the people of God. The minority — ordained ministers — are at their service" (EG 102). Even the Second Vatican Council which really set the renewal of the laity in the life and mission of the Church, had defined the laity negatively in the sense that their identity is contrasted with the priests and religious. "The term laity is here understood to mean all the faithful except those in holy orders and those in the state of religious life specially approved by the Church."(LG 31). The CCC also follows the same formula, while describing the role of laity in the Church. (Cf. 897).

Its decree on laity emphatically stated that the mission of laity is given to them directly, by the Holy Spirit, not indirectly through the ordained office: "(The laity) are assigned to the apostolate by the Lord Himself. They are consecrated for the royal priesthood and the holy people not only that they may offer spiritual sacrifices in everything they do, but also that they may witness to Christ throughout the world." (AA 3).

This negative sort of definition has given room for a mistaken and misguided understanding about the laity's call and mission. By describing the laity that 'they are not priests' and that 'they are not religious' it gives an impression that the priests and the religious are the primary membership-holders of the Church, in reference to whom the laity are to be understood. Conceptually then the laity are to be assumed as second class members in the Church. Their role is mainly to serve the hierarchy who really constitute the Church.

Thanks to such negative way of understanding the laity, there is still another impression that has already crept into minds of the people that that the only real vocation in the Church is the priesthood and to the consecrated life. They alone have a real mission to fulfil in life. Even 50 years after Vat. II laity see themselves merely as helpers to the clergy and religious. Their mission lies in going round the parish priest and doing what he commands to do.

All these mistaken and misguided understanding of the laity are washed off by Pope Francis, as his Apostolic Exhortation describes the laity as the vast majority of the people of God whom the minority of ordained ministers are called to serve (EG 120). In such a description laity are made the focal point of

Church's very existence the priests and religious are called to serve them. Here, Pope Francis is making a Copernican revolution in the understanding of the Church. As against the erstwhile understanding of the Church mainly from the standpoint of the hierarchy, and the laity being defined in terms of the hierarchy, Pope Francis emphasises that laity form the pivotal point at whose service the call of hierarchy is destined to be.

The Pope reiterates the same idea much more pointedly in a letter to the President of the Pontifical Commission for Latin America.[19] First he asserts sympathetically that "lay people are immersed in those struggles, with their families, trying, not only to survive, but who, in the midst of contradictions and injustices, seek the Lord and want to witness this". Then he tells the pastors that their task "should be that of seeking a way to be able to encourage, accompany and stimulate all their attempts and efforts to keep hope and faith alive in a world full of contradictions especially for the poorest, especially with the poorest". He further explicates that, they "as Pastors must be committed in the midst of our people and, with our people, sustain their faith and their hope – opening doors, working with them, dreaming with them, reflecting and especially praying with them."[20] Moreover He invites the pastors to continually "to look at, protect, accompany, support and serve the laity."

In fact, the very identity of the clergy is defined by Pope Francis only in correlative terms to the laity, rather than identifying laity in relation to the hierarchy. He explains the correlative relationship through a simple but telling illustration. A father is not understood on his own without his children. He might be a very good worker, professional, husband, and a friend. But it is only his children that makes him a father. So also, Francis writes: "A Pastor is not conceived without a flock, which he is called to serve. The Pastor is Pastor of a people, and the people are served from within. Often one goes forward indicating the path, at other times behind so that no one is left behind, and not infrequently one is in the middle to hear well the people's palpitation."[21]

"It is only when the Pastors feel themselves an integral part of the laity that they are positioned as pastors in life," Francis says. That alone gives them a proper perspective to address the problems of laity in a different way. Otherwise, there is a danger of the hierarchy falling "into reflections that can be very good in themselves but that end up by functionalizing the life of laity or theorizing so much that speculation ends by killing action." In fact Francis believes that the pastors of the Church have already fallen into this danger.

No doubt, Vat. II affirms the specific call of the laity as well as their special role in society, when it states that "there are certain things which pertain **in a special way** to the laity, both men and women, by reason of their condition and mission" (LG 30).

What **specifically** characterizes the laity is their secular nature… (they) by their very vocation, seek the kingdom of God by engaging in temporal affairs and by ordering them according to the plan of God. They live in the world, that is, in each and in all of the secular professions and occupations.... They are called there by God that by exercising their proper function and led by the spirit of the Gospel they may work for the sanctification of the world from within as a leaven (LG 31).

Likewise CCC says: "By reason of their special vocation it belongs to the laity to seek the kingdom of God by engaging in temporal affairs and directing them according to God's will. . . . It pertains to them in a special way so to illuminate and order all temporal things." (CCC 898).

However, they all remain in books. Francis is convinced that the laity are not given the necessary autonomy to play their role effectively. It is all because of the 'clericalism' that is still dominant in the Church. He is so anxious to remove this 'deformity'. Hence, his open denouncement of clericalism:

Clericalism leads to the functionalization of the laity, treating them as "messengers," restricts different initiatives and efforts and I even dare to say the necessary boldness to be able to take the Good News of the Gospel to all the ambits of the social and especially political endeavor. Far from stimulating the different contributions, proposals, little by little clericalism extinguishes the prophetic fire that the Church is called to witness in the heart of her peoples. Clericalism forgets that the visibility and sacramentality of the Church belongs to the whole People of God (cf. LG 9-14), and not just to a few chosen and enlightened.

Obviously therefore Francis warns the clergy and bishop of identifying the 'Church as an elite of priests, of the consecrated, of the Bishops'. Identifying himself as one belonging to the pastor's community he tells his fellow-pastors: "it is good to remember... we all form part of the Holy People faithful of God. To forget this brings in its train various risks and deformations both in our own personal as well as in communal living of the ministry that the Church has entrusted to us". Quoting *Lumen Gentium,* he reminds the clergy that the Church is "the People of God, whose *identity is the dignity and the freedom of the children of God, in whose hearts dwells the Holy Spirit as in a temple"* (LG 9). From this then it is easy for Pope Francis to draw out that the faithful, Holy People of God is anointed with the grace of the Holy Spirit' and thus, as we (the clergy) reflect, think, evaluate, discern, we must be very attentive to this annointing."[22]

As against the pastors, clergy and the bishops, who would assume that they alone are consecrated people, Francis urges them to see baptism as the primary sacrament on account of which the whole church has been consecrated as the People of God. To his fellow bishops, the Pope says:

To look at the People of God is to remember that we all entered the Church as lay people. The first Sacrament, the one that seals our identity forever and of which we should always be proud is Baptism. By it and with the *anointing of the Holy Spirit,* (the faithful) *are consecrated as spiritual house and holy priesthood* (LG n. 10). Our first and fundamental consecration sinks its roots in our Baptism. No priest or Bishop has baptized anyone. Lay people have baptized us and it is the indelible sign that no one will ever be able to eliminate.[23]

Thus, it is good for the pastors 'to look to the faithful, Holy People of God, and to feel themselves an integral part of the same', Pope says.[24] That alone positions them in life and, therefore, in the themes they treat in a different way. Only in this way they can be really helped not to fall into reflections that can be very good in themselves but that end up by functionalizing the life of the lay people or theorizing so much that speculation ends by killing action.

'Looking continually at the People of God', this alone would save the pastors from merely declaring some slogans that are fine and beautiful phrases but are unable to sustain the life of the laity. One such phrase is, as remembered by Pope is this: "The hour of the laity has come" But, Francis plainly acknowledges that "it seems that the clock has stopped."[25]

This situation has arisen because clericalism was playing a dominant role, making the laity 'totally clergy-dependent' and treating them merely as 'the extended arm of hierarchy'. So, the role of laity cannot be discussed ignoring one of the greatest distortions of the Church:

This approach (clericalism) not only nullifies the character of Christians, but also tends to diminish and undervalue the Baptismal grace that the Holy Spirit put in the heart of our people. Clericalism leads to the homologization (functionalization) of the laity, treating the laity as "representatives", restricts different initiatives and efforts and I even dare to say the necessary boldness to be able to take the Good News of the Gospel to all the areas of the social and above all political sphere. Clericalism, far from giving impetus to the diverse initiatives, efforts, little by little extinguishes the prophetic flame that the entire Church is called to witness in the heart of her peoples. Clericalism forgets that the visibility and sacramentality of the Church belongs to the whole People of God (cf. LG nn. 9 -14), and not only to the few chosen and enlightened.[26]

Contrastingly Pope Francis says: "The Council does not consider the laity as though they were members of a second tier, at the service of the hierarchy and merely carrying out their orders issued from high up but instead as Christ's disciples who are called to animate every place and human activity in the world according to the spirit of the Gospel."[27] In virtue of their baptism, they "are protagonists in the work of evangelization and human promotion …. Incorporated in the Church, each member of the People of God is **inseparably a disciple and a missionary**. Lay movements in their dynamism are a resource for the Church?"[28]

At one time missionary activity was seen as work of some professionals in the Church. The missionaries' life-long work was to proclaim the Gospel to other nations and convert the people into our Church. Pope Francis proposes a contrary view in his Apostolic Exhortation: "In virtue of their baptism, all the members of the People of God have become missionary disciples (cf. Mt 28:19). All the baptized, whatever their position in the Church or their level of instruction in the faith, are agents of evangelization. It would be insufficient to envisage a plan of evangelization to be carried out by professionals while the rest of the faithful would simply be passive recipients. The new evangelization calls for personal involvement on the part of each of the baptized. Every Christian is challenged, here and now, to be actively engaged in evangelization; indeed, anyone who has truly experienced God's saving love does not need much time or lengthy training to go out and proclaim that love. Every Christian is a missionary to the extent that he or she has encountered the love of God in Christ Jesus: we no longer say that we are "disciples" and "missionaries", but rather that we are always "missionary disciples" (#120).

To corroborate it, EG cites the instances of those first disciples who went forth to proclaim him joyfully. Philip immediately after encountering the gaze of Jesus, exclaimed to Nathanael: "We have found the Messiah!" (Jn 1:41). The Samaritan woman became a missionary immediately after speaking with Jesus and many Samaritans come to believe in him "because of the woman's testimony" (Jn 4:39). So too, Saint Paul, after his encounter with Jesus Christ, "immediately proclaimed Jesus" (Acts 9:20; cf. 22:6-21). Every Christian, in so far as one has really encountered Jesus and has truly experienced God's saving love, one is called to offer others an explicit witness to the saving love is challenged, here and now. (#120)

So, the role of the laity has now become much more intense and gravely responsible. New-evangelization can be taken up at any time or anywhere, by anybody, provided that one is ready to bring the love of Jesus to others. This can happen unexpectedly and in any place: on the street, in a city square, during work, on a journey (#127). One can always be respectful and gentle to others, one can enter into personal dialogue, when the other person speaks and shares his or her joys, hopes and concerns for loved ones, or so many other heartfelt needs. Later, if possible one can bring up God's word, perhaps by reading a Bible verse or relating a story, but always keeping in mind the fundamental message: the personal love of God who became man, who gave himself up for us, who is living and who offers us his salvation and his friendship.

Of course, this message has to be shared humbly as a testimony on the part of one who is always willing to learn, in the awareness that the message is so rich and so deep that it always exceeds our grasp. At times the message can be presented directly, at times by way of a personal witness or gesture, or in a way which the Holy Spirit may suggest in that particular situation. If it seems prudent and if the circumstances are right, this fraternal and missionary encounter could end with a brief prayer related to the concerns which the person may have expressed. In this way they will have an experience of being listened to and understood; they will know that their particular situation has been placed before God, and that God's word really speaks to their lives. (#128)

In other words, it is the real experience of having encountered Christ that should be the real source of our joy. Such a joy would spontaneously exude in anything one does or speaks. This should be the real method of evangelizing, rather than devising an organized plan to be carried out by professionals. If at all some professionals pursue oral proclamation, they should always be respectful of the other, prayerful in their approach and humble in their attitude to the other.

Apart from that general role laity could play in the New-Evangelization, Pope Francis wants the laity to play an active role in the world, with its complex social and political issues. In a message to the participants of a conference for laity,[29] the Pope, citing the teaching of the Second Vatican Council and underlined that the lay faithful, in virtue of their baptism, "are protagonists in the work of evangelization and human promotion". Particularly, he urges the laity to work for the 'social inclusion' of the poor, maintaining always priority-attention to religious and spiritual needs. In so doing, they are "to use regularly the Compendium of the Social Doctrine of the Church, which he called a "complete and precious tool."[30] Moreover, Pope admonishes that the laity "must also maintain a vital link to the diocese and to parishes, so as not to develop a partial reading of the Gospel or to uproot themselves from the Church". The parishes and lay movements should not counter each other.

Pope Francis, during his USA visit in March 2014, pointed out in Philadelphia that changing times for the Church called for a greater role for the laity. To quote his words: "We know that the future of the Church in a rapidly changing society will call, and even now calls, for much more active engagement on the part of laity."[31]

During the same visit Pope Francis talked about the special role for women in the future. Referring to the call given to Saint Katharine Drexel, the patroness of the local parish church at Philadelphia, Pope esteemed the immense work she had realized, even when she was a young girl. He recalled the particular instance in which she was challenged to do her part to which, of course, she responded positively. In that connection Pope raised the following pertinent questions regarding the present day situation:

> How many young people in our parishes and schools have the same
> high ideals, generosity of spirit, and love for Christ and the Church!
> Do we challenge them? Do we make space for them and help them to
> do their part? To find ways of sharing their enthusiasm and gifts with
> our communities, above all in works of mercy and concern for others?
> Do we share our own joy and enthusiasm in serving the Lord?[32]

Even much before such pronouncements in USA, Pope had outlined the special role women could play in the Church. When asked by his interviewer "What should be the role of women in the church? How do we make their role more visible today?" Pope Francis replied to him thus:

It is necessary to broaden the opportunities for a stronger presence of women in the church. I am wary of a solution that can be reduced to a kind of 'female machismo,' because a woman has a different make-up than a man. But what I hear about the role of women is often inspired by an ideology of machismo. Women are asking deep questions that must be addressed. The church cannot be herself without the woman and her role. The woman is essential for the church. Mary, a woman, is more important than the bishops. I say this because we must not confuse the function with the dignity. We must therefore investigate further the role of women in the church. We have to work harder to develop a profound theology of the woman. Only by making this step will it be possible to better reflect on their function within the church. The feminine genius is needed wherever we make important decisions. The challenge today is this: to think about the specific place of women also in those places where the authority of the church is exercised for various areas of the church. "It is necessary to broaden the opportunities for a stronger presence of women in the church.[33]

On the occasion of the 200th anniversary of Argentina's independence in 2016, the Pope wrote on July 9 a letter to the Argentine Bishops' Conference. In it he remarked:

> I am convinced that our motherland needs to bring alive the prophecy of Joel. Only if our grandparents dare to dream and our young people dare to prophesy great things can the motherland be free. We are in need of the dreaming elderly to drive the young who, inspired by those same dreams, run forward with the creativity of prophecy.[34]

Obviously the Pope also highlighted the suffering of the sick, the poor and prisoners, as well as those exploited through child abuse, drugs and human trafficking, describing them as "the most afflicted children of the motherland" and therefore in need of the laity's involvement in alleviating their sufferings.[35]

In an address delivered to the young people on 16th Feb. 2016, Pope Francis asked specifically the young to "dare to dream", of course in the context of family. The role of the laity in the Catholic Church cannot be fully dealt with unless their family context is referred to. Pope Francis certainly gives immense importance to Family. To quote just but one instance of his remarks about family:

> In the family we learn solidarity, how to share, to discern, to walk ahead with each other's problems, to fight and to make up, to argue and to embrace and to kiss. The family is the first school of the nation, and in the family you will find that richness and value that you have. The family is like the custodian of that great value, in the family you will find hope.[36]

Especially in the context of the changing times for the Church, the Pope is calling for a greater role for the laity to be played in Church's mission. Just an excerpt from the homily he gave in the Cathedral Basilica of Sts. Peter and Paul in Philadelphia[37] will help us to understand the mind of the Pope on this point:

> One of the great challenges facing the Church in this generation is to foster in **all the faithful** a sense of personal responsibility for the Church's mission, and to enable them to fulfill that responsibility as missionary disciples, as a leaven of the Gospel **in our world**. This will require creativity in adapting to changed situations, carrying forward the legacy of the past not primarily by maintaining our structures and institutions, which have served us well, but above all by being open to the possibilities which the Spirit opens up to us and communicating the joy of the Gospel, **daily and in every season of our life**.

> Pope Francis is convinced of the transformative power of the laity. This he brought out in the Plenary Assembly of the Pontifical Council for the Laity, on June 17, 2016: "The Church should always value the transformative power of faith-filled laity who are willing to serve the Gospel." He also agreed that "we need well-formed lay people, animated by a sincere and clear faith, whose life has been touched by the personal and merciful love of Christ Jesus". But his emphasis is upon the daring propensity required of the laity: "We need lay people who take risks, who get their hands dirty, who are not afraid of making mistakes, who go forward. We need lay people with a vision of the future, not confined to the little things of life." Above all, he said that the "Church needs lay people who "dare to dream."[38]

Conclusion

From the foregoing discussion it is evident that Pope Francis has a new vision for the Church and is determined to change the existing sick and deformed Church into a healthy and glowing Church. He is convinced that the main cause of the distortion is the wrong understanding of the Church, as an institution of clergy and the religious, ignoring their basic call to be people of God, and forgetting the identity and potentiality of laity and that it has failed to shine owing to its self-referent and self-glorifying and clergy-centered approach. Hence, Pope Francis envisions a new Church in which the role of the laity, including the women and the young, will decisively be the central, and focal subject. In this vision, the laity's call and mission, arising out of the baptismal vocation, determines even the role of the hierarchy.

So the need of the hour is a double pronged change of mind-set, required of both clergy and the laity. On the one hand there is urgency to evoke among the laity realization of their vocation and mission to be carried out on their own, and get themselves immersed in the struggle of transforming the world into the reign of God in the light of the Gospels. On the other hand the clergy ought to accompany the laity, encourage them and work in their midst, far from separating themselves from the laity, and reflecting on the laity's problems independently of involvement in laity's struggles, still worse 'using them' for their own designs and according to their abstract reflections which are often cut off from their actual involvement.

Would that the whole Church cherish Francis' vision of Church as a correlative, cooperative, collaborative, collegial, and co-inclusive People of God with its task of 'mystery of moon," and really radiating the light of her Master, outgoing and evangelizing the world. It is in realization of this vision that the laity play the key role. They are the basic, central and focal point. Hence, Pope Francis proposes this dictum: "To evoke the faithful, holy people of God is to evoke the horizon to which they are invited to look and from whence to reflect."[39] Moreover, Pope Francis is challenging all sections of laity: men, women, the young, the elderly, and the family as a whole, in season and out of season, while at the same time taking all efforts to reform the church structures! Not that there is no opposition to this visionary and a pastoral minded Pope.[40] This impels the authentic faithful to pray that his Copernican revolution in the Church is accepted by all and that the laity pay heed to his call, and wake up from slumber and begin to play their rightful role effectively.

Endnotes

1   In Behavioural Psychology the term 'apperception' is used to mean "the process by which new experience is assimilated to and transformed by the residuum of past experience to form a new whole".

2   Paul VALLEY, *Pope Francis: Untying the Knots,* (London: Bloomsbury, 2013), 160, emphasis added.

3   Paul VALLEY, *Pope Francis: Untying the Knots,* (London: Bloomsbury, 2013), 162.

4   Michael COLLINS, *Francis Bishop of Rome, A Short Biography,* (Bangalore: Claretian Publication, 2013), 90-99.

5   Paul VALLELY, *Pope Francis: Untying the Knots,* (London: Bloomsbury, 2013), 167.

6   http://en.radiovaticana.va/storico/2013/03/27/bergoglios_intervention_a_diagnosis_of_the_problems_in_the_church/en1-677269, accessed 27 June 2017.

7   http://en.radiovaticana.va/storico/2013/03/27/bergoglios_intervention_a_diagnosis_of_the_problems_in_the_church/en1-677269, accessed 27 June 2017.

8   Paul VALLELY, *Pope Francis: Untying the Knots,* (London: Bloomsbury, 2013), 177.

9   After a month he assumed the office, Pope Francis appointed a group of eight cardinals "to help him reform the Roman Curia and to help him govern the Catholic Church". A few months later, the group of eight cardinals welcomed a new member, the new Secretariat of State, Cardinal Pietro Parolin. Hence, they become known as the C9. The first group of eightcardinals consists of (1) Cardinal Oscar Andres Rodriguez Maradiaga of Honduras (2) Cardinal Francisco Javier Erráuriz, Chile (3) Cardinal Sean Patrick O'Malley of Boston (4) Cardinal Reinhard Marx, of Munich, (5) Cardinal Laurent Monsengwo, the Democratic

Republic of the Congo (6) Cardinal Oswald Gracias of Bombay (7) Cardinal George Pell, secretary for Economy and the Governor of Vatican, Giusseppe Bertello (8) Italian Bishop Marcello Semeraro acts as the coordinator and secretary.

10 As reported by Anne THOMPSON, NBC (National Broadcasting Company) The Nightly News, Sept. 19, 2013, http://www.nbcnews.com/video/nightly-news/53056224/#53056224, accessed 14th June, 2017.

11 Pope Francis, *Evangelii Gaudium : Apostolic Exhortation on the Proclamation of the Gospel in Today's World* (Nov. 2013).

12 The XIII Synod of Bishops gathered from 7-28 October 2012.

13 Abigail Frymann ROUCH "Pope Francis publishes radical vision for Church", in *The Tablet: The International Catholic News Weekly,* 26 November 2013, http://www.thetablet.co.uk/news/145/1/pope-francis-publishes-radical-vision-for-church, accessed 6.6. 2017.

14 Randy DAVID, "The pope of the peripheries", in *Philippine Daily Inquirer* January 15, 2015, accessed 17.6.2017 http://opinion.inquirer.net/81724/the-pope-of-the-peripheries#ixzz4kgyhOXB6, accessed 17.6. 2017.

15 Austen IVEREIGH, *The Great Reformer: Francis and the Making of a Radical Pope,* (New York: Holt, Henry & Company, Inc. 2014).

16 Antonio SPADARO, "A Big Heart Open to God", in *Thinking Faith,* the online journal of the Jesuits in Britain 19th September 2013, http://www.thinkingfaith.org/articles/20130919_1.htm accessed 10.11.2016.

17 A former Vatican bureau chief for Catholic News Service, wrote "The Vatican Diaries".

18 Laurie GOODSTEIN and Elisabetta POVOLEDO, "Pope Sets Down Goals for an Inclusive Church, Reaching Out 'on the Streets'", http://www.nytimes.com/2013/11/27/world/europe/in-major-document-pope-francis-present-his-vision.html NOV. 26, 2013, accessed 16 June, 2017 http://www.nytimes.com/2013/11/27/world/europe/in-major-document-pope-francis-present-his-vision.html

19 The Letter dated 16 March 20116 is released in *L'Osservatore Romano,* NUMBER 17, (2444), 29 April 2016, with the title: "The Hour of the Laity has Come" pp. 4 & 5.

20 *L'Osservatore,* op.cit, p. 4, Column 4.

21 *L'Osservatore,* op.cit, p. 4, Column 1.

22 *L'Osservatore,* op.cit, p. 4. Colum 2-3.

23 *L'Osservatore,* op.cit, p. 4. Column 2.

24 *L'Osservatore,* op.cit. p. 4 column 1 at the bottom.

25 *L'Osservatore,* op.cit., Column 2, at the top.

26 *L'Osservatore,* op.cit. 4, Column 3.

27 Vatican Radio, "Pope Francis message on Laity Vocation" http://en.radiovaticana.va/news/2015/11/12/pope_francis_message_on_laity_vocation/1186245, accessed 20. June 2017, This was part of the message addressed to Cardinal Stanislaw Rylko, President of the Pontifical Council for the Laity, Pope Francis sent on 12th November 2015, to the participants of a seminar jointly organized by the Pontifical Council for the Laity and the Pontifical University of the Holy Cross to discuss the theme: "Vocation and mission of the Laity: Fifty years after the Decree: *Apostolicam actuositatem".*

to mark the 50th anniversary of the Second Vatican Council's Decree on the Apostolate of the Laity.

28   In a message to the participants at a conference in Rome on the laity (March 7-8, 2014), held at the Pontifical Lateran University organized under the theme, "The Mission of Lay Christians in the City."

29   Conference, held at the Pontifical Lateran University, was organized under the theme, "The Mission of Lay Christians in the City", March 7-8, 2014, Cf. Vatican Radio, 2014-03-07, "Pope Francis: laity are 'protagonists' in Church's mission" http://www.news.va/en/news/pope-francis-says-laity-are-protagonists-in-church, accessed 5.5.2017.

30   Vatican Radio, 2014-03-07, op. cit.

31   Tom McGRATH, "In Homily, Pope Francis Calls for Greater Role for Laity ... and Women?",http://www.phillymag.com/news/2015/09/26/pope-francis-philadelphia-homily/#qRcdocpWMcwK7ySE.99 September 26, 2015, accessed 5.10.2016.

32   Tom McGRATH, "In Homily, Pope Francis Calls for Greater Role for Laity ... and Women?",http://www.phillymag.com/news/2015/09/26/pope-francis-philadelphia-homily/#qRcdocpWMcwK7ySE.99 September 26, 2015, accessed 5.10.2016.

33   Antonio SPADARO, S.J, "A Big Heart Open to God", op.cit.

34   Junno Arocho ESTEVES, 'Dare to dream,' Pope Francis urges Argentines on 200th anniversary of independence" http://www.catholicherald.co.uk/news/2016/07/12/dare-to-dream-pope-francis-urges-argentines-on-200th-anniversary-of-independence/ 12 Jul 2016, accessed 15.6.2017.

35   Junno Arocho ESTEVES, *Ibid.*

36   L'Osservatore Romano, Vatican City, No. 7 (2434), 19, February 2016, p. 20.

37   Tom McGRATH, "In Homily, Pope Francis Calls for Greater Role for Laity ... and Women?",

       http://www.phillymag.com/news/2015/09/26/pope-francis-philadelphia-homily/#qRcdocpWMcwK7ySE.99 September 26, 2015, accessed 5.10.2016.

38   "For Pope Francis, the Catholic Laity can transform the World", Catholic News Agency, Vatican City, Jun 18, 2016 http://www.catholicnewsagency.com/news/for-pope-francis-the-catholic-laity-can-transform-the-world-86987/ accessed 4.6.2017.

39   *L'Osservatore*, op.cit. p. 4 Column1.

40   Myron J. Pereira, "Reforming the church: Inside the mind of the pope", in UCAN India,posted on June 14, 2017, http://www.ucanindia.in/news/reforming-the-church:-inside-the-mind-of-the-pope/34980/daily, accessed 10.7.2017.

Chapter 10

Reinventing Religious Life
The Challenge of Pope Francis

Rajakumar Joseph SJ
Vidyajyoti College of Theology, Delhi

The good Pope Francis, a religious with a difference, makes a tremendous impact on the religious life of the consecrated men and women all over the world.[1] His interest and commitment to this cause was visible, when he dedicated the year 2015, as the year of 'consecrated life'. As an ardent religious, "he brings a particular understanding of the dynamics of religious life and its relationship to the church."[2] He does not offer mere single line rules to follow but presents perspectives and patterns to reinvent religious life and become relevant and prophetic in the contemporary context of the World. As an auxiliary bishop of Buenos Aires, he participated in the Synod on consecrated life in the year 1994. There he made a significant intervention with regard to the ecclesial character of the consecrated life. He said, "Consecrated life is a gift to the Church, it is born of the Church, it grows in the Church, and it is entirely directed to the Church."[3] Thus, he views consecrated life at two interrelated levels, namely, its relationship to the church in its missional dimension and its own integrity, in living out various aspects of being a religious. In his apostolic exhortation *Evangelii gaudium* he writes, "It is not by proselytizing that the Church grows, but by attraction"[4] and this attraction is not drawing people through various creative programme and strategies, but by the way the consecrated people live their authentic discipleship.

In his Apostolic Letter addressed "To all Consecrated People," Pope Francis refers to Saint John Paul II's Post-Synodal Apostolic Exhortation, *Vita Consecrata,* which says,"You have not only a glorious history to remember and to recount, but also a great history still to be accomplished! Look to the future, where the Spirit is sending you in order to do even greater things."[5] This affirms the role of religious life in the past and encourages the religious to rededicate once again in strengthening and supporting the church in its mission to build the Reign of God. Pope Francis, who beautifully builds on the tradition and yet creatively responds to the contemporary needs, in his Apostolic Letter, under the section, 'aims of consecrated life,' illustrates the need "to look to the past with gratitude… to live the present with passion….to embrace the future with hope."[6] Let this be a mantra to every religious to be grateful for all the works of the Holy Spirit, to be imbued with the fire of God's love to rededicate oneself completely for God's mission and to walk ahead with hope towards the future.

1. Called to be Joyful Witnesses

During his meeting with Seminarians and Novices, Pope Francis said, "I want to say one word to you and this word is "joy".Wherever there are consecrated people, seminarians, men and women religious, young people, there is joy, there is always joy! It is the joy of freshness, the joy of following Jesus; the joy that the Holy Spirit gives us, not the joy of the world.There is joy!"[7] The joy of responding to the call through the inspiration of the Holy Spirit is the key to the effectiveness of consecrated life. According to Pope Francis,

The consecrated life will not flourish as a result of brilliant vocation programs, but because the young people we meet find us attractive, because they see us as men and women who are happy! Similarly, the apostolic effectiveness of consecrated life does not depend on the efficiency of its methods. It depends on the eloquence of your lives, lives which radiate the joy and beauty of living the Gospel and following Christ to the full.[8]

Thus, Pope Francis distinctly states that there are two things very crucial to the fruitfulness of consecrated life.They are; true happiness and the witnessing of that joy in living the Gospel values in our apostolates and communities. He also emphasizes the need to build community life, like a family, keeping Holy Spirit and Communion in the middle. He says, "A joyless community is one that is dying out. […] A community rich in joy is a genuine gift from above to brothers and sisters who know how to ask for it and to accept one another, committing themselves to community life, trusting in the action of the Spirit."[9] The joy of following Jesus and the joy of being filled with Holy Spirit animates the community to accept one another as God's gift and to be open to one another in true love and sharing as our gift to God. "Joy is confirmed in the experience of community, that theological space where each one is responsible for their fidelity to the Gospel and for the growth of all. When a community is fed by the same Body and Blood of Jesus, it gathers around the Son of God, to share the journey of faith, guided by the Word. It becomes one with him, together in communion, experiencing the gift of love and festive celebration in freedom and joy, full of courage."[10] The religious community is sacramentally united in Christ and becomes faithful to the gospel by its evangelical living for the growth of all.

Pope Francis is never tired of challenging every catholic and specially the religious to be joyful people. He writes that the religious are called, "to know and show that God is able to fill our hearts to the brim with happiness; that we need not seek our happiness elsewhere; that the authentic fraternity found in our communities increases our joy; and that our total self-giving in service to the Church, to families and young people, to the elderly and the poor, brings us life-long personal fulfilment."[11] The religious are people, who have deep God-experience and have encountered God in their prayer, liturgy and in their apostolates. These experiences of God and encounter with the Word of God become the fount of joy for the religious to emanate inner happiness in their community living and in their self-giving service in the church.

Joyful witness does not mean that the religious are free of troubles, disappointments, the experiences of dark night of the soul and infirmities. "But in all these things we should be able to discover "perfect joy." For it is here, that we learn to recognize the face of Christ, who became like us in all things, and to rejoice in the knowledge that we are being conformed to him who, out of love of us, did not refuse the sufferings of the cross."[12] The ingredient of "perfect joy," is the 'gospel joy' which is rooted in the good News of salvation brought about by Christ, through his own death on the cross and resurrection. Hence, the religious learn to look at the negativities of the world as transient elements and focus themselves on the 'gospel joy' of Christ, which is deeper and everlasting.

"The joy of the gospel fills the hearts and lives of all those who encounter Jesus,"[13] very specially the consecrated people, who have dedicated themselves to the service of God. The acceptance of the message of salvation sets them truly "free from sin, sorrow, inner-emptiness and loneliness. With Christ joy is constantly born anew."[14] This joy is continues and contagious. The more we put on Christ, the more will we experience self-fulfilment andreadiness to go out to empower the needy and the weak. The cause of our inner joy is not any external reality, on the other hand, the presence of Christ within us. Christic influence transforms the religious so much that the religious does not put his or her heart on the worldly values and measures, but on the values of the Kingdom of God (cf., Mt. 12:48) and lives joyfully.

2. Religious as Contemplatives in Action

The good Pope Francis underscores that "the interior pilgrimage begins with prayer," and he goes on to define that this prayer becomes "the source of the fruitfulness of the mission."[15] The moment of engagement in prayer and the effect of prayer constitute the life of a religious. The engagement in prayer and liturgy empowers the religious to be a person of God and at the same time to relate to the world without being lost in the worldliness of the world. The effect of contemplation liberates the religious to totally commit oneself to actions, which bring about the reign of God. In this process, "The first thing for a disciple is to be with the Master, to listen to him and to learn from him," and they need to realize the more they remain in Him, the more they bear fruit, like 'the Vine and the branches' (Jn 15: 5). Because it is "the warmth of God, of his love, of his tenderness" that is "in our hearts" that helps us "who are poor sinners, warm the hearts of others."[16] If we think that we do things because of our own strength, then we are mistaken and end up either with self-glory or in frustration.

The way of "being with Jesus" moulds our contemplative approach to existential realities of life and eventually our response becomes free of ego and self-will. The time in contemplation inspires and enlightens our vocation and makes us understand the choice that God has made in calling us. "The Lord calls us to follow him with courage and fidelity; he has made us the great gift of choosing us as his disciples; he invites us to proclaim him with joy as the Risen one, but he asks to do so by word and by the witness of our lives, in daily life. The Lord is the only God of our lives, and he invites us to strip ourselves of our many idols and to worship him alone."[17] Such a deep realization of our total commitment to the Lord and to the Mission of God can take place only by the grace and inspiration of the Holy Spirit in our regular contemplation and prayer. Our face to face experience with the risen Lord makes us remain ever conscious of our own call to consistently let go and bear witness in our own day to day lives. The more we bring prayer to our living, the more we free ourselves of external attachments and enter deeply into missionary activities. These missionary activities flowing from the grace of the Lord, not only heal the world, but also bring us back to God in prayer. The time in contemplation becomes the source of one's own inner disposition to listen to others, to touch the lives of others and to cause gradual transformation in the society like the leaven and salt.

Pope Francis who blends these both dimensions in his own life urges us to "cultivate the contemplative dimension, even amid the whirlwind of more urgent and heavy duties. And the more the mission calls you to go out to the margins of existence, let your heart be the more closely united to Christ's heart, full of mercy and love."[18] The contemplative dimension sharpens our faith and enlightens our discipleship, so that it is not mere package of actions, but more of sharing the grace and love of communion with the Lord and simultaneously sharing in true solidarity and communion the pain and agony of the suffering humanity.

3. Always Promoting Growth in Communion

The communion with the Lord through sacramental practices by the religious is not merely a ritual practice, but one that makes them "experts in communion." Pope Francis reiterates the message of "spirituality of Communion" effectively illustrated by John Paul II, in his apostolic letter. According to John Paul II:

A spirituality of communion indicates above all the heart's contemplation of the mystery of the Trinity dwelling in us, and whose light we must also be able to see shining on the face of the brothers and sisters around us. A spirituality of communion also means an ability to think of our brothers and sisters in faith within the profound unity of the Mystical Body, and therefore as "those who are a part of me". This makes us able to share their joys and sufferings, to sense their desires and attend to their needs, to offer them deep and genuine friendship.[19]

Such an understanding of communion needs to be first lived out within the respective communities of each congregation by treating our own brothers and sisters as part of the Mystical Body and avoiding uncharitable criticism, gossip, envy, jealousy and hostility. In *Evangeli gaudium*, Pope Francis says, it is the" mystique of living together" by way of fraternal correction and respect for those who are weak, makes our life "a sacred pilgrimage."[20]

Consecrated men and women are called to grow in communion with the Lord and with its members and with others. The Christian understanding of communion, like Christian faith, is a dynamic and growing communion. If it remains stable, it is a sign that it begins to deteriorate. The growth of communion and encounter between various charisms, congregations, institutes, vocations and leaders "can open up a path of hope. No one contributes to the future in isolation, by his or her efforts alone, but by seeing himself or herself as part of a true communion which is constantly open to encounter, dialogue, attentive listening and mutual assistance. Such a communion inoculates us from the disease of self-absorption."[21]

A growing spirituality of communion moves towards seeing what is positive in others."A spirituality of communion implies also the ability to see what is positive in others, to welcome it and prize it as a gift from God: not only as a gift for the brother or sister who has received it directly, but also as a "gift for me."[22] Thus communion is not only coming into union among one another but also encouraging one another to grow in their gifts and talents, in order to be effective instruments in the Vineyard of the Lord. "A spirituality of communion means, finally, to know how to "make room" for our brothers and sisters, bearing "each other's burdens" (Gal 6:2) and resisting the selfish temptations which constantly beset us and provoke competition, careerism, distrust and jealousy."[23] The growth in spirituality of communion ultimately moves us from being passive supporter to become an active supporter and go to the extent of making room for our brothers and sisters to grow and flower forth. This is the effect of synergy, which begins within the communities and flows over to lay faithful and ecclesial community and even beyond its boundaries.[24]

4. Formation of Heart than Personality Development

Identifying the crucial role of formation for a meaningful consecrated life, Pope Francis says, "The formation of candidate is fundamental. There are four pillars of formation: spiritual, intellectual, communitarian and apostolic... The four pillars should be integrated right from the first day of entrance into the noviceship and should not be arranged sequentially. They must be interactive."[25] A holistic formation not only forms the individual but also defines the dynamic of community living and the mission in which they get involved. In the complex world of today, the formees should be helped, not to avoid problems by forbidding doing this or that, but assisted in confronting them and entering into a healthy dialog to find a constructive solution. He further says, it would be hypocrisy, if the formees suppress all their questions and wait for the day, when they will be told, 'Good. You have finished formation.' Such hypocrisy is the result of clericalism. According to Pope Francis, clericalism is one of the causes of the "Lack of maturity and Christian freedom" in the People of God.[26]

Pope Francis eloquently says, "Formation is a work of art, not a police action. We must form their hearts. Otherwise we are creating little monsters. And then these little monsters mould the People of God."[27] Thus, Pope Francis emphasizes the need to focus on the formation of heart, than on the formation of personal growth or personality development. The formation of heart is oriented towards the People of God as its goal. Therefore the formation for a consecrated life should focus on "following Christ, the crucified and risen one[28] ...to take up his way of life, to adopt his interior attitude, to allow oneself to be invaded by his Spirit, to absorb his surprising logic and his scale of values, to share in his risks and his hopes."[29] The formation of the heart to vibrate with the sacred heart of Jesus is the true formation and they will bear witness to the life, death and resurrection of Jesus in their lives. If the hearts of the religious are as sour as vinegar, then they are not made for the people of God. We are not forming administrators and managers, but fathers, brothers, sisters and travelling companions, to accompany the people of God, always drawing strength and inspiration from the intimacy with the Lord.

5. Discernment and Consolation as a Way of Life

"Being with Jesus shapes the contemplative approach to history which knows how to see and hear the presence of the Spirit everywhere and, in a special way, how to discern the spirit's presence in order to live in time as God's time."[30] A religious is called to form a heart that can rightly discern the will of God, by listening to the promptings of the Spirit and convert one's living space as divine space. In this horizon of divine space, a religious learns to "test everything, hold fast to what is good; abstain from every form of evil" (1 Thesol. 5:21). The art of discernment always helps the religious not to "believe every spirit, but test the spirits to see, whether they are from God" (1 Jn 4:1). The religious, thus, through the practice of discernment both personal and communitarian, identifies what is from God and always seeks to do good by listening to the promptings of the Spirit.

The fruit of discernment in life is spiritual consolation. "In Jesus' view, consolation is a gift of the Spirit, the *Paraclete*, the Consoler who comforts us in our trials and awakes a hope that does not disappoint. Thus, Christian consolation becomes comfort, encouragement, hope. It is the active presence of the Spirit (cf. Jn 14:16-17), the fruit of the Spirit."[31] A religious, who responds to the inspiration of the Holy Spirit experiences consolation in one's life and becomes a source of comfort and hope for others. Thus personal consolation spills out to the community and eventually to the wider society. In this way, the consecrated people lead a fruit bearing life and they bear witness to the fruits of the Spirit - love, joy, peace, patience, kindness, generosity, faithfulness, gentleness, and self-control (Gal 5:22). The consolation of a religious is the sign of our consecrated life, which comforts others and instils hope.

The Pope says, "The men and women of our time are waiting for words of consolation, the availability of forgiveness and true joy. We are called to bring to everyone the embrace of God, who bends with a mother's tenderness over us – consecrated women and men, signs of the fullness of humanity, facilitators and not controllers of grace,[32] stooped down in a gesture of consolation."[33] The religious who reflects this spiritual and internal consolation of the personal intimacy with the Lord will be a sign and symbol of God's mercy and reconciliation in the world. As symbols of reconciliation, they will not only embody compassion and reconciliation, but also enter into the mission of bringing reconciliation to unfortunate ones in the periphery of the society. The Pope also strongly believes that spiritual consolation and "contemplation opens out to prophetic aptitude. The prophet is one "whose eye is opened, and who hears and speaks the words of God;...a person of three times: the promise of the past, the contemplation of the present, the courage to point out the path toward the future."[34] The religious, as contemplatives in action, live in the world with this prophetic and missionary nature.

6. Prophetic Living and Missionary Discipleship

According to Pope Francis, "the distinctive sign of consecrated life is prophecy,"[35] and "Prophecy of the Kingdom, (which) is non-negotiable."[36] The role of Prophecy is not only announcing the message of God, but also being the messenger of God. Hence it is not appearing to be prophets, but truly being prophets and being religious men and women who light the way to the future. In his address to the Superiors General: "Radical evangelical living is not only for religious: it is demanded of everyone. But religious follow the Lord in a special way, in a prophetic way." This is the priority that is needed right now: "to be prophets who witness to how Jesus lived on this earth... a religious must never abandon prophecy."[37] Several great religious saints and monks, even at the face of persecution, never gave up prophesising and it includes sometimes making noise or disturbing, but always from a good conscience and personal integrity. In reality, the charism of religious people is like yeast, unassuming yet always affecting and transforming through a prophetic life based on the spirit of the Gospel.[38]

A religious is a religious, only when he or she passionately lives out this prophetic dimension and condemns any act of mediocrity or compromise (cf., Rev. 3:16 "So because you are lukewarm, and neither cold nor hot, I am about to spit you out of my mouth"). In the words of Abraham Heschel, prophecy is "the exegesis of existence from a divine perspective."[39] The prophets interpret the existential situation of the community and constantly accompany the people by challenging and leading towards God experience.

Prophets receive from God the ability to scrutinize the times in which they live and to interpret events: they are like sentinels who keep watch in the night and sense the coming of the dawn (cf. Is 21:11-12). Prophets know God and they know the men and women who are their brothers and sisters. They are able to discern and denounce the evil of sin and injustice. Because they are free, they are beholden to no one but God, and they have no interest other than God. Prophets tend to be on the side of the poor and the powerless, for they know that God himself is on their side.[40]

However the pope is aware that the religious also can become wearisome or experience apparent fruitlessness, desperation or fall into the temptation to flee, like Elijah and Jonah. But the prophets should "know that they are never alone," God keeps encouraging them, as He did with Jeremiah, "Be not afraid of them, for I am with you to deliver you" (Jer 1:8).[41] The prophetic life of a religious is a participation in the mission of God. For it is God, who will go before you and speak for you, "Now go, I will be with your mouth and teach you what you are to speak" (Ex. 4:12).

The Christian discipleship begins to blossom and take root in the form of mission, when the religious listen to God in contemplation and respond to God in their prophetic role. The disciple in his or her faithfulness commits oneself for the mission and service by self-emptying and self-giving deeds. Thus, faithful discipleship culminates in missionary discipleship. Both are intertwined and interrelated. "Faithful discipleship is grace and love in action; it is the practice of sacrificial charity."[42] And missionary discipleship is martyrdom and *kenosis*. "When we journey without the Cross, when we build without the Cross, when we profess Christ without the Cross, we are not disciples of the Lord, we are worldly. We may be bishops, priests, cardinals, popes, but not disciples of the Lord."[43] The consecrated people in being prophets bear witness to missionary discipleship by willingly choosing to carry the cross and go through the pain of persecution and agony.

7. Going to the Frontiers

For Pope, "Ours is not a 'lab faith,' but a 'journey faith,' an historical faith. God has revealed himself as history, not as a compendium of abstract truths. [...] You cannot bring home the frontier, but you have to live on the border and be audacious."[44] Hence, Pope Francis reiterates that the faith of the catholic and very specially that of the religious is existential and ever dynamic. It calls us to be alert to the spirit and alive to the needs of the suffering humanity at the frontiers. In that regard, Pope Francis says,

> I am convinced of one thing: the great changes in history were realized when reality was seen not from the center but rather from the periphery. It is a hermeneutical question: reality is understood only if it is looked at from the periphery, and not when our viewpoint is equidistant from everything. Truly to understand reality we need to move away from the central position of calmness and peacefulness and direct ourselves to the peripheral areas. Being at the periphery helps to see and to understand better, to analyze reality more correctly, to shun centralism and ideological approaches.[45]

The conviction of the need to perceive the reality from the periphery is the key to understand the language, suffering and culture of the humanity at the periphery. It demands that we leave the comfort of our nests and structures, in order to become acquainted with the life-experiences of people at the periphery.

The Pope also distinguishes between geographical frontiers and symbolic frontiers. There are geographical frontiers, which demand our physical availability to move from the centre to the periphery. "But there are also symbolic frontiers that are not predetermined and are not the same for everyone; rather they "need to be sought on the basis of the Charism of each Institute."[46] The symbolic frontiers illustrate that going to the frontiers also imply, besides reaching out to the poor and the marginalized, we also need "to visit the frontiers of thought and culture, to promote dialogue, even at the intellectual level, to give reasons for hope on the basis of ethical and spiritual criteria, questioning ourselves about what is good. Faith never restricts the space for reason, but opens it to a holistic vision of the human person and of reality, and defends it against the danger of reducing the human person to "human material."[47] The consecrated people need to include both these kinds of frontiers in their discernment and decision making process, before they send their brothers and sisters on frontier missions.

The Pope also spoke about the "frontiers of thought."[48] The frontiers of thought refer to the education ministry of consecrated people, through which they can transform the society and redefine values based on the Reign of God. Therefore "he insisted education today is a key, key, key mission!" and it needs to "convey understanding, convey ways of doing things, convey values."[49] Ultimately the education ministry of the religious should attempt to convey a different value system and understanding centred on the Kingdom of God. Though the realities of marginalization and exclusion take upper most priority in terms of determining the frontier missions, the religious also need to enter into adequate discernment vis-à-vis their own charism and the existential need of the people. Such a clear discernment would help in finding out our target group and selecting apt personnel for such a mission, or else we may end up sending religious who have good will, but are not prepared for situations that they may face in the frontier missions.

8. Religious Life: Still a Place of Hope and Future

The apostolic letter of Pope Francis refers to Benedict XVI in urging us not to "join the prophets of doom who proclaim the end or meaninglessness of the consecrated life in the Church in our day; rather clothe yourselves in Jesus Christ and put on the armour of light – as Saint Paul urged (cf. Rom 13:11-14) – keeping awake and watchful."[50] This letter invites us to place our hope in the Lord. This hope is not based on the strength of our achievements, but on the One who is risen and for whom "nothing is impossible" (Lk 1:37). "This is the hope which does not disappoint; it is the hope which enables consecrated life to keep writing its great history well into the future. It is to that future that we must always look, conscious that the Holy Spirit spurs us on so that he can still do great things with us."[51] Thus religious life becomes a beacon of hope, as it re-invents[52] and re-orients itself in its radical following of the Lord, to be able to speak a new language for these changing times.

Pope Paul VI in his decree on the adaptation and renewal of religious life writes, consecrated life is the following of Christ as presented in the gospels.[53] It implies living the life of compassion and communion, forgiveness and reconciliation, and healing and life-giving. In this light, the good Pope Francis emphasizes the need to create "alternate spaces" rather than living in some utopia. The 'alternate space' should create an ambience for "Gospel approach of self-giving, fraternity, embracing differences, and love of one another"[54] to thrive. This space becomes the source of creativity rooted in fidelity to one's own charism, yet finding new ways to respond to the signs of times. "The Pope invites us to renew our vocation and to fill it with joy and passion, so that the increase in loving activity is a continuous process – "it matures, matures, matures."[55]

The consecrated life is a loving activity, that never stops but continues to mature by giving itself in love and service. According to Pope Benedict XVI, "Love is never finished and complete; throughout life it changes and matures, and thus remains faithful to itself."[56] The consecrated life embodies such a love, which is faithful to itself and because it is faithful to itself, it is unconditional, self-giving and outgoing. That's why Pope Francis in his hope-giving words to the consecrated people says, "Don't be closed in on yourselves, don't be stifled by petty squabbles, don't remain a hostage to your own problems. These will be resolved if you go forth and help others to resolve their own problems, and proclaim the Good News. You will find life by giving life, hope by giving hope, love by giving love."[57] Consecrated life attains completion in constantly giving, prophetically challenging and leading people to God and to new life. Reiterating this dimension of consecrated life, Joan Chittister, in her book on religious life writes, "We must teach again that religious are meant to be the wake-up call for the Church."[58] Let the religious re-invent themselves to be relevant and to be the wake-up call for the society towards being a better world.

Endnotes

1   Jeffrey A. KRAMES, *Lead with Humility: 12 Leadership Lessons from Pope Francis*, (New York: American Management Association, 2015), 37.

2   Pope FRANCIS, "On Religious Life," (19 August, 2013), in *La Civilta Cattolica*, no. 2.

3   J. M. BERGOGLIO, *Intervention at the Synod on the Consecrated Life and its Mission in the Church and in the World*, (XVI General Congregation, October 13, 1994).

4   Pope FRANCIS, *Evangeli Gaudium*, (Rome: November 2013), no. 14.

5   JOHN PAUL II, *Vita Consecrata*, (Rome: Pose Synodal Apostolic Exhortation, March 25, 1996), no. 110.

6   Pope FRANCIS, *To All Consecrated People*, (Rome: 30th November 2014), no. I: 1-3. Cf., John Paul II, Apostolic Letter *Novo Milleniio Ineunte* (6 January 2001), no. 1, "to remember the past with gratitude, to live the present with enthusiasm and to look forward to the future with confidence."

7   Pope FRANCIS, *Meeting with Seminarians and Novices*, (Rome: 6 July, 2013), in *L'Osservatore Romano*, Monday-Tuesday, 8-9 July 2013, CLIII (155), p. 6.

8   Pope FRANCIS, *To All Consecrated People*, no. II. 1.

9   Congregation for Institutes of Consecrated Life and Societies of Apostolic Life, Instruction: *Fraternal Life in Community*. "*Congregavit nos in unum Christi amor*", (2 Febreaury 1994), n. 28: in *Ench Vat* 14, 345-537 in Congregation for Institutes of Consecrated Life and Societies of Apostolic Life, *Rejoice! A Letter to the consecrated men and women. A Message from the Teachings of Pope Francis*, (2 February, 2014), no. 9.

10   Congregation for Institutes of Consecrated Life and Societies of Apostolic Life, *Rejoice! A Letter to the Consecrated Men and Women. A Message from the Teachings of Pope Francis*, no. 9.

11   Pope Francis, *To All Consecrated People*, no. II. 1.

12   Ibid., no. II, 1.

13   Pope FRANCIS, *Evangeli Gaudium*, no. 1.

14   Ibid., no. 1.

15   Congregation for Institutes of Consecrated Life and Societies of Apostolic Life, *Rejoice! A Letter to the Consecrated Men and Women. A Message from the Teachings of Pope Francis*, no. 6.

16   Pope FRANCIS, *Address to the Participants at the International Congress on Catechesis*, (Rome: 27 September 2013), in *L'Osservatore Romano*, Sunday 29 September 2013, CLIII (88), p. 8.

17   Pope FRANCIS, *Homily at the Eucharistic Celebration at St. Paul Outside the Walls*, (Rome: 14 April 2013), in *L'Osservatore Romano*, Monday-Tuesday 15-16 April 2013, CLIII (88), p. 8.

18   Pope FRANCIS, *Homily for Holy Mass with Seminarians and Novices*, (Rome: 7th July 2013), in *L'Osservatore Romano*, Monday-Tuesday 8-9 July 2013, CLIII (155), p. 7.

19   JOHN PAUL II, Apostolic Letter *Novo Milleniio Ineunte,* (6 January 2001), no. 43.

20   Pope FRANCIS, Apostolic Exhortation, *Evangeli Gaudium,* no. 87.

21   Pope FRANCIS, *To All Consecrated People,* II, II. 3.

22   JOHN PAUL II, Apostolic Letter *Novo Milleniio Ineunte,* no. 43.

23   JOHN PAUL II, Apostolic Letter *Novo Milleniio Ineunte,* no. 43.

24   POPE FRANCIS, *To All Consecrated People,* II.3

25   Antonio SPADARO, *Wake up the World: Conversation with Pope Francis about Religious Life,* trans. Donald Maldari, in *La Civilita Cattolica* (2014), I, 3-17.

26   Ibid., I, 3-17.

27   Ibid., I, 3-17.

28   John PAUL II, Post-synodal Apostolic Exhortation *Vita Consecrata* (25 March 1996), no. 22, in: AAS 88 (1996), 377-486.

29   Congregation for Institutes of Consecrated Life and Societies of Apostolic Life, *Rejoice! A Letter to the Consecrated Men and Women. A Message from the Teachings of Pope Francis,* no. 5.

30   Ibid., no. 6.

31   Ibid., no. 8.

32   Pope FRANCIS, Apostolic Exhortation *Evangelii gaudium,* no. 47.

33   Congregation for Institutes of Consecrated Life and Societies of Apostolic Life, *Rejoice! A Letter to the Consecrated Men and Women. A Message from the Teachings of Pope Francis,* no. 8.

34   Pope FRANCIS, *Daily Meditation in the Chapel of Domus Sanctae Marthae,* (16 December, 2013), in: *L'Osservatore Romano,* Monday-Tuesday 16-17 December 2013, CLIII (229), p. 6.

35   Pope FRANCIS, *To All Consecrated People,* no. II. 2.

36   Antonio SPADARO, *Wake up the World: Conversation with Pope Francis about Religious Life,* trans. Donald Maldari, in *La Civilita Cattolica* (2014), I, 3-17.

37   Pope FRANCIS, *Address to all Superiors General,* (Rome: 29 November 2013). In Pope Francis, *To All Consecrated People,* no. II. 2.

38   Cf., Antonio SPADARO, *Wake up the World: Conversation with Pope Francis about Religious Life,* trans. Donald Maldari, in *La Civilita Cattolica* (2014), I, 3-17.

39   Abraham J HESCHEL, *The Prophets,* Vol. 1, (New York: Harper & Row, 2001), XIV.

40   Pope FRANCIS, *To All Consecrated People,* no. II. 2.

41   Ibid., no. II. 2.

42   Congregation for Institutes of Consecrated Life and Societies of Apostolic Life, *Rejoice! A Letter to the Consecrated Men and Women. A Message from the Teachings of Pope Francis,* no. 6.

43   Pope FRANCIS, Apostolic Exhortation *Evangelii gaudium,* (24 November 2013), LEV, Citta del Vaticano, 2013, n.1.

44   Antonio SPADARO, *Interview with Pope Francis,* in: *La Civilta Cattolica,* 164 (2013/III), 474.

45   Cf. J.M. Bergoglio, *Nel cuore dell'uomo. Utopia e impegno,* (Milan: Bompiani, 2013), p. 23. Antonio Spadaro, *Wake up the World: Conversation with Pope Francis about Religious Life,* trans. Donald Maldari, in *La Civilita Cattolica* (2014), I, 3-17. In *Evangelii guadium* (no. 236), Pope Francis writes, "Here our model is not the sphere, which is no greater than its parts, where every point is equidistant from the centre, and there are no differences between them. Instead, it is the polyhedron, which reflects the convergence of all its parts, each of which preserves its distinctiveness...There is a place for the poor and their culture, their aspirations and their potential."

46   Antonio SPADARO, *Wake up the World: Conversation with Pope Francis about Religious Life*, trans. Donald Maldari, in *La Civilta Cattolica* (2014), I, 3-17.

47   Cf. FRANCIS, *Meeting with the World of Culture*, Cagliari, 22 September 2013, in *L'Oservatore Romano*, Monday-Tuesday 23-24 September 2013, CLIII (218), p. 7.

48   Antonio SPADARO, *Wake up the World: Conversation with Pope Francis about Religious Life*, trans. Donald Maldari, in *La Civilta Cattolica* (2014), I, 3-17.

49   Ibid., I, 3-17.

50   Pope BENEDICT XVI, *Homily for the Feast of the Presentation of the Lord*, (2 February 2013).

51   Pope FRANCIS, Apostolic Letter *To All Consecrated People*, no. I. 3.

52   Jeffrey A. KRAMES, *Lead with Humility: 12 Leadership Lessons from Pope Francis*, (New York: American Management Association, 2015), 37.

53   Pope PAUL VI, *Perfectae Caritatis*, (Rome: October 28 1965), no. 2.

54   Pope FRANCIS, *To All Consecrated People,* no. II. 2.

55   Pope FRANCIS, *Meeting with Seminarians and Novices*, (Rome., 6 July 2013), LEV, *Citta del Vaticano*, 2013, no. 47.

56   BENEDICT XVI, Encyclical Letter *Deus Caritas est* (25 December 2005), no. 11, in: AAS 98 (2006), (217-252).

57   Pope FRANCIS, *To All Consecrated People,* no. II. 4.

58   Joan CHITTISTER, *The Fire in These Ashes*, (Franklin, Wisconsin: Sheed & Ward, 1999), 23.

IV. DIALOGUE AS WAY OF LIFE

Chapter 11

Dialoguing with Religions
The Impact of Pope Francis on 'Inter-Cultural and Inter-Faith Interactions'

John Peter Vallabadoss OFM Cap
St. Joseph's Capuchin Philosophical College, Kotagiri, Tamil Nadu

Introduction

Contemporary society has become keenly aware of multi-cultural and multi-religious contexts. Sensitivity towards co-existence, and mutual interaction, with others professing different creeds, ideologies and life-style, have become the norm of the day. Narrow-mindedness and exclusivist paradigms do not seem to have a rightful place in the current global situation and interaction with the Other in total openness is encouraged. In such a current context, the Catholic Church looks forward to recognizing and respecting other faiths and ideologies with open-mindedness. As evidenced by Second Vatican Counciliar, and Post-Counciliar, documents such a positive approach makes the Church ever more significant and relevant today. The papacy of Pope Francis has shown signs of continuing the optimism of healthy interaction. His outgoing life-style, outreach to others, and his effective transmission of the Gospel message of Jesus of Nazareth, clearly communicate to the world the good news of Christ's unconditional embrace of all humans. Following in the footsteps of his patron Saint Francis of Assisi, Pope Francis has felt the call from within, to 'rebuild my falling house,' amidst ever brewing community fragmentation in the name of religion and tradition. Our global human community has been positively impacted by the open-mindedness of Pope Francis. This article highlights the approach and effectiveness of both Francis of Assisi and Pope Francis, in dealing with the Other, and the impact both have had on the Church in particular, and society at large.

1. Called to Rebuild and Reach out

The Divine call felt by Francis of Assisi in the ruined chapel of San Damiano to 'rebuild the falling house' is a call for everyone. For Pope Francis too this is a call not only to rebuild the Church, but our entire society. Our global society is falling apart by assertions of individual identities in terms of caste, ethnicity, race, religion and tradition. Consequently, war and terrorism, racial and ethnic cleansing, genocide and hatred towards others continues to fragment humanity. Pope Francis responds to this Divine call to rebuild, by reaching out to all people without prejudice, in an all embracing genuine love.

With an awareness of the challenge of living in a plural society, Pope Francis calls for inter-religious, inter-faith and inter-cultural dialogue. Taking Francis of Assisi as his patron, the Pope says, "He is the man who gives us this spirit of peace - the poor man... Oh, how I wish for a Church that is poor and for the poor."[1] By his love of the poor which is more than just philanthropy, and by capturing the gospel poverty as Francis of Assisi did, Pope Francis has exhibited tremendous courage. "I am confident that Pope Francis' love for the poor and his passion for the social gospel will help galvanize the Church to greater fidelity to the gospel and a renewed commitment to building a civilization of love."[2]

Accepting individuals in their personal set of circumstance, was the way of Christ and Francis of Assisi. Francis of Assisi seems the perfect guide to lead so many in our times where both secularization and a search for spirituality collide. An encounter of Francis of Assisi with the Sultan of Egypt at Damietta in 1219 during the fifth crusade, illustrates the classic experience of relating to other traditions.[3] Initially Francis' approach to the Sultan was contextually presented as to preach the gospel and to convert him to Christianity. The factors remained that it took courage to preach the good news to the opponent of the Christian world at that time of war and enmity with the Muslims. The Damietta experience has turned out to be an evangelizing effort which taught Francis as it is not to give but to receive, not to preach but to witness to one's faith and conviction. Dialogical encounter is where one learns from the other and shares his conviction with the other. "Perhaps the new way of evangelizing is not so much through confrontation and argument but through conversation, dialogue, and affirmation, a way that allows us to reach out to people..."[4] In the changing context of mission today, witnessing to the gospel is not by preaching the good news with words, but by living it with action.

2. Embracing All

Francis' relation with other traditions is an act of embrace, as the Jesus of the Gospels did by way of touching all despite differences.[5] The all-embracing approach of Jesus encourages us to accommodate others who are not part of our own communal and personal religious traditions, ideologies, ethnicities, or nationalities. Surely an exclusivist orientation is not compatible with our present-day thinking and action, though fanatics may find it comfortable and useful. Contemporary Catholics can no longer assert an exclusivist paradigm. As Michael Amaladoss rightly points out, "After the Second Vatican Council and the event of Assisi, October 1986, when the Pope came together with the members of other religions, to pray for peace, no Catholic can be an exclusivist."[6] Holding on to one's own faith formulations and lifestyle need not make one exclusionist. This attitude leads one to avoid, segregate and ostracize the Other as not only different, but unwanted and rejected. Negative approaches toward traditions not our own, and believers of different faiths, ultimately denies the Catholic core of universality; it ignores the possibility and opportunity of salvation for all.[7] Pope Francis encouraged the Egyptian Christians in April 2017 referring to his predecessor's document saying, "You have shown, and continue to show, that it is possible to live together in mutual respect and fairness, finding in difference a source of richness and never a motive of conflict."[8]

Acknowledging that other religions have 'seeds of the gospel,' as 'anonymous Christians,' or as knowing 'partial revelation,' can make a positive feeling in oneself and others as well. Moving beyond rejection of the other, inclusivists are able to respect the other as related to, and the Other as part of the self. Such a move is the most common undertaking today and to some extent a 'successful' position.[9] Assimilation can, however, certainly become elitist, patronizing, and self-serving unless approached with real humility and acceptance. Problems with inclusivism can lay in its denial of the other person simply as one is, in the here and now.[10] Real acceptance enables Catholic Christians to move beyond ecclesio-centrism and Christo-centrism to a truly Theo-centric approach where God becomes the centre of revelation and the Divinity that manifests in as He elects. The biblical story of the Tower of Babel (Gen 11:1-9) illustrates the human dream of building a stone tower of unity by homogenizing the differences in community. Plurality is indeed, part of God's plan, even though mono-cultural tendencies have predominated throughout human history.[11]

3. Pluralistic Attitude towards Others

Pluralism plainly accepts that there is more than one kind of existence and holds that all existence is ultimately reducible to a multiplicity of distinct and independent beings or elements, emphasizing the qualitative diversity within reality. Pluralistic approaches are born out of the existential dilemma of everydayness when encountering mutually incompatible worldviews.[12] Living amidst many options, points of view, conflicting and opposing positions, in a globalized contemporary multicultural context, can result in not merely viewing the other as different, in merely tolerating, or in reducing the other, but recognizing plurality and accepting them. Recognition of and sensitivity to radical diversity emerges from the conviction that no single unit or group is capable of embracing the totality of human experience.[13]

Pope Francis at Assisi in Sep, 2016, said, "Our religious traditions are diverse. But our differences are not the cause of conflict and dispute, or a cold distance between us."[14] Postmodern approaches to creating a space for 'free play' of opposites, of the different, enables one to have a pluaristic attitude. No tradition can claim to be universal, perennial and certain. Pluralistic attitudinal changes call for a change from the presumption of 'exclusiveness' and 'self-sufficiency' regarding one's own, to an openness and respect others. No thought is so rich that it does not need to be complemented by others, and no thought is so 'poor' that it has nothing with which to complement others.[15] To be sure, there is a plurality of versions of reality, however there is always a danger of relativism; claiming that all versions are true, right, or equally good.[16] Pope Francis favours dialogue; a positive encounter that helps people of different generations, citizens of different ethnic origins, and different convictions live together.[17]

4. Condemning Polarization

Fanaticism, and fundamentalism are symptoms of a human tendency to polarize. Pope Francis is against such claims of fanaticism. In his homily during mass at Cairo, Egypt on 29 April, 2017 Pope Francis said, "God is pleased only by a faith that is proclaimed by our lives, for the only fanaticism believers can have is that of charity! Any other fanaticism does not come from God and is not pleasing to him."[18] Arguing for a pluralistic all-embracing attitude His Holiness realizes that what we need is neither uniformity nor multiplicity, but a unity that expresses itself in diversity. In his meeting with Muslim community in Central Mosque of Koudoukou, Bangui in Central African Republic on 30 November 2015, Pope Francis spoke: "Together, we must say no to hatred, no to revenge and no to violence, particularly that violence which is perpetrated in the name of a religion or of God himself."[19] The Pope recounted the journey of religious leaders to Assisi from the reigns of Pope John Paul II and Pope Benedict XVI, as a sign of embracing each other with differences. He declared that whoever uses religion to foment violence contradicts religion's deepest and truest inspiration and that violence in all its forms does not represent the true nature of religion. It is the antithesis of religion and contributes to its destruction. He emphatically said, "Peace alone is holy. Peace alone is holy, not war!"[20]

Conflicts among humans in the name of God and religion are incompatible and unacceptable from the point of view of authentic religious experience and of the Divine-human relationship. While voicing out contempt for discrimination and violence in name of religion, the Pope also distances religion from terrorism. To counter the spread of extremist ideology, he calls for protecting religious and individual freedoms. He reiterated this point in Cairo by referring to "unconditional respect for inalienable human rights such as equality among all citizens, religious freedom and freedom of expression, without any distinction."[21] Authentic religious experience prevents anyone becoming a sectarian, narrow-minded religious fanatic. Viewed from this conviction, for any committed religious person, every religion is complementary in nature not contradictory to each other. A pluralistic religious context helps persons to enrich, deepen and strengthen their belief in a particular tradition.[22]

Pope Francis urges the faithful to transcend their divisions. During his visit to Egypt he "managed the delicate balance of embracing Islam while condemning Islamic extremists in the Muslim majority country."[23] A true believer must be broad-minded and open-hearted to learn from the other. No theology of religion should negate the specificity and the absoluteness of another religious commitment. Similarly, none has a right to subordinate other religions to its own claims or rewrite other religious languages, to align with its own terms. Embracing the other enables one to allow the other to be the other. Wherever he goes, Pope Francis spreads peace and joy by embracing all, by embracing the marginalized. He always feels happy to be in contact with people. He visits all countries with suffering, countries with problems. His firm refusal to cancel his visit to Egypt in April, 2017, after the church bombings weeks before is evidence of his firm conviction by showing solidarity with the victims of violence, and to send a strong message to extremists that he loves peace, not violence. It takes courage to stand against people whose main weapon is fear.

5. From Confrontational to Conversational Mode

In dialogue, the communicator not only speaks but listens as each party relates a version of truth.[24] The Church understands itself and others better in a pluralistic world through interreligious dialogue.[25] Inter-religious dialogue has helped Christians, to some extent, to enter into the depths of religious experience of non-Christians, especially by dropping triumphalist language.[26] The encounter of Francis of Assisi with the Sultan took place not in a context of fear and insecurity. Francis approached the Sultan in total openness. Pope Francis continues to speak of this open attitude as 'the duty to respect one's own identity and that of others,' and 'the courage to accept the difference.' "Those who are different, ... should not be seen or treated as enemies."[27]

While many of his contemporaries were overwhelmed by surface differences and politics, Francis of Assisi cast his net into deeper waters. Befriending an enemy of the Crusaders turned out to destroy the enmity without eliminating the person. In the footsteps of the Master Jesus, and his Patron Francis of Assisi, Pope Francis avoids confrontation with the Other by fully engaging a conversational method of resolving conflict. "May Saint Francis of Assisi, who eight centuries ago came to Egypt and met Sultan Malik al Kamil, intercede for this intention."[28] In his speech to the Peace Conference in Egypt in April 2017, Pope Francis concluded by stating, "the future also depends on the encounter of religions and cultures."[29]

6. Engaging with the Other

Pope Francis calls for countering the barbarity of those who foment hatred, by advocating an education in respectful openness and sincere dialogue. The only alternative to the incivility of conflict is the civility of encounter.[30] Saint Francis' exhausting mission journey to the Saracens met with little success. Francis did not achieve any of his goals: he neither obtained the martyr's crown nor the Sultan's conversion; neither peace between Christians and Muslims, nor a new concept of a Crusade without weapons. It is not the visible results that count but witnessing and risking one's own life. In his contacts with the Muslims, Francis became aware that they were not the 'cruel beasts' that European war propaganda for the Crusades made them out to be. On the contrary, he saw their high moral standards, and admired, above all, their deep veneration and submission to God. He clearly understood that the Muslims had to be respected for who they were. The Muslims were his brothers and he wanted his friars to go and live among them as witnesses to their faith.[31]

Pope Francis calls for learning from others; "As Christians, we can also benefit from these treasures built up over many centuries, which can help us better to live our own beliefs."[32] The attitudinal changes in Saint Francis were also attributed to his meeting with the Sultan. He later adapted the list of praises of God after the model of Islamic prayer of praises. Such would have been inconceivable to the ears of those accustomed to the Crusading sermons, and to hearts blinded by hatred for Islam. Francis also noted the way Muslims praised God five times a day, prostrated themselves on the ground, and paid reverence to the Almighty with deep bows. In his Letter to the Entire Order, Francis urged his friars to adopt a similar prayer posture.[33] The deepening awareness of the transcendence of God is clear in Francis' songs and there is a clear development towards the Transcendent after his return from Damietta to Italy: 'All-powerful, most holy, Almighty and supreme God, Holy and just... He alone is true God, Who is perfect and good, and He alone is good, loving and gentle, kind and understanding. He alone is holy, just, true and right...'[34] In his Letter to the Faithful and in the Praises of God at La Verna, Francis speaks in similar terms of the Omnipotence and Sublimity of God, but at the same time stresses God's goodness, a goodness he praises again and again.[35]

Pope Francis is of similar opinion in learning from others as he says, "True openness involves remaining steadfast in one's deepest convictions, clear and joyful in one's own identity, while at the same time being 'open to understanding those of the other party' and 'knowing that dialogue can enrich each side.'"[36] The respect for persons and cultures made Saint Francis not merely to 'go to,' or 'go against' the Muslims, but to 'go among' them as a messenger of peace with a greeting: "The Lord give you peace." Francis was received by the Sultan with the same wish: "*Assalamaleikum.*"

Religions are dynamic and aspire to peace; yet they are often involved in conflict and violence. Islam is literally the religion of peace; Vedic blessing of *śanti* is very emphatic in Hinduism; Jesus greeted people with word of peace 'Peace be upon you.' There is absolute emphasis on compassion *'ahimsa'* in Buddhism, and Judaism has given the world the word and concept *'shalom.'* Pope Francis is always comfortable in greeting people belonging to the Islamic faith; "*As-salamu alaykum!*" in all his speeches. It is by sharing with each other who we are as believers that we can enrich one another.

7. Pope Francis: Model of Inter-Faith Openness

When considering the people of Islam, what comes foremost in the minds of many is an experience of Islam in its fundamentalist form, as projected by media in the wake of many terrorist attacks. In April, 2017, when Pope Francis visited Egypt, he sent a strong message of peace to strengthen communal ties. He spoke of Islamophobia and religious and individual freedoms.[37] His visit amidst the terrorist attack on Coptic churches in Egypt, especially on Palm Sunday in March 2017, brought back the memory of the visit of Francis of Assisi in 1219. The special significance of Pope Francis' visit to Egypt in the aftermath of recent attacks on Christians in the region, lays in his understanding of Islam with respect to violence and terrorism. He reiterated that terrorism has no religion. In his speech to the Egyptian authorities on the first day of his visit to Egypt, Pope Francis said, "It is our duty to dismantle deadly ideas and extremist ideologies while upholding the incompatibility of true faith and violence, of God and acts of murder.'[38]

Today communities all over the world face a crisis of unrest, chaos, diminishing human values, respect for fellow humans, loss of dignity and integrity, and exploitation. In his address "Thirst for Peace: Faiths and Cultures in Dialogue," at Assisi, on the world day of prayer for peace, on 20th Sep., 2016, Pope Francis said that people today thirst for peace and they know that there is no tomorrow in war, and that the violence of weapons destroys the joy of life."[39] "An ethics of fraternity and peaceful coexistence between individuals and among peoples cannot be based on the logic of fear, violence and closed-mindedness, but on responsibility, respect and sincere dialogue."[40] The search for the good and the positive must continue on both sides. There are good and sincere people in every religion.

Violence in the name of religion has become daily news in our time. In the process of eradicating violence and promoting peace we need to promote fellowship. In his address to the Rabbis in Jerusalem, Pope Francis said, "Mutual understanding of our spiritual heritage, appreciation for what we have in common and respect in matters on which we disagree: all these can help to guide us to a closer relationship."[41] Inter-faith openness and fellowship will help us focus on the finest characteristics of our counterparts, and to discover the depth and richness of our religious traditions. Inter-faith interaction is really intercommunication among truly religious people. The required attitude consists primarily of humility. Communicating one's own God experience to others would be made effective only when we develop a listening attitude to the others' Divine experiences.

On his visit to Istanbul in November, 2014, Pope Francis prayed with key Muslim and Orthodox Church leaders in a gesture of inter-faith harmony.[42] For Pope Francis, inter-religious/faith dialogue 'should not be an isolated event' that makes us resigned in the face of the pain of people who are hostages of war, poverty and exploitation. In an interview with journalists on his return from Turkey, Pope Francis said that interreligious dialogue should take a qualitative leap in not just talking about theology, but religious experience.[43] One cannot be indifferent and impotent before those struck by violence. 'We cannot allow terrorism to imprison the hearts of a few violent people,' bringing pain and death to many. Pope Francis wants everyone to assume responsibility and to contribute to peaceful reconciliation. He wishes, "May a new season finally begin, in which the globalized world can become a family of peoples… Nothing is lost when we effectively enter into dialogue… Everyone can be an artisan of peace."[44]

8. Mission as Encounter with the Others

Pope Francis speaks of today's mission as more to listen to the world than to speak to it. The need of our time is a response, "to the existential issues of people today, especially the young, listening to the language they speak."[45] A heart level listening to the issues of affected people can lead to a fruitful change. Mission involves an attitude of respect for cultures, hence a heart ready to listen to others with respect. Regarding his visit to the Mosque in Turkey, Pope Francis said that he went there as a pilgrim. When he entered the Mosque he felt that he was not a tourist, but felt the need to pray and prayed together with the Mufti for all, most of all for peace, 'Lord, let's put an end to these wars.'[46] His prayer for peace is an adequate response to his listening to the conflicted zone of the Middle-East he was visiting at that time. A great gesture and attitude of respecting the sacred space of the other religions was shown by Pope Francis. Having sensitivity to the sacredness of the place of worship of other believers is the fruit of interreligious conviction of a search for the Divine.

Pope Francis has been a consistent voice of reason with "an appeal not to build walls, but bridges,"[47] when political leaders of some countries wanted to build walls across their borders. Francis mentioned that those who build walls and not bridges are not Christians. Even in meeting the American president, Donald Trump he has given the message of peace, urging him to be a peace-maker, giving him an olive branch, saying "It is my desire that you become an olive tree to construct peace."[48] Each one of us is called to be a peacemaker, uniting and not dividing, extinguishing hatred and not maintaining it, opening paths to dialogue and not building new walls, the Pope said. During his visit to Jerusalem, he pressed for pursuing peaceful solutions to every controversy and conflict, and to avoid initiatives and actions that contradict their faith in God, and to tirelessly work for peace, with decisiveness and tenacity.[49] Peace requires a process of dialogue that is "tenacious, patient, strong and intelligent," he said, and it refuses to give up no matter what happens.

9. Concluding Remarks

Relating with other faiths and traditions is Jesus' way of embracing others in his life and ministry. Francis of Assisi had taken that insight from Jesus and approached the Sultan of Egypt with openness and returned as a transformed person, making peace and learning from Islam. Looking at Pope Francis in his words and activities from the perspective of Francis' encounter with the Sultan, makes one aware of Franciscan influence of making peace in and through dialogical modes. Imparting gospel charism in the context of today is the great challenge Pope Francis places before each of the followers of Christ. His interaction with other faiths, other cultures, embracing the plight of immigrants, imparts a new way of being Catholic today. Gospel values of humanity, compassion and love, service and reaching out those in need, are found in the person and activity of Pope Francis. His visits to mosques, synagogues, other denominational churches and receiving and visiting with patriarchs, archbishops, high priests and religious leaders of other faith traditions, has revived the hopes of witnesses to the gospel in multi-religious and secularized world. The impact of Pope Francis is in shaking up the rigid structures of the narrow-minded, 'navel gazing' Catholic Church, to become open-minded in embracing others with the differences.

Endnotes

1   Andrea TORNIELLI, *Jorge Mario Bergoglio, Francis: Pope of a New World* (Bangalore: ATC and San Francisco: Ignatius Press, San Francisco, 2013), 67.

2   Sean P O'MALLEY, Foreword, *Reclaiming Francis: How the Saint and the Pope are Renewing the Church,* by Charles M Murphy (Mumbai: Pauline, 2014), 3.

3   Francis' experience with the Sultan in Egypt had been narrated by various biographers and authors according to the need and context of their times. Differences are on what aspect of Francis' mission is emphasized by the writer. It makes interesting reading to study the differences of authors within the Order, like Thomas of Celano and Bonaventure, and authors outside the Order, like Jacques de Vitry, the Bishop of Acre, Ernout and Henri d'Avranches, who wrote his *Versified Life of St. Francis.* The accounts are as follows, Celano - (1Cel 57), (2Cel 30); Bonaventure (LMj IX:8); Jacques de Vitryin *History of the Orient* (HO 32); Refer, Regis J. Armstrong, et.al. *Francis of Assisi: Early Documents – The Saint, The Founder, The Prophet,* 3 Vols. (New York: New City Press), 2000.

4   Charles M MURPHY, Intro. *Reclaiming Francis,* 17.

5   Jesus' encounter with different people as referred in the Gospels vouch for this: Talking on faith issues with Samaritan woman (Jn 4:1-41), non contempt of other beliefs but an approach with human love with Roman Centurion (Lk 7:1-10), shedding traditional prejudice and appreciating others' faith with Syro-phonecian woman (Mk 7:24-29), perfecting faith perspective with Nicodemus (Jn 3:1-21), confronting and contempt of religious hypocrisy with Pharisees (Mt 5-6; 23), dialoging and presenting one's own views with differing Sadducees (Mt 22:23-46), correcting the misinterpretations out of conveniences with Scribes and Lawyers (Mt 12:38-42).

6   Michael AMALDOSS, "The Pluralism of Religions and the Significance of Christ," in *Asian Faces of* Jesus, ed., R.S. Sugirtharajah, 5th Print (New York: Orbis Books, 2001), 86.

7   *Ibid.*

8   BENEDICT XVI, *Post-synodal Apostolic Exhortation Ecclesia in Medio Oriente*, 24-25.

9   Francis X. CLOONEY, "Reading the World in Christ: From Comparison to Inclusivism," in *Christian Uniqueness Reconsidered: The Myth of Pluralistic Theology of Religions,* ed. Gavin D'Costa (New York: Orbis Books, 1990), 79.

10 Michael AMALDOSS, "The Pluralism of Religions and the Significance of Christ," 86.

11 Johnson J. PUTHENPURACKAL, "Pluralism: A Philosophical Clarification of the Notion," in *Pluralism of Pluralism: A Pluralistic Probe into Philosophizing* (Bangalore: ATC, 2006), 17.

12 *Ibid.*

13 SELVARAJ, "Harmony in Religious Plurality: Panikkar's Approach," in *Raimon Panikkar – Being Beyond Borders* (Bangalore: ATC, 2012), 246-248.

14 http://w2.vatican.va/content/francesco/en/speeches/2016/september/documents/papa-francesco_20160920_assisi-preghiera-pace.html accessed 10 May, 2017.

15 Johnson J. PUTHENPURACKAL, "Pluralism: A Philosophical Clarification of the Notion," 19-21.

16 Refer, George KARUVELIL, "Religious Pluralism: A Philosophical Critique," in *Pluralism of Pluralism: A Pluralistic Probe into Philosophizing* (Bangalore: ATC, 2006), 207-228.

17 Cindy WOODEN, "Dialogue for peace is an obligation, Pope tells religious leaders," in *Catholic Herald.co.uk* accessed on 30 Dec. 2013.

18 http://en.radiovaticana.va/news/2017/04/29/pope_francis_in_cairo_full_text_of_homily_at_sat_am_mass _/1308944. accessed 10 June, 2017.

19 http://w2.vatican.va/content/francesco/en/speeches/2015/november/documents/papa-francesco_20151130_repubblica-centrafricana-musulmani.html accessed 28 June, 2017.

20 http://w2.vatican.va/content/francesco/en/speeches/2016/september/documents/papa-francesco_20160920_assisi-preghiera-pace.html accessed 10 May, 2017.

21 http://w2.vatican.va/content/francesco/en/speeches/2017/april/documents/papa-francesco_20170428_egitto-conferenza-pace.html accessed 20 July, 2017.

22 Paulachan Kochappilly, "Celebration of Interfaith Experience," in *Pilgrims in Dialogue: A New Configuration of Religions for Millennium Community,* ed. Antony Kalliath (Bangalore: Dharmaram Publications, 2000), 295.

23 http://www.latimes.com/world/middleeast/la-fg-egypt-pope-francis-leaves-20170429-story.html accessed on 10 August, 2017.

24 R.T. BROOKS, *Communicating Conviction* (London: Epworth Press, 1983), 82-83.

25 A. PUSPARAJAN, "Prospects of Christian Dialogue with Other Religions,"in *Journal of Dharma,* Vol. 8, No. 3 (1983), 248.

26 A. Pusparajan, "Dialogue: Crisis and Solution," in *Mission Today,* Vol. IV, No. 4 (2002), 177.

27 http://w2.vatican.va/content/francesco/en/speeches/2017/april/documents/papa-francesco_20170428_egitto-conferenza-pace.html accessed 20 July, 2017.

28 http://w2.vatican.va/content/francesco/en/speeches/2017/april/documents/papa-francesco_20170428_egitto-conferenza-pace.html accessed 20 July, 2017.

29 http://w2.vatican.va/content/francesco/en/speeches/2017/april/documents/papa-francesco_20170428_egitto-conferenza-pace.html accessed 20 July, 2017.

30 http://w2.vatican.va/content/francesco/en/speeches/2017/april/documents/papa-francesco_20170428_egitto-conferenza-pace.html accessed 20 July, 2017.

31 Benen FAHY, trans. "Chapter 16: Missionaries among the Saracens and other unbelievers – the Rule of 1221," in *The Writings of St.Francis of Assisi* (Chicago: Franciscan Herald Press, 1963), 43.

32 Pope FRANCIS, *Evangelli Gaudium* – 254.

33 "Letter to the Entire Order," no.4 in *Francis and Clare: The Complete Works,* trans. Regis J. Armstrong & Ignatius C. Brady (New York: Paulist Press, 1982), 56.

34 "The Earlier Rule," no.23.1, 9 in *Francis and Clare,* 133.

35 "Letter to the Faithful," No.61-62, in *Francis and Clare,* 71.

36 Pope FRANCIS, *Evangelli Gaudium* - 251.

37 http://www.aljazeera.com/indepth/opinion/2017/04/pope-francis-egypt-voice-reason-170429115853335.html accessed on 30th Sep, 2017.

38 http://en.radiovaticana.va/news/2017/04/28/pope_francis_addresses_egypts_civil_authorities_full_ text/1308759

39 http://w2.vatican.va/content/francesco/en/speeches/2016/september/documents/papa-francesco_20160920_assisi-preghiera-pace.html accessed 10 May, 2017.

40 Pope Francis, "Nonviolence: A Style of Politics for Peace," *Message for the 2017 World Day of Peace, 5.*

41 http://w2.vatican.va/content/francesco/en/speeches/2014/may/documents/papa-francesco_20140526_terra-santa-visita-presidente-israele.html accessed 21st July, 2017.

42 http://www.bbc.com/news/av/world-europe-30259206/pope-francis-visits-blue-mosque-in-istanbul-turkey accessed on 1st June, 2017.

43 http://w2.vatican.va/content/francesco/en/speeches/2014/november/documents/papa-francesco_20141130_turchia-conferenza-stampa.html accessed on 1st June, 2017.

44 http://w2.vatican.va/content/francesco/en/speeches/2016/september/documents/papa-francesco_20160920_assisi-preghiera-pace.html accessed 10 May, 2017.

45 "Address of Pope Francis to CELAM," in *Unto the Margins: Pope Francis and his challenges,* ed., John Chathanattu (Delhi: Media House Delhi, 2013), 249.

46 http://w2.vatican.va/content/francesco/en/speeches/2014/november/documents/papa-francesco_20141130_turchia-conferenza-stampa.html accessed 1st June, 2017.

47 http://w2.vatican.va/content/francesco/en/audiences/2017/documents/papa-francesco_20170208_udienza-generale.html accessed 20 Sep., 2017.

48 http://www.jpost.com/Christian-News/Report-Jerusalem-Vatican-in-talks-on-pope-visit-to-Israel-493924 accessed 20 Sep., 2017.

49 http://w2.vatican.va/content/francesco/en/speeches/2014/may/documents/papa-francesco_20140526_terra-santa-visita-presidente-israele.html accessed 21st July, 2017.

Chapter 12

Dialoguing with Science
Science and Religion for Human Growth

S. Stephen Jayard
Faculty of Philosophy, Jnana-Deepa Vidyapeeth, Pune, Maharashtra

Introduction

In the 21st century it is not difficult to find common platforms for Science and Religion. Gone are those days when these two powerful human enterprises were seen opposing each other; it was unimaginable then to think of common interests between these two disciplines. But now the findings from both the macro and the micro worlds reveal that science alone cannot answer many of the questions that humanity comes across.

The Church has been taking keen interests in science, especially in astronomy, since the 16th century, when Pope Gregory XIII brought in reform of the calendar. Later in 1890s Pope Leo XIII founded Vatican Observatory; it has now acquired a good reputation, with 1.8 meter telescope for exploring the vast dark space out there; quite a few astronomers of the observatory engage in several significant studies and researches in many fields of Cosmology; they study asteroids, meteorites, extrasolar planets, stellar evolution, and so on. Further, in the recent past, the Church did not keep aloof from science and it always encouraged its followers to do serious science. Priests and monks have been ardent partners in the scientific enterprises; we find a priest or a religious, at every crucial turn in the progress of science in the modern era; for instance, the famous geneticist Gregor Mendel was a Christian monk and the epoch-making theory of Big Bang in Cosmology was the brain child of Georges Lemaitre, a Belgian mathematician and Catholic priest. This priest indeed had a great reputation too. He travelled to California in January 1933 for a series of lectures and in one of them he elaborated his Big Bang theory. Einstein could not resist his desire to openly applaud him; he gave him a standing ovation and announced: "This is the most beautiful and satisfactory explanation of creation to which I have ever listened."[1]

Pope John Paul II always encouraged dialogues between Science and Religion and appealed to theologians that they be sufficiently informed of the recent developments in science; he advised them to be equipped with the basics of science so that they could avoid making shallow statements and uncritical reflections regarding scientific theories, like the Big Bang. He sincerely invited scientists also to be aware of the recent developments in the theological trends and the Scriptural researches. In short, as mentioned in his letter to George V. Coyne, the then Director of Vatican Observatory, on 1 June, 1988, that he was always convinced and he invited others too to be convinced that "Science can purify religion from error and superstition; Religion can purify science from idolatry and false absolutes. Each can draw the other into a wider world, a world in which both can flourish."[2]

Thus, though a few centuries ago the Church had a wrong understanding of science, now the Church has realized that there would not be real contradiction between these two powerful enterprises. With the modern tools of interpreting the Bible and the new theological understandings science is not seen as a threat to faith. Science, in fact, can be seen as something that strengthens one's faith.

1. Interaction between Science and Religion

The need for interaction between Science and Religion seems to be on the steady increase. Several developments in the recent science call for a revision of our traditional notions; for instance, the traditional understanding of 'reality' is forced to be re-visited.

Contemporary science questions the classical understanding of 'reality'. The new discoveries and observations, both in the macro and the micro worlds, challenge the dogmas of scientism and they "radically alter the status of knowledge and the place of the knowing subject."[3] *The mysterious nature of matter:* Heisenberg's principle of uncertainty and Bohr's principle of complementarity suggest that the actual nature of reality escapes our complete understanding, because, "The elementary particle is neither a wave nor a corpuscle but a 'thing' that combines the two images."[4] Therefore, at that level, matter ceases to be 'material' and "Matter has lost its substance."[5] *The Mystery of the 'Fine-tuning':* The study of biotic coincidences and the anthropic principles seem to suggest that the universe has been very meticulously fine-tuned to be ready to receive conscious human beings; being convinced of this Dyson, asserts that "the universe knew we were coming"[6] and Paul Davies declares that "We are truly meant to be here."[7] Fine-tuning in the universe is, though may not be a proof, but a strong indicator for an intelligent design; for instance, the initial density of the universe had to be meticulously fixed to an accuracy of 10^{-60} and this precision is like an archer hitting a one-centimeter-square target placed fifteen billion light-years away.[8] Several scientists-turned theologians, like John Polkinghorne, Arthur Peacock, Ilya Prigogine, etc., also find something more to the evolution process than mere chance. They have gone beyond reductionism and are open to mystical and metaphysical overtones in their approach to reality. Even great minds, like Einstein, are also convinced that such fine-tuning in the universe cannot be the outcome of a mere chance. If one argues that all these fine-tunings are just fixed by laws of physics, the question arises: "Where do the laws of physics come from? And why *those* laws rather than some other set?"[9] Therefore, the mystery still remains!

Further, as science proceeds we realize that we lose our grip over reality. The classical notions of certainty, causality, absolute measurability and stability are significantly challenged. We are forced to get reconciled with arbitrary nature of the initial conditions, irreducibility, uncertainty, and unpredictability. By this "we are reminded of the contingence and finite nature of man."[10] Such realization of our finitude makes us wise and humble. We are cautioned not to meddle with the wisdom of nature that has been there for about fourteen billion years.

One of the fundamental ways to define humans is to see them as 'seekers of meaning'. As Victor Frankl shows, the search for 'meaning in life' becomes more fundamental to life than food, shelter and clothing. Philip Clayton shows that the meaning-quest is related to the very nature of human being and sciences alone will not be sufficient to comprehend human nature, and therefore, the quest for meaning cannot be satisfactorily fulfilled by science, though science may contribute something in the process of meaning-seeking.

Though humans are biologically very much a part of creation and share a lot with other creatures, yet they seem to be far different from all of them, in terms of reason, will power, ability to imagine, the exercise of control over natural passion and above all the ability to go beyond the immediate environment. However, we cannot easily define life, nor its meaning or purpose, ***because the "questioner" and the "questioned" are one and the same here***. Modern neuroscience may succeed in mapping the areas of the brain to find out what happens when one is filled with love or hatred, fear or tranquility; Psychology may come up with convincing theories about the good effects of love and the bad effects due to its absence. *But science cannot exactly define what love is, and since it is this love that makes one find meaning in life, science can comprehend neither love nor meaning.*

2. Pope Francis' Commitment to Science

As Pope Francis has done some studies in Chemistry he is not a stranger to science. He has always been encouraging priests and religious to involve more and more in serious science. He expressed his deep desire, in a meeting with the participants of

Symposium Sponsored by Vatican Observatory, that the Church must have many more religious men and women to bridge the gulf between faith and science.[11] Knowing about our cosmos is indeed the satisfaction of the innate desire to know. According to Guy Consolmagno, a Jesuit brother, appointed by Pope Francis as the new director of the Vatican Observatory, in 2015, makes it clear that Vatican is eager to investigate in the field of astronomy because astronomy satisfies our quest, as it is a part of being human.[12]

Pope Francis always cautions about the dangers of the literal reading of the Bible, especially the account of creation in the book of Genesis. So in his address to the Pontifical Academy of Sciences on the Big Bang Theory and Evolution. (27 October, 2014), he alerts: "If we take this story literally we run the risk of "imagining that God was a magician, complete with an all powerful magic wand." But, he affirms, "that was not so."[13] The theories on the origin of matter and life, like the Big Bang and the evolutionism, leave several questions unanswered. Science does not provide any satisfactory, provable answers to the questions like, the wherefrom of the primeval atom, the cause of the big bang, the mode and the purpose of the Big Bang and so on. Pope goes on to announce that "The Big Bang theory, which is proposed today as the origin of the world, does not contradict the intervention of a divine Creator but, rather requires it."[14]

Pope Francis explains how God has chosen to create nature with the inherent power to evolve further. The scientific theory of evolution implies creation, because unless there is something in the first place it would not evolve. God did not want a 'finished product' when he created the world, rather he wished his creation to evolve towards 'perfection. Creation implies a "Creator" as an art implies an artist, a dance a dancer! Catholic teaching says God created all things from nothing, but it doesn't say how and that leaves open the possibilities of evolutionary mechanisms like random mutation and natural breeding.

Pope Francis has high hopes with scientists. They need to instruct the policy makers and the general public regarding the critical situation of the ecological crisis. But they are very often influenced and hijacked by very many other forces, from within and without, in such a way that they are not able to do justice to their vocation to do science in a moral way. "I would say that it falls to scientists, who work free of political, economic or ideological interests, to develop a cultural model which can face the crisis of climatic change and its social consequences," he said, "so that the vast potential of productivity will not be reserved for only a few."[15]

It was a very interesting meeting between Pope Francis and Stephen Hawking, known as the 2nd Einstein, during a session of the Pontifical Academy of Sciences convened to discuss the impact of scientific knowledge and technology on people and the planet (November 25-29, 2016). Pope sincerely wants to remind the world that "We are not custodians of a museum and its masterpieces that we have to dust off every morning, but rather collaborators in the conservation and development of the existence and biodiversity of the planet and human life."[16] He insists upon moral basis for all our human endeavours, including scientific ones. Authentic collective living has to be based on morality. He *critiques consumerism and irresponsible development; he strongly suggests a holistic vision rooted in spirituality which would ensure a healthy environment for everyone and a better care for the environment itself.*

3. Pope Francis and Eco-Spirituality

Pope Francis' involvement with science and his hopes with the scientists came out very clearly in his encyclical, *'Laudato Si: On Care for our Common Home'* (18 June, 2015); it is an Encyclical on Ecology by Pope Francis; it is acclaimed by several as the, may be described as the most significant contribution of the Catholic Church to ecology. As he assumed his office, he took the name of St. Francis of Assisi (1181-1226) precisely because of the latter's love for nature and admiration for God's creation. St. Francis of Assisi had deep love for nature; he treated all that is in nature as his brothers and sisters. Inspired by this ardent love, Pope Francis wrote the encyclical. It is for the first time that a Pope dedicated an entire encyclical letter to the issues of environment and climate change. He deliberately and affectionately addresses to 'every' person who lives on earth, as we all share the 'common home'. It is the moral responsibility of everyone in caring for the earth. Oftentimes a wrong reading of the creation account absolves humans of their sin of exploiting the earth; but actually *in the beginning God gave humanity the earth to "till and keep" (Gen 2:15), where tilling refers to 'cultivating, ploughing, or working' and keeping means, 'Caring, protecting, overseeing and preserving'.*

Pope Francis is greatly concerned about the ecological crisis. He is deeply convinced that all need to work on a war-footing in order to save the earth, our common home. He gave a clarion call to the world of scientists to establish "a regulatory system that includes inviolable limits and guarantees the protection of ecosystems before new forms of power derived from the technological-economic paradigm produce irreversible damage not just to the environment but also to coexistence, democracy, justice and freedom."[17]

There have been also serious voices of blame and accusations of Pope transgressing the areas of morality and theology to go into the unfamiliar and unnecessary terrain of science; for instance, the Republican presidential candidate Rick Santorum openly suggested that Pope Francis to "leave science to the scientists" in order to show his displeasure about Pope's constant reminder and efforts to fight against climate change.[18] Since Pope openly challenges the irresponsible ways of the nations and societies that add up to the environmental crises, there are attacks on him. Of course, there also powerful voices that support his genuine concern for the eco-welfare of humanity at large. His efforts to point out to the world, the rich and the poor nations, the highly educated elite and the poor ignorant, about the urgent need to act collectively and proactively to protect the mother Earth are greatly appreciated by many world leaders.

Pope demands a right understanding of stewardship, rather than ownership, regarding our role in taking care of the earth. He has supported his arguments for the immediate need to protect the Earth from the environmental degradation with enormous scientific accuracy. As David M. Lodge points out, he has situated the environmental crisis in a much broader context, by linking it "to economic exploitation and the plight of the poor."[19]

a. Poverty and Ecology

His concern for the poor is well-known. He invites humanity to work together to remove poverty from the face of the earth. He feels that the earth has also been impoverished by the careless actions and greedy attitude of humanity. Therefore, as he voices out for the poor in humanity, in the same breath he draws our attention to the impoverished earth; he calls for a caring treatment for the earth urgently, because "the earth herself, burdened and laid waste, is among the most abandoned and maltreated of our poor."[20] Thus, he sees the link between poverty and the ecological crisis. Most of the ecological problems like the increase in the global temperature or the pollution of the atmosphere are the result of the careless attitude and reckless activities by the rich and the affluent. But the poor and the underprivileged, as the sharers of the common home, are forced to suffer from those ecological crises. The air conditioning machines blow hot air adding slowly and steadily to the global temperature; the burning of the fossil fuels and other travel mechanisms pollute the air; but the poor, who are generally add much less to these, suffer more because of the ill effects. When they are afflicted with related diseases, those diseases have a great impact on their lifestyle and even their very survival.

b. Ecological Conversion

Pope Francis sees the urgency in taking care of nature; he invites the whole of humanity to engage in this with the utmost dedication. To dedicate ourselves to work for nature is like dedicating oneself to a new religious or social ideology. One needs to "convert oneself" to this new mission; one needs a profound interior conversion; no one can keep oneself aloof from this important mission of saving the environment. If one decides to participate in this global mission, one has to be ready to change one's life style which adds to the environmental crisis in some way or the other; if one likes to participate in the global drive for saving the earth but at the same time if one continues in one's old ways of life that are damaging the earth, then it is an inconsistent and self-contradicting behavior. Therefore. he is convinced that "*what they all need is an 'ecological conversion', whereby the effects of their encounter with Jesus Christ become evident in their relationship with the world around them*" (*Laudato Si'*, No. 217).

c. New Spirituality

Pope Francis proposes a 'new spirituality' that enables us to see the Creator in the Creation, to realize that wasting the natural resources is an insult to their creator and to realize that we are not the 'owners' of this earth, but 'responsible stewards' who are called to be 'co-creators' with God. Thus one realizes that saving water and natural resources is also a spiritual virtue. Each creature has its own beauty, dignity and purpose; their purpose is not to be assessed in terms of their usefulness to human existence. His new spirituality enlarges its vision and includes social structure and environment. Thus, not only caring for the poor but also valuing manual labour, denouncing consumerism and the tyranny of the market forces are certainly spiritual activities. Excessive use of plastics, consuming natural resources and fossil fuels, wasting energy, increase in the global temperature are some of the blunders that modern humanity is engaged with.

Conclusion

It is high time that we all realized that we are very much part and parcel of cosmos. Nature is never hostile to us, nor that are we strangers to it. Sometimes when we are struck by natural disasters like earthquakes, floods or tsunamis, we are made to think that nature works out against our survival and well-being. In fact, in many of such cases it can be traced out that nature, in its efforts to maintain its fine balance, just reacts to our actions, which are very often highly detrimental to itself. We all are very much part of nature. The inter-connectedness between us and nature is so much that, it is said, very many minerals, salts and chemical elements, like iron, carbon, oxygen, calcium, potassium, magnesium, iodine, etc., that are in our bodies are also abundantly found in nature, in the plants, animals and even the distant stars, millions of light years away. As we are very much part of nature, the mother earth never rejects us; for example, when we are buried after death, the earth very comfortably accommodates us, nor the atmosphere rejects the smoke that comes our when we are cremated. We often don't realize the significance of our being part of the unimaginably vast universe. For instance, when one holds a litre of water a part of the whole cosmos is in it. If only all the molecules of that water are kept as a string one by one it will be long enough to reach the moon from the earth, up and down for about seven times. [There are about 10^{25} molecules in one litre of water; each molecule is 10^{-10} meter, and the length of the whole string will be 10^{15} meter].

Though, humanity has not sufficiently realized the cosmic significance, which results in ecological crises, yet Pope does not lose hope with humanity. Since God has given us the reasoning power we can certainly reflect upon our own responsibility towards protecting nature. As God never loses hope with us let us also not lose hope for the betterment of the current situation. But the only concern is that we all have to be convinced of the dire need for immediate action. *Pope invites all brothers and sisters, living on the planet earth to make a pledge to save the earth and to protect the environment.* We hope that the Pope Francis' sincere efforts to work towards a better environment will bring forth lasting fruits. As David M. Lodge is hopeful, "if Pope Francis can persuade the communist Raúl Castro to reconsider Catholicism,"[21] he could easily create an atmosphere for the scientific consensus, whereby various communities of faith, science and the rulers can come together for open sharing and mutual learning.

Humanity needs to realize that God is truly present in all his creation, not only in human beings. This very realization is the foundation of eco-spirituality, which will motivate everyone to deal with nature in a cautious and respectful manner, to ensure its inner worth and undeniable dignity. S. Ignacimuthu explains the fundamental role of eco-spirituality in his book: Eco-spirituality is the basis for all our efforts to find solutions for the ecological crisis. In our present times we are facing huge challenges and crises in ecology and in this context the need and relevance of eco-spirituality is very high and important.[22]

As Francis Bacon wished, science must take us back to the glorious state of the pre-fallen state. It should make us wise, not otherwise. If we are not humble enough to "learn how to learn from nature", as Dudley Shapere puts it, we may end up using science as a tool of desolation and it would be like chopping off the very branch of the tree upon which we are sitting and, as Claude Levi Strauss fears, "the world began without the human being, and will end without him."[23]

The substance of Pope Francis' analysis of science and his exhortation to the world of science can be summed up as follows: "We need science with the human face." Only such science will enrich humanity. Enriching humanity would mean, among many other, making humans wiser, more sensible to mysteries and enabling them to find more meaning in their existence. Though humans have enormous cognitive power, yet they are cosmically very insignificant in the vast dark universe, known and unknown. As Blasé Pascal has it, "Man is only a reed, more frail than nature, but he is a thinking reed. It does not need the whole universe to wipe him out; a breath, a drop of water, is enough to kill him." But still humans are more powerful and noble than the universe, because, "he knows that he dies and knows the advantage the universe has over him,"[24] whereas the universe that kills him does not, cannot know anything.

With due admiration and respect to science, joining with Pope Francis, let us dearly expect science to collaborate with other disciplines to enrich humanity and protect nature. It is high time that we realized, as Philip Clayton declares, "… science alone will never provide the answer."[25] Thus, the efforts and mission of Pope Francis to integrate science with other social and spiritual disciplines are very essential and relevant in paving the way for better humanity and safer environment.

Endnotes

1   See: Mark BIDMON, "A Day without Yesterday: Georges Lemaitre and Big Bang"; http://www.catholiceducation.org/en/science/faith-and-science/a-day-without-yesterday-georges-lemaitre-amp-the-big-bang.html; accessed on 11 May, 2017.

2   See: https://w2.vatican.va/content/john-paul-ii/en/letters/1988/documents/hf_jp-ii_let_19880601_padre-coyne.html

3   Thierry MAGNIN, "Moral Philosophy – A Space for Dialogue between Science and Theology", in *Science and the Search for Meaning – Perspectives from International Scientists*, Jean Staune (ed.), (PA, USA: Templeton Foundation Press, 2006), p. 140.

4   Ibid., p. 146.

5   Trinh Xuan THUAN, "Science and Buddhism", in *Science and the Search for Meaning – Perspectives from International Scientists*, Jean Staune (ed), (PA, USA: Templeton Foundation Press, 2006), p. 181.

6   Freeman DYSON, *Disturbing the Universe* (NY: Harper & Row, 1979), p. 250.

7   Paul DAVIES, *The Mind of God* (NY: Simon & Schuster, 1992), p. 232.

8   Trinh Xuan THUAN, "Science and Buddhism", p. 184.

9   Paul DAVIES, "Glimpsing the Mind of God", in *Science and the Search for Meaning – Perspectives from International Scientists*, Jean Staune (ed.), 2006, p. 31.

10 Thierry MAGNIN, "Moral Philosophy – A Space for Dialogue between Science and Theology", p. 142.

11 See: https://zenit.org/articles/pope-francis-church-needs-religious-who-bridge-the-gap-between-science-and-faith/; accessed on 17 April, 2017.

12 For the full interview with him, see: http://www.sciencemag.org/news/2015/09/talking-science-and-god-popes-new-chief-astronomer; accessed on 5 May, 2017.

13 See: http://www.independent.co.uk/news/world/europe/pope-francis-declares-evolution-and-big-bang-theory-are-right-and-god-isnt-a-magician-with-a-magic-9822514.html; accessed on 10 May, 2017.

14 See: http://www.pressreader.com/australia/ daily-mercury/20170424/281801398846412; accessed on 11 May, 2017

15 See: https://www.washingtonpost.com/news/energy-environment/wp/2016/11/29/pope-francis-urges-world-leaders-not-to-delay-climate-change-efforts/?utm_term=.787f92d71df8; accessed on 9 May, 2017.

16 See: http://www.catholicherald.co.uk/news/2016/11/29/pope-francis-meets-stephen-hawking-at-vatican-science-conference/; accessed on 7 May, 2017.

17 See: http://en.radiovaticana.va/news/2016/11/28/pope_francis_address_to_pontifical_academy_of_sciences/1275273; accessed on 10 January, 2017.

18 See: http://time.com/3907567/pope-francis-rick-santorum-science/; accessed on 10 May, 2017.

19 See: http://www.nature.com/news/faith-and-science-can-find-common-ground-1.18083; accessed on 17 April, 2017.

20 See: https://www.washingtonpost.com/news/energy-environment/wp/2016/11/29/pope-francis-urges-world-leaders-not-to-delay-climate-change-efforts/?utm_term=.787f92d71df8; accessed on 11 February, 2017.

21 See: http://www.nature.com/news/faith-and-science-can-find-common-ground-1.18083; accessed on 10 Dec, 2017.

22   IGNACIMUTHU, S., *Eco-spirituality* (Dindigul: Vaigarai Publications, 2011), p. 159. (The title of the book in Tamil - *Sutruchuzhal Aanmigam*).

23   Claude LEVI-STRAUSS, *Tristes Tropiques* (Paris: Librarie Plon, 1955).

24   Blasé PASCAL, *Pensees*, ed. Philippe Sellier (Paris: Mercure de France, 1976), p. 231 & 145.

25   Philip Clayton,"*Foreword*", in *Science and the Search for Meaning – Perspectives from International Scientists*, Jean Staune, (ed.), 2006, p. xvi.

Chapter 13

Ian Barbour's Models for Science-Religion Dialogue
A Re-reading Inspired by Pope Francis

Gregory Mathew Malayil CMI
Dharmaram Vidhya Kshetram, Bengaluru, Karnataka

Introduction

"It cannot be maintained that empirical science provides a complete explanation of life, the interplay of all creatures and the whole of reality. This would be to breach the limits imposed by its own methodology."[1] Pope Francis points out the fact that the existence of human life on earth remains as a mystery in spite of the advancements in science. The unparalleled developments in communication technology, medicine, biotechnology and information technology are admirable. However, a complete explanation of life is not provided by any of the sciences so far. It seems that the scientific methodology itself imposes certain limits to its operational domain. Though science tackles many phenomena successfully, a realm of qualities which are non-computable; to mention a few, aesthetic sensitivity, love, pain, poetry, consciousness, etc., cannot be sensed or analysed within the frame of science. From a logical point of view, science doesn't have any means to ensure the truth of the knowledge it finds out. Godel's two incompleteness theorems state this fact very clearly.[2] The theorems speak about the limits of provability in formal axiomatic theories.[3] It seems that science is in a state of saturation and it needs a break-through to go further ahead. At the same time, we must remember that science is a discipline in which one studies the features of the world around us, and tries to describe the observations systematically and critically.[4]

Religious scriptures remain relevant and have been sources of inspiration for many, even after several decades of centuries. Pope Francis asks us whether it is reasonable to dismiss certain writings just because of the fact that they evolved in the context of religious belief.[5] As Pope rightly observes ethical principles which are being apprehended by reason can always reappear in different guise. He highlights the fact that too much compartmentalism or absolutization of any domain would reduce the effectiveness in confronting common problems which threat humanity.[6] Here the Holy Father, in the context of environmental problems and ecological movements, points out the necessity of dialogue between Science and Religion. Though Science–Religion dialogue has become almost like a cliché, still there will be room for more insights. A re-reading of conventional thoughts would help us to grasp more nuances of the realities related to the relation between Science and Religion. Interdisciplinary studies between Science and Religion, may acquire an academic nature and would not provide any output relevant to real life. As Holy Father rightly reminds, Science-Religion studies should help a human being to imbibe an integral vision of the two that both Science and Religion are for the well-being every living being.

Science reduces any observation or phenomenon to a scientific realm and this reduction is unavoidable in scientific methodology. When life is reduced as cells or atoms, the dimension of creation will be lost. When we say that distance can be calculated by multiplying speed with time, there is a reduction to the realm of computation and we lose the real concept of space. Many a time the reduction takes away the metaphysical dimensions of reality and Science and Religion end as academic disciplines; without contributing any meaning to human life. Holy Father's attempt is to provide certain convictions which may help us to realize that our mission in this regard is prophetic.

1. A Glimpse into the Relevant Literature

Whatever be the nature of the relationship between Science and Religion, it has always been a topic which attracted many thinkers and philosophers. After having been written a lot in this line, still it remains as new and enlightening thoughts that are being shared by several authors. In spite of all this literature it seems that the ice-berg remains unravelled. A few recent works which are pertinent to the theme of this paper are mentioned here: *Spiritual Information,* edited by Charles L. Harper, presents hundred perspectives on Science and Religion, where a spectrum of various dimensions such as psycho-somatic-pneumatic, socio-anthropo-philosophic and several other aspects of Science and Religion are discussed.[7] Cognitive science of religion is presented as an exciting new development in the understanding of the spiritual aspect of human nature.[8] It has been observed that reductionism as a danger began with scientific studies; which would tamper with the metaphysical dimensions of scientific observations.[9] Andrew B. Torrance observes that interdisciplinary studies in Science and Religion many a time favouring science and thus leading to methodological naturalism and he reminds us that a scientist who is a Christian, should keep away from Methodological naturalism.[10] As the evolution theory says about the survival of the fittest and chance, again material scientists speak about chances of combination of matter, the question remains, how such a product of chance can think rationally and be able to acquire knowledge at all. Stacey E. Ake establishes that the said conflict between Science and Religion is a euphemism and the actual conflict is between a few practitioners of both the disciplines; or the conflict is among people.[11] The history of the dialogue between Science and Christianity is well elucidated by Job Kozhamthadam.[12]

2. Certain Features of Science and Religion

The terms Science and Religion are very generic; and so the questions, which branch of science or which religion, would arise immediately. It could be said that all religions have certain common and unique characteristics and all sciences also have certain features shared by all. Religion is defined variously as a service in adulation of God as expressed in a system of faith and worship, and an awareness or conviction of the existence of a supreme being.[13] The existence of the supernatural is beyond the laws of science. The beginning and growth of any religion is connected to a god-man. Science does not accept the existence of a high priest, a god-man or any other authority that cannot be questioned. In fact science denies the existence of the supernatural and miracles which are the very essence of religion.[14] For certain events those who are religious can have a supernatural explanation; which would be outside the scope of science. In view of science all such events, assuming that they have occurred, which at times is doubtful, do have a scientific explanation, often simple and ingenious. In this write-up Science and Religion are used in the generic sense; and in case they denote anything particular, it would be specifically mentioned.

In both the disciplines, we believe that there is an objective world, and one reality that can be observed. Ian Barbour rightly claims "There are striking similarities between Science and Religion but also significant differences and both need discussion if we are to represent these two areas of human life fairly."[15] Though Science and Religion have their own operational space, it is to be noted that, both of them, all through the history of human beings, have attempted to answer the same questions; the concerns or foci might be different but the essence of the questions are the same. The primitive man did not have Religion or Science. But he had the quest to know what was around? He might be taken up by the phenomena of nature and its different functions. The feeling of wonder and the questions why and how which arose with the evolution of his intelligence and expansion of brain, enhanced his intuitive and imaginative potentials and widened his vision. In his search for truth he had revelation which led him to God and Religion. His attempt at finding immediate cause might be the beginning of scientific enquiry. So it could be reasonably speculated that Science and Religion had a common origin. At the same time, the two were entirely different with their frames and perspectives characteristic of them. Religion which was enhanced with revelations transcended the immediate observations to a higher realm without bothering about the causes or mechanisms which worked behind it.

3. Methods for Relating Science and Religion

Science as a critical enterprise may be described with the terms, correctness, critique and challenge and religion as a creative experience can be presented in terms of its three significant features namely, values, vocation and vision.[16] Science and Religion are two human endeavours of understanding the same reality. In their truest form Science and Religion presuppose an absolute commitment to truth, rely on judgment and discernment in their practice and allow a similar attitude of questioning and process testing which in the long run leads to continuously improving representation and understanding of reality.[17] Religion interprets and correlates experience whereas scientific theories interpret and correlate experimental or observational data. Both Science and Religion have an element of tradition in which each generation does not start from scratch, but proceeds on the basis of past research. Further Science and Religion as human enterprises are accomplished within a community of scholars either a scientific community or a religious assembly.[18] Both have cognitive and practical elements.

Science investigates the nature and tries to unravel the hidden. Religion proclaims that the nature is the creation of God. Religion has the answer in its own way for the existence of this universe. Though science comes forward with theories, no theory is a final word. Theories are only possibilities. So, Religion need not try to accommodate theories as such by inserting God at the beginning of the evolution theory or interpreting the singularity of the Big Bang as the presence of God. Since faith is leap into the darkness it doesn't require any scientific validation. This does not mean that religion should ignore the theories of science. It is commendable to welcome and appreciate theories as Pope Francis did with Big Bang Theory.[19] If religion tries to get the attestation from science, faith will become a part of scientific theories which may be revised with future inventions of science. Research in Science and Religion necessarily involves asking what sort of enterprise is in question? Philosophers in their descriptions tend to stress the practice of science as the activity of a particular community, a particular type of rational enterprise. Most scientists simply think of themselves as finding out more about the way things really are.

It was in 1960's that the major developments in the philosophy of science and the philosophy of religion, new theories and discoveries of natural sciences as well as complex shifts in the theological landscape, were evolved. These new trends made possible constructive interaction between Science and Religion which seem often separate or even hostile intellectual communities.[20] Scientist turned theologian Ian Barbour provided the initial bridge between Science and Religion in his *Issues in Science and Religion*. Barbour's crucial insight was to recognize the similarity between the methodological, linguistic and epistemological structures of science and theology which led him to 'critical realism.'[21] Several scholars followed it and their major concern was to create a framework for dialogue that allows for methodological reductionism as a legitimate scheme for scientific research but respecting the irreducibility of the processes and properties referred to by theology.

4. Science Challenges Religion

It seems that conceptual developments in the contemporary sciences challenge religions and their dogmas. Special Theory of Relativity proves that space and time are not absolutes and it confronts our ordinary sense of time flow and assumption of universal 'present moment'. Newtonian Mechanics describes nature as a closed causal system and divine action was reduced to human subjectivity. Determinism evolved from Newtonian theory led to the conclusion that nature is governed by its laws which are eternal. Since Quantum Mechanics, chaos and related theories are probabilistic they could be interpreted in favour of religion too. Theory of evolution questions the role of God and the existence evil, calamities and sufferings, challenges the thoughts of God's action in the world namely the theistic evolution. Cosmology challenges the religious concepts of redemption, and the doctrines of incarnation, resurrection and eschatology. The challenges may be apparent and a deeper understanding of the theories and insightful interpretations of the dogmas would bring clarity.

5. Limitations of Science

The entire cosmology of 20th century is built on the Big Bang theory, which is the most popular one among the various theories on the origin of the universe. The moment of creation, known as 'singularity' is intrinsic in the model. This model in juxtaposition with standard model of particle physics, serves to interpret the cosmic evolution of the universe.[22] Both the models, - one describing the universe on macroscopic scale and the other on microscopic scale, generate a few parameters which cannot be derived from theory alone, but which have to be experimentally determined and then inserted into the governing equations. As of now these parameters are free and therefore could be arbitrarily assigned without violating the basic laws of nature.[23] However, in our observable universe in which we are a part, these parameters as determined experimentally have a specific set of values. It turns out that these values are precisely those which are found to be critical for the existence of life in the universe. Even a small deviation of any one of them from the normal value would throw everything out of gear and the existence of life on earth would be put in jeopardy.[24]

Now the question is why nature should have chosen precisely those values of parameters which in turn resulted in the creation of life on the earth. Was there any conscious entity or purpose behind it? Many scientists think that this is merely a chance or accidental coincidence and that the existence of life in the Universe could be considered to be a mere consequence of the evolutionary process. Pope Francis is very clear in his articulation in this regard:

> ....the world came about as the result of a decision, not from chaos or chance, and this exalts it all the more. The creating word expresses a free choice. The universe did not emerge as the result of arbitrary omnipotence, a show of force or a desire for self-assertion. Creation is of the order of love. ..A fragile world, entrusted by God to human care, challenges us to devise intelligent ways of directing, developing and limiting our power.[25]

Science interprets life and associated phenomena, as a consequence of an accidental evolution, which took place among certain complex molecules. This is a kind of reduction and definitely it would result in the loss of certain original characteristics of the system. Assuming life as a product of chance, is equal to reducing human beings to material objects whose life is a meaningless one without any kind of values. Science is unable to accommodate any conscious decision behind the evolution of this universe and human life.

Another school of thought does not subscribe to this view and it thinks that there is a grand designer behind the entire episode of cosmic creation who deliberately and with great precision adjusted the parameters at the moment of creation to ensure the existence of life. A third group mostly comprising of Physicists, working on theoretical Cosmology has put forward the audacious hypotheses that ours is only one among the ensemble of universes created at the moment of Big Bang.[26] Each of these universes has its own governing laws. A subset of this ensemble has laws and parameters which support life and we happen to be members of this subset; again pointing to life as an outcome of chance. The inherent limitations and imperfections of science are very clear, despite all its outstanding success and achievements.[27] These limitations open the door for interaction and collaboration with other fields of knowledge. Such a collaboration is not an encroachment of another's turf; but only an assistance to science to achieve its goals: fulfillment of human and cosmic aspirations.

6. Relationship between Religion-Science: Models

The scattered and less focussed thoughts and features related to religion and science are classified and made oriented to practice with the help of several models. Prominent among them are the Ian Barbour's Conflict-Independent-Dialogue-Integration models.[28] Barbour's models became significant by providing a framework for modelling the interaction between the two seemingly disparate fields. John Haught has suggested the categories of conflict, contrast, contact and confirmation. A more detailed eight-fold classification has been offered by Ted Peters.[29] Barbour's models are outlined here for our reflection.

Conflict Model

The conflict model claims that, a priori, either science or religion is true and the other is necessarily false. The confrontation between Galileo and the Catholic Church is typically recalled as a classic example of confrontation between Science and Religion. Galileo's trial in 1633 marked the beginning of what has since then become proverbial, an idea that Science and Religion must inevitably be in conflict. Darwin's evolutionary theory was another historical example cited for the conflict between Science and Religion (or rather the Church and science). The evolutionary origins of humanity, seemed a threat to human dignity, especially when survival of the fittest was used by social philosophers to justify ruthless economic competition and colonialism. After all, the idea of an impersonal process of variation and natural selection challenged the traditional idea of purposeful design. The conflict thesis is represented today by two views at opposite ends of the theological spectrum; creation science and scientific materialism. Creation science, which originated as a fundamentalistic view in United States since the early in the twentieth century, took a strong stand defending biblical innerancy. Its proponents claimed that there is scientific evidence against evolutionary theory. Scientific materialism is the assertion that matter is the fundamental reality in the universe and scientific method is the only reliable path to knowledge.

Independent Model

The second model is the freedom display, which expresses that Science and Religion can both be valid as long as they are kept in their different spaces. Both Science and Religion can be valid in the meantime as long as they regard their points of confinement and remain consistent with their territory. Science reveals to us how and religion discloses to us why and some other utilization of either is wrong. Neo-orthodoxy which arose in early 20th century as a fresh theological move, opts for independent model because the objects of study in science and theology are completely distinct. Theology deals with transcendent and hidden mysterious God, who is radically unlike the world which is the object of scientific research.

Two language theory, which is an innovative reflection on language, says that we are not to look for the meaning of words but to be concerned with their functions. There is no neutral meaning for any sentence and hence its function is more important than meaning. Scientific language is informative because it deals with facts which are measurable and can be shared by all. The goal of science is to understand the universe, its laws and the way it works and scientists base their beliefs on evidence and rational argument. Scientific language is used for explanation, prediction or control and theories primarily taken as calculating devices for accurate prediction and practical tools for technical application.

As Barbour points out 'The distinctive features of religious language, according to linguistic analysts, are to recommend a way of life, to elicit a set of attitudes and to encourage allegiance to particular moral principles."[30] The religious language serves a wide range of functions some of which have no parallel in science. Religious language may include; declaration of one's commitment to a way of life, and death problems; personal religious experience, wonder and worshipful attitude.

Dialogue Model

Dialogue portrays more constructive relationships between Science and Religion than does either the conflict or independence view but it does not offer the degree of conceptual unity claimed by advocates of integration. Independence emphasizes differences between Science and Religion whereas dialogue emphasizes several kinds of similarity including the presuppositions and boundary questions of the scientific enterprise and methodological and conceptual parallels between the two fields.

Boundary questions are raised but not answered by science. Boundary questions or limit questions are those which arise at the speculative boundary of science and cannot be answered with the help of scientific methodology alone. Barbour suggests that dialogue may arise when science raises at its boundaries, limit questions that it cannot itself answer.[31] Why is the universe intelligible? Why is there a universe at all? Stephen Hawking writes "What is it that breaths fire into the equations and makes a universe for them to describe?"[32] The usual approach of science of constructing a mathematical model cannot answer the questions of why there should be universe for the model to describe. Shortage of personnel who are sufficiently versed in both, is the major difficulty in dialogue. Discussion can be awesome or productive depending on the attitudes of parties. Another interesting thing is that religions have their own communities and spokesmen, whereas science is not owned by such particular well defined group.

Integration Model

This model posits that the truth of Science and Religion can be integrated into a more complete or full "whole." Academics of Science and Religion like this model too but it also suffers from sounding good but being immensely difficult to put into practice. This model was exemplified in the works of Pierre Teilhard de Chardin who sought to integrate evolution, Christianity redemption, and perfection, and saw all of this fulfilled in his vision of the 'Omega Point.'[33] Advocates of integration call for formulations of traditional theological ideas that are more extensive and systematic than those envisaged by advocates of dialogue. Natural theology claims that the existence of God can be inferred from the evidence of design in nature.In a theology of nature, the main source of theology lies outside science, but scientific theories strongly affect the reformulation of certain doctrines. In a systematic synthesis, both Science and Religion contribute to the development of an inclusive metaphysics such as that of process philosophy.

7. The Four Models: A Unified Approach

The relationship between Science and Religion would be more realistic when we approach the models proposed by Barbour from a different perspective, in which the relation cannot be ascribed to any single model, say conflict or integration. It is not appropriate to fix any particular model in order to describe the relationship between Science and Religion. In any human relationship, social or personal, there are elements of conflict or dialogue and it will be a part of the functioning of the relations; the same way it is with Science and Religion.

On analysing the four models it could be seen that they are not as one of the four possibilities in the relationship between Science and Religion. In fact, the Science–Religion association includes all the four aspects together. Certain conflicts will always exist between them due to the very nature of each one. In certain other aspects, in the methodology and postulates or fundamental assumptions, if any, there are several elements in which they are independent. Dialogue is necessary between the two as process of understanding each other. Integration is not expected as an event of a combination of the two; but as an attitude which should be developed with each individual; especially for religious leaders and scientists. Common man is not obsessed with religiosity or scientism. Integration is an attitude of balance which should be attained as a part of our education. Integration is never meant to produce a combinational product of Science and Religion.

John Paul II summarizes the criteria for historical research by concluding that the Church must not be afraid of the truth that emerges from history and is ready to acknowledge mistakes wherever they have been identified, especially when they involve the respect that is owed to individuals and communities. She is inclined to mistrust generalizations that excuse or condemn various historical periods. She entrusts the investigation of the past to patient, honest, scholarly reconstruction.

The Church and science must not seek a seamless integration, but a respectful recognition of disciplinary boundaries and differences. John Paul II observed, "The Church does not propose that science should become religion nor religion science. . . . To be more specific, both religion and science must preserve their autonomy and their distinctiveness. Religion is not founded on science nor is science an extension of religion. Each should possess its own principles, its pattern of procedures, its diversities of interpretation, and its own conclusions."[34]

In *Fides et Ratio* John Paul II observes that Scientific reductionism would lead to Scientism which dismisses values as mere products of the emotions and rejects the notion of being in order to clear the way for pure and simple facticity.[35]

8. Scientists and Spirituality

Pope Francis observes that the Church is in need of religious men and women who can bridge the gap between faith and modern science.[36] In this context, the attitude among eminent cosmologists and physicists, regarding challenging questions relating science and spirituality deserves special attention. It is fair to state that there is no consensus in this regard one way or the other even among scientists. Within their ranks there are both believers and non-believers:,[37] to mention a few outstanding figures; Galileo, Newton, Schrodinger, Einstein were believers, and to certain extend mystics too. The non-believes assert that there are no deeper meaning to or scheme behind cosmic evolution. Laplace and Lagrange, great mathematicians and scientists of the 18th century, considered God as a 'fine hypothesis which explains several things'. Nobel laureates Steven Weinberg and Richard Feynman were of the conviction that the universe is pointless and meaningless. In their world view, life in general, and human being in particular are totally irrelevant against the backdrop of a vast and meaningless universe. The believers, in general, on the other hand see a grand designer at work who is identified by them as God or Creator of the universe.

A balanced approach taken by the British astrophysicist Arthur Edington, renowned for classic work on relativity and stellar structures is worth recalling.[38] His stand resembles more or less Immanuel Kant's *phenomena* and *noumena* in certain aspects. According to Edington, scientific theories are based on computation and they could address only those parts of the universe which are quantifiable. By the same token, those parts of human experience which could not be described by mathematics such as religion, love, compassion, consciousness and aesthetics are by definition outside the purview of science. According to him religious experience is no real less than physical experience. Based on this premise he rejected any claim to prove or disprove religion by scientific methodology. These are entirely two realms of experience that could neither validate nor support each other. He observed that Science and Religion shared a motivation and a method. Both were engaged in continual searches for knowledge, the former in the physical world and the latter in the spiritual world. Searching and not finding is the basis of both Science and Religion. He asserted that scientific enquiry and practice of religion are two basic impulses of human mind and what made a good scientist could also make a good religious minded person. Coming from major a scientific figure, the opinion voiced by Edington was tremendously popular during his time.

Here, it is once again clear that the dialogue and integration must happen within each individual. A scientist realizes the breach of science at its boundaries and philosophise the boundary problems. His further stance may be influenced by several factors for which he cannot be blamed.

Conclusion

Apart from academic level, the integration between Science and Religion, could be actualized only through fostering the right attitude. Ignoring the historical events which are cited as conflicts, there are still certain dimensions of conflict which are inherent. In a sense conflicts are also positive, productive and contributive, if there is fruitful dialogue. When we speak of Science and Religion taking the aspect of dialogue; we cannot ignore the inter-religious dialogues and interdisciplinary research programmes going on in science. For the growth of religions or sciences, in the initial stages, specialization would help and is a necessity to a great extent. Otherwise it is very difficult to start with research in Religion or Science. But at certain stages of its development, each one recognizes the need of collaborating with others.

Finally, it is the human being who takes care of all these things. Creative and effective dialogue between Science and Religion discovers the deep and ultimate truth in human's lived experience. At the heart of human experience, there is a solid unity, the consciousness of which would create a healthy and positive attitude. Whether it is inter-disciplinary or intra-disciplinary, the integration happens in the human mind. In fact, Science-Religion conflicts and as well dialogues are taking between the ardent practitioners of these things. Though it is an academic level activity, it may help us to tune our attitudes more generous and keep it unbiased. It would deepen our faith with a critical openness and enable us to act firmly for the good. The prayer of Pope Francis is apt in this context. "....Touch the hearts of those who look only for gain at the expense of the poor and the earth. Teach us to discover the worth of each thing, to be filled with awe and contemplation, to recognize that we are profoundly united with every creature as we journey towards your infinite light..."[39]

Endnotes

1   Pope FRANCIS, *Encyclical Laudato Si,* 199.

2   SMORYNSKI C., "The incompleteness theorems," in Handbook of Mathematical Logic, ed. J. Barwise (Amsterdam: North-Holland, 1977), 821–866.

3   The first incompleteness theorem states that in any consistent formal system, within which a certain amount of arithmetic can be carried out, there are statements of the language of the system which can neither be proved nor disproved within it. According to the second incompleteness theorem, such a formal system cannot prove that the system itself is consistent.

4   John COLLINS, *Science and Faith: Friends or Foes* (Illinois: Crossway Books, 2003), 34.

5   Pope FRANCIS, *Encyclical Laudato Si,* 199.

6   Ibid., 201.

7   Charles L. HARPER, *Spiritual Information: 100 Perspectives on Science and Religion* (Philadelphia: Templeton Press, 2005), xv.

8   Fraser N WATTS, "The New Cognitive Science of Religion", in *Spiritual Information: 100 Perspectives on Science and Religion*, ed Charles L. Harper (Philadelphia: Templeton Press, 2005), 101.

9   Stuart A KAUFFMAN, *Reinventing the Sacred* (New York: Basic Books, 2008), 10.

10   9Andrew B TORRANCE, "Should a Christian Adopt Methodological Naturalism?" *Zygon: Journal of Religion and Science*, 52 No. 3 (2017), 691-725.

11   Stacey E. AKE, "Scientists in the Cosmos: An Existential Approach to the Debate between Science and Religion" *Zygon: Journal of Religion and Science*, 51, No. 4 (2016), 1011-1022.

12   Job KOZHAMTHADAM, *Science, Technology and Values* (Pune: ASSR Publications, 2003), 3-30.

13   BHARGAVA P.M, "Does Science Refute Religion?" in *Angels, Devils and Science*, ed. Bhargava (New Delhi: National Book Trust India, 2016), 139.

14   14George COMBE, *Between Science and Religion* (New York: Cambridge Univ. Press, 1857, digital print-2009), 20-34.

15   Ian BARBOUR, *Religion in an Age of Science* (New York: Harper and Row, 1990), 66.

16   Kuruvilla PANDIKATTU, "Dialogue Between Science and Religion for Preserving and Fostering Life," in *Science, Technology and Values,* ed. Job Kozhamthadam (Pune: ASSR Publications, 2003), 35-39.

17   Sarojini HENRY, *Science Meets Faith* (Mumbai: St. Paul's, 2009), 150.

18   Ibid.

19   Pope FRANCIS, *Plenary Session of the Academy of Sciences*: *Vatican*, October of 2014.

20   Robert John RUSSEL, "Methods Relating Science and Religion," *Encyclopedia of Science and Religion*, vol. 2, (New York: Macmillan Reference, 2003), 746.

21   Ibid.

22   CHANDRASEKHARAN, P. C., *Understanding the Universe* (New Delhi: Global Vision, 2011), 206.

23   Ibid.

24   Ibid.

25   Pope FRANCIS, *Encyclical Laudato Si*, 77.

26   CHANDRASEKHARAN, *Understanding the Universe,* 207.

27   Job KOZHAMTHADAM, *Contemporary Science and Religion in Dialogue* (Pune: ASSR, 2002), 41.

28   Ian BARBOUR, *When Science Meets Religion* (New York: Harper Sanfransisco, 2000), 10-27.

29   Ian BARBOUR, "Science and Religion: Models and Relations," *Encyclopedia of Science and Religion*, vol. 2, (New York: Macmillan Reference, 2003), 746.

30   Ian BARBOUR, *When Science Meets Religion*, 20.

31   Ian BARBOUR, *When Science Meets Religion*, 3.

32   Stephen HAWKING, *A Brief History of Time*, 192.

33   TEILHARD DE CHARDIN, The Phenomenon of Man (New York: Harper & Row Publishers, 1961), 259.

34   Pope JOHN PAUL II, "Letter to George V. Coyne," M 8., *See* Phillip M. Thompson, *Between Science and Religion* (Maryland: Lexington Books, 2009), 188.

35   Pope JOHN PAUL II, *Fides et Ratio*, 88.

36   Pope FRANCIS, at *Symposium Sponsored by Vatican Observatory*, 18 September 2015.

37   CHANDRASEKHARAN, *Understanding the Universe*, 203.

38   Ibid., 205.

39   Pope FRANCIS, *Encyclical Laudato Si*, 246.

V. LISTENING TO THE CRY OF THE POOR

Chapter 14

Pope Francis' Challenge
Listening to the Cry of the Marginalized

Paul Thelakat
Editor, Sathyadeepam, Kochi, Kerala

1. Man of the Periphery

Shortly after his election to Papacy, Pope Francis made an apparently scandalous statement that shocked me. It was something that even the sharpest critics of the church would not have made: "Court is the leprosy of papacy." He refuses to enter the court and its palace; he stays at the periphery. It is in the Papal court that the recently revealed sexual scandal of Fr. Marcial Maciel was kept under wraps by top Vatican officials. The harassing of many innocent Christians even by princely prelates was part of the cover up. Are we in a Church of the Grand Inquisitor where you have a purely ideological religion, in which there are, as Dostoevsky's Zossima complains, "no more Churches left…, but only clergymen and magnificent church buildings."[1]

By his election on 13 March 2013 Cardinal Jorge Mario Bergoglio was brought to centre stage in the Church, but he preferred to remain at the periphery. That was a scandalous behaviour of defiance and refusal. As for him, he is in the shoes of the carpenter, who was always at the periphery. He did not get a place to be born; the event of his birth was with the cattle, not a house of human culture "for there was no place in the inn." He was an outcaste to the culture and language of his time. He became a fugitive running away for fear of being killed. He lacked an abode, a hearth and place of his own. He had no land, he was always a migrant.

His way of life merited banishment from the land as a heretic and an anti-national. The culture and the religion of his place cast him out to be crucified. On the cross he cried out "*Eli, Eli, lema sabachthani?*" that is, "My God, my God, why have you forsaken me?" (Mt 27:46). It is first of all a cry apparently of Godlessness. It is cry of the God-forsaken, or the cry of a man in whose world God is dead. A world in which God is absent is a violent world devoid of the hospitality of ethics. It is indeed a world of war on the other. Who is the Christian who does not feel himself an atheist in moments of his dark night? The history is no more shadowed by eternity; it is the loss of the sense of history itself.

2. The Outlook from the Periphery

Pope Francis took a stand with the marginalized who are at the periphery of human exstence. Those cast out into the periphery are the women, the poor, the low caste, the underprivileged, the sick, the orphaned, the homosexuals, the third gender. These are the people who cry to "God why have you forsaken me." It is taking a position with the godless. These men and women feel the agony of the absence of God. In other words, the absence of justice is the absence of the divine. These arethe 'exhausted subjects" with the loss of the Father, human beings have become 'less "identities" than journeys', transitory beings who have a collective, unreflected 'passion', with no *Heimat* of face-to-face human relations. This situation manifests the 'death of God' in the sense that the 'love of the Father' cannot be reconstructed from a social memory which has been undergoing the most devastating 'cultural forgetting'. The words of the Pope "better to be an atheist than a hypocritical Catholic" therefore become very relevant. "This is true of the individual man, of an entire nation, of all humanity, of the mending of all being whose corruption always proceeds from self-oblivion."[2]

It is here that the Pope makes a relevant 'cultural mourning' for the lost Father, a theodicy (justification of goodness) which brings back an ethical home. The lost father is one of hospitality, who himself is among the outcasts in his only son Jesus Christ. It is the god of the world who has cast them out of the world. The only way out from the crisis rests in the ability to recover and identify with the loving 'Other'. The cultural situation of the 'silenced Father' posits challenges for theology; theology has to 'mourn' in its language on God. Mourning entails critical understanding of the self and the world. The Church and Christians have to learn to stand in the periphery and witness mourning prayer engendering a grammar of life of other centredness into the secular subject without colonizing it. Discourse of periphery is an alternative to globalization.

Christians need to see 'Christ' in the 'other' in a genuine way. It is not only suffering which is common, as a consequence of the self's becoming 'ungrounded', but Love is also shared, which gives rebirth. Love is indeed solely redemptive. This latter is the claim of ecce homo. 'Love is the time and space in which 'I' assumes the right to be extraordinary... I am, in love, at the zenith of subjectivity. Faith states the Cross as the highpoint of the union with the Father, the subject is a 'being toward death'. The Christian God in 'suffering' emerges as the real Other to the self. "My God, my God, why have you forsaken me?" What solitude has not been haunted by this cry and this silence! Christian suffering is shareable: this is the first way in which Christianity has effected a revolution in the approach to suffering. Shareable, first of all, between humans and Christ, who, in assuming it, confers upon it extraordinary dignity, at the interface of the human and the divine; shareable next, and consequently, among human beings themselves, who only allow themselves to look for a way to relieve it on the condition that they can look it in the face, give it a name, and interpret it. The 'death of God', in terms of the suffering of the human self, is seen as a condition of rebirth through thought and action.

'...Compassion brings about a historically unprecedented moral solidarity with vulnerable humankind. For two thousand years, right up to the most recent Christian humanism, Christian morality comes to drink at the source of this compassion, and one can only salute the generosity of the works that put this compassion into practice. I have seen for myself, notably in the care for the handicapped, the extraordinary vitality of Christians, and Christian institutions dedicated to compassion, that courageously supplement the weaknesses of legislator and politics.'[3] Does Jesus in his suffering speak only to human nature? Son of God, but allowing himself to be annihilated, does he not turn the divine itself to nothing? Theological debates leave the question open. Is it possible to take it up again today? The question remains: is the suffering to death only due to Christ's humanity, or does it affect the very nature of his divinity? And thus of Divinity? After the Last Supper, and the night before the Passion, doesn't Christ tell Philip: "He that hath seen me hath seen the Father?" Protestants and Orthodox apparently attend more closely to this "descent" (of the Father himself) "into the lowest earthly regions."[4]

3. The Malady of the World

At the heart of the world is the crisis the disappearance of the Father as an all permeating cultural loss. 'Homeland' in all its traditional sense is lost. Technology and politics have increasingly detached us from our natural habitats and have turned us into nomads once again. In a world where the effects of globalization render us homeless and a resurgent tribalism threatens to give us a home in which there is violent suppression of difference of the other. Homelessness in an unprecedented scale, rootlessness to an unprecedented depth provided an atmosphere conducive to the rise of modern totalitarianism. Human beings have become 'less "identities" than journeys, transitory beings. The medium of history has been radically altered."To lack infinitude is despairing, reductionism, narrowness."[5] As in Samuel Beckett it 'totalises despair'. It is a situation of 'symbolic mourning' and apply it to the situation of the 'lost Father'. This 'madness', the loss of the genuine Father's genuine love, "along with the questioning of authority, the law, and values – which has been interpreted as an attack on the role of the father – the loss of habitat that characterises our fate undermines the original place, assaults maternal support, and threatens to destroy identity itself.'"[6]

It engenders totalitarianism, by corrupting the 'Father's love' in Nazism, in Khaliphate, Hindutva and communism, produced the fatal inability to trust in the historical 'Other'. Arendt creates a veritable anthropology, even a political psychology, of totalitarian massification by describing the destruction of the psychic space of humans under totalitarian regimes, proof of which may be found in the fact that when movements lose their power, their formerly fanatical supporters immediately stop believing in the dogma and throw themselves instead into the quest for another promising fiction.[7] Place has become one of pain itself because of the original uprooting –the dehabitation and the primordial separation. The symbolic mourning applies to the situation of the 'lost Father'. Pope Francis intends to anchor his reflections on the direct experience of the true life and in the periphery. "This is really very important to me: the need to become acquainted with reality by experience, to spend time walking on the periphery in order really to become acquainted with the reality and life-experiences of people. If this does not happen we then run the risk of being abstract ideologists or fundamentalists, which is not healthy."[8] This unhealthy tendency is already visible in certain areas of the church in dealing with the situations of uprootedness and nostalgia. They subordinate justice to freedom. Such politics of homecoming can be accused of ontological chauvinism and ethical insensitivity.

"Symbolic loss refers to the loss of an attachment to a political ideology or religious creed, or to some aspect or fragment of one, and to the inner work of coming to terms with this kind of loss. In this sense it resembles mourning. However, in the case of symbolic loss the object that is lost is, ordinarily, socio-historical, cognitive, and collective. The lost object is a symbol or rather a system of symbols.'"[9] There is death of language which creates 'Semiotic Passion' as an anticipation of the 'ontic' suffering of the subject and the present cultural conditions. This is initiated by 'an analysis of religion in absentia'. Consumerism or 'economical growth' as the end of culture with the same force denies finitude, individual fragility, and death, its own transience. Our post-Freudian culture has created a hyperactive superficial symbolism though, in practice, it only distracts its 'exhausted subjects' from their 'ontological' pain. We are at the cross-roads of the fiascos of the Enlightenment. The tragedy of concentration camps opens: 'Everything has to be measured by the possibility of Auschwitz.'[10] It is not a tragedy that conservative theologian emeritus Pope expresses veiled criticism that the progressive pastoral pope succumbs to "the dictatorship of the *Zeitgeist*" (cfr. tribute to the late Cardinal Joachim Meisner by Pope-emeritus Benedict XVI on July 17, 2017). The church still lives in a situation monologue in the centre and such monologues cannot be proved lies except under mortal crime of death in the church. The crisis of modernity is an opportunity of to get rid of soliloquies and be cured by 'going before the crisis' of multilingual discourse. Pope Francis wrote, "The Church is called to come out of herself and to go to the peripheries, not only geographically, but also the existential peripheries: the mystery of sin, of pain, of injustice, of ignorance and indifference to religion, of intellectual currents, and of all forms of misery."[11] It was imposition of a soliloquy, and modernity calls for polyphony of dialogical discourse. Truth will arrive in from the bridges and the peripheries of dialogue. The semantic content of the notion of periphery is quite wide and obviously not limited to urban marginalities, although the image of the misery of the suburbs of Buenos Aires certainly is always in the background."Francis uses 'peripheral' in different ways, always positive. He warns the church not to become so fixated on the centre that it neglects the periphery—those people who live on the edge of mainstream society, whether within the economically advanced nations, or globally. That 'edgy' quality might result from poverty, from racial categories, or from sexuality and life-style. Although, not calling for any kind of relativism, he urges the church to reach out to everyone."[12] "There is a tension between the centre and the periphery. We must get out of ourselves and go toward the periphery. We must avoid the spiritual disease of the Church that can become self-referential: when this happens, the Church itself becomes sick. It's true that accidents can happen when you go out into the street, as can happen to any man or woman. But if the Church remains closed onto itself, self-referential, it grows old. Between a Church that goes into the street and gets into an accident and a Church that is sick with self-referentiality, I have no doubts in preferring the first."[13] Modern humanity is both homely and homeless at the same time. We dwell, and yet we do not dwell; we belong to being, yet we are separated from being; we are in place, and yet we find ourselves displaced; we are home, and yet nevertheless remain homeless. Exodus is a fundamental and necessary element of homecoming. The Christian stands between home and homelessness, between Ulysses and Abraham. The story of Abraham's departure from home is emblematic of the self's journey from interiority to exteriority.

4. The Theology of the Crucified

The cultural situation of the 'silenced Father' posits the challenge of theology. This need to recover the lost universalism of the 'Father' is the moment for the *theologia crucis*. There is only one way out of the crisis, if the ability to identify with the loving 'Other' is recovered. For the theology of the cross the categorical imperative is failed history itself. The self-sufficient Enlightenment replaces the lost universal, compromised 'autonomous' reason, with the eschatological scandal of the forgotten victims. It is at the time experience of one who is my silenced brother. 'The starry sky above and the moral law within', which inspired genuine awe in Kant, is replaced by the memory-lit sky of the victims of the past wars and atrocities, and seen as God interrupting human morals from without.

Instead of compromised human reason, it is apocalyptic time or apocalyptic consciousness that transforms history. Pope Francis stands to contribute to a second anthropological revolution, as these questions bring about a genuine distance from the post-modern situation. 'To give meaning to suffering and begin the associative speech that will transform malady and death into a narrative of life, a new life: this is how the value of analytical interpretation as pardon can be defined. If you prefer, you can call this experience a healing. An endless one.'[14]

Pope Francis' discourse sounds as a critical appraisal of the world order or disorder. The Papal narrative on the periphery takes several theoretical approaches to the international relations. Today globalization implies an increasing "westernization" of the economic, technological and communicational patterns on interactions in the world. By world politics it is rather meant a more pluralistic system of the relation between religions. Globalization is sometimes represented in terms of religions capitalizing on global "vectors". The tools of liberal globalization—ironically—are seen as means for promoting and disseminating a radical anti-Western ideology. Western technology is seen in combination with an instrumental approach to transnationalism. It is opposed by the surge of the terrorism of khaliphate in Iraq and Syria. It takes more and more the form of a "sacred violence."

The global order decimates cultures and differences imposing the sameness every where. Global market does away with local differences to the point of a totalitarian imposition of Western ways. The universal claims of religions has been put under stress in the case of the so-called "transnational religions", meaning "religious traditions with universal pretensions and global ambitions."[15] Religions are supposed to be the potentially universal glue for an increasingly post-global world, where identities are being crafted as societal structures that resist globalization. Different religions in the world will be essential for there to be some overarching sense of order and respect. The worldview that is emerging for the global world, therefore, is in essence a kind of higher order.[16] Although, the idea of a "higher order" becoming a shared worldview is speculative, "yet the necessities of global interaction may force it upon us. The threat of globalization is that it tries to get everyone doing the same thing and thinking alike. In some ways the world is becoming too compact. The idea of a global higher order has the advantage of not imposing a single ethic or ethos on the rest of the world, except for the higher-order pattern of civility. It may be the coming global civilization."[17]

The "welcome of and advocacy for the marginalized" is the key component of God's hospitality in the Christian Scriptures. For Francis, the worst effect of widespread inequality is exclusion. He writes this: "It is no longer simply about exploitation and oppression, but something new. Exclusion ultimately has to do with what it means to be a part of the society in which we live; those excluded are no longer society's underside or its fringes or its disenfranchised—they are no longer even a part of it."[18] He says: "When a society ... is willing to leave a part of itself on the fringes, no political programmes or resources spent on law enforcement or surveillance systems can indefinitely guarantee tranquility."[19] He is critical of the economic theory of free market system. "Some people continue to defend trickle-down theories which assume that economic growth, encouraged by a free market, will inevitably succeed in bringing about greater justice and inclusiveness in the world." And he calls this view an "opinion, which has never been confirmed by the facts."[20] He decries "ideologies which defend the absolute autonomy of the marketplace,"[21] and says "no to a financial system which rules rather than serves."[22] Human dignity should be absolute, but the current financial system sees money and power as absolute and human dignity as relative.

"To sustain a lifestyle which excludes others, or to sustain enthusiasm for that selfish ideal, a globalization of indifference has developed. Almost without being aware of it, we end up being incapable of feeling compassion at the outcry of the poor, weeping for other people's pain, and feeling a need to help them. ... The culture of prosperity deadens us; we are thrilled if the market offers us something new to purchase. In the meantime all those lives stunted for lack of opportunity seem a mere spectacle; they fail to move us."[23] Hospitality is also practised in a way that "deforms" it from its purpose when "it is practised as a way of caring for so called 'inferior people' by those who are more advantaged and able to prove their superiority by being 'generous,'" a model of hospitality of the 'lady bountiful.'[24] Without the ability to love "man becomes the living sepulchre of himself, and what yet survives is the mere husk of what once he was."[25] "Love is the extremely difficult realization that something other than oneself is real. Love, and so art and morals, is the discovery of reality."[26]

For Biblical scholar Laurie Brink, Jesus' encounters with the Syro-Phoenician woman (Mark 7:24–30) and the Samaritan woman at the well (John 4) reveal that "we are always the other encountering the other," sometimes host and sometimes guest.[27] "Hospitality is the practice of God's welcome by reaching across difference to participate in God's actions bringing justice and healing to our world in crisis."[28] Hospitality as "unity without uniformity"[29] "the best experiences of hospitality are often those in which guests take on some of the roles of hosts and hosts also experience the presence of their guests as refreshment and gift."[30] Russell concurs: "Hospitality is a two-way street of mutual ministry where we often exchange roles and learn the most from those whom we considered 'different' or 'other.'"[31] To shelter the other in one's own land or home, to tolerate the presence of the landless and homeless on the ancestral soil, so jealously, so meanly loved – is the criterion of humanity.

5. Crying Protest Contained in Prayer

Everything has to be measured by the possibility of Auschwitz, the marginalsied and the outcast. The Passion is not just there as an object of our investigation, but is a challenging and unsettling fact for all of us, interrogating us without mercy, questioning our understanding of God and ourselves. The truth is that God is the only real and authoritative iconoclast.[32] The epiphany of a face is holy language. Awakening of the soul in the excess of evil. The excess of evil by which it is a surplus in the world is also our impossibility of accepting it. The soul which, awakened by evil, should manifest an absolute resistance by its apparition, its epiphany, it opposes to all evil powers.

Pope Francis makes an option to be an iconoclast. He is for "an epochal shift... a revolution." He challenged "lukewarm Christians" and "couch potato" Christians to engage much more energetically in spreading the Church's message, not to "take refuge... in a cozy life," but to get beyond our "comfort zones" and live with greater "apostolic fervor." He challenged his Church to be more forthrightly, "poor, and for the poor." He challenged his own fellow bishops to be "Men who love... poverty, simplicity and austerity of life." He asked Brazilian bishops bluntly, "Are we still a Church capable of warming hearts?" Cardinal Timothy Dolan of New York, reacting to the pope's challenges, told an interviewer, "I find myself examining my own conscience... on style, on simplicity, on lots of things." Pope Francis warned Vatican diplomats-in-training that "careerism is leprosy." He challenged a global culture in which "money... for the mighty of this earth, is more important than people." "I prefer a Church which is bruised, hurting and dirty because it has been out on the streets, rather than a Church which is unhealthy from being confined and from clinging to its own security" he wrote to the Synod of Bishops. "I don't want token consultations," he explained in an interview, "but real consultations." The five words that have come to define both the promise and the limits of Francis' papacy came in the form of a question: "Who am I to judge?" He also recognizes that Catholic doctrine, as it is currently formulated, cannot be made to justify women as priests. "The feminine genius is needed wherever we make important decisions," he has said. Pope Francis has made no secret of his intention to radically reform the administrative structures of the Catholic Church, which he regards as insular, imperious, and bureaucratic. He understands that in a hyper-kinetic world, inward-looking and self-obsessed leaders are a liability.

The Pope addressed the leaders of the Roman Curia — the Cardinals and other officials who are charged with running the church's Byzantine network of administrative bodies. The Pope's message to his colleagues was blunt. Leaders are susceptible to an array of debilitating maladies, including arrogance, intolerance, myopia, and pettiness. When those diseases go untreated, the organization itself is enfeebled. To have a healthy church, we need healthy leaders, not leaders who hide indolent laziness of silencing women and the weaker sections with the masks of ghar vapasi communalisms and oriental traditions.

The Pope was not looking for management experts but spiritual men and women. He doesn't even have a "leadership philosophy" – instead, he focuses on one priority only: he is a follower of Jesus, and his Jesuit formation helps him to follow Jesus more closely. "Today's world stands in great need of witnesses, not so much of teachers but rather of witnesses. It's not so much about speaking, but rather speaking with our whole lives."[33] "How much filth there is in the Church," said Cardinal Joseph Ratzinger during a memorable Way of the Cross at the Colosseum (Ninth station, Via Crucis, 2005). How can one begin to change the Church? "You and I are the starting point," said Mother Teresa of Calcutta to an interviewer (quoted by Pope Francis, Prayer Vigil, World Youth Day, July 27, 2013). "I can start with my life being illuminated by God's grace."

Leadership diseases Pope names as narcissism, excessive busyness, mental and emotional "petrification", excessive planning and functionalism, poor coordination, "leadership Alzheimer's disease." Rivalry and vainglory, existential schizophrenia, gossiping, grumbling, and back-biting, idolizing superiors are to be cured not by management executives but one must be open to a profound paradox about great leadership: it is deeply spiritual. It is simply following the passion, the cry of the crucified. "Crying' is a powerful metaphor. It would be worth developing it as one of the central images of theology's 'post-modern' reading of the Passion. It is not forcing it to relate it to the 'semiotic' state of language. 'Crying contained in prayer' can be seen when the ethical language of a culture is being formed. It recalls… language being in ferment, the struggle to mature into expression, when 'love is neither merely semiotic nor merely Symbolic.'[34] The Passion presented is the interruption of the narcissistic claim for 'self-redemption' or narcissistic-suffering. "'I' exist if, and only if, I suffer; the feeling of pain alone makes me exist; it is pain that makes my existence meaningful; without it my being would lack employment, utter boredom."[35] "Again and again prayer is a cry of lament from the depths of the spirit. But this cry is in no sense a vague, rambling moan. It calls out loudly, insistently. Nor is it merely a wish or desire, no matter how fervent. It is a supplication. The language of prayer finds its purpose and justification in the silently concealed face of God. Hence the lament, supplication, crying and protest contained in prayer, as also a silent accusation of the wordless cry, can never simply be translated and dissolved into a discourse.'[36] Being attuned to the cry in the society and the church and responding to the value of analytical interpretation is pardon and this experience is a healing. Prayer and hearing of prayer are not impotent and sterile unless manifests through the ethical deed. Speaking to the other is a form of prayer. "Ethics is an optic, such that everything I know of God and everything I can hear of his word and reasonably say to him must find an ethical expression."[37]

Endnotes

1   Mikhail BAKHTIN, *The Dialogic Imagination*, ed. and trans., Michael Holquist,Vadim Liapunov, and Kenneth Brostrom, Austin: University of Texas Press Slavic Series, 1982, p. 72.

2   E. LEVINAS, Published in *Orot ha-Teshuvah, Jerusalem: Or Etzion*, 5th ed, 1970, 15:10.

3   Julia KRISTEVA, *This Incredible Need to Believe*, Columbia University Press, New York 2009, pp. 91-92.

4   *Ibid.*, p. 93.

5   J. KRISTEVA, *Tales of Love*, Columbia University Press, New York 1987, pp. 99-100.

6   Julia KRISTEVA, *Hannah Arendt*, Columbia University Press, New York 2001, p. 195.

7   *Ibid.*, p. 137.

8   Philip JENKINS. "A Peripheral Vision." Available online: http://www.patheos.com/blogs/ anxiousbench/2014/02/a-peripheral-visionp. 4.

9   Peter HOMANS, 'Introduction', in *The Ambiguity of Mourning and Memory at Century's End*, Edited by Peter Homans, University Pressof Virginia, Charlottesville, London 2000, p. 20.

10   Johann Baptist METZ, 'Christians and Jews After Auschwitz', in *The Emergent Church*, translated by Peter Mann, Crossroad Publishing Company, New York, 1981, p. 21.

11   Pope FRANCIS. "Remarks at the pre-Conclave General Congregation meetings of the Cardinals." Available online: HYPERLINK "http://en.radiovaticana.va/storico/2013/03/27/ bergoglios_intervention_a_"   http://en.radiovaticana.va/storico/2013/03/27/bergoglios_ intervention_a_ diagnosis_of_the_problems_in_the_church/en1-677269

12   Pope JOHN PAUL II. "Discorso." 16 October 1978. Available online: http://www.vatican. va/holy_father/john_paul_ii/speeches/   1978/documents/hf_jp-ii_spe_19781016_primo-saluto_it.html

13   Andrea TORNIELLI. "Tentazione sudamericana per il primo Papa extraeuropeo." Interview with Cardinal Jorge Bergoglio. La Stampa, 2 March, 2013.

14   J. KRISTEVA, *Intimate Revolt, The Powers and Limits of Psychoanalysis*, Columbia University Press, New York 2002, p. 24.

15   Mark JUERGENSMEYER, *Global Religions*, New York: Oxford University Press, 2003, p. 7.

16   *Ibid.*, p. 124.

17   Pasquale FERRARA, *Global Religions and International Relations: A Diplomatic Perspective*, New York: Palgrave MacMillan, 2014. p. 131.

18   Pope FRANCIS "*Evangelii Gaudium: Apostolic Exhortation on the Proclamation of the Gospel in Today's World.*"Vatican.va, 24 November 2013, no. 2.

19   *Ibid.*, 2, p. 59.

20   *Ibid.*, 2, p. 54.

21   *Ibid.*, 2, p. 56.

22   *Ibid.*, 2, p. 57.

23   *Ibid.,* 2, p. 54.

24   *Ibid.* 20, Letty M. RUSSELL, *Just Hospitality: God's Welcome in a World of Difference*, Edited by J. Shannon Clarkson and Kate M. Ott. Louisville: Westminster John Knox Press, 2009, pp. 80–81.

25   Percy Bysshe SHELLEY, "On Love," Romanticism: *An Anthology*, ed. Duncan Wu, Oxford: Blackwell, 1994, p. 860-861.

26   Iris MURDOCH, "The Sovereignty of Good Over Other Concepts," *Existentialists and Mystics: Writings on Philosophy and Literature,* ed. Peter J. Conradi, New York: Allen Lane, 1998, p. 215.

27   Laurie BRINK, OP. "In Search of the Biblical Foundations of Prophetic Dialogue: Engaging a Hermeneutics of Otherness."*Missiology*, 41, 2013, p. 19.

28   M. Russell LETTY, *Just Hospitality: God's Welcome in a World of Difference*, Edited by J. Shannon Clarkson andKate M. Ott. Louisville: Westminster John Knox Press, 2009, p. 19.

29   *Ibid.*, p. 80.

30   Jessica WROBLESKI, *The Limits of Hospitality*, Collegeville: Liturgical Press, 2012. p. 73.

31   M. Russell LETTY, *Just Hospitality*, p. 20.

32   Rowan WILLIAMS, *Open to Judgement, Sermons and Addresses*, Darton, Longman & Todd, London 2004, pp. 109-110.

33   Pope FRANCIS, address St. Peter's Square, May 18, 2013.

34   Kelly OLIVER, *Reading Kristeva: Unraveling the Double-Bind*, Indiana University Press, Bloomington, 1993, p. 122.

35   J. KRISTEVA, *This Incredible Need to Believe*, p. 91.

36   Johann Baptist METZ and Karl RAHNER, *The Courage to Pray*, translated by Sarah O' Brian Thowig, Crossroad, New York 1981, p. 13.

37   E. LEVINAS, *Basic Philosophical Writings*. Ed. Adriaan T. Peperzak, Simon Critchley, and Robert Bernasconi. Bloomington: Indiana University Press, 1996, p. 17.

Chapter 15

Pope Francis' Plea
Critiquing the Capitalist Order

Victor Ferrao
Dean, Rachol Seminary, Goa

'Capitalism is terrorism against all of humanity' says Pope Francis.[1] How are we to understand this unprecedented and scathing critique of capitalism from the head of the Catholic Church? His holiness names the excesses of global capitalism as 'the dung of the devil.'[2] Maybe someone might describe Pope Francis as an anti-Oedipus. He does not seem to fit the mould of Popes of old. He has brought in fresh life in the Catholic Church. There is a discernable Francis effect that is sweeping the catholic world and beyond like a storm. In this short study, an attempt is made to understand this strong teaching on capitalism through the prism of the work French thinkers, Gilles Deleuze and Felix Gauttari.[3] These thinkers offer us different modes of thinking. We cannot apply them entirely but have to modify their findings. This means their thought stands in need of evangelization. Perhaps, using the conceptual apparatus of these thinkers, we may be enabled to understand the evils of contemporary capitalism that has teamed up with race, caste, patriarchy, consumerism, anthropocentrism and religions and unearth how it is reproducing a dehumanising world order. Several scholars have already celebrated the unbound and free character of the thought of Deleuze and Gauttari. Their thought is said to be free from the burdens of representation, primacy of cogito, of intentional consciousness of phenomenology as well as pathology of the Oedipus-complex.[4] This does not mean other critical ideas of Freud and Lacan within the field of Psychoanalysis are of no use to understand the earth shattering critique of Pope Francis. We shall also travel the road of the thinking pursued by these thinkers and critically follow their analysis of desire to understand how it is manipulated by capitalist world order. Capitalist driven world is profoundly unequal. It debases both its victims as well as its perpetrators[5] and has a devastating impact on our common home.[6] It continuously produces and maintains its unequal power hierarchies. The pope rightly teaches that trickle-down economics fails as it only keeps the poor waiting.[7] Pope Francis has rightly put our focus at the centre of its reproductive power by naming it as the worship of the God of money. This worship of money is driven by our desire. This is why the analysis of desire[8] that drives the worship of the God of money can open several windows on the ruthless manner in which capitalism reproduces and grows. Staying within this analysis of desire, we have to analyse our dynamic becomings. The capitalist society drives our becoming human that is unbecoming of all Humans. Having studied our becoming, we shall try to manifest Christic becomings that can become catholic responses to the dehumanising capitalist order.

1. Cartographies of Desire

a. Surrogating the Desire

Desire is viewed as the root of all suffering by Buddha. Desire for wealth and power is certainly the cause of the misery of humanity. Desire is studied with profound depth by Psychoanalysis. Sigmund Freud resolves the restlessness of our desire through the Oedipus complex. Persuaded by castration phobia, the child has to oediepalise (let go its desire) and desire the desire (sublimate) of the father. This means child has to become the father. There is no other choice for the poor child. The law of the father becomes the only model of living an adult life. Though, the theory of Freud has it merits, we can see how its oedipal solution of the desire is reproducing the desire of the father.That is why one who owns the phallus in a society sets the desire of that society. Maybe our caste laden society can be seen as trapped into a desire of the Brahmins. Everyone seems to mimic (sorrogate) the desire of the Brahmin. It just demonstrates that somehow caste castrates us in our country. It rates and ranks us and we fail to be ourselves as we chase the desire to become a Brahmin. Following this line of thought, we may be enabled to understand the phyllo-centrism of the capitalist society. In a capitalist society everyone has to chase the Phallus of the big Other. This mimicking of the desire of the big Other of the capitalist Other is one that reproduces and maintains the fertility of capitalism and is at the heart of the worship of the God of Money. In some way, the Big Other of the capitalist order becomes the God of money. Pope seems to put this teaching with Gospel-centric wisdom when he says, 'money must serve and not rule.'[9]

b. The Insatiable Desire

Freudian resolution of the desire only reproduces the desire of the one who owns the Phallus in the society. In a capitalist society, the Phallus is owned by the big Other. This is why capitalism keeps on reproducing itself by surrogating its desire in its subjects. Hence, French Psychoanalyst Jacques Lacan attempts to revisit the Oedipal tangle of Freud. Lacan views human desire as insatiable. He asserts that it can never be satisfied. This means that our desire is poised to fail.[10] Caste castrates us in India. We cannot become Brahmins. We are simply surrogates. Similarly, those subjected to the desire of the big Other in a capitalist society cannot reach the fulfilment of their desire. But this frustration of our desire produces a lack. This sense of lack produces further desire. Thus, a capitalist driven society entangles its subjects in a chain of unlimited desires that can never reach fulfilment. This is why the lack that drives the desire for more drives our consumerist and materialist society. Hence, Pope Francis is right. Capitalism is terrorising all humanity. The dynamism of capitalism is based on circulation and accumulation of wealth that always gets attracted to the rich and the powerful. Capitalist driven world is a stereotypical and boring. There are no real choices. We enjoy only those freedoms that are allowed by the capitalist order of things.

c. Anti-Oedipal Desire

Deleuze and Gauttari donot accept the oedipal resolution of our restless desire. They do not view desire as lacking as Lacan would want us to believe. They suggest that desire is anti-oedipal. It refuses to surrender to the law of the father. It does not have to mimic the phyllo-centrism of the dominant big Other. One can choose to ride one's unique desires or even try several other waves of desire.[11] This means desire is productive. It lacks nothing and does not have to oedipalize. It is a positive force. This opening of desire to a wild ride cannot be fully reconciled with the position of Pope Francis. But the fact that desire does not have to surrender to the desire of the dominant other already opens the possibility of choice that can reject the worship of the God of money and prepare room for an effective response to the terror unleashed by capitalism on all humanity. This means somehow the work of Deleuze and Gauttari set us free from the phallic logic that chains us to the Oedipus complex. Phallic logic prohibits what one desires. One cannot have one's desire. One has to mimic the desire of the dominant big Other. Deleuze and Gauttari open the way of breaking this bondage to the desire of the big Other, the worship of the God of money. Thus, desire as productive can be channelled to contest as well as seek an emancipative and Christian response to the heartless capitalism solely driven by a heartless profit making market principle.

2. Cartographies of Human Becoming
a. Libidinal Becomings

Freud stays within the realm of anthropocentrism when he teaches that human beings are afflicted by an unconscious. He seems to teach that the unconscious is biological and is embedded in each person. It is like an iceberg and we cannot fully know it. It rules our conscious life. We are all moved by the unconscious in search of the satisfaction of our drive for pleasure (libido).[12] This pleasure is chiefly physical. The capitalist society is a libidinal society. It provides unlimited ways of exciting the libido of a person. Freud provides us with the developmental theory of an individual that is based on the libido. We may find how consumerism that is embedded within a capitalist order often reinforces our fixations in the developmental stages identified by Freud. The personality structures that Freud presents can also drive this imprisonment to the capitalist driven consumerism. Freud says that a human person is composed of three structures which he calls Id, ego and superego. We can notice how from the Freudian point of view, a capitalist society is condemned to the unlimited satisfaction of the id. It means the capitalist society keeps us perpetual children who cry for the satisfaction of their thirst for libido. Hence, the worship of the God of money is oppressive and promotes the infantalization of humanity but stays within the bondages of anthropocentrism.

b. Lack Driven Becomings

Lacan liberates Freud from his biological reductionisms of libido. He expands the operation of libido. It is not merely biological pleasure. It is more. He calls it jouissance. With Lacan pleasure drive becomes unlimited enjoyment. It can be derived from anything. If my rival fails in a project, it brings me pleasure. With this expansion of the domain of pleasure, we can also understand Lacan's transformation of the nature of unconscious. He teaches that the unconscious is not within us but is between us. He teaches that it is the discourse of the other.It triggers in us mimetic desire. We imitate the desire of the other. This is foundational to the race of competition which is the driving force of capitalism. He views the self as a lacking self. It is the lack that is constantly born in relation to the desire of the other that is driving the capitalist society. To understand this thirst irrupting from a lack, we will have to enter his teaching about the unconscious. He says that the unconscious is structured like a language.[13] It is by becoming a speaker that the self that is struck by a relationship of lack is thrown into a world of the unconscious. Capitalist order also works like a signification system (language) and therefore merges with the unconscious that afflicts each individual placed within it. Thus, Lacanian analysis also stays within the limitation of anthropocentrism and does not seem to provide enough resources to reject the worship of the God of money.

c. Machine Like Becomings

The biological unconscious of Freud and the language structured unconscious of Lacan is replaced by Deleuze and Gauttari. They teach that the unconscious is constructed by us in relationship with our society and the world. They do not represent the unconscious but are interested in what it does. Our unconscious is a productive machine which drives our desire.[14] It simply connects and disconnects us to people and things. The desiring production that connects the pen to the paper with the help of the hands and the mind of the author in the course of writing is an example of desiring machine. Writing transforms the pen, paper, mind and hands of the author into a machine. Several such connections are possible. We have many such machines operating within our bodies. Besides these, our bodies connect to other bodies and things and become desiring machines. Capitalism is one gigantic desiring machine that connects several other smaller desiring machines. We humans connect ourselves to these machines and drive our becomings. But we are not condemned to the desiring machines of capitalism. I do not have to take a MacDonald sandwich and connect it to my mouth and become a desiring machine. The moment mouth connects to the sandwich it disconnects to another desiring machine that makes me a speaker. Thus, it is within these limitless possibilities of connections and disconnections that Deleuze and Gauttari finds the emancipative potentials for human beings becoming free from the limitations of racism, casteism, patriarchy, anthropocentrism, etc. From among these limitless becomings, they propose three types of becomings: becoming women, becoming animal, becoming child.[15] These becomings lead us to become a minoritarian. We may find resources within these kind of teachings of Deleuze and Gauttari to reject the God of money and abandon the becomings that are forced on us by the capitalist order. Similarly, we will have resources within this mode of thinking to embrace Christic becomings.

3. Cartographies of Our Response to Capitalist Order

a. Christic Becomings

Deleuze and Gauttari are radicals. They need to be modified and adapted and within this modified perspective, we can find a catholic response to the exploitative capitalist order. Pope Francis has rightly called it a terrorist order because the inequalities that it creates also creates the terrorist violence. Terrorist violence is a reactive violence to the invisible violence of the capitalist order. Deleuze and Gauttari teach that becomings do not mimic. They imitate no one. It is here that we have problems with the work of Deleuze and Gauttari. We require the imitating of our Lord Jesus Christ. This is fundamental to Christianity. How are we to remove this blockade? Is it possible to adopt their doctrine of becoming? Maybe there is a way. They teach that all becomings are molecular. Becomings cannot be molar. Molar becomings are logocentric and fixed into sameness. In fact no authentic becomings can be molar. Molecular becomings are dynamic and not static and fixed. They are never the same. Now that there is no one way but several catholic ways of imitating Christ who is God and Saviour, it is possible to molecularize in our imitation of Christ. There are limitless Christic becomings forus to choose. Hence, becoming Christic is a way of rejecting the God of money that is promoted by the capitalist order. Becoming Christic is both plural as well as minoritarian. It is an option for the minority as well as a choice to be a minority like Jesus Christ. It is choice to stay on the margins of society. It can be a great antidote to the call to stay in the limelight which is a temptation to become the majoritarian. Becoming a majoritarian is call to follow the crowd and become faceless.

b. Becoming the Body-of-Christ

I buy therefore I AM is the subject of the capitalist order. Capitalist order is a signification system wherein one becomes what one has. Deleuze and Gauttari can illumine this kind of becomings for us. We connect and disconnect in any form of becoming. We connect to capitalist mode of becoming by disconnecting to other forms of becomings. Let us take an example. The capitalist order has destroyed our ecology. But to save our planet earth they suggest that we have to down-size our demography. This means to connect to what they describe as planet saving capitalist order, we have to delink and plug human fertility. In a similar manner, in order to connect to the capitalist God of money we have to disconnect from the triune God and the catholic community in several ways. Pope Francis reading the signs of the times reinterprets the fifth commandment, 'Thou shall not kill' as 'Thou shall not do an economy of exclusion and inequality.'[16] Hence, if we ride our desire and direct it to connect to the living body of Christ, we can become the vibrant body-of-Christ. Pope exhorts us to overcome what he calls globalization of indifference and invites us to resist the new tyranny of the market.[17] But to link to Christ and his living body, one has to disconnect in several ways one's linkages to the capitalist order and completely delink one's connections with the God of money. Pope Francis being the Vicar of Christ becomes the nodal point for us to bring about this communion. This becoming of the Body-of-Christ is not inward looking but is one that is leading us to connect with God's creation and other humans so that we can together becomes God's family saved in Christ.

c. Becomings of the Kingdom

Catholic becomings animated by the Christ and His Gospel and the Magisterium of the Church can open up several forms of becomings to serve the Kingdom. We can imagine these various forms of becomings as waves. We can ride these different waves depending on our aptitude, charisms as well as our likings (aesthetic orientations) and work to build God's kingdom in our world. It will again require us to be a minority unto the image and likeness of our Lord Jesus Christ. The becomings of the kingdom are profoundly marked by the call to become a minority for the sake of Christ and his Gospel. This would require us to be both mystical and prophetic. As mystics, we will have to discover and discern in the power of catholic faith the presence of Christ amidst us and then join him in building his kingdom. This requires faith and courage. Faith takes us into the mystical realm to see Christ in our world and courage gives us the prophetic spirit to choose what it takes to join Christ and become an active servant of the Kingdom. This choice of the servant-hood of Kingdom will enable us to determine the kind of gospel becomings or the becomings of the Kingdom that we can choose and live our life in the Church. Thus, strengthening our links with Christ, Church and his mission, we shall delink and dismantle our links with capitalist order and it's God of money. In this context, we need to be cautious about the fact that the ruthless capitalist order often destroys our links with tradition, culture and religion. We seem to get uprooted as we cling to the capitalist world order. In such situations, we often find people becoming fanatic holding on to the last straws of the culture, tradition and religion. The becomings of the Gospel are not those that sprung forth from the fear of the loss of the original or the fundamental. They are authentic becomings of love that follow from the call of Christ.

Conclusion

Pope Francis has waged a relentless war on capitalism and its Gods of money. This humble effort is join this battle. We think that capitalism succeeds by manipulating our desire. Hence, we have chosen the path of psychoanalysis in the context of this study to understand how we can interrupt, disrupt and dismantle the worship of the God of Money and open ways that we can continue the war against terror unleashed by capitalism.

Endnotes

1   https://www.commondreams.org/news/2016/08/02/pope-francis-capitalism-terrorism-against-all-humanity accessed on 29/09/2017.

2   https://www.nytimes.com/2015/07/12/world/americas/in-fiery-speeches-francis-excoriates-global-capitalism.html?mcubz=3 accessed on 29/09/2017.

3   See Gilles DELEUZE and Felix GAUTTARI, *Anti-oedipus: Capitalism and Schizophernia*, trans. Robert Hurley, Mark Seem and Helene R. Lane (Minneapolis: University of Minnesota Press, 1983) and See Gilles Deleuze and Felix Gauttari, *A Thousand Plateaus: Capitalism and Schizophernia*, trans. Brain Massumi (Minneapolis: University of Minnesota Press, 1987).

4   See Leen DE BOLLE, ' Preface: Desire and Schizophrenia' in Leen De Bolle, Ed. (Leuven: Lueven University Press, 2010), 7.

5   https://www.newyorker.com/news/john-cassidy/pope-franciss-challenge-to-global-capitalism accessed on 29/09/2017.

6   See encyclical *Laudato Si'*. Also see 'Why Pope Francis wants us to stop worshiping capitalism' http://www.pbs.org/newshour/bb/pope-francis-wants-us-stop-worshipping-capitalism/ accessed on 29/09/2017.

7   Ibid.

8   See Kristyn GORTON, *Theorising Desire: From Freud to Feminism to Film* (New York: Palgrave Macmillan, 2008) 8. Ibid., 11-13.

9   https://www.newyorker.com/news/john-cassidy/pope-franciss-challenge-to-global-capitalism. accessed on 29/09/2017.

10 See Kristyn GORTON, *Theorising Desire*, 16-18.

11 Ibid., 22-24.

12 See Ibid., 14-15.

13 See Kristyn GORTON, *Theorising Desire*, 17.

14 See Leen DE BOLLE, ' Preface: Desire and Schizophrenia', 8-18.

15 Becoming-women contests man/woman binary of psychoanalysis. There is no becoming-man as it cannot become-molecular. Just because women is positioned as oppositional to man/phallus/ masculine, the absolute representative of standard or norm, all becomings have to come through becoming-woman. They further teach that becoming-woman is not limited to man but women also have to become-woman. Woman also has a molar identity. It concerns what is expected from a normal woman. This is imitative while becoming-woman cannot be mimetic. No one can become a woman by wearing a dress or makeup. Becoming-woman is molecular transformation and is different to every person. Becoming-woman involves dismantling of molar identities, like wife, mother, sister, virgin, prostitute, etc. It involves staying in a continues process of transformation, always changing. All becoming is becoming a minoritarian. Hence, becoming-child as well as becoming-animal contest the privileged binaries of adult/child and human/animal respectively. By these becomings Deleuze and Gauttari try to dismantle the imposition of molar identities of man and woman. See Kathryn M Blake, *A Contemporary Feminist Critique of Psychoanalysis through Gilles Deleuze and Felix Gauttari*, A thesis submitted to the graduate school-New Brunswick, Rutgers, the State University of New Jersey, in partial fulfilment of degree of Masters of Art, 38-46.

16 https://www.newyorker.com/news/john-cassidy/pope-franciss-challenge-to-global-capitalism accessed on 29/09/2017.

17 Ibid.

Chapter 16

Pope Francis' Mission
Prophetic Commitment

Mariapushpam Paul Raj
Department of Scriptural Studies, Jnana-Deepa Vidyapeeth, Pune

In the parishes of the diocese of Rottenburg-Stuttgart, Germany a signature-campaign called *Pro Concilio* was initiated in early 2017 in support of making a request to the Holy See to get the so-called *viri probati* ordained as ministers for the different parish communities. This and many other such initiatives are happening in the Catholic Church today under the leadership of Pope Francis, though not all members of the Church including a few of those who play the leading roles agree with him in every point.[1] In spite of the opposition and the objection he is facing from some of his fellow-Christians, Pope Francis continues to make a difference and send out waves of positive energy through his *uncomplicated faith* in the Gospel, his *unassuming attitude towards others*, his *simple life*, through his *insightful perception of reality* with its problems and chances, and the *simple, direct and distinct language* he uses to preach the Good News to everyone.

His life-style represents a new way of living faith, hope and charity as did the prophetic figures of the Old Testament, challenging the powerful both inside and outside the Church to care for the neglected and the underprivileged. What he says and does is so surprising and disturbing that one begins to ask oneself whether he is the Pope or a Prophet of God who has been sent to warn us and call us all to return to the Lord. In spite of the many dissenting voices which consider him as ambiguous and confusing and request him to 'behave himself' as a Pope and guard the traditional faith of the Church, he goes about his business with much conviction and certainty advocating and promoting more radical ways of living the faith.

It is not easy for an ordained minister to integrate the demands of the sanctification, leadership and prophetic ministries especially when a conflicting situation arises. Further in the life of every minister one of the three functions stands out though the other two are not neglected. When we observe the way Pope Francis carries out his holy office, what stands out, in my opinion, is the 'prophetic' aspect, though as a Pope he does not neglect his sanctifying and leading responsibilities. This short essay attempts to focus on the prophetic dimension of the ministry of Pope Francis. Since our understanding of what is 'prophetic' is based on the biblical understanding of prophet and prophetic ministry, let us first make a few clarifying observations on this matter.

1. Biblical Prophets and the Word of God

The most fundamental thing about the biblical prophets is that God's word was personally made known to them (cf. Jer 11:18) whereby the Sprit of the Lord played a central role (cf. Hos 9:7; Mic 3:8; 2 Sam 23:2; Ezech 3:12-14). The primary function of the biblical prophets is not *foretelling* or *predicting*, something which is popularly expected of a prophet, but *forth-telling*, that is, proclaiming what has been received from the Lord and doing it in his name.[2] In fact, the Greek term *prophets* contains the verbal stem *phe* meaning to 'say' or to 'speak' and the prefix *pro* meaning both 'forth' and 'fore.'[3] Its Hebrew equivalent *nabi*[4] refers both to a "speaker" or "proclaimer" and to the "one called" or "appointed"[5] (cf. Amos 7:14-16; Is 6:1-13; Jer 1:2-10; Ezech 1:2-3.11). In any case, every biblical prophet is a called proclaimer as is attested to by the call narratives in which God is the one who calls[6] the prophets and commissions them with a specific mission. However, the Bible also contains a number of instances of prophets 'foretelling' or 'predicting' which serve as a sign of prophetic authority (cf. Deut 18:22; Is 41:22; 43:9). Such proclamation of prophets took different forms like judgements and assurances of salvation (Hos 4:1-5; 2 Kg 1:6; 20:6; Is 66:7-15), oracles of woe or of assurance (Is 5:8-24; Jer 30:10-11), admonitions (Amos 4:4-5) and prophetic symbolic acts (Is 20:2-4; Jer 28:10).[7] Texts like Deut 18:18-22 and Jer 28:8-9 also make a distinction between true and false prophets.[8]

Though it is the Old Testament which has a separate section on prophetic literature, we also find a number of occurrences of this term in the New Testament having the same meaning as declaring an inspired or revealed statement (Mt 7:22; 13:14; 1 Cor 14:6; Acts 2:17), or predicting something that is hidden (Mt 26:68; Lk 22:64) or lies in the future (Mk 7:6; 1 Pet 1:10). Apart from calling John the Baptist (Lk 1:76) and Jesus (Jn 4:19) as prophets, the New Testament also speaks of Early Christian missionaries as prophets (cf. Mt 10:41; 23:34; Lk 11:49).[9] Today as was in the biblical times, we are faced with the difficulty of identifying and assessing authentic prophets. We are faced with the questions: Does God continue to inspire or speak to certain men and women even today? Does what is called prophecy today really communicate God's word? The Bible instructs its readers to 'test' (1 Thess 5:20-21) prophets and their prophecies.

2. The Manner the Prophets Spoke

The prophets of the Old Testament appear to "make much ado about paltry things, lavishing excessive language upon trifling subjects" and "even a minor injustice assumes cosmic proportions" and they were breathlessly impatient with injustice (cf. Amos 8:4-8).[10] Indifference and incapacity to sense the depth of misery caused by the plight of human beings was a matter of serious concern for them. Their language was not charged with harmony but with agitation, anguish and a spirit of non-acceptance, but also with firmness and compassion. They were impatient of excuse and contemptuous of pretence and self-pity. The mouth of a prophet is "a sharp sword" and a "polished arrow" taken out of the quiver of God (Is 49:2).[11]

The prophets were not faithfully defending the traditionally cherished beliefs and institutions such as sacrifices, priesthood and temple but questioned their scandalous pretensions (cf. Amos 6:8; Jer 6:20; 7:4.8.9-15.21-23). They even called the enemies of the Israelite people like Assyria (cf. Is 10:5; 5:26; 7:18, 8:7; 13:5) and Nebuchadnezzar (cf. Jer 25:9; 27:6; 43:10) as God's 'instruments' which he would use against his own people.[12] The prophets preferred to speak the truth even though it appeared to go against their own people of Israel.[13] Neither modesty, compromise, satiety, tolerance nor understanding but honesty, critique and challenge were the values predominant in the lives of the biblical prophets, though sometimes they exaggerated the guilt of the people and made them appear hard to believe (e.g. Jer 8:10; cf. Jer 5:1.5; 6:6.13).

The prophets also emphasized the mercy and love of God for the people. For example, the prophets present God as the Good Shepherd (cf. Ezech 34) and as a loving parent (cf. Hos 11:1; Is 42:1-9; 46:3; 49:15; 66:13). A number of prophetic texts bear witness to this mercy of God. For example we read in Is 54:10: *For the mountains may go away and the hills may totter, but my faithful love will never leave you, my covenant of peace will never totter, says Yahweh who takes pity on you* (Cf. Is 54:7-8; 55:3; 63:7; Jer 31:3; 33:11; Mic 7:20).

And finally the prophets of the Bible had to face threats and challenges from the people and had to suffer a lot. The best example of such sufferings of a prophet was found in Jer 11:18-12:6 which was one of the so called confessions of Jeremiah[14] where Jeremiah lamented over the betrayal of his friends and family in Anathoth. Amos was also hated for reproving the people on behalf of God (cf. Amos 5:10). Loneliness, misery and frustration were part of the prophetic ministry and they had to go on even though the people would not listen to them (cf. Ezech 2:4-5).

Thus we see that the biblical prophets were "extra-institutional charismatic leaders" who were called by God "through a special call experience" and they were sent to "recall" the people of Israel and its leadership, namely the kings and priests, "from the errant ways" into which they had strayed, and to "re-new" their God experience.[15] They, in turn, "lived the faith with radical example. Embracing poverty, extreme religious vows and calling for renewed commitment, they spoke out against injustice" of the powerful and "defended the poor."[16] They were not defenders of the institution against all odds but went to the extent of questioning the institutional structures in order to re-establish justice and harmony among the people and to renew the covenantal relationship between God and the people.

3. Pope Francis' Prophetic Mission

When Pope Benedict XVI stunned the world by resigning from his Papal office he honestly admitted that it was due to his lack of strength of mind and body. Such an honest admittance of one's dwindling energies also speaks volumes about the seriousness of the difficulties and problems the Church was facing, both internally and externally, and about the radical response such a crisis moment demanded from the Papal Chair. Declining number of vocations, increasing examples of scandalous behaviour from clergy and religious including accusations of sex abuse against Church leaders, reports of corruption inside Vatican itself, issues of abortion, contraception, same-sex marriages, communion to the divorced, ecumenical and inter-religious relations, ruthless killing of the innocents and the growing misery of the migrants and the profit-oriented market economy which epitomizes money as the almighty were only a few of the challenges inherited by Pope Francis, the successor to Pope Benedict XVI. In the following we make an attempt to understand the 'prophetic' response of the present Pontiff.

a. Through Simplicity in Life

The popularity of Pope Francis is derived from the simplicity of his life. The plastic watch, iron cross, frayed cassock, black shoes and socks instead of the expensive handmade scarlet silk slippers, ring of the fisherman in silver, Ford Focus instead of the Papal Limousine, the missing traditional shoulder-cape and the gold-embroidered ceremonial stole are the loud *signs* of his simplicity which attract the ordinary person. When Pope Francis saw the Papal Apartment after his election to Papacy in March 2013 he commented saying "the entrance is so narrow that people could enter only in dribs and drabs."[17] Since he wanted to live with the people, he chose to live in the Papal guest house Casa Santa Maria. This was not a strategy adopted by him after he was elected Pope but had practiced it in his years of ministry in the *villas miseria*, the teeming slums of his native city, Buenos Aires.[18] "A church of the poor, for the poor" is the motto of his Papacy he made on the day of his election. He never likes to be portrayed as a 'superman' or as a star but prefers rather to be considered a normal man who laughs, cries and has friends like everyone. To a question asked by Mathilde Imberty of the Pope being a star, he answered, "Stars are beautiful … But the Pope must be, must be the servant of the servants of God."[19]

His simplicity is not limited to how he lives his personal life but is extended in the concern he has for the poor and the afflicted. In his address to the bishops of Brazil the Pope clarified saying "Without the grammar of simplicity, the Church loses the very conditions which make it possible 'to fish' for God in the deep waters of his Mystery."[20] He is convinced that the poor have a special place in God's people. This is what he says about the poor in *Evangelii Gaudium* 197:[21] "God's heart has a special place for the poor, so much so that he himself "became poor" (*2 Cor* 8:9; cf. *Lk* 2:24; *Lev* 5:7); … He made himself one of them: "I was hungry and you gave me food to eat", and he taught them that mercy towards all of these is the key to heaven (cf. *Mt* 25:5ff.)."

According to him it is the poor who teach us "the *sensus fidei*," and we need to let ourselves be evangelized by them. Our commitment to them should not consist exclusively in activities or programmes of promotion and assistance but in loving attentiveness which considers the other "in a certain sense as one with ourselves" (EG 199). The worst discrimination the poor suffer is the lack of spiritual care and therefore our preferential option for the poor must mainly translate into a privileged and preferential religious care (EG 200). Whatever be our lifestyle no one can think we are exempt from concern for the poor and for social justice (EG 201).

The Pope expressed his option for the poor already during his first pastoral visit of his Papacy outside Rome which he made to Lampedusa in South Italy on 8 July 2013 which is indicative of his special concern for the dislocated refugees and migrants who are on a permanent search for a place to live in. When he went there he threw a wreath of flowers into the sea and wore purple colour mass vestments (which is usually worn during the time of fasting in the Church) in remembrance of those who had drowned in the Mediterranean while attempting to cross over to Europe. In his homily he also came down heavily upon the indifference of the powerful and the rich to the plight of the poor and called for a "reawakening of consciences" to counter the "globalization of indifferences" being shown to the migrants. Inspired by the appeal made by him, a wealthy Italian American couple who now live in Malta, Regina Catrambone and her husband Christopher, founded an association named Migrant Offshore Aid Station and bought a 131 foot rescue boat, the *Phoenix* spending their own money of 3.7 million UD dollars.[22]

Pope Francis calls every Christian to care for the vulnerable and help the slow, the weak or the less talented to find opportunities in life (EG 209). He identifies the homeless, the addicted, the refugees, indigenous peoples, the elderly, and particularly the migrants as belonging to this group of vulnerable (EG 210). He exhorts that on the face of human trafficking we should not look the other way like Cain (EG 211). Special attention should be paid to women who are doubly poor and the unborn children who are the most defenceless (EG 212-213) by accompanying women in difficult situations, even when abortion appears to be the only way (EG 214).

b. Through Deep Faith in the Gospel

In his Encyclical *Lumen Fidei*[23] (LF) the Pope refers to Jn 12:46 and 2 Cor 4:6 and asserts that faith is *light brought by Christ* and it illuminates the entire journey of the believers (LF 1) and every aspect of human existence (LF 4). This faith is in a living God who calls us and loves us through Jesus Christ who demonstrates God's love for us through his death (LF 4). The death and resurrection of Christ is the proof of utter reliability of God's love for us (LF 16-17). This faith is transmitted by those who have seen God's light and heard his voice from generation to generation through an unbroken chain of witnesses. It is the lived memory of the life bringing act of Jesus' love kept alive in the Church and taught under the guidance of the Holy Spirit (Jn 14:26) that makes the believers contemporaries of Jesus (LF 37-38). This faith is absorbed and deepened in the family (LF 52-54).

Without this faith in God our mutual trust would be weakened, we would remain united only by fear and our stability would be threatened (LF 55). This faith involves painful testing, trials, suffering and weakness which can become an act of love and entrustment into the hands of God (LF 56). It is *a lamp which guides our steps in the night*. God's response to those who suffer is that of *an accompanying presence,... Christ is the one who, having endured suffering, is "the pioneer and perfecter of our faith"* (*Heb* 12:2; LF 57). Suffering reminds us that ... only from God, ... can our society find solid and lasting foundations. .... The dynamics of faith, hope and charity (cf. 1 Th 1:3; 1 Cor 13:13) thus leads us to embrace the concerns of all men and women on our journey ... *Let us refuse to be robbed of hope*, or to allow our hope to be dimmed by facile answers and solutions which block our progress (LF 57).

In his Apostolic Exhortation *Evangelii Gaudium* in which the focus is on the *Joy* of the Gospel, the Pope identifies consumerism, desolation and anguish born of a complacent yet covetous heart, feverish pursuit of frivolous pleasures, and a blunted conscience as the danger of the world today makes the believers callous to the joy of God's love (EG 2). This joy can be regained through a renewed personal encounter with Jesus Christ (EG 3). This regained joy urges (2 Cor 5:14) and obliges (1 Cor 9:16) everyone to share with others (EG 10) the message that God has *revealed his immense love in the crucified and risen Christ* (EG 11). The Church must carry on this proclamation (EG 169).

Thus he sees faith as a challenge calling for changing the human predicament. He posed the same challenge to the priests in his homily during the Chrism mass at St. Peter's Basilica on 28 March 2013 admonishing them "to *go out* to the *outskirts* where there is suffering, bloodshed, blindness that longs for sight." He also said that the priest who seldom goes out of himself, ends up as sad priests instead of being shepherds living with *the odour of the sheep*. Finally he asked the priests to "be shepherds, with the *odour of the sheep*" and so be "fishers of men."[24]

The depth of his faith can be understood from the very title of his Encyclical, *Evangelii Gaudium* (EG) which discloses his fundamental attitude of joy for the Gospel message. That he is immersed and filled with this joy finds its expression in his address to the Jesuits during their General Congregation on 24 October 2016 in which he warned them not to allow the enemy of human nature[25] to rob oneself among other things of the joy of evangelizing, because joy is constitutive of the Gospel message and one cannot give a good piece of news with a sad face.[26] It looks as if the Gospel message alone is sufficient for him to be happy in life.

According to Pope Francis the Gospel continues to be a vital source of eternal newness for the Church, against all those who would "indoctrinate" it in dead stones to be hurled at others."[27] In his opinion one of the three temptations against missionary discipleship is to "transform the Gospel message into an ideology" which refers to "the attempt to interpret the Gospel apart from the Gospel itself and apart from the Church."[28]

In one of his informal letters to the German youth admonishing them to remain faithful to reading and living the Bible, the Pope narrates his own association with his 'old, well-worn' copy of the Bible. All that he tries to explain in the contents of this letter is how the Bible contains words God wishes to speak to every human being and how it can be read on all occasions and in every circumstance. In lieu of a 'theological introduction' to and critical questions on the Bible, he evokes interest for the Bible in the young people by describing his own personal experience and the attachment to his Bible which is naturally the source of his faith.

As he understands his faith in an uncomplicated manner, so also is his view on prayer and meditation as tools for daily life and as acts of speaking and listening by which humility has to be the governing attitude. The only way one could grow in relationship with God is to pray with humility.[29] For him prayer is when he makes his decisions and it should be an experience of giving way, of surrendering, where our entire being enters into the presence of God. Further he believes that prayer is the place where dialogue, listening and transformation occur, looking at God, but above all sensing that we are being watched by him.[30] It is inspiring to recall that on the first day of his office as the Bishop of Rome one of the first things he did was to go to the Mary Major Basilica to pray.[31]

c. Through Insightful Perception of Contemporary Reality

Like the prophets who saw what the others failed to see and who always had an insight into the reality and called for a renewed relationship with it, Pope Francis too proves himself again and again to be creative and innovative. In the pre-conclave meeting before his election to Pope, he spoke forcefully to the Cardinals that the Church "must go to the peripheries" in both a geographic and existential sense and must beware of "theological narcissism."[32] Narcissists are those who are blinded by the radiant glow of their self-perceived greatness and they don't see what havoc they create or what misery they inflict on others.[33] He repeats the same clarion call in EG 20: "Each Christian and every community must discern the path … to go forth from our own comfort zone in order to reach all the 'peripheries' in need of the light of the Gospel." This reflects his vision of the Church as a 'centrifugal Church.'[34] Such a vision of the Pope was also reflected in his warning to the Vatican diplomats-in-training that careerism is leprosy and in his invitation to his fellow bishops to be men who love poverty, simplicity and austerity of life.[35]

Twenty months later into his Papal office four days before Christmas 2014 he presented the Roman Curia with a list of fifteen ailments from which the Curia had to heal itself. This list voiced the prophetic call for conversion from the sicknesses of "leading double life," "of teaching others with severity and leading a hidden, sometimes dissolute life," "of gossiping," "of rivalry and vain glory," and "of worldly profit and exhibitionism" among the other things.[36] In order to arrive at a fairer representation at the Vatican he first created a council of eight (later nine) cardinals from across the world to reform the Roman Curia, and has started appointing new Cardinals to the College of Cardinals more and more from countries like Ivory Coast, Burkina Faso, Ethiopia, Haiti, Nicaragua, New Zealand, Vietnam, Myanmar and Thailand. Such actions reveal the direction of correcting Eurocentric imbalance in the College of Cardinals by adding a number of curial Cardinals from poorer countries.

d. Through Doing Justice to Women

His concern for including women in the Church activities is also evidenced by a number of activities. On 4 May 2015 he welcomed the female head of Sweden's Lutheran Church Archbishop Antje Jackelen of Uppsala on an official visit to Vatican.[37] On 5 December 2014 when he appointed new members to the Vatican's International Theological Commission, for the first time seven female theologians were included as part of the twenty member commission. He has also spoken repeatedly of the need for the Church to develop a deeper theology of women and of his determination to promote women to senior positions in Rome. Though he has no intention of modifying the Church teaching on ordination of women priests still he intends to promote the participation of women in Church life. On 11 May 2017 he told the Canadian bishops that it is "vital" that more women be involved, including in decision making, and that we need to "bring the voice of women into the responsibility structures of the church."[38] A number of people all over the world believe that a radical decision with regard to ordination of women priests cannot be ruled out with the ever-surprising Pope Francis at the helm.[39]

e. Through Putting Own House in Order

The dragging and nagging corruptions at the Vatican bank is known to many of us under the headword *Vatileaks*. Pope Francis has not hesitated to invite a number of agencies consisting of renowned lay financial experts to review the operations of the Vatican bank. Though it is suspected by some Vatican Cardinals that such external scrutiny might amount to voluntary renouncement of Papal sovereignty and might lead to attack from outside to destabilize the Holy See, Pope Francis goes ahead with the reforms.In February 2014 he handed over the authority for running the Vatican finances to Cardinal George Pell one of the so called "Group of Eight" who since 2014 releases the balance sheets about the Vatican financial situation with facts and figures and who since January 2015 has introduced draconian new accounting rules for every Vatican headquarters department. Total financial transparency is the order given by Pope Francis.[40]

f. Through Discerning Mercy as Foundational

The great jubilee year of mercy lasting from 8 December 2015 to 20 November 2016 which was declared by Pope Francis on the fourth Sunday of Lent in 2015 was a seminal idea that was born out of a deep conviction that the Church and the world today are very badly in need of becoming 'merciful' towards fellow humans and towards nature. The official document *Misericordiae Vultus* which contained the message of the Pope on this theme of mercy is founded on the principle that God is rich in mercy (Eph 2:4) and he is "a God merciful and gracious, slow to anger, and abounding in steadfast love and faithfulness" (Ex 34:6).

This declaration created a 'hype' about mercy and at least in the ecclesial circles to say the least, it initiated a renewed awareness and a reawakening about the nature of God and the nature and the mission of the Church. In a situation of indecisiveness, ambiguity, indifference, profit-oriented market, achievement based entrepreneurs, conformity promoting education and political systems which reduces human beings to instruments of usefulness and leaves behind anxiety and uncertainty, it was highly necessary to remind humanity of the God of the Bible who has revealed himself as someone who cares, loves and is merciful. The call for a year of mercy was a prompt and appropriate response of Pope Francis to the situation humanity was in at the moment. In EG 114 the Pope also invited the Church to be a place of mercy, where everyone can feel welcomed, loved, forgiven and encouraged to live the good life of the Gospel. Thus the Church is supposed to become a 'mother' and a 'shepherdess.'[41]

Quoting the *Summa Theologica* (I-II, q. 66, a. 4-6; q. 108, a.1) in EG 37, Pope Francis made the following assertion: "… as far as external works are concerned, mercy is the greatest of all the virtues."[42] It becomes clear from the context of the Exhortation that mercy was considered to be the same as the 'works of love' mentioned by Paul in Gal 5:6.[43] By equating mercy with the works of love, the Pope was actually qualifying mercy as *the* 'Christian' way of relating to one's neighbor. He also referred to this mercy in his address to the Jesuits on the occasion of their General Congregation describing that this mercy is not an abstract word but a lifestyle of concrete gestures and an expansion of the colloquy with the Lord placed on the cross.[44] In the same address he also stated that the "Lord who looks at us with mercy and chooses us, sends us to bring with all its effectiveness, that same mercy to the poorest, to sinners, to those discarded people, and those crucified in the present world, who suffer injustice and violence.[45]

The visit of Pope Francis to the migrant camp in the Greek island Lesbos on 16 April 2016 to highlight the humanitarian crisis was a concretization of this message of mercy the Pope intended to drive home in the hearts of his contemporaries. The Pope spent five hours on Lesbos with Bartholomew I, the spiritual leader of the world's Orthodox Christians and with the Archbishop of Athens and on his return journey he took with himself twelve refugees to Vatican all of whom were Syrian Muslims. It was indeed a symbolic gesture from the Pontiff to tell the people in plight that they are not alone in their struggle. He also appreciated the efforts made by Greece to take care of them. At the same time, it also posed a challenge to the international community to become more sensitive to the issue of migrants and refugees.

g. Through Hearing the Cry of Mother Earth

Much acclaimed is also the concern of the Pope for creation. Already in EG he has expressed this concern pointing out that creation as a whole is 'frequently at the mercy of economic interests or indiscriminate exploitation' (EG 215) and that desertification of the soil and extinction of species is a painful disfigurement and has invited all Christians to watch over and protect the fragile world following the example of Saint Francis of Assisi (EG 215).

Further his Encyclical *Laudato Si'* (LS) came as a pointed expression of his concern for creation and nature. First of all it must be said that this Encyclical is a timely response to the international situation when the countries of the world are discussing climate change and environmental protection. His calling the earth as 'common home' for human beings is very surprising, because here is a Pope who calls not the heaven but the earth which is usually considered as 'banished' in Christian theology as a common home. Of the twenty nine occurrences of the word "home" in this Encyclical, sixteen of them are used to call the earth as the common home of humanity. He rightly identifies that this common home is falling into serious disrepair (LS 61) and it is human beings who have "hurt and mistreated" the common home in the last two hundred years (LS 53). The Encyclical also attests to the discoveries of science and technology (LS 102-136), appreciates the efforts made by the international community to save the earth and calls for more serious and committed action (LS 164-198) and calls for a dialogue between religion and science (LS 199-201).

h. Through Identifying Family as the Nucleus

The Pope has rightly and prophetically identified that the future of the Church lies actually in the 'family' the most fundamental unit of the society where the making or the breaking of the society begins and ends. Realizing its importance for the Church he decided to call a synod on family this time using a new method of first consulting the local Churches followed by a discussion among the Cardinals on the results of the consultation and then a first synod (in October 2014) to formulate the questions and another one (in October 2015) to vote on concrete proposals. His aim in the synods has not been to change the doctrines of the Church on the sacraments or indissolubility of marriage but find ways of integrating those alienated from Church life due to some tragic personal situations.[46] The Church has the responsibility, in his opinion, 'not to lose the saved' and 'to save the lost.'

The post-synodal document *'Amoris Laetitia' On Love in the Family*, moves in the direction of caring for the alienated ones, especially in chapter eight which actually addresses the concern the Pope had before the council, namely, integrating those who are alienated from the Church. The chapter begins by articulating the desire of the Church to show mercy and to help those who are struggling to live according to God's plan for marriage and family because of moral weakness (AL 291). The pastors must lead those living without proper marriages to live according to the Gospel and motivate them to live according to the law helped by grace (AL 293-295). Following Jesus, the Church must show mercy (AL 296) by first understanding those who are into 'irregular' scenarios (AL 298) and then discerning ways of integrating the "divorced and civilly remarried" into the community, without compromising the faith or causing scandal (AL 299). Instead of condemning people based on general laws, pastors should seek to bring those people out of their disordered state regardless of their culpability (AL 305).

i. Through Remaining Open

Another important concern the Pope has is to relate with other denominations and religions. Speaking to the leaders of the Protestant Salvation Army he mentioned to them that he learned the spirit of ecumenism from his grandmother way back in 1940 when she commented about two Salvation Army women walking on the other side of the road saying, 'they are good Protestants!'[47] The joint-declaration "From Conflict to Communion" made by the Lutheran World Federation (LWF) and the Pontifical Council for Promoting Christian Unity (PCPCU) to commemorate the 500 years of Reformation, is a significant milestone in the ecumenical history of the Church. This document calls for mutual positive appraisal of the Reformation movement and the Catholic response and engages itself in the theological discussion instead of a political conflict to promote further encounter among the Christians.

Pope Francis is also emerging as a model of dialogue both in word and deed.[48] The Pope looks at truth and love as intimately related and as caught up in the dynamism of life, relationships and history rather than in abstract speculation.[49] Such a perception of reality could help as a common platform for a dialogue with other religions.

The insightful perceptions of Pope Francis can be summarized in his six foundational commitments as formulated by Chris Lowney: Know yourself deeply, live to serve others, immerse yourself in the world, withdraw from the world daily, live in the present and revere tradition and create the future.[50] As he himself mentioned in his homily on the inauguration of his ministry as the Bishop of Rome, every leader must follow the example of Joseph in exercising the role of the protector "discreetly, humbly and silently, but with an unfailing presence and utter fidelity, even when he finds it hard to understand" and "By being constantly attentive to God, open to the signs of God's presence and receptive to God's plans, which calls for … "a capacity for concern, for compassion, for genuine openness to others, for love."[51] According to him "authentic power is service, and that the Pope too, when exercising power, must enter ever more fully into that service … and must open his arms to protect … the hungry, the thirsty, the stranger, the naked, the sick and those in prison (cf. *Mt* 25:31-46). Only those who serve with love are able to protect!"[52]

j. Through Unassuming Attitude towards Others

Pope Francis is a person who approaches other human beings in an unassuming manner. This was evident already when he, as a twenty eight year old young priest at Immaculate Conception College in in Buenos Aires, went out of his way to help the young boys to form a musical band because they wanted one. His desire to bring human beings together finds its expression in his address to the Jesuits on 24 October 2016 calling for "harmonizing the tensions brought about by the diversity of men."[53]

One of the main accusations made against Pope Francis is that he behaved in a conservative and authoritarian way when he was the provincial superior of the Argentinian Jesuits when he had banned guitar-songs, insisted on clerical dress and discouraged the Jesuits from learning subjects like politics, sociology and engineering in order to prevent them from becoming involved in political activities. He is also accused of not having protected the Jesuits Francesco Jalics and Orlando Yorio who were among the kidnapped during the military regime.[54] It was even said that Bergoglio even gave the 'green light' to arrest them.[55]

When we consider all this, it appears odd to imagine that such an unassuming Pope was so authoritarian then. However, one should consider the context in which all this happened. It was a situation of a deep economic crisis in Argentine[56] which led the country into a military dictatorship that ruthlessly killed even priests and nuns.It was in this context that the then Jesuit provincial warned the two above mentioned Jesuits to leave *Bajo Flores* where they were working for the poor. When they refused to comply with his instruction, thereby also defying the obedience vow of the Jesuits, he withdrew their religious license in order save their life from the military dictatorship. Evidently, the two Jesuits refused to obey because of their 'preferential option for the poor' as one of the serious follow-up actions of the then much acclaimed 'liberation theology.'[57] One can understand that the efforts of the provincial only helped to prevent victimization of the Jesuits by the then military regime. Later on one of the two Jesuits Francesco Jalics clarified in a statement saying, "The fact is: Orlando Yorio and I were not denounced by Father Begoglio."[58]

The Pope's unassuming attitude towards life becomes vivid from a few instances such as celebrating his first mass as Pope in a surplice and greeting the congregation one by one as they came out, kissing the Argentinian President Cristina Kirchner thereby abandoning the tradition that Popes never kiss or receive kisses, rejoicing at a small boy taking over his Papal seat on an occasion, washing and kissing the feet of prisoners on Maundy Thursday and hugging and kissing the face of a disfigured poor man the photo of which went viral in the social media. These and many other things which he does express the joy he finds in accepting and relating to the underprivileged and unfortunate people.

k. Through Simple, Direct and Distinct Language

About himself the Pope has said that he is a sinner upon whom the Lord has looked and forgiven. About the Church he says that it 'is a field hospital after battle.' About following the principle of collegiality and moving towards a synodal Church he says, "Periphery shapes the centre."[59] He does not hesitate to name the difficulties of the Church such as 'functionalism' and 'clericalism.' 'Who am I to judge?' was his answer, when he was asked about his opinion on homosexuality. He is sensitive to the difficulties and challenges that people go through. He does not judge but understands their struggle.[60] One can make an endless list such concise but vivid statements made by the Pope which are examples of his direct and distinct language.

Conclusion

Prophetic character demands transparency and credibility. The important question to be asked is: 'Are the institutions of the Church transparent and credible?'[61] Through his life and ministry the Pope seems to direct the Church towards this goal of being transparent and credible. "Pope Francis' courage coupled with humility and firmness offers great hope that he will lead the church like Jesus who was a great agent of change."[62] The main reasons for this hope and positive energy which he instils in the hearts and minds of the poor as well as in all human beings of good will who dream of establishing the Kingdom of love, peace and justice which Jesus preached are the following: how he proves his solidarity with the poor again and again, the pastoral concern he has for the people of God and which he attempts to instil into the hearts and minds of his fellow clergymen by asking them to move to the peripheries, the joy and happiness he discharges both in his faith life and in his relationship with fellow human beings and above all his conviction about God's mercy and compassion which he tries to translate into everyday life. May all who see him also perceive his prophetic invitation and commit themselves to cause of God!

Endnotes

1   It is not an unknown fact that four Cardinals wrote the so called 'dubia' a letter on 19 September 2016 to the Pope with five questions seeking clarification on the Apostolic Exhortation *Amoris Laetitia* and on 23 September 2017 a document "formal correction" to the alleged errors in the above said Exhortaiton has been published on blogs and online newspapers which accurse the Pope of seven heresies.

2   D. J. Mccarthy, "Prophecy in the Bible," in *The New Catholic Encyclopedia* 11 (1967), 861.

3   Helmut KRÄMER, "Prophet" in *Theological Dictionary of the New Testament* 6, 784. The understanding of a prophet as one who "foretells" is usually derived from the practice of considering the Old Testament prophets as 'foretellers' of Jesus the Messiah. However, it must also be noted that such messianic proclamations are relatively few in number in the Old Testament. Cf.Erich Zenger,"Die Bücher der Prophetie," in Erich Zenger (ed.), Einleitung in das Alte Testament (Stuttgart: W. Kohnhaller, 2008), 417.

4   Cf. Hatch EDWIN, Redpath A HENRY, *A Concordance to the Septuagint and the Other Greek Versions of the Old Testament Including the Apocryphal Books* (Grand Rapids – Michigan: Baker Academic, 1998), 1231-1233.

5   In the recent times the passive meaning is preferred to the active one. Cf. R Rendtorff, **aybn** in the Old Testament, in: *Theological Dictionary of the New Testament* 6, 796.

6   C BROWN, "Prophet", in *New International Dictionary of New Testament Theology* 3 (1986), 77.

7   Cf. Ake VIBERG, *Prophets in Action: An Analysis of Prophetic Symbolic Acts in the OT* (Stockholm: Almqvist and Wiksell, 2007), 27-45. In this book we find a definition and a list of such prophetic symbolic acts.

8   Cf. Willem A. Vangemeren, *Interpreting the Prophetic Word: An Introduction to the Prophetic Literature of the Old Testament* (Grand Rapids: Zondervan, 1990), 63-66. On page 63 of this book the author is making a table comparing the characteristics of false and true prophets.

9   For more info on the origin and development of early Christian prophecy kindly see Ulrich LUZ, "Stages if Early Christian Prophetism," in *Prophets and Prophecy in Jewish and Early Christian Literature, ed. Joseph Verheyden* et. al. (WUNT 2.286, Tübingen: Mohr Siebeck, 2010), 57-75. Further see David E. AUNE, *Prophecy in Early Christianity and the Ancient Mediterranean World* (Oregon: Wipf and Stock, 2003), 189-232.

10   Cf. Abraham J. HESCHEL, *Prophets* (Peabody: Prince Press, 2000), 3-4.

11   Cf. Abraham J. HESCHEL, *Prophets*, 5-7.

12   Abraham J. HESCHEL, *Prophets*, 8-12.

13   We read in Jer 38:3 where the prophet prophesies saying that the city of Jerusalem will certainly be handed over to the army of the king of Babylon, and he will capture it. Such prophecies were very much displeasing to the people and the kings who ruled over them.

14   Traditionally five such confessions are identified in the Book of Jeremiah: Jer 11:18-12:6; 15:10-21; 17:14-18; 18:18-21 and 20:7-13. See Georg Fischer, Knut Backhaus, *Beten – Die Neue Echter Bibel Themen 14* (Würzburg: Echter, 2009), 41-42.

15   G.M. SOARES-PRABHU, "The Dharma of the Biblical Prophet," in Scaria Kuthirakkattel (ed), *Biblical Spirituality of Liberative Action: Collected Works of George M. Soares Prabhu,* vol. 3, Jnana-Deepa Vidyapeeth Theological Series, Pune 2000, 110.

16   Dwight LONGENECKER, "Francis is a great prophet, but he also needs to be pope," accessed on 12.05.2017 from: https://cruxnow.com/commentary/2016/12/08/francis-great-prophet-also-needs-pope/.

17   Pope FRANCIS interview by Fr. Antonio SPADARO, "A Big Heart Opens to God," in *La Civilta Catholica,* September 2013.

18   David WILLEY, *The Promise of Francis: the Man, the Pope and the Challenge of Change* (New York: Gallery Books, 2015), 23-50.

19   Radio Vatican Asia Newsletter, vol. 3, no. Spl 4, Sept. 29, 2015.

20   Pope Francis Address to the bishops of Brazil in Rio De Janeiro on July 27, 2013 (Zenit.org).

21   Pope Francis, *Apostolic Exhortation Evangelii Gaudium: The Joy of the Gospel* (Trivandrum: Carmel International Publishing House, 2013). All the subsequent references to *Evangelii Gaudium* is taken from this volume and will be referred to by the abbreviation EG with the respective number referred to.

22   Ibid, 135-136.

23   All subsequent references to this document are made to an online version of the document downloaded from http://w2.vatican.va/content/francesco/en/encyclicals/documents/papa-francesco_20130629_enciclica-lumen-fidei.html on 10.10.2017.

24   Pope Francis' homily at the Chrism Mass atSaint Peter's Basilica Holy Thursday, 8 March 2013 accessed on 12.10.2017 fromhttp://w2.vatican.va/content/francesco/en/homilies/2013/documents/papa-francesco_20130328_messa-crismale.html

25   The 'enemy ofhuman nature' is the way Ignatius calls the force of evil in human beings in his Spiritual Exercises 140.

26   Pope Francis' Address to the Jesuits, in Asian Journal of Religious Studies, 62/1-2 (January-April 2017): 9-10.

27   From the Address of His Holiness Pope Francis on 24 October 2015 on the occasion of the Conclusion of the Family Synod, accessed on 15.08.2016, from: http://w2.vatican.va/content/francesco/en/speeches/2015/october/documents/papa-francesco_20151024_sinodo-conclusione-lavori.html.

28   Pope Francis' address to the coordinating committee of CELAM in Rio De Janeiro on 29 July 2013 (zenit.org).

29   Cf. Mario ESCOBAR, *Francis: Man of Prayer* (Nashville: Thomas Nelson, 2013), 165-167.

30   Paul VALLELY, *Pope Francis: Untying the Knots* (London: Bloomsbury, 2013), 144.

31   Cf. Chris LOWNEY, *Pope Francis: Why He Leads the Way He Leads* (Chicago: Loyola Press, 2013), 79-80.

32   David WILLEY, *The Promise of Francis,* 12.

33   Cf. Chris LOWNEY, *Pope Francis: Why He Leads the Way He Leads,* 2.

34   Alphonse AROCKIASWAMY, *Decoding Pope Francis: The Man, the Pastor and the Missionary* (Bangalore: SFS Publications, 2016), 43.

35   The statements of this sentence are taken from Chris Lowney who has collected them from different news agencies in Chris Lowney, *Pope Francis: Why He Leads the Way He Leads,* 7.

36   David WILLEY, *The Promise of Francis,* 17-18.

37   Ibid, 73.

38   Cindy WOODEN, "Go out now, share the Gospel, get messy, pope tells Quebec bishops," in *Crux. Taking the Catholic Pulse*, accessed on 12.05.2017 from: https://cruxnow.com/vatican/2017/05/12/go-now-share-gospel-get-messy-pope-tells-quebec-bishops/.

39   Cristina ODONE, "For the Sake of the Priesthood's Future, Catholics Need to Talk about Women Priests,"*Daily Telegraph*, January 21, 2015.

40   David WILLEY, *The Promise of Francis*, 50-71.

41   Paulraj MARIAPUSHPAM, "God Who is Rich in Mercy (Eph 2:4): Mercy in the Bible,"*Asian Journal of Religious Studies* 64/1 (July-August 2016), 18-20.

42   Pope FRANCIS, *Apostolic Exhortation Evnaglii Gaudium: The Joy of the Gospel* (Trivandrum: Carmel International Publishing House, 2013), 36.

43   This verse Gal 5:6 expresses, in my opinion, Paul's most complete understanding of religion, namely as 'faith working through love.'

44   Pope Francis' Address to the Jesuits, 11.

45   Pope Francis' Address to the Jesuits, 12.

46   Austen IVEREIGH, *The Great Reformer: Francis and the Making of a Radical Pope* (New York: Herny Holt and Company, 2014), 374-375.

47   Cf. David WILLEY, *The Promise of Francis*, 28-29.

48   Michael AMALADOSS, "Pope Francis and Dialogue," *Vidyajyoti Journal of Theological Reflection* 79 (March, 2015), 165.

49   Ibid, 181.

50   Chris LOWNEY, *Pope Francis: Why He Leads the Way He Leads*, 9-10.

51   "Homily of Pope Francis for the Beginning of the Petrine Ministry of the Bishop of Rome," 19 March 2013 accessed on 11.10.2017 from https://w2.vatican.va/content/francesco/en/homilies/2013/documents/papa-francesco_20130319_omelia-inizio-pontificato.html.

52   Ibid.

53   Pope FRANCIS' Address to the Jesuits, 7.

54   Cf. Mario I AGUILAR, *Pope Francis: His Life and Thoughts* (Cambridge: The Luther Worth Press, 2014), 72-77.

55   Austen IVEREIGH, *The Great Reformer*, 130.

56   Cf. Mario I AGUILAR, *Pope Francis*, 63-65.

57   Cf. Gustavo GUTIERREZ, *A Theology of Liberation* (New York: Orbis, Maryknoll, 1971).

58   Austen IVEREIGH, *The Great Reformer*, 130.

59   Austen IVEREIGH, *The Great Reformer*, 374.

60   Michael AMALADOSS, "Pope Francis and Dialogue," 166.

61   Michael AMALADOSS, "Is Prophecy Still Alive?: Institution and Charism in the Christian Community in India," *Vidyajyoti Journal of Theological Reflection* 69 (Feb – 2005), 94-96.

62   ARASAKUMAR R, "Pope Francis An Agent of Change,"*Indian Currents*, 22-28 April 2013, 41.

Chapter 17

Is Pope a Communist? A Critical Response

Francis Arackal
Professor of Journalism and Mass Communication,
Amity University, Gurgaon, Haryana

Introduction

Since Pope Francis' election on 13 March 2013 he has been a very popular leader[1] around the globe for people of all religions because he came across as a man for all without any kind of distinctions. Besides, he was for peace and dialogue wherever conflict situations arose and existed such as in Ukraine, Crimea, Syria, Columbia, in the Middle East and so forth. What was most noticeable at the very beginning of his pontificate was his emphasis on compassion, love for the poor, refugees, immigrants, prisoners, and women and children caught up in serious and unfortunate situations. It is said that when one takes up issues of injustice one automatically gets perceived as dabbling in politics – often the leftist kind. In fact spirituality and politics are not entirely separable. While automatic political immersion may not be necessary and need not be true always while taking up causes of justice, people's perceptions cannot be easily erased. Now perceptions are also borne out of certain prejudices individuals and groups harbour about others, especially about a person or group/community that has a different ideology than your own. Conservative Christians, especially in United States of America, are led by a right-wing ideology with all the ramifications that go along with it (This will be spelt out later in the paper). Anyone who is opposed to this ideology, which is often not helpful for the cause of the poor, the marginalized, and the minorities, is easily labeled as a leftist or Marxist/Communist. Pope Francis being perceived, by Conservative Christians, as a left-leaning Marxist/Communist emerges from their right-wing ideological mental makeup. The present paper would like to do a deeper study about this perception. Is Pope Francis a Communist?

1. Origin of the label 'Communist' for Pope Francis

Rush Limbaugh[2], a conservative US radio talk show host, called Pope Francis a Marxist. He did so while commenting on Pope Francis' encyclical "Evangelii Gaudium" ("the Joy of the Gospel") on his top-rated radio show, which according to reports has an audience of 15 million in the United States (US). Limbaugh is reported to have castigated the Pope's economic principles and denouncement of Capitalism. He referred to the "sad" and "unbelievable" papal proclamation the Pope wrote "about the utter evils of Capitalism," and said the pontiff didn't understand how economics worked. "Look, folks, you know, I hate saying I told you so all the time," said Limbaugh. "But when it needs to be said, I do not shrink from it. ... This guy sounds like a Marxist."[3]

It is evident that Limbaugh was rushing to attack the Pope through mischaracterization of Francis' comments about economics. According to Horn (2013) the fundamental problem was that Limbaugh chose to quote not what Pope Francis wrote but a *Washington Post* article on the exhortation, which stated:

"Pope Francis attacked unfettered capitalism as 'a new tyranny' and beseeched global leaders to fight poverty and growing inequality, in a document setting out a platform for his papacy and calling for a renewal of the Catholic Church. . . . In it, Francis went further than previous comments criticizing the global economic system, attacking the 'idolatry of money.'"[4]

Limbaugh responded by saying, "This is just pure Marxism coming out of the mouth of the Pope. Unfettered Capitalism? That doesn't exist anywhere. 'Unfettered capitalism' is a liberal socialist phrase to describe the United States."[5]

If Limbaugh as a media person, and his many conservative Catholic supporters in the US, is to remember Pope John Paul II, in his 1991 encyclical *Centesimus Annus*, reflected on Socialism and Capitalism in the light of the fall of Communism in Soviet Union and Eastern Europe: "While acknowledging that profit has a "legitimate role" in the function of business and that "the Marxist solution" to economic inequality had failed, the Pope also spoke of the "inadequacies of Capitalism"and said that profit is not the only indicator that a business is doing well. The human dignity of workers also matter and if Capitalism is left unchecked it becomes "ruthless" and leads to "inhuman exploitation." Pope Francis' words are very much consistent with John Paul's."[6] Was Pope John Paul II a Marxist?

2. Significance of Choosing the Name Francis

To understand Limbaugh's accusation and to understand Pope's position we need to delve deep. We go back to the very moment of Cardinal Jorgo Mario

Bergoglio's election as the Pope. Cardinal Bergoglio deliberately, may be after much thought and meditation, and seemingly based on his life-motto, chose the name of St. Francis of Assisi (and not St. Francis Xavier, who belonged to his own Jesuit Society). St. Francis as a young man left home and chose to be the poor son of a rich father. St. Francis may have been hearing the echo of the words of Jesus to the rich young man: "Go sell, what you have and give it to the poor, and then follow me" (Mathew 19:21). Accordingly St. Francis gave away all he had, even the clothes he was wearing, to the poor and became almost naked, imitating the almost naked Jesus hanging on the cross to save humankind. Francis then, following the voice he heard from the crucifix in San Damiano, proceeded to build the crumbling and dilapidated church. At St. Francis' time "crumbling and dilapidated church" had both literal and figurative significance. True, the physical structure of the church of San Damiano was crumbling and dilapidated, perhaps due to neglect of the ecclesiastical authorities of his time. Figuratively too, the Church was crumbling and dilapidated due to the various scandals involving the ecclesiastical hierarchy of his time. Similarly, a situation of administrative, financial, and moral scandals were prevailing at the Vatican at the time of Bergoglio's election as Pope. Scandals involving the founder of the Legionaries of Christ, whom the previous Pontiffs seem to have protected, were raging. (The scope of this paper does not allow me to go into the details of these scandals). Cardinal Walter Kasper gives us some clue to the situation of the Church in to which Bergoglio was elected Pope, "a Pope of Surprises": "The cases of abuse had unleashed a shock wave and caused serious damage, above all in the United States, Ireland, Belgium, and Germany. Additionally, there arose the impression of mental fatigue and exhaustion, a lack of confidence and enthusiasm. The Church was increasingly occupied primarily with itself; it suffered and moaned about its situation or occasionally celebrated itself. Its prophetic power appeared extinguished and its missionary vitality appeared to languish. A world that had become secular and that was no longer communist, but rather consumerist and determined by the economy, appeared to make the Church marginal. Booming Pentecostal churches and esotericism throughout the world threatened to outstrip it. A relentless downward spiral appeared to be in motion."[7]

In Bergoglio's case choosing the name Francis meant various things: A desire to imitate the life of St. Francis in its multi-dimensional aspects: Poverty, humility, building the Church which was collapsing under the weight of doctrinal overload and misplaced and misinterpreted rituals and practices. At the time the progressive documents of Vatican II were put on the back burner. The Roman Missal translation (to get it closer to the original Latin version) was a disaster. Tridentine Latin Mass was being promoted by some authorities in the Vatican – liturgy was getting an ideological bend. The Catholic Church had been almost turned into an exclusive sect whereby only those adhering to the rigidity of doctrines could properly belong to it; those feeling alienated due to existential exigencies and struggles of life could very well go away. The very word 'Catholic' (meaning embracing everyone) had become a misnomer.

Imbibing the spirit of the Beatitudes, and the spirit of St. Francis, to near perfection Pope Francis began to speak for the world's poor, hungry, the sick, the lonely, the unloved. As St. Mother Theresa would do Pope Francis saw in all of them the face of Jesus. Imitating the foot-washing example of Jesus, Francis washed the feet of prisoners, differently abled, and Muslim women. Like a loving and caring father he would hug them and kiss them. At no juncture these gestures were thought to be or interpreted to be photo-op moments as it may be in the case of many other world leaders. Rather, these acts of kindness and compassion sprang out from a heart full of empathy, and sympathy.

Nor was he displaying these public gestures just because he is now Pope, the Vicar of Christ on earth, rather it is the very stuff that Bergoglio is made up of. His simplicity and humility had become a legend in his home Archdiocese of Buenos Aires and country (Argentina) even before he was elected Pope.

3. Influence of Liberation Theology

One of the great influences on Pope Francis' thinking was theologian Lucio Gera (1924-2012); Gera was the father of Argentine theology. At the 1964 Latin American Episcopal Conference (CELAM) held in Petropolis, Gera gave a paper on the theme 'The Meaning of the Christian Message in the Context of Poverty and Oppression.' This theme has become foundational for all forms of Liberation Theology. They all operate according to the method of "see, judge, act."[8] In a pastoral situation this means: observe the situation, make a judgment about what could be done, and then take action to try to correct the problem.[9]

It is at this Conference that Liberation Theology is said to have been born. Gustavo Gutierrez from Peru, now a member of the Dominican Order, is considered as the father of Liberation Theology. Liberation Theology tries to look at Christian revelation from the perspective of the poor in order to see what light Christian revelation can shed on poverty.

It was felt that Theology had gradually become a topic of only debate and discussion amongst clerics, abstract from ordinary life because of two isolations: Isolation of Theology from public life and isolation of people from social products of religion. These two isolations seem to have turned religion into a historical 'museum types of ideas'. Liberation Theology tried to overcome this isolation and became an attempt for liberating people of the world from poverty and oppression. Liberation Theology interprets the Gospel of Jesus Christ in light of the oppressed. Liberation theology looks at justice from the point of view of the oppressed in light of standards of love and justice envisioned in Christianity.

Liberation Theology was largely a response to the three coexistent social, political, and religious changes in Latin America:

First, worsening social and economic conditions for the majority of people in Latin America in the 1950s created a desire and expectations for change.

Second, the structural causes of poverty were addressed in Latin American Dependency Theory, and class-based inequities were identified in Marxist critiques of capitist systems. By the late 1950s a revolutionary climate was apparent in the region, exemplified by the Cuban Revolution of 1959.

The Second Vatican Council (1962-1965) was the third Major reason. Pope John XXIII opened the Council by expressing the hope that the Catholic Church "might become once again...the Church of the poor."

Since the emergence of Liberation Theology, it had become a unique and permanent political movement throughout Latin America; from Mexico to Chile, from Nicaragua to Brazil, this movement had been politically effective in merging together traditional, religious values with a commitment to social activism on behalf of the "poor[10] and Oppressed."

According to Liberation Theology the role of the Church therefore is to meet the needs of the poor; push for structural changes; and speak out against injustice. From the very outset of his pontificate Pope Francis' has been in the forefront addressing these issues. And during Francis papacy so far Liberation Theology has been freed from the doctrinal suspicions it faced from some ecclesiastical authorities in the Vatican in the past decades.

4. Making Sense of the Perception of Pope Francis being a Communist

It is not that this perception is so-widespread; at the same time it exists, especially among conservative Christians and Catholics in the United States. These conservative Christians are reported to have been driven by a one-point agenda: Anti-abortion. When we examine this one-point agenda we would find that it is a reductionist view: To conservative Christians, pro-life equals anti-abortion. To them all other issues directly connected to preservation of human life – poverty, hunger, war, unjust structures (economic, social, religious) – do not seem to belong to pro-life issues. According to reports most pro-life conservative Christians have been supportive of George Bush's Iraq invasion in which thousands of US soldiers (some of them in their youthful prime) and millions of civilians lost their lives. Even when the whole world thinks that Bush's Iraq invasion was one of the greatest tragedies of the 20th century with so many disastrous consequences such as the rise of terrorism, conservative Christians in the US, to this day, justify Bush's monumental misadventure. Whereas, to progressive Christians and Catholics pro-life embraces all these multifarious issues. To conservative Christians anyone speaking for the poor, speaking against injustices and oppressions, supporting the rights of the immigrants is seen as being left-leaning tantamount to being a Communist and a Socialist. Since his election to the Chair of St. Peter, Pope Francis has been the primary spokesperson on all these issues, which gives the impression that he is left-leaning and is close to being a Communist and a Socialist, if not an out-right Communist as Limbaugh labeled him.

Of course, it has to be noted that for the conservative Christians the words 'communist' and 'socialist' are baggage from the cold-war time, when the Communist and Socialist Soviet Union (and her Communist allies in Europe and elsewhere) was seen as the arch-enemy of the Capitalist United States of America. To many conservative Christians the very word 'socialist' is anathema. One of the main objections of conservative Republican Christians against President Barrack Obama was that he was introducing 'socialism' in the US or he is taking the US on the path to 'socialism', which was totally unacceptable to them.

This brings us to take a deeper look at the political under-pinning of both Conservative and Progressive Christians in the US. The US is mainly a two-party political system: Democrat and Republican. It has been generally agreed that the Democratic Party maintains more progressive ethos and policies than the Republican Party, which is led by conservative ideals. The Democratic Party is thought to be mainly a party of the poor (predominantly Blacks) and the Republican Party is mainly a party of the rich (predominantly Whites). The Democratic Party is generally pro-choice and Republican Party pre-dominantly pro-life. But in economic policies there seems to be a divergence from this usual binary: The Democratic Party is more conservative than the Republican Party, which is more liberal. The former is for more government control while the latter stands for almost unbridled freedom for businesses. It may be added here that it is this unbridled freedom for businesses (Capitalism) that resulted in the economic recession that began in 2007, from which the US and the world is yet to recover.

This takes us to the consideration of a Theory, which has been the standard-bearer and justifier for unbridled Capitalism. It is the Trickle-down Theory of economic operation.

5. Trickle-down Economic Theory

a. Origin of the Term 'Trickle-down'

In its origins the term 'Trickle-down' seems to have been a populist political term in the context of US politics. The first reference to trickle-down economics came from American comedian and commentator Will Rogers who used it to derisively describe President Herbert Hoover's stimulus efforts during the Great Depression.[11] Rogers commented that money was all appropriated for the top in the hope that it would trickle down to the needy. Rogers' joke became economic dogma within two generations, thanks in large part to Reagan, about whose economics we shall deal later on. Rogers' comment is like a foreshadowing of similar economic deal that happened during the economic recession in the US in 2007: bailout of banks and the paying of bonuses and perks to the high-end CEOs, who in themselves had a great part in the making of the problem. The poor and the middle-class in the US who were reeling under the great impact of recession (especially unemployment) were left to fend for themselves. It is said that "any policy can be considered 'trickle-down' if the following are true: first, a principle mechanism of the policy disproportionately benefits wealthy business and/or individuals in the short run. Second, the policy is designed to boost standards of living for all individuals in the long run."[12]

b. Forms of Trickle-down

There are two broad understanding of Trickle-down Theory, both seeming to favour the wealthy: Supply-side arguments, normally associated with tax cuts for the rich, suggest that the wealth creators would be more incentivized to raise output and create more and better jobs. Demand-side arguments, associated with subsidies and tariffs, claim that the wealthy need protections in order to keep paying their employees or to invest more.

c. The Laffer Curve

Laffer[13] Curve is a bell-curve style analysis that showed the relationship between changes in the official government and actual tax receipts. The Laffer Curve suggested taxes could be too light or too onerous to produce maximum revenue; in other words, a 0% income tax rate and a 100% income tax rate each produce $0 in receipts to the government. At 0%, no tax can be collected; at 100%, there is no incentive to generate income. This should mean that certain cuts in tax rates would actually boost total receipts by encouraging to create more taxable income.

Laffer's idea that tax cuts could boost growth and tax revenue was quickly labeled 'trickle-down'. Between 1980-88, the top marginal tax rate in the US fell from 70 to 28%. Between 1981-89, total US federal receipts increased from $599 to $991 billion. This seems to empirically support one of the assumptions of the Laffer Curve. However, it neither shows nor proves correlation between a reduction in top tax rates and economic benefits to the lower classes.[14]

d. Reaganomics to Trumponomics

The Trickle-down Theory is an economic idea which states that decreasing marginal and capital gains tax rates[15] - especially for corporations, investors and entrepreneurs - can stimulate production in the overall economy. According to trickle-down theory proponents, this stimulus leads to economic growth and wealth creation that benefits everyone, not just those who pay the lower tax rates. President Reagan's economic policies, commonly referred to as "Reaganomics" or supply-side economics, were based on trickle-down theory. The idea is that with a lower tax burden and increased investment, business can produce (or supply) more, increasing employment and worker pay. Reagan initially slashed the top income-tax rate from 70% to 50%. Trickle-down policy's detractors see the policy as tax cuts for the rich and don't think the tax cuts benefit lower-income earners. At the center of Reagan's economic doctrine was the idea that economic gains primarily benefiting the wealthy—investors, businesses, entrepreneurs, and the like—will "trickle-down" to poorer members of society, creating new opportunities for the economically disadvantaged to attain a better standard of living. Prosperity for the rich leads to prosperity for all, the logic goes.[16]

President Donald Trump has been following a similar economic policy. In November 2017 the US Congress passed the largest tax overhaul (through a tax-cut bill for the rich) in a generation in the US. "Using highly questionable supply-side arguments, which history has shown to be wrong, the bill's [Republican] advocates argue that it will spur so much economic growth, with so many businesses and individuals paying so much more in taxes on their higher earnings, that the measure will largely or entirely pay for itself."[17]

Democrats repeatedly slammed the bill as a give away to the rich at the expense of the poor. In addition to lowering taxes for businesses and many individuals, the Senate bill also makes a major change to health insurance that the Congressional Budget Office (CBO) projects would have a harsh impact on lower-income families. By 2019, Americans earning less than $30,000 a year would be worse off under the Senate bill, CBO found. By 2021, Americans earning $40,000 or less would be net losers, and by 2027, most people earning less than $75,000 a year would be worse off. On the flip side, millionaires and those earning $100,000 to $500,000 would be big beneficiaries, according to the CBO's calculations.[18]

e. Does it Work?

Proponents of Trickle-down model, especially Simon Kuznets,[19] reach the following conclusions: First, when the rate of capital accumulation is sufficiently high, the economy converges to a unique invariant wealth distribution. Second, even though the trickle-down mechanism can lead to a unique kind of distribution under laissez-faire, there is room for government intervention: in particular, redistribution of wealth from rich lenders to poor and middle-class borrowers improves the production efficiency of the economy both because it brings about greater equality of opportunity and also because it accelerates the trickle-down process. Third, the process of capital accumulation initially has the effect of widening inequalities but in later stages it reduces them: in other words, this model can generate a Kuznets' curve.[20]

It is Kuznets' hypothesis that as a country develops, there is a natural cycle of economic inequality driven by market forces which at first increases inequality, and then decreases it after a certain average income is attained.

f. Trickle-down Critique

The social problems of developed nations were spreading concern about the costs of economic growth. This is very evident in the US where there is racial polarization between the White and the Blacks. A vast section of the black population has not benefitted from the economic growth. Also from the 1980s the middle income levels have continuously come down.

Despite substantial transfers of capital and technology from the developed nations to the Third World, the gap between per capita incomes between the two blocs was growing. This shows the trickle-down economics has not worked.

Unemployment rates were refusing to go down in spite of impressive growth rates. This down-right belies the expectations of the trickle down proponents.

Power was concentrated among an elite coterie who benefited from the growth, who then used that power to preserve the inequality in their societies. It would seem that the Theory was used to cover up the economic manipulations of the rich and the elite in society. All trickle-down policies basically transfer wealth and advantages from all taxpayers towards an already wealthy few.

One major flaw of the Theory is that other economic indicators that were equally important, besides per capita incomes and GNP, were given a short shrift.

In a devastating report, International Monetary Fund (IMF) declared the idea of 'trickle-down' economics to be as much a joke as Rogers' humourous comment.Increasing the income share to the bottom 20 percent of citizens by a mere one percent results in a 0.38 percentage point jump in GDP growth. The IMF report, authored by five economists, presented a scathing rejection of the trickle-down approach, arguing that the monetary philosophy has been used as a justification for growing income inequality over the past several decades. "Income distribution matters for growth," they wrote. "Specifically, if the income share of the top 20 percent increases, then GDP growth actually declined over the medium term, suggesting that the benefits do not trickle down."[21]

6. Pope Francis and Trickle-down Theory

In November 2013 in his Apostolic Exhortation *Evangelii Gaudium* Pope Francis denounced 'Trickle-down' Economic Theories. In this 50,000-word paper outlining a philosophy that would guide his papacy, Pope Francis decried an "idolatry of money" and warned it would lead to "a new tyranny." He used tough language in attacking what he views as the excesses of Capitalism. Using a phrase with special resonance in the United States, he strongly criticized the Trickle-down Economic Theory — often affiliated with Republican Conservatives — that discourages taxation and regulation.

"Some people continue to defend trickle-down theories which assume that economic growth, encouraged by a free market, will inevitably succeed in bringing about greater justice and inclusiveness in the world," Francis wrote in the papal document.[22] "This opinion, which has never been confirmed by facts, expresses a crude and naive trust in the goodness of those wielding economic power and in the sacralized workings of the prevailing economic system."[23]

Commenting on Francis' Exhortation Michael Sean Winters, a fellow at Catholic University's Institute for Policy Research and Catholic Studies, said,

"There's no way a Catholic who is a serious intellectual can ever again not address the issue of income inequality, of the structural sins of our economic system. This is so front and center" … "This is a pastor's voice. He's saying, 'If we're serious Christians, we need to be knee-deep in this stuff.'"[24]

7. Pope Francis' Response on Being Labelled a 'Communist'

From history we know that Communism came in to fill the vacuum created by Christianity. Christianity in many ways failed the historical Jesus; it lost out on the Kingdom values that Jesus came to establish. The Church, the visible symbol of Christianity, got entangled in man-made doctrines, rules, and regulations, observances, and rituals. The Church almost everywhere, knowingly or unknowingly, neglected the poor, the needy, the working class, and played into the hands of the rich and the powerful. Persons (Christians and others) belonging to the above categories only got easy access to Apostolic palaces, Bishops palaces, Presbyteries, Rectories, high-walled and often well-barricaded convents, and religious houses. In this situation Communist slogans and thoughts became very attractive especially to the working class in many parts of the world. Communists took up and plunged into the daily struggles of the people even if it was for party interests. Therefore, sometime ago when Pope Francis was accused of being a Communist he retorted: It is Communists who have borrowed from Christian ideals and principles and certainly it is not the other way round. Jesus is the one who loved the poor and spoke for them. Hence, speaking for the poor and the down-trodden is to follow the ideals of the gospel and not a case of following Communism.

Conclusion

From the foregoing pages it is very clear that it is a total misconception on the part of Limbaugh and conservative Christians to label Pope Francis a 'Communist' just because he speaks for the poor, for women, for refugees, for environment, against injustice, against war, against the "tyranny of money", against big tax-cuts for the rich, against Capitalism, and against global warming. There couldn't be a worse representation of Pope Francis when people associate him with a leftist ideology or call him out rightly a Communist. Conservative Christians ensconced in the one-point agenda, anti-abortion, do not look or think beyond. Sometimes many of them give the impression that their capacity to think and reflect is totally lost. Or else how could one possibly explain the election of the billionaire businessman Donald Trump as the US President when he doesn't even come anywhere close to the Gospel values except latching on to the one-point agenda of conservative Christians? This is also the case, unfortunately, with many members of the Catholic hierarchy. Such an attitude cannot be described as one inspired by the life of Jesus or the Gospel. Whereas Pope Francis deeply immersed in the Gospel values, especially that of the Sermon on the Mount (which is the very core of the New Testament), proclaims the reign of the Kingdom of God. Indeed, Pope Francis is an image of Jesus in our world today.

Endnotes

1 Pope Francis was declared Time's Person of the Year in 2013 itself. This is what *Time* wrote while declaring Pope Francis as Person of the Year 2013: "Rarely has a new player on the world stage captured so much attention so quickly—young and old, faithful and cynical—as has Pope Francis. In his nine months in office, he has placed himself at the very center of the central conversations of our time: about wealth and poverty, fairness and justice, transparency, modernity, globalization, the role of women, the nature of marriage, the temptations of power." http://poy.time.com/2013/12/11/pope-francis-the-choice/> 09 December 2017.

2 Rush Hudson Limbaugh III is an American radio talk show host and conservative political commentator.

3 Bradford THOMAS. (2015). "Limbaugh: I Told you that Pope Francis is a Marxist" <http://www.truthrevolt.org/news/limbaugh-i-told-you-pope-francis-was-marxist> 10 November 2017.

4 Trent HORN. (2013). "Rush Limbaugh doesn't Get Pope Francis" <https://www.catholic.com/magazine/online-edition/rush-limbaugh-doesnt-get-pope-francis> 10 November 2017.

5 Cheryl K. CHUMLEY. (2013). "Rush Limbaugh decries Pope Francis' 'pure Marxism' teachings" <http://www.washingtontimes.com/news/2013/dec/3/rush-limbaugh-decries-pope-francis-pure-marxism/> 15 November 2017.

6 Trent HORN. (2013). "Rush Limbaugh doesn't Get Pope Francis" <https://www.catholic.com/magazine/online-edition/rush-limbaugh-doesnt-get-pope-francis> 10 November 2017.

7 Walter KASPER. (2015). *Pope Francis' Revolution of Tenderness and Love* (Translated by William Madges). Paulist Press: New York, P. 02.

8 Ibid., P, 16. Cardinal Kasper suggests that the method developed by the founder of the Young Christian Workers, Cardinal Joseph Cardijn (1881-1967), had a strong influence on Pope Francis before he became pope. The method of the Young Christian Workers was to observe, judge and act.

9 Some in the Church think that that Pope Francis is using the method of observe, judge, act as he leads the Church.

10 The poor are any forgotten, oppressed, and abandoned people.

11 http://www.investopedia.com/terms/t/trickledowntheory.asp (accessed on 22 July 2016).

12 http://www.investopedia.com/terms/t/trickledowntheory.asp (accessed on 22 July 2016).

13 A US economist, who was an advisor to President Ronald Reagan's administration.

14 http://www.investopedia.com/terms/t/trickledowntheory.asp (accessed on 22 July 2016).

15 CGT is a tax on capital gains, the profit realized on the sale of a non-inventory asset that was purchased at a cost amount that was lower than the amount realized on the sale.

16 https://psmag.com/the-imf-confirms-that-trickle-down-economics-is-indeed-a-joke-207d7ca469b#.4399e6dre (accessed on 23 July 2016).

17 Robert E. RUBIN. (2017). "No Serious Lawmaker should Support this Tax Bill". https://www.washingtonpost.com/.../no-serious-lawmaker-should-support-this-tax-bill/.../ 30 November 2017.

18 Heather LONG. (2017). "Senate GOP Tax Bill Hurts the Poor More Than Originally Thought, CBO Finds" https://www.washingtonpost.com/news/wonk/wp/2017/11/26/

senate-gop-tax-bill-hurts-the-poor-more-than-originally-thought-cbo-finds/?tid=hybrid_
collaborative_2_na&utm_term=.cadddcb1f744> 30 November 2017.

19   Simon Kuznets was a Belarusian-American economist, statistician, demographer, and
      economic historian who won the 1971 Nobel Memorial Prize in Economics.

20   A Kuznets curve is a graph with measures of increased economic development on the
      horizontal axis and measures of income inequality on the vertical axis.

21   https://psmag.com/the-imf-confirms-that-trickle-down-economics-is-indeed-a-joke-
      207d7ca469b#.4399e6dre (accessed on 23 July 2016).

22   Pope FRANCIS. (2017). *Evangelii Gaudium*, Pp. 53-60. <http://w2.vatican.va/content/
      francesco/en/apost_exhortations/documents/papa-francesco_esortazione-ap_20131124_
      evangelii-gaudium.html> 30 November 2017.

23   Ibid., pp. 53-60.

24   Zachary A. GOLDFARB and Michelle BOORSTEIN. (2013). "Pope Francis denounces
      'trickle-down' economic theories in sharp criticism of inequality" <Source: https://www.
      washingtonpost.com/business/economy/pope-francis-denounces-trickle-down-economic-
      theories-in-critique-of-inequality/2013/11/26/e17ffe4e-56b6-11e3-8304-caf30787c0a9_
      story.html?utm_term=.f630d35551ad> 30 November 2017.

VI. PROTECTING ENVIRONMENT

Chapter 18

Laudato Si'
Its Trinitarian and Christological Dimensions

Jacob Parappally MSFS

Professor, Systematic Theology, Tejas Vidya Peeth, Bengaluru, Karnataka

Introduction

What has the Trinity to do with ecology? The same question can be raised about the relation between Jesus Christ and the ecological issues of our times. What has Jesus Christ to do with ecology? Everything! This may surprise us because in the past the Christian faith has very systematically separated itself from the concerns of the environment or ecology. Living in the midst of people who worship nature in general and the forces of nature like winds, fire, thunder, etc., as gods, Christianity insulated itself from any form of pantheism which says that everything is god. Pantheism grew in the primitive societies and pantheistic ideas were integrated into the belief systems of the people of the Greco-Roman and Mediterranean world as well as of the eastern religions. The God-experience of the Old Testament times as articulated in the bible challenged the worship of the powers of the nature as gods and secularized them as created by God through his word. However, the attraction to pantheism was a real temptation even to those who had faith in One God. The other extreme of considering nature as mere objects to be conquered, subordinated and manipulated to satisfy human greed has brought in irreparable damage to nature and eco-system causing dangerto all living creatures including humans. A deeper understanding of the inter-relationship between humans and the entire creation based on the foundational Christian experience of God as

Trinity and Jesus Christ, the Logos or, God became human as the link between God and the world gives us a comprehensive, integral and liberative vision of the entire creation. In fact, Pope Francis, in his encyclical, *Laudato si* has already attempted to show the relation between God and creation especially in the last two prayers found in the encyclical.

What is environment? Environment is the external surroundings in which we humans, animals and plants live and it affects the development of everyone and everything that lives and grows in that environment. Ecology tries to study by analyzing and understanding the complex net-work of relationships and interdependencies in a given environment. It all boils down to how to the understanding of relationships among living beings and their relation to non-living or *a-biotic* realities in the entire creation. In fact, religion is all about relationships: relationship with oneself, God, others and creation.

The term 'religion', according to many is derived from the Latin word, *religare* which means 'to bind together'. Therefore, any religion that divides and separates people from people, people from the Absolute or God and people from the entire creation is a not a religion and even ifit has a semblance of a religion. For the Cosmic religions like Hinduism and many of the ancient religions of the Near East, relationship with the world and all in it was easy as it was an essential part of their religion. But they perverted it according to Paul. He says, " Claiming to be wise, they became fools, and exchanged the glory of the immortal God for images resembling mortal man or birds or animals or reptiles" (Rom 1:22).While, Cosmic religions have a predilection for everything in nature and believe it as divinize supported by a cyclic view of time derived from the course of nature, the Judeo-Christian tradition believes that everything is created by God and it has beginning and an end. Therefore, this religious tradition has a linear view of time which emphasizes history. When the cosmic religious traditions went to the extreme of making the organic and inorganic things and powers of nature as gods, the prophetic religious traditions went to the extreme of absolutely separating the entire cosmos or creation from God emphasizing God's transcendence neglecting the immanence of God. However, the biblical experience of God and the world as articulated in the different books of the bible, Jesus' own relation to creation, the teachings of the Fathers of the Church, the Magisterium and the recent Popes present an integral and balanced understanding of the relation between God, human beings and the created world.

Nowhere in the Bible it is unambiguously stated that God is absolutely separated from the world though God is supreme creator, ruler, controller, protector and provider of the needs of the world. God is related to the world as its creator. This relationship between God and the world need to be affirmed in order to understand the mysteries of creation, incarnation and resurrection and the sacraments and God's presence in human communion. We have to say, God is distinct from the creation but not separate from the creation. They are not one and they are not two either! This is not a philosophical or theological puzzle but the meaning of our existence and the existence of the world founded on the Trinitarian and Christic experience of God. This faith-experience can lead us to an understanding of our integral and liberating relationship with God and the creation and to develop a responsible attitude towards our environment and eco-system.

In this paper I am attempting to show how our Christian experience of God as Trinity and our relationship with God in Jesus Christ is the foundation of our right relationship with the entire creation and the demands it makes to care for the creation as well as to respond to the ecological crisis we face today based on the Encyclical *Laudato Si* by Pope Francis.

1. The Trinitarian Dimension of Ecology

It is the Christian experience of God that God is a communion of three Persons, the Father, Son and the Holy Spirit. Church's experience of God as Trinity from its originary experience of Jesus Christ as Lord and God after his resurrection, the experience of the Holy Spirit at Pentecost and the experience of the apostles that Jesus called God as Abba, Father. They expressed this faith-experience by baptizing those who believed in the name of the Father and Son and the Holy Spirit, confessed the Triune God in their creeds and prayers, etc. It is this foundational faith that has entered into the Christian understanding of humans and the world in their relation to the Trinitarian God. The later theological reflections on the Trinitarian God would explain that humans are created in the image and likeness of God, but God the Trinity. So every human being is an image of the Father, the Son and the Holy Spirit. Every human being has a Father dimension, that is transcendence, the Son dimension that is transparence, and the Spirit-dimension that is immanence. Therefore, all humans are by nature communitarian as they are the images of the Trinity or the Absolute communion. They are inter-related and inter-connected as persons. What is the relation of the rest of the creation other than humans with the Trinity?

According to the Christian tradition the vestige or dress of the Trinity is in the creation (*vestigia trinitatis in creatura*).[1] John Paul II says, St. Augustine wrote: "It is necessary that we, viewing the Creator through the works of his hands, raise up our minds to the contemplation of the Trinity, of which creation bears the mark in a certain and due proportion."[2]

Pope Francis has expressed the similar understanding of the relation between the Triune God and the creation in the Christian prayer in union with the creation in his encyclical *Laudato Si* "Triune Lord, wondrous community of infinite love, teaches us to contemplate you in the beauty of the universe, for all things speak of you. Awaken our praise and thankfulness for every being that you have made. Give us the grace to feel profoundly joined to everything that is."[3] The relation between the Trinity and the creation is not mere presence of God in the creation or creation revealing the beauty and grandeur of the Trinity. It is more than a mere reflection but a deeper relationship that can be explained only in relation through the Son who became human and thus became a part of creation.

The Trinity is the source and model of the entire creation. The Trinity is the source because everything is created by the Triune God. Irenaeus of Lyons says that God has created the world with his two hands, the Logos and the Pneuma or the Word and the Spirit. The stamp of the Trinitarian God can be discovered in the creation. According to John Paul II, "It is a truth of faith that the world has its beginning in the creator, who is the Triune God. Although, the work of creation is attributed especially to God the Father—this we profess in the creeds of the faith ("I believe in God the Father Almighty, Creator of heaven and earth")—it is also a truth of faith that the Father, the Son and the Holy Spirit are the unique and indivisible "principle" of creation.[4] The Trinity is the model of creation because everything in the world are distinct and are inter-related, both living and non-living. Everything in this universe is unique. The marvelous plurality of everything that exists, every plant and every animal, every bird in the sky and every fish in the sea reveal the plurality and distinctiveness of everything that exists.

How can we explain the meaning of this plurality? They are all modeled after their maker, the Triune God. In the absolute communion of the Trinity one person is not the other. The Father is not the Son or the Spirit. The same could be said of the Son and the Spirit. Yet there is only One God. The unity in the diversity of the creation is modeled after the Trinity. What Tertullian says the Trinity explains the difference and communion among them. He says that in the Trinity there is difference without division, there is distinction without separation. Such a great plurality and unity we can find in the creation. Therefore, any contemplation of the creation leads us to the contemplation of the eternal communion of the Father, the Son and the Spirit. Therefore, everything in the creation must be approached with a contemplative attitude not with a pragmatic attitude. If we have a contemplative attitude to Nature or Creation everything in the universe becomes a symbol or a sacrament for us, raising our minds to God and filling our hearts with love and thankfulness to God like the Psalmist who sang, "when I see the heavens, the work of your hand...(Ps 8).

At the conclusion of his general audience speaking about the creation John Paul II said, "Creation is the work of the Triune God. The world "created" in the Word-Son, is "restored" together with the Son to the Father, through that Uncreated Gift, the Holy Spirit, consubstantial with both. In this way the world is created in that Love, which is the Spirit of the Father and of the Son. This universe embraced by eternal Love begins to exist in the instant chosen by the Trinity as the beginning of time."[5]

The ecological crisis today is created by our pragmatic attitude towards creation. We relate to the things in the universe for their usefulness. How a thing is useful to us is our concern. So the world as a sacrament is manipulated, used and abused for the selfish greed of humans. Thus we not only disfigure the creation but also disfigure the Triune God who created the world. Therefore, it is a tremendous responsibility placed on to treat the things of creation with certain reverence due to it because everything in the universe is reflecting the glory of God.

2. Christological Dimensions of Ecology

It is easier for us to understand how Jesus Christ is related to the entire creation. We have not only the witness of the Gospel but also the Fathers of the Church and the teaching of the Magisterium about the Christic dimension of the creation because everything created 'through him' and 'for him' (Col 1:15f). John would say, the Word was God and the world was made through him (Jn 1:10). In fact, all things were made through him and without him nothing was made (Jn 1:3). The Letter to the Hebrews affirms the same when it says that God through the Son "also created the world" (Heb 1:2). It is true that everything created through the Son but is he related to the universe only as its creator? It would have been a relation between the creator and the creature if the Word or the Logos had not become human. The incarnation or the hominization of the Word made the entire creation a new creation. After the incarnation the universe or the cosmos is no more the same. Every mighty star to the tiniest atom, every non-living and the living being was transformed by humanity's unity with divinity. The world has become sacred. The world has become a sacrament.

Paul expresses this intimate union of the Logos with the creation in the Christological hymn in Colossians. "He is the image of the invisible God, the first born of all creation. For by him all things were created, in heaven and on earth, visible and invisible, whether thrones or dominions or rulers or authorities—all things were created through him and for him. And he is before all things, and in him all things hold together" (Co 1:15-16). This hymn summarizes the biblical revelation about the relationship of the creation with God revealed through Jesus Christ. Jesus Christ is the Alpha and the Omega of creation, the beginning and the end and indeed, the meaning of the universe. In Jesus Christ God reveals not only what humans are and what they can become but also what the world is. The world too has its origin and end in Christ. When one encounters Jesus Christ as the beginning and the end or source and final destiny of one's life, she or he will find meaning in life. The hominization of the Word, or God becoming human and thus becoming a part of this worldly reality gives meaning also to this universe. John expresses this revelation by synthesizing the Greek philosophical term Logos which means word, reason or meaning and the Hebrew term *dabar* or word. In the Hellenistic or Greek world-view logos is the beginning and the end of the world or the meaning of the world and for the Hebrews dabar Yahweh or God's word is God's presence and action in history. Therefore, when John combines these two world-views to reveal who Jesus is, he uses the term Logos which means that Jesus Christ is the meaning of the universe and God's presence and action in history. According to Athanasius, a great Father of the Church before incarnation the Logos was the governing principle of the universe from outside but after the incarnation he is the governing principle of the universe from within the universe. So we can legitimately affirm that everything living and non-living has its beginning and end in Christ, indeed, its meaning is Christ. In other words, there is no-thing outside the reality of Christ. After the incarnation or hominization of the word, everything and everyone is a Christophany, a manifestation of Christ in its own unique way.

The incarnated Son of God or Jesus the human lived a life in right relationship with the entire creation. He did not run away from the world considering it evil. Everything created by the Father who makes the sun shine and rain fall on everyone without any discrimination was found to be revealing his Father's care and love. Pope Francis affirms this in his encyclical *Laudato Si'*. He says: "Jesus lived in full harmony with creation, and others were amazed: "What sort of man is this, that even the winds and the sea obey him?" (*Mt* 8:27). His appearance was not that of an ascetic set apart from the world, nor of an enemy to the pleasant things of life. Of himself he said: "The Son of Man came eating and drinking and they say, 'Look, a glutton and a drunkard!'" (*Mt* 11:19).[6] Further he says, "He [Jesus] was far removed from philosophies which despised the body, matter and the things of the world. Such unhealthy dualisms, nonetheless, left a mark on certain Christian thinkers in the course of history and disfigured the Gospel. Jesus worked with his hands, in daily contact with the matter created by God, to which he gave form by his craftsmanship.[7] What a harmonious relationship with the creation!

In the during the apostolic times when the NT was taking shape and during the post-apostolic times heretical schools like that of the Gnostics and Docetics taught that matter was evil and the spirit was good. They would not accept that God became truly human because God cannot assume evil matter. Docetics said Jesus appeared to be human but not really human. The Fathers of the Church like Ignatius of Antioch, Irenaeus and others fought against such heresies and affirmed that whatever God has created was good and God became truly human. However, their heretical doctrine had a negative influence on the Christian understanding of the world and on the Christian spirituality. The slogan of some spiritual masters was "*fuga mundi*" or run away from this world. The Christian vocation is not to run away from the world but remain in it with a contemplative attitude and transform it with a prophetic commitment empowered by the Holy Spirit who makes everything new.

In the resurrection of Christ, the humanity of Christ is glorified and through the glorified body of Christ the entire creation is transformed and glorified. Therefore, the material reality can be transformed to become the medium of God's presence. The sacraments, especially the Eucharist, which we celebrate is a celebration not only of our communion with God and one another but also our communion with the entire universe. In a single piece of bread we use at the Eucharistic celebration the entire universe is at work, the sun, the earth, water, the wheat plant, the seed, the farmer, the baker and finally those who receive it. The universe plays its role in the miracle of the Eucharist, along with Christ, the priest and the community.

Conclusion

It is the Son of God who made this creation new with his incarnation and resurrection and it is the Holy Spirit guides the creation to its final destiny as willed by the Father. I would like to conclude my paper with the prayer of Pope Francis presented at the conclusion of the his encyclical *Laudato Si'*, "Son of God, Jesus, through you all things were made. You were formed in the womb of Mary our Mother, you became part of this earth, and you gazed upon this world with human eyes. Today you are alive in every creature in your risen glory. Praise be to you!"

Endnotes

1   *De Trinitate*, VI, 10, 12

2   JOHN PAUL II, *Creation is the Work of the Trinity*, General Audience, 5 March, 1986 & *Laudato si*, No. 98

3   Pope FRANCIS, *Laudato si'*, No. 246

4   JOHN PAUL II, *Creation is the Work of the Trinity*, General Audience, 5 March, 1986.

5   Ibid.

6   *Laudato si'*, No. 98.

7   *Laudato si'*, No. 98.

Chapter 19

Laudato Si'
Its Philosophical Foundation

Thomas Kalary MSFS
Suvidya College, Bengaluru, Karnataka

Introduction

Pope Francis' encyclical *Laudato Si'* has definitely provoked ripples in the collective conscience of humanity. An interesting question in this context would be: who is the immediate philosophical mind behind *Laudato Si'*? In answering this question, it would be apt to turn our attention to another historical event that took place on February 28, 2013. In his last act as Pope, while officially renouncing the Papacy and bidding farewell to the College of Cardinals in the Vatican's Clementine Hall, Pope Benedict XVI quoted Romano Guardini in the short speech he delivered. Quoting from Guardini's book *The Church of the Lord*, he said "the Church is not an institution devised and built at table, but a living reality. She lives along the course of time, evolving, like any living being, transforming herself. Yet her nature remains the same."[1]

1. Guardini's Critique of Technological Approach to Nature

Guardini, as we know,was a known modernist, who was even under suspicion of heresy before Vatican II. After the Council, Guardini found a warm reception in the Church. In fact, Paul VI wanted to elevate him to the college of Cardinals, something that he politely refused. Thinkers like Martin Buber, Martin Heidegger and Max Scheler were instrumental in fashioning the liberal thinking of Guardini.

In turn, he had a definitive influence on Pope Paul VI, Karl Rahner, Joseph Ratzinger and the present Pope Francis.It is common knowledge that Guardini played a key role in the theological and liturgical movements of the '30s and '40s of the twentieth century that led to Vatican II. He had redesigned a chapel at Burg Rothenfels. Discarding the Gothic altars and elaborate décor, he stripped the church, painted the walls white and installed a moveable altar surrounded on three sides by simple stools. The focus was entirely on the congregation and the priest, together forming a community gathered for worship with no separation between them. We see that he was a worthy precursor of the Council's Constitution *Sacrosanctum Concilium* and Paul VI's liturgical reform. Guardini feared that the popular devotions that had energized the Catholic revival of the nineteenth century had fostered anarchic spiritual individualism in which prayer had become simply a tool for attaining merit in the quest for individual salvation. Communism offered an alternative to this anarchy, but only at the expense of eliminating individual freedom. Against these extremes, he emphasised that the idea of the Church as the Body of Christ, an organic union of persons that made possible the full flourishing of the "free personality," which is "the presupposition of all true community." The spirit of the liturgy is above all a spirit of community, uniting the faithful with each other even as it unites them to God. This side of Guardini is known to all.

But there is another unknown side of Guardini that is made remarkably visible by the encyclical *Laudato Si*. Guardini loved nature and took particular delight in the lake region around Milan. Besides being enchanted by the physical beauty of the area, what intrigued him above all was the manner in which human beings, through their architecture and craftsmanship, **interacted non-invasively and respectfully with nature**. When he first came to the region, he noticed, for example, how the homes along Lake Como imitated the lines and rhythms of the landscape and how the boats that plied the lake did so in response to the swelling and falling of the waves. But by the 1920's, he had begun to notice a change. The homes being built were not only larger, but more "aggressive," indifferent to the surrounding environment, no longer accommodating themselves to the natural setting. And the motor-driven boats on the lake were no longer moving in rhythm with the waves, but rather cutting through them indifferently.

In these unhappy changes, Guardini noted the emergence of a distinctively modern sensibility. He meant that the attitudes first articulated by Francis Bacon in the sixteenth century and René Descartes in the seventeenth were coming to dominate the mentality of twentieth-century men and women. Consciously departing from Aristotle, for whom knowledge was a modality of contemplation, Bacon opined that knowledge is power, more precisely power to control the natural environment. This is why he infamously insisted that the scientist's task is to put nature "on the rack" so that she might give up her secrets. Just a few decades later, Descartes told the intellectuals of Europe to stop fussing over theological matters and philosophical abstractions and to get about the business of "mastering" nature. This shift in consciousness gave rise to the modern sciences and their attendant technologies. It is the Guardinian worries about the disastrous consequences of this shift that is shared by Pope Francis in his encyclical.

The Encyclical *Laudato Si* with the thematic title "On Care for our common Home" moves away from the customary practice of being addressed to the bishops of the Church or the lay faithful, but similar to Pope Saint John XXIII's *Pacem in Terris*, is addressed to all people in order" to enter into dialogue with all people about our common home" (#3). The primary focus is not the ecological dangers that the modern world faces, but our mistaken understanding of nature, and of our place and role in nature. We have of ourselves an inflated image and a criminally commodified vision of nature. We regard it, in essence, as a kind of accident demanding technological mastery and manipulation for our own self-centered purposes. Attempts were also made to justify such a criminal approach by referring to the creation account in Genesis (1:28) that apparently grants man "dominion" over the earth. It is not without reason that the objection was raised that the Judaeo-Christian tradition based on this account has encouraged the unbridled exploitation of nature by man.

The encyclical sets out first to correct such mis-readings of the biblical accounts. "The creation accounts in the book of Genesis contain, in their own symbolic and narrative language, profound teachings about human existence and its historical reality. They suggest that human life is grounded in three fundamental and closely intertwined relationships: with God, with our neighbour and with the earth itself. According to the Bible, these three vital relationships have been broken, both outwardly and within us. .. The harmony between the Creator, humanity and creation as a whole was disrupted by our presuming to take the place of God and refusing to acknowledge our creaturely limitations. This in turn distorted our mandate to "have dominion" over the earth (cf. *Gen* 1:28), to "till it and keep it" (*Gen* 2:15). As a result, the originally harmonious relationship between human beings and nature became conflictual (cf. *Gen* 3:17-19)." (LS, 66)

As the next step, the encyclical turns to the problem of modern ecological crisis? It begins by acknowledging the contribution of modern technology as it "has remedied countless evils," and the genuine progress it has effected, "especially in the fields of medicine, engineering, and communications" (102). But the cost that is being paid for it is unjustifiably high. The Pope writes, "Technology tends to absorb everything into its ironclad logic"; "in the most radical sense of the term, power is its motive—a lordship over all" (108). This results in a serious problem. It manipulates and commodifies everything in nature. This commodification poisons everything, not only our environment but our self-understanding. It affects our use of our own bodies, our grasp of the meaning and purpose of our sexuality, the relations between the sexes, and our attitude toward children, marriage and family life. This commodification of nature causes us not only to abuse and dispose of the poor and marginalized through sheer selfishness. And worse still, it causes us to abuse and dispose of ourselves.

The problem for modernity is that it vacillates between two extremes— between envisioning humanity as lord and master over the raw material that is nature and seeing the human animal as the enemy of the rest of the natural order. Francis focuses on the former error: "Modernity," he writes, "has been marked by an excessive anthropocentrism" (116). Separating the human from the natural, one direction in modernity promotes manipulation of nature without limits (118), whereas another direction sees humans as the chief threat to the cosmos. Accordingly, Francis observes, we find ourselves in a "constant schizophrenia, wherein a technocracy which sees no intrinsic value in lesser beings coexists with the other extreme, which sees no special value in human beings."

Now to return to our initial question: who is the philosophical inspiration behind these insights? It is no doubt that in his elucidations Pope Francis is heavily influenced by Romano Guardini's *End of the Modern World*, which presents a sort of nightmarish vision of humanity, in which human power gives rise to a kind of technology which itself operates by its own logic of progress, liberating itself from human control in the process, and eventually returns to plague the inventor. But how many readers of Guardini will know that in these technological views Guardini was himself heavily indebted to Martin Heidegger's critique of modernity's technological view of thinking? It is here that this essay proposes to make a small note.

2. Heidegger and the Machinational and Relational Interpretation of Beings

Heidegger begins his reflections on modern technology with the candid observation that today, all over the world the humans remain "unfree and chained to technology."[2] This has resulted in a dangerous situation, viz. the further the technology advances, the more it "threatens to slip from human control." (QT, 5) It is this sad situation that necessitates a questioning of the essence of modern technology and the threat it poses. Pointing out the current understanding of technology in its "instrumental character" "as a means to an end" or in its "anthropological character" as "a human activity", though correct, still fails to show what is really *ownmost* to technology. "Technology is a mode of revealing. Technology comes to sway [essences] in the realm where revealing and unconcealment take place, where *alētheia*, truth, happens." (QT, 13) Heidegger calls our attention to the essential difference between modern and past technologies. Whereas in its original sense technology was a mode of revealing, a "bringing-forth in the sense of *poiēsis*," the "revealing that rules in modern technology is a challenging." (QT, 14) The windmill is a classic example of the old technology. It needs wind to turn its sails. But it does not unlock energy from the wind. It just goes along the play of things as they are. Or, placing a bridge across a river does not do violence to the river, but rather it allows the river to be what it is. In coal production, in contrast, what is aimed at is to extract the energy stored in coal to generate heat, which in turn is meant to generate steam out of water, with which the wheels of some machines can be turned for some other purpose. Or, take the case of installing a dam across a river for generating hydroelectric energy. In both cases, violence is done to the things and they are manipulated. It is this characteristic of the modern technology that becomes the object of scrutiny by Heidegger.

According to Heidegger, our age is characterized by a machinational interpretation of beings. That is, modern technology comes across to us predominantly in a "machinational" character, that includes such activities of objectifying, making, producing, ordering, etc. (GA 65:115/91) In the process, what is ownmost to technology gets disguised (of course not eliminated). Here, technology becomes absolutely anthropocentric, representing absolute human domination and mastery over everything, all beings and nature. This total subjugation by man, naturally abetted by technology, leaves no room for other things to be on their own. Everything is there to be exploited to serve the needs of the human subject. This machinational perspective of beings as mere makeable and exchangeable objects is nothing short of nihilism, where man is made the ground of everything amidst a negation of all transcendent ground and values. When man considers himself the measure of everything else in the cosmos, man becomes an unbridled monster, who replaces every transcendental values with technological powers.

In the 50s Heidegger speaks of the essence of modern technology in terms of another "disclosive framework", viz. Ge-stell which is variously translated as "en-framing" or "positionality." The World War II heralded a new framework of "standing reserve" (GA 79:32/31) in the place of the subject-object framework that let everything including humans be understood in terms of how it can be represented, arranged, mobilized, exchanged, or replaced for a specific goal, a framework in terms of which everything gets degenerated into mere raw-materials. Everything is positioned or framed into a horizon, where everything, including humans, is just replaceable commodities for global consumption. Just recollect the times we grew up with small riverlets, paddy fields, ponds, where life was really lived. Everything had an intrinsic worth, they formed an essential aspect of that "home" for the humans and other living beings around it. And today?

While machinational interpretation of beings revolved around the subject-object relation that exalted the hegemony of anthropocentrism and reduced everything else to orderable and makeable objects, in enframing the subject-object framework disappears and everything is assimilated into a frame for which everything comes to presence as part of a stockpile that can be manipulated. In the former, human beings as the productive agents or representing subjects had some sort of a prominence, whereas in the enframing technological attitude human beings are just resources within the totalising technological disclosure of reality. As standing reserve everything is pieces of stockpiles to be ordered or replaced, parts to be assembled or disassembled. There is no such thing as a part-whole relation as in a living organism, but everything is a mere part that can be exchanged or replaced. We know how our electronic gadgets come to us today. They come to us as packets of various pieces. If one piece does not work, it gets replaced. Neither parts, nor the whole as such, has any individual identity. They are all parts of a stockpile that can be consumed, exchanged, or replaced.

Human beings are no exception to this circuit of orderability. Days may not be far off, where the attention moves from cloning human beings to erecting factories that produce human beings. The essence of technology as enframing does not leave man alone as in charge of technology. He himself is devoured by the same process of framing, that had in fact facilitated man's domination of the rest of the nature. Not only that a worker is seen as an instrument for production, but even the top brass of companies, who plan and organize, are so easily and ruthlessly fired and replaced. They are mere resources to be ordered, arranged, disposed of or replaced. For Heidegger, the tragedy of such a technological interpretation is that every person and everything in the world loses its individual identity, distinctive independence and uniqueness. Everything is positioned within a horizon of global commodification. Each and every being is transformed into mere replaceable stockpile.

What then is the main danger of modern technology? For Heidegger, the primary danger is not so much the atomic or other destructive weaponry or even the environmental disasters resulting from the application of modern technology. They can only bring about a physical destruction. But the real problem is the spiritual destruction of man living under the sway of such technological attitude. Through an abject surrender to such a technological attitude, man lives under the illusion that they are the masters and everything is in their perfect control. This illusion is the result of their belief that everything before them is just objects and means to be ordered and organized by them. But they are oblivious to the truth that under this illusion, they reduce themselves to mere resources, subject to the same process of being ordered or replaced. To dispel the illusion that we are the masters of the world and to respond appropriately to the domination of technology, what is needed first is to realize that we are not before or beyond the complex of technological relationships, but rather we are inescapably chained to such relationships.

How do we respond to this technological interpretation of being appropriately? Technology can never be overcome, because it is no more under our power; we are not its masters. Heidegger favours rather a free relation to technology. This free relation to technology begins with the realization that today the first challenge is to disclose technology in its one dimensionality, where the humans are dangerously enslaved by technology, negating any role for their free will. Becoming aware of this danger opens up the possibility for a free relation to technology in the sense that it will free us from any compulsion to continue with it unconditionally or to rebel against it as something devilish. We can use technology or any technical devices, without being enslaved to them, without being controlled by them. This amounts to experiencing the 'technological' in terms of its limitations. Experiencing the limits of technology would make us so free in our dealings with them that we can let go of them at any time. Such a free relationship implies an "yes" and "no" at the same time, an yes to the unavoidable use of technical devices, but with a no to any right on their part to dominate us, to enslave us.

Indeed, technology has its inherent danger. The way to overcome its danger is not by rejecting technology, but by perceiving the danger it poses and allowing ourselves to be ourselves. Realizing its danger itself opens the possibility of a "turn" away from it. It is in this sense that he quotes the German poet Friedrich Hölderlin: "But where the danger is, there grows also what saves." (QT, 28) What is decisive in the process, warns Heidegger, is to remember that "despite all conquest of distances the nearness of things remains absent."[3] This could easily be illustrated with what happens in most of our human communities today. A cell phone easily reduces distances across the globe. But for that we often sacrifice the nearness of one another, say at a dining table, when each one is busy with their electronic gadgets. In order to truly experience and maintain nearness, we must encounter things in their respective truth, understand them in what they are. Only then will we be saved from the danger of technology, from being reduced, both things as well as ourselves, to mere supplies and reserves.

Having taken this detour, let us ask the question: Is the encyclical a corrective to the excesses of modern technology? No. It is true, that the Pope gently but firmly states that modern technology is fundamentally flawed. The very philosophy behind it is cancerous. However, the key thrust of the encyclical is much more than being a cry of protest against the evils of modernity or modern technology. For the Encyclical the ecological crisis is as much a crisis of human person, who is now lost in the cosmos, increasingly alienated from self, others, nature, and God. "If the present ecological crisis is one small sign of the ethical, cultural, and spiritual crisis of modernity, we cannot presume to heal our relationship with nature and the environment without healing all fundamental human relationships" (119). What makes this a truly great and moving and beautiful encyclical is the magnificent exposition of another view of reality: a description of the true nature of the created order, in all its marvellous and interconnected glory, and of the true role of man as the gardener of this garden of wonders. The heart of the encyclical revolves around the question of how to move away from an exploitative technological relation to a caring relation to our entire environment.

It is again here that the Heideggerian insights on the relational character of everything finite could throw further lights on the encyclical. With the notion of the "fourfold" (Thing, 173f.)[4] Heidegger attempts to highlight how the entire finite existence -- that includes humans as well as every aspect of the entire universe -- stands so interrelated that it opens ways of authentic relationships away from the dangerous technological one that consider things as mere stockpile under our domination.

With the notion of the fourfold, Heidegger tries to show that what we encounter in our universe is not lonely objects out there, but essentially things that "gather" in themselves earth, sky, mortals, and divinities. In every finite existence, "earth and sky, divinities and mortals dwell *together all at once*. These four, at one because of what they themselves are, belong together. Preceding everything that is present, they are enfolded into a single fourfold." (Thing, 173) "Earth" stands for the very "matter" of existence, but not in the sense of the solid ground, but in the sense of non-quantifiable sensuous appearing. It is not the substantial basis from which everything evolves, but rather, it is that which shines or radiates in a thing while making it appear. This shining or radiating of a thing requires a medium to appear and that medium is the sky. The sky represents the mediation of the appearance of a thing in terms of such elements like the weather patterns, variable lighting, as well as the temporal exposure to night and day and seasonal changes. Thus, one can say that the appearance of a thing is always 'weathered' by the sky. But these two constitutive elements are not all that is there to the appearance of a thing. There is, then, the dimension of the divinities that indicates the disclosure of the finite, mediated appearance as essentially meaningful. According to Heidegger, the reason why every single thing is inherently meaningful is because of the participation of divinities in its constitution. We know that it is the relatedness among things that give things their initial meaning. But such relatedness is possible only because they are exposed to a beyond and are addressable by it, viz. the mystery of grace. When Heidegger says that divinities are a constitutive element of a thing, he is underlining the fact that all things, not just humans, are exposed to the surprise of grace. All finite existence is always already immersed in a "hermeneutics of message." It is this exposure to grace, it is this immersion in a message that makes any meaningful existence possible at all. The fourth constitutive element for a thing is the mortals. Things appear as meaningful to man. In turn, they cannot appear as meaningful if man is not exposed to them. For Heidegger, what is unique to man is that he is a being-in-the-world, whose ownmost possibility is death. No one can die our deaths for us. Death is a possibility that we can neither evade, nor possess. It is a possibility that makes all our other possibilities impossible. It is this fact that what is most my own remains outside me that draws me outside of me and opens me essentially to the world. As mortals, we exist as members of a community who participate in the world. With this notion of the 'fourfold' Heidegger highlights how everything finite stands essentially interrelated into a onefold. "Each of the four mirrors in its own way the presence of the others" and in doing this, each of it "sets each of the four free into its own" in their "essential being toward one another." (Thing, 179)

Heidegger's thinking of a thing in its mediational and relational character is in effect a thinking of finitude itself. When we speak of something as finite, we think of it as limited and this limitation as something negative. But for Heidegger, the finitude of a thing is to be understood positively as that surface or interface of its exposure to the world beyond it. Taken this way, finitude stands for the extension of a thing beyond itself and the many relations it has entered into and is open to. For Heidegger, thus, for a thing to be finite means for it to exist beyond itself. This beyond that supports this ecstatic character of things is the world. To appear as a thing is to be exposed to other things as well as to the world as the beyond that facilitates this exposure. Everything that shares finite existence does so in its interrelatedness to everything else around it within the world that surrounds them.

It is the fourfold that opens the thing to this beyond and makes it addressable by that world in turn. The world that addresses things in this age of technological domination is precisely that one-dimensional framework that robs the things of their relationality and reduces them to a status of mere replaceable pieces of a stockpile solely at the service of the consumeristic and power-hungry self-interests of man. An appropriate response to the dangers of such a technological approach would realize the essential interrelatedness of all finite existence and allow the things to disclose themselves as they are. It would be a response that opens the possibility for them to show themselves not only as existing within a cluster of relations that draws them out into innumerable directions of varying degrees (spatial, temporal, affective, associative, etc.) of relations, but also as bridges between our surroundings and ourselves, touching us and transforming us in the process. A response in terms of such a "releasement" from the will to dominate would also enable man to "dwell" within the world, not as its master or its exploiter, but as its "servant" allowing everything to presence themselves in their own glory and as its "shepherd" concern fully nurturing and protecting them *to be* what they are. Thus, things in the world "do not appear *by means* of human making. But neither do they appear without the vigilance of mortals. The first step toward such vigilance is the step back from the thinking that merely represents . . . to the thinking that responds and recalls." (Thing, 181). This step back will begin, when the mortals really learn to dwell, in the sense of cherishing, protecting, preserving and caring for, and "build out of dwelling, and think for the sake of dwelling" (BDT, 161).

Conclusion

In an age, where most of the initiatives to protect our environment against its senseless exploitation and mindless destruction still share the assumption that man has a "right" to manipulate nature without causing much damage to it, Heidegger's views challenge this very assumption. We need a kind of conversion, a conversion from being harbingers of the technological attitude, driven by the hunger for power over all things and a compulsion to reduce everything to mere commodities to a new vision of reality and ourselves that would facilitate everything in the world to manifest themselves in their own intrinsic worth. That could be the first step, according to Heidegger, for the emergence of an authentic ecological consciousness.

On similar ontological foundations, and in the true spirit of the author of the book of Genesis, the Biblical prophets, Irenaeus, Thomas Aquinas, Francis of Assisi, Pope Francis wants to recover a properly cosmological sensibility, whereby the human being and her projects are in vibrant, integrated relation with the world that surrounds her. "The earth was here before us and it has been given to us. The biblical texts are to be read in their context, with an appropriate hermeneutic, recognizing that they tell us to "till and keep" the garden of the world (cf. *Gen* 2:15). "Tilling" refers to cultivating, ploughing or working, while "keeping" means caring, protecting, overseeing and preserving. This implies a relationship of mutual responsibility between human beings and nature. (67) Clearly, the Bible has no place for a tyrannical anthropocentrism unconcerned for other creatures. (68) Everything has its place, everything is relational.

Endnotes

1   Cf. https://w2.vatican.va/content/benedict-xvi/en/speeches/2013/february/documents/hf_ben-xvi_spe_20130228_congedo-cardinali.html.

2   Martin HEIDEGGER, "The Question concerning Technology," in *The Question Concerning Technology and Other Essays*, trans. William Lovitt, New York: Harper & Row Publishers, 1977, p. 4. (hereafter cited as QT and will be incorporated into the text).

3   Martin HEIDEGGER, "The Thing," in *Poetry, Language, Thought*, trans. Albert Hofstadter, New York: Harper & Row Publishers, 1971, p. 166. (Hereafter referred to as Thing/ and will be incorporated into the text).

4   This notion of the 'fourfold' is further elaborated in his essay "Building Dwelling Thinking," in *Poetry, Language, Thought, op. cit.,* pp. 150ff. (Hereafter BDT). For a very detailed presentation of this theme, cf. Andrew J. Mitchell, *The Fourfold: Reading the Late Heidegger*, Evanston, Illinois: Northwestern University Press, 2015.

Chapter 20

Laudato Si'
Eco-Vision of Pope Francis

Isaac Parackal OIC
Jnana-Deepa Vidyapeeth, Pune, Maharashtra

The hallmark of the contemporary age is development and rapid growth in all levels of life. Ours is especially an age of scientific and economic progress and growth. However, there is a degeneration in relationships and value system. Progress leads us to a kind of alienation. There is a growing awareness that this alienation is caused not only by arms race, regional conflicts, human right violations and continued injustices among the peoples and nations, but also by a lack of due respect for nature. The sense of precariousness and insecurity makes humans greedy and selfish. The scientific mind feels threatened at the very thought of *mystery*. It wants to *master* everything and conquer the mysteries of nature.[1] *Experiment* has taken the place of *experience*. The contemporary human person wants to experiment rather than to experience in the heart level. *Human beings try to misuse nature for the selfish motives.* They do not recognize the intrinsic value of nature and try to exploit her in all possible ways. So, *agriculture* has become *agribusiness*. Previously it was a love-making with the soil with optimum yield but now it has become the maximum level of exploitation with modern technologies.[2] The egoistic mentality makes humans forget their ultimate role in the universe. They fail to realize that *nature is not a slave to be raped but a partner to be cherished*. Nowadays, even the deserts are not deserted as they are locus of dangerous atomic experiments. The fact that many challenges facing the world today are interrelated confirms the need for carefully coordinated solutions based

on a morally coherent world-view. The radical relativity in the universe urges us
to think in terms of an environmental spirituality that integrates all beings in the
thread of harmony and love. In view of this environmental crisis, Pope Francis
raises his prophetic voice in his encyclical letter *Laudato Si'*. It was an awakening
call to realise the interconnectedness among God, human beings and nature, and
reminds us of our vocation to be catalysts in bringing back the lost relationship.
The Pope reaffirms the role of the human person in creating an environment of
harmony and concord. Pope Francis urges us to make the earth a real home, a
family for all beings. This article is an analysis of Pope Francis' eco-vision depicted
in the encyclical, *Laudato Si'*.

1. Present Scenario of Ecological Crisis

Pope Francis in his encyclical elaborates the theme of ecology starting with the
present terrible condition of the earth: "The sister (earth) now cries out to us
because of the harm we have inflicted on her by our irresponsible use and abuse
of goods with which God has endowed her."[3] The "mastery mentality" of human
beings made her sick in all possible ways. Humans have disfigured the face of
the earth by plundering her at will. "The earth, our home, is beginning to look
more and more like an immense pile of filth."[4] The soil, water, air and all forms
of life have been sickened by the constant exploitation. Human beings have,
the Pope writes, forgotten the fact that they are made up of earthly elements.
Pollution caused by non-biodegradable waste from the industrial sources
and business establishments is a matter of great concern because it covers the
beautiful landscapes with toxic rubbish.[5] The laxity in recycling and reusing waste
causes pollution of the soil. Climatic change and global warming aggravate the
situation. The green gases that cause global warming are released mainly as a
result of human activity. Intensive use of fossil fuels and deforestation add to the
pollution levels.[6] A rise in the sea level due to the melting of the polar ice caps can
create a serious situation as a quarter of the population lives in the coastal areas.[7]
Climate change, the Pope observes, is a global problem with crucial implication:
"It represents one of the principal challenges facing humanity today."[8] Water
pollution is another serious problem. The contamination of water resources by
industrial toxic materials causes dramatic consequences. "Every day, unsafe water
results in many deaths and the spread of water related diseases, including those
caused by microorganisms and chemical substances."[9] The oceans that contain
the bulk of our planet's water supply are contaminated and the variety of marine
creatures is badly affected and drastically depleted. The uncontrolled fishing
threatens marine organisms such as plankton, coral reefs, and thereby breaks
the ocean food chain. The oceans, Pope Francis feels, have been turned into a
cemetery of species by human unbridled exploitation. The same is true of rivers
and lakes.[10] Deforestation, for the Pope, is another area of serious concern. The
vast forests, the bio-diverse lungs of the planet, are burned down or levelled for

purposes of cultivation and have frequently become wastelands. This entails the loss of countless species of beings.[11] Many cities and urban areas are congested with huge inefficient structures, excessively wasteful of energy and water and they really lack sufficient green space. He cautions, "We were not meant to be inundated by cement, asphalt, glass and metal, and deprived of physical contact with nature."[12] These structures are so chaotic that they create visual and sound pollution, too. The multinational companies, he observes, operate their business establishments in the developing countries and leave behind great human and environmental liabilities such as unemployment, abandoned towns, the depletion of natural reserves, deforestation, the impoverishment of agriculture and local stock breeding.[13] The selfishness of human beings makes the planet be squeezed dry beyond every limit.[14] "Never have we so hurt and mistreated our common home as we have in the last two hundred years."[15]

Pope Francis draws a picture of modern media and digital world so beautifully that it many a times hinders us from hearing the wise advice of the great sages of the past. "The overloaded accumulation of unwanted information by media and digital world aggravates the situation by preventing people from thinking and reflecting wisely, respecting the other and loving generously. Personal relationships are replaced by internet relations that lead people to a sort of mental pollution."[16] The Pope writes: "Efforts need to be made to help these media become sources of new cultural progress for humanity and not a threat to our deepest riches."[17] True wisdom, he reminds us, is not a product of mere accumulation of overloaded data but it is the fruit of self examination, dialogue and generous interactions between persons. In this scenario, the Pope analyses the role of human person in the world to overcome the present crisis. He affirms without doubt that the human person has the sacred vocation to fulfil the mission of God.

2. Human Being's Role in Creation

The human being has a privileged role in creation as s/he is the only creature capable of relating with the Creator. The traditional term 'dominion' connotes exploitation. It does not adequately convey the 'caring' component inherent in the Biblical understanding.[18] Since God is immanently present in the world, the world is to be seen as the manifestation of God's action. God is everywhere and at all times in the processes and events of the world which are to be seen as the vehicle and instrument of God's action and as capable of expressing His intentions and purposes – as our bodies are agents of ourselves. Then, the human attitude towards nature should be of respect. Human being's role in nature should not be a 'dominion' but a 'caring' which promotes the betterment of the created world. The human being is not dominator but priest, trustee, and protector of creation.

2.1. Human Being as Priest of Creation

Human being's role in creation can be seen as that of priest of creation. Pope Francis observes that the complex of proper responses of humans to nature suggests that the human being's role in nature may be perceived as that of priest of creation, as a result of whose activity the sacrament of creation is reverenced and dignified.[19] Since s/he alone is conscious of God, him/herself and nature, can mediate between insentient nature and God – for a priest is characterised by activity directed towards God on behalf of others. Human beings alone can reflect on the purposes of God and s/he alone can fulfil those purposes cooperating with God.[20] Humans alone can contemplate and offer the action of the created world to God. However, a priest is also active towards others on God's behalf and in this sense, too, the human being is the priest of creation. S/he alone, having reflected and contemplated on God's intentions and plans, can be active in and with the created world consciously seeking to enhance and fulfil God's purposes.[21] S/he is to live with reverence for all creation giving equal value to all.[22] The ultimate destiny of the universe is the fullness of God which is realized in the resurrection of Christ. Human being endowed with intelligence and love, and drawn by the fullness of Christ has the sacred duty to revere the nature as s/he does to other persons and lead the whole universe back to the Creator.[23]

The Pope brings out the cosmic characteristic of the Eucharist which joins heaven and earth. It embraces and penetrates all creation.[24] To be a priest means to be a mediator. So human beings as priests of creation have been entrusted with the sacred vocation to gather together the offering of creation and present it back to God.[25] In this sense, the human being is an intermediary between God and Nature and this divine vocation matures and sanctifies the human person.[26] S/he is cooperating with God in the creative activity and fulfils God's purposes within it.[27] "Thus, the Eucharist is also a source of light and motivation for our concerns for the environment, directing us to be stewards of all creation."[28]

2.2. Human being as Steward of Creation

For Pope Francis nature is a divine gift given to the "care" of humanity.[29] He repeats this "caring notion" to assert the responsibility of humankind towards God, the giver of the gift.[30] He reminds us, "The destruction of human environment is extremely serious, not only because God has entrusted the world to us men and women, but because human life itself is a gift…"[31] In the story of Genesis, the human being is presented as having 'dominion' over the creation. This has encouraged unbridled exploitation of nature.[32] However, it is a "caring dominion" rather than an "authoritative domination." The term 'dominion' has a kingly reference. Caring and preserving are part of kingly qualities. A king is supposed to look after his kingdom and the subjects. He is not expected to exploit his people for his own selfish purposes.[33] The human being would fail in his/her royal office of dominion over the earth, were s/he to exploit the earth's resources to the detriment of the land, plant life, animals, rivers and seas, etc. The Pope reminds us that the two biblical concepts "tilling" and "keeping" also should be understood in the proper context. "Tilling" refers to cultivating, ploughing or working, while "keeping" means caring, protecting, overseeing and preserving."[34] What is decisive is the responsibility of humans for the conservation of what has been entrusted to them. S/he can show this responsibility by exercising his/her royal office of mediator of prosperity and well-being, like the kings of the ancient world.

In this sense, creation is entrusted to the proper care and concern of human beings and they are answerable and accountable to God for the faithful preservation and maintenance of it.[35] Pope Francis gives a spirituality by drawing a "Father figure" of God who creates and owns the land and to whom human beings are accountable.[36] This spirituality, he thinks, is the best way to restore humans to their rightful and proper place in the universe.[37] He re-affirms that the tyrannical anthropocentrism is completely alien to the Bible and each being has its own intrinsic value and worth.[38] He speaks of a "universal fraternity' which encourages care for nature and fellow beings. It is a fraternal love that inspires us to accept the other with gratitude.[39] We, humans, need to regain the conviction that we need one another, that we have a shared responsibility for others and the world.[40] The Pope affirms: "The natural environment is a collective good, the patrimony of all humanity and the responsibility of everyone."[41] A fragile world entrusted by God to human care clearly affirms human responsibility to protect it and manage it wisely with careful discernment.[42] Authentic human progress has a moral character. It assumes full respect for the human person together with great concern for nature.[43] The world we live in is a common home which is entrusted to the care of human beings.[44]

2.3. Human Being as *Symbiont* with Reverence for Creation

The world, according to Pope Francis manifests God's continuing presence and so it commands admiration and awe.[45] Emphasizing the interdependent, symbiotic character of life he suggests that our attitude to nature should not be manipulative. It is a partnership between human beings and the world where s/he acts as a *symbiont - the one who makes harmony*. "Nature cannot be regarded as something separate from ourselves or as a mere setting in which we live in. We are part of nature, included in it and thus in constant interaction with it."[46] The Pope elaborates this marvellous harmonious relation: "An integral ecology includes taking time to recover a serene harmony with creation, reflecting on our life-style and our ideals, and contemplating the Creator who lives among us and surrounds us…"[47] Further, he adds, "The human person grows more, matures more and is sanctified more to the extent that he or she enters into relationships, going out from themselves to live in communion with God, with others and with all creatures."[48]

Quoting from the book of Genesis, the Pope argues that human life is grounded in three fundamental and closely intertwined relationships with God, with our neighbour and with earth itself.[49] However, this vital relationship has been broken and outwardly and within. This rupture he calls sin, and it has resulted in the loss of harmony.[50] The originally harmonious relations have become conflictual and confrontational. In this context, the call to be a *symbiont* to regain the lost relationship becomes significant. The Pope stresses the interconnectedness of the cosmic family as he states: "Because all creatures are connected, each must be cherished with love and respect, for all of us as living creatures are dependent on one another."[51] The Buddhist concept of *radical relatedness of all beings* (*pratītyasamudpāda*) is much echoed here in the words of Pope Francis.[52] Creatures exist only in dependence on each other, to complete each other and in the service of each other that "throughout the universe we can find any number of constant and secretly interwoven relationships."[53] All life is interdependent, indeed many creatures can only live in concert with, and often literally on, particular other organisms (*symbiosis*).[54] Although we are often not aware of it, we depend on other beings for our own existence.[55] "Everything is related, and we human beings are united as brothers and sisters on a wonderful pilgrimage, woven together by the love God has for each of his creatures..."[56] This love of God, the Pope states, "unites us in fond of affection with brother sun, sister moon, brother river and mother earth"[57]

The Pope affirms that the human being has the sacred duty to conserve and protect nature which is unique and irreplaceable.[58] The Earth is a precious home for all of us and it deserves our love.[59] It is our duty to preserve it from degradation and destruction for the future generations. "It is on loan to each generation, which must then hand it on to the next."[60] It is "a gift which we have freely received and must share with others."[61] He urges us to strengthen undoubtedly our conviction that we are one family.[62] It is the duty of the human being as *symbiont* to care for what is of value to God. We are *"one world with a common plan."*[63] As children we are called to be instruments to carry out the plans of God, our Father, to make the earth beautiful, peaceful and serene.[64] "Living our vocation to be protectors of God's handiwork is essential to a life of virtue."[65] This living up, for him, is not an optional life-style, but the essential aspect of Christian experience- "an ethical imperative essential for effectively attaining the common good."[66]

2.4. Human Being as the Interpreter and Prophet of Creation

God as Creatoris expressing His intentions and purposes and is unveiling the divine meaning, in the various and distinctive levels of the created natural world and in its processes. The human being is capable of seeing and hearing it. The natural world is seen as the symbol of God's meaning and it is conceived as the means whereby God's intentions and purposes are made known. In other words, the world is seen as a sacrament.[67] "Hence, there is a mystical meaning to be found in a leaf, in a mountain trail, in a dewdrop and in a poor person's face."[68] This concept of sacrament, according to Pope Francis "serves to emphasize another aspect of human function, namely, human being as *interpreter* of creation's meaning, value, beauty and destiny. He beautifully writes: "Standing awestruck before a mountain, he or she cannot separate this experience from God and perceives that the interior awe being lived has to be entrusted to the Lord."[69] As Jesus made his way throughout the land, he contemplated the beauty of creation and invited others to perceive a divine message in it.[70] The flowers of the field and the birds which his human eyes contemplated and admired are imbued with his radiant presence.[71] Every creature presents then the radiance of God.

As interpreter of God's meaning in creation, human being has the prophetic function which is a complementary aspect of the priestly role of human person.[72] A prophet is one who reads the sign of the times and interprets them for the future. So, the human being is the interpreter of God, and as such, s/he acts as a *prophet*, a role which historically has always complemented the priestly in human's corporate relation to God. The human being as prophet reads the signs of nature and interprets them for the betterment of the world. Faith allows us to interpret the divine meaning and the beauty of what is unfolding. The whole universe is open to God's transcendence within which it develops.[73] "The universe unfolds in God, who fills it completely."[74] The Pope observes that God has written a precious book whose letters are the created things present in the universe.[75] From electromagnetic to Divine and from vegetal to human, all are intertwined and every creature manifests the continuous divine revelation.[76] This contemplation of creation allows us to discover each thing as a teaching which God wishes to hand on to us. Humans have to listen to this subtle voice, understand the message and interpret the meaning for the whole world.[77] Pope asserts that "the divine and the human meet in the slightest detail in the seamless garment of God's creation, in the last speck of dust of our planet."[78]

2.5. Human Being as Co-creator, Co-worker and Co-explorer with God

God respects human freedom and is intimately present to every being without impinging on its autonomy. "God wishes to work with us and, he, who counts on our cooperation, can also bring good out of the evil we have done."[79] The Holy Spirit has filled the earth with various possibilities and therefore from the very heart of being something new can always emerge. So there is creativity and novelty in nature as in the case of an art work.[80] Human excellence could be seen as the human being making his/her distinctive human contribution as *co-creator* to that ceaseless activity of creation which is God's action in and for the world.[81] Creating a world in need of development God in some way sought to limit Himself so that the so-called evils, sufferings and dangers are part of the childbirth which God uses to draw humans into the act of cooperation with Him.[82] In the scene of creation the human being stands with his/her creative energies within him/herself and in relation to nature. Creation is of an order- an order of love (*rta*).[83] This order extends a free choice before human beings. The Pope's vision could be rightly placed in the following way: does the human being join in with the creative work of God harmoniously integrating his/her own material creations into what God is already doing? Or does s/he make a disorder, an entanglement and confusion within the creation process? "We are free to apply our intelligence," Pope Francis states, "towards things evolving positively, or towards adding new ills, new causes of suffering and real setbacks."[84] The human being can either create a world "in which freedom, growth, salvation and love can blossom, or lead towards decadence and mutual destruction."[85]

The Pope cautions us that, in a technocratic paradigm, human freedom to take decisions and make space for creativity is substantially diminished. The technological culture has become so dominant that it tries to absorb everything with power motive – "a lordship over all."[86] The Pope observes, "Once the human being declares independence from reality and behaves with absolute dominion, the very foundations of our life begin to crumble..."[87] In this context he urges us to take a balancing position that would enhance human creativity and lead to new advancement of science and technology on the one hand, and creating an attitude to control the negative effects of intervention in the eco-system on the other hand. In other words, our intention should not be merely profit oriented but other-oriented. Quoting his predecessor, Pope Francis undoubtedly affirms that the scientific and technological progress is an evidence of "the nobility of the human vocation to participate responsibly in God's creative actions."[88] He acknowledges that technology has remedied countless evils that used to harm and limit human beings. He also appreciates the work of many scientists who contributed to the welfare of the human race.[89] In this sense, the human being is acting as a creative participant in creation as it were the leader of the orchestra of creation in the performance which is God's continuing composition. Moreover, the human being is offering him/herself with dedication in the creative process. Techno-science, the Pope admits, can produce important means to improve the quality of human life.[90] In short, humans have the opportunity of consciously becoming *co-creator* and *co-worker* with God in His work on earth.[91]

The human being recognizes that God is always active 'making things new', then his/her response to created nature should be flexible and open-minded. S/he should then expect change and adjust him/herself to modifications in the world's ecosystems as s/he observes sensitively the changing processes.[92] The Pope urges us to uncover (or dis-cover) God's presence in creation.[93] Technology helps the human being fulfil his/her personal and social development in cooperation with God. "Human creativity cannot be suppressed."[94] For him, science and technology are wonderful products of a God-given creativity.[95] Techno-science "can produce art and enable men and women immersed in the material world to 'leap' into the world of beauty."[96] He gives the example of an artist who cannot be stopped from using his or her creativity. In the same way, human beings who possess particular gifts for the progress of science and technology cannot be prevented from using their God-given talents for the welfare of the world. S/he through science and technology is exploring with God the creative possibilities within the universe, God has brought into being. This is to see human beings as *co-explorer* with God.[97] This cooperation of humans in the creative processes is not a passive involvement but an intelligent and active participation – an authentic collaboration with the Creator. "It is an attitude of the heart, one which approaches life with serene attentiveness, which is capable of being fully present to someone without thinking of what comes next, which accepts each moment as a gift from God to be lived to the full."[98] In order to do this, humans have to discern God's meaning in nature.[99] This is a vocation to cultivate the human abilities to protect the earth and develop its potential.[100]

3. Human Work as Sanctifying

Work, according to Pope Francis has an ennobling and sanctifying role that contributes to the overall well-being of the whole world. It matures and sanctifies the life of human beings.[101] Quoting from the Bible he shows how Jesus being a carpenter sanctified human work. Through his work Jesus lived in full harmony with nature and lent it an attention, full of fondness and wonder.[102] The correct understanding of work, Pope reminds us, is an essential aspect of integral ecological relationship between human beings and the world. The meaning and purpose of work play an important role in the understanding of our interconnectedness. "This has to do not only with manual or agricultural labour but with any activity involving modification of existing reality."[103] In this perspective every work can be seen as God's work for the development and progress of human society and of the whole creation.[104] Even an unimportant job in society, when it is done with love and commitment, has a great significance and it serves for the upliftment and better shaping of human society.[105] Freedom belongs to human creativity, to create oneself and to build up the world. The experience of contemporary humans finding themselves, and moreover believing themselves, not as masters of universe, but in a certain sense, its builder, its responsible partner, is a fundamental religious experience. The Pope observes that work is part and parcel of our rich Christian monastic tradition together with awe-filled contemplation of creation. The great monastic communities combined work with prayer because of its great spiritual significance.

Seeing work as spiritually meaningful has proved revolutionary. Through the interplay of recollection and work the monks sought their personal growth and sanctification. This monastic model inspires us to envisage work as a way to re-build the ruptured interconnectedness.[106] "This way of experiencing work makes us more protective and respectful of environment; it imbues our relationship to the world with healthy sobriety."[107] This intentionality includes faith in human freedom, hope for the ultimate peace, and love of universal justice. Human quest also is for the well-being of the human race here on earth as s/he is committed to the challenges of times and thereby the ultimate realization of life. The main concern of him/her is to promote harmony with the cosmos, communion among all humans and confidence in the Divine. This is the sacredness of the human labour where one experiences the splendour of his/her creative freedom. "Work is a necessity, part of the meaning of life on this earth, a path to growth, human development and personal growth."[108] The human being has the capacity to improve his/her lot, to further the moral growth and develop their spiritual endowments. Pope Francis observes, "Work should be the setting for this rich personal growth, where many aspects of life enter into play: creativity, planning for the future, developing our talents, living out values, relating to others, giving glory to God."[109] In this context, the Pope puts forward the idea of human work that is for the consecration of the whole world and offering it back to God.[110] Here, the world is seen not only as a gift from God but also a task to be fulfilled by human beings. Being a priest it is the primary duty of a human person to do service of God - to offer the world back to God. In this sense, whatever he/she does for the betterment of the world is a sacred service thereby, s/he becomes the celebrant of nature.[111] Human creative freedom is meant for the building up of the universe and for the welfare of the people. Every discovery is a result of human creativity through which reality is revealed. Every revelation is a source of salvation and welfare for society. Human life justifies itself by being of service to the human race and working together towards the progress of society.

Humans, for Pope Francis, are created with a vocation to work.[112] While immersed in humanitarian work, by helping the poor and the needy we need to enlarge our horizons and transcend the boundaries of our limited circles by productive diversity and business creativity.[113] Today we need to take seriously the world and its concerns, and to act responsibly for the total welfare of the entire human community.[114] The Pope states, "The effects of the present imbalance can only be reduced by our decisive action here and now."[115] This will affirm the basic dignity and freedom of everyone. Our actions should be enlightened actions so that through our actions we resonate, radiate and create an atmosphere of spirituality in and around so that world itself becomes a sanctuary. We listen to the world and the shouts and cries of the human milieu. Through our actions, we will integrate ourselves, experience the Divine and serve the cosmos.[116] This spirituality of human work, the Pope asserts, is able to provide motivation for people to act for the future good of humanity and the whole ecosystem.[117]

4. A Spirituality of Radical Conversion (*Metanoia*)

We have seen how Pope Francis raises his prophetic voice against the egoistic tendencies of human beings who try to exploit the natural resources for the selfish motives. "When People become self-centred and self-enclosed, their greed increases."[118] He observes that the current global situation engenders a feeling of insecurity and uncertainty which can become 'a seedbed for collective selfishness. He beautifully notes: "The emptier a person's heart is, the more he or she needs things to buy, own and consume."[119] He cautions that obsession with consumerist life style can only lead to violence and mutual destruction especially when it is a monopoly of a few.

However, Pope Francis encourages us to rise above all these limitations by choosing what is good. He urges humanity to make a new start and turn away from our destructive tendencies of self-centredness.[120] He calls for a spirituality of radical *metanoia* (turning back). It is a commitment and conviction.[121] It is a radical conversion of heart, mind and spirit.[122] He calls it the ecological conversion or *metanoia*.[123] It is a *metanoia* from our old life styles and selfish attitudes to a new understanding of reality (from dualism to inclusivism- *dvaita* to *advaita*). It is a *metanoia* from self elevation to self expending. It is a *metanoia* from our mental and social conditioning to a new path of freedom and openness towards goodness, truth and beauty.[124] It is a *metanoia* from life-negation to life-affirmation.[125] It is a *metanoia* from individualism to togetherness.[126] It is a *metanoia* from self-affirming to other-affirming.[127] It is a *metanoia* from knowing the instrumental value of nature to knowing the intrinsic value of nature.[128] It is a new awareness that makes us awaken to new horizons of freedom and joyful celebration of life.[129] This ecological conversion "can inspire us to greater creativity and enthusiasm in resolving the world's problems and in offering ourselves to God 'as living sacrifice, holy and acceptable'."[130] This conversion calls for a number of attitudes which together foster a spirit of generous care, love and full of tenderness.[131] It is a spirituality that listens to the groaning of mother earth with great compassion and helps us move into concrete actions that would in turn heal the wounded planet.[132] This spirituality calls us to abandon our destructive and disrespectful attitudes towards mother earth. It is a spirituality that reminds us of our mission, sacred duty to be instruments of spreading the ecological consciousness. This spirituality calls us to replace consumption with sacrifice, greed with generosity and wastefulness with a spirit of sharing.[133]

Pope Francis emphasizes the significance of education that can bring this new awareness.[134] He observes, "There is a nobility in the duty to care for creation through little daily actions, and it is wonderful how education can bring about real changes in life style."[135] Education in environmental responsibility can encourage ways of acting that can directly and significantly affect the world around us. He elaborates a number of practical ways such as avoiding the use of plastic, reducing water consumption, planting trees, care for other beings, etc.[136] This ecological awareness through education must be translated into new habits andbe made into practical at different levels - at schools, in families, in the media, in the political institutions, in catechesis and elsewhere.[137]

Pope Francis urges everyone to take up an ancient lesson found in different religious traditions together with the Bible. It is a life style with the conviction that "less is more."[138] He cautions, "A constant flood of consumer goods can baffle the heart and prevent us from cherishing each thing and each moment."[139] So, a life of simplicity marked by moderation can help us to appreciate small things and be grateful for the same. It helps us live our life to the full and be serenely present to the beauty of reality with humility.[140] Quoting Saint Francis of Assisi, Saint Therese of Lisieux, Saint John of the Cross and Saint Bonaventure, Pope Francis proposes a spirituality that cherishes a "culture of care" towards the "other" as each creature bears in itself a Trinitarian structure.[141] To be totally open to this "Trinitarian epiphany" of reality is the sum and substance of the ecological spirituality that leads us to a life of fulfilment: "Everything is interconnected, and this invites us to develop a spirituality of that global solidarity which flows from the mystery of the Trinity."[142] This eco-vision is not only to pass "from the exterior to interior to discover the action of God in the soul but also to discover God in all things."[143] This eco-vision is in a way learning to encounter God in all creatures which bear in themselves a specifically Trinitarian structure and reveal the mystery of the Trinity in a unique manner.[144] It is a vision that "entails learning to give, and not simply to give up."[145] The Pope writes, "When we can see God reflected in all that exists, our hearts are moved to praise the Lord for all his creatures and worship him in union with them."[146] I conclude this article with a prayer of our great ancient sages of the Indian tradition, *Lokāsamasthā sukhino bhavanthu* which means, "*Let there be peace and happiness in the whole world.*" Together with Pope Francis, let us also wish the same for the whole world with the prayer, "*Praise be to you, Lord.*"

Endnotes

1   Pope FRANCIS, *Laudato Si'*, Trivandrum: Carmel International Publishing House, 2015, No. 116. Henceforth, this book would be referred as L.S.

2   L.S. 190.

3   L.S. 2.

4   L.S. 21.

5   L.S. 21.

6   L.S. 23.

7   L.S. 24.

8   L.S. 25.

9   L.S. 29.

10   L.S. 40-41.

11   L.S. 38.

12   L.S. 44.

13   L.S. 51.

14   L.S. 106.

15   L.S. 53.
16   L.S. 47.
17   L.S. 47.
18   L.S. 67.
19   L.S. 83.
20   L.S. 66.
21   L.S. 233-236.
22   L.S. 69.
23   L.S. 83.
24   L.S. 236.
25   L.S. 80-81.
26   L.S. 231.
27   L.S. 83.
28   L.S. 236.
29   L.S. 228.
30   L.S. 55.
31   L.S. 5.
32   L.S. 67.
33   L.S. 5, 6, 11, 106.
34   L.S. 67.
35   L.S. 200.
36   L.S. 92, 53.
37   L.S. 75, 68.
38   L.S. 68, 69, 95.
39   L.S. 228.
40   L.S. 229.
41   L.S. 95.
42   L.S. 78, 161.
43   L.S. 5.
44   L.S. 232.
45   L.S. 93-96; 233-234, 238.
46   L.S. 139.
47   L.S. 225.
48   L.S. 240.
49   L.S. 66.
50   L.S. 66.
51   L.S. 42.
52   L.S. 164, 240.
53   L.S. 240.
54   L.S. 86, 138.
55   L.S. 140.
56   L.S. 92.

57   L.S. 92.

58   L.S. 34.

59   L.S. 164.

60   L.S. 159.

61   L.S. 159.

62   L.S. 52.

63   L.S. 164.

64   L.S. 53.

65   L.S. 217.

66   L.S. 125.

67   L.S. 234.

68   L.S. 233.

69   L.S. 234.

70   L.S. 97, 100.

71   L.S. 100.

72   L.S. 222.

73   L.S. 79.

74   L.S. 178.

75   L.S. 85.

76   L.S. 138.

77   L.S. 85, 225. The Pope laments that the subtle words of love in nature are not heard in today's noisy, busy, imbalanced and distracted life style. It is a call to recover the serene harmony with creation and thereby with the Creator Himself.

78   L.S. 9.

79   L.S. 80.

80   L.S. 80.

81   L.S. 53.

82   L.S. 80.

83   L.S. 77. It is a cosmic order of love, see 236.

84   L.S. 79.

85   L.S. 79.

86   L.S. 108.

87   L.S. 117.

88   L.S. 131.

89   L.S. 102.

90   L.S. 103.

91   L.S. 117.

92   L.S. 42.

93   L.S. 225.

94   L.S. 131.

95   L.S. 102.

96   L.S. 103.

97   L.S. 131-132.
98   L.S. 226.
99   L.S. 78.
100   L.S. 79.
101   L.S. 231.
102   L.S. 98.
103   L.S. 125.
104   L.S. 230-231.
105   L.S. 125, 231.
106   L.S. 70.
107   L.S. 126.
108   L.S. 128.
109   L.S. 127.
110   L.S. 83.
111   L.S. 98.
112   L.S. 128.
113   L.S. 129.
114   L.S. 162.
115   L.S. 161.
116   L.S. 128.
117   L.S. 216.
118   L.S. 204.
119   L.S. 204.
120   L.S. 207.
121   L.S. 52, 216-218.
122   L.S. 217.
123   L.S. 220.
124   L.S. 205.
125   L.S. 9.
126   L.S. 9, "It is a way of loving, of moving gradually away from what I want to what God's world needs."
127   L.S. 208.
128   L.S. 140.
129   L.S. 207.
130   L.S. 220.
131   L.S. 220.
132   L.S. 49, 2.
133   L.S. 9.
134   L.S. 211-215.
135   L.S. 211.
136   L.S. 210-211.
137   L.S. 209-215.

138 L.S. 222.
139 L.S. 222.
140 L.S. 223.
141 L.S. 218-240.
142 L.S. 240.
143 L.S. 233.
144 L.S. 234, 239.
145 L.S. 9.
146 L.S. 87.

VII. SERVANT LEADERSHIP

Chapter 21

Pope Francis
His Leadership Style and Impact

Kurien Kunnumpuram SJ
Christ Hall, Kozhikode, Kerala

Introduction

Two years back Chris Lowney published a book on the leadership style of Pope Francis.[1] In it he points out that the Pope did not receive any special training to lead the Catholic Church as Pope. The training he got was to be a Jesuit. Lowney contends that his Jesuit training has a huge impact on the way Pope Francis leads the Church.[2] "His Jesuit background has informed his leadership values and principles."[3] As the Pope confesses: " I feel like I am a Jesuit in terms of my spirituality, what I have in my…heart… Also, I think like a Jesuiit."[4]

Jesuit spirituality can be understood only in the context of Ignatius' vision of the religious life in the Society of Jesus. As Lowney points out:

> The Jesuit founder envisioned a religious order plunged into the world, not sheltered in monasteries. Hence, he had to develop practices conductive to success amid the chaotic, distracting, tempting, confusing busyness that characterizes the work world. No wonder, then, that Ignatius' ideas are useful not only to Jesuits but to the rest of us as well, whatever our religious beliefs may be.[5]

The Spiritual Exercises of St Ignatius plays a crucial role in the spiritual formation of the Jesuits. Jesuit novices make these exercises for 30 continuous days. During these days they meditate on the life of Jesus, their personal life history and the way in which they have to follow Jesus.

Pope Francis made these exercises at least twice: once as a novice and a second time as tertian. For several years, as Novice Master he guided the month's retreat of his novices. So it is quite certain that his spirituality is well grounded in the Spiritual Exercises of St Ignatius. His life and activities as Pope bear witness to it.

Some of the elements in the training of the novices are uniquely Jesuit. For example, Ignatius prescribed that each novice spend "a month in making a pilgrimage without money, but begging from door to door at times...in order to grow accustomed to discomfort in food and lodging." Ignatius wanted to shake the trainees free from their reliance on "money or other created things" and spur them to rely on God alone. The pilgrimage helped develop that attitude.[6] Besides, Ignatius wanted "tough, resilient Jesuits who could struggle through discomfort and overcome adversity". It is very likely that the idea of a pilgrimage has had a great impact on Pope Francis, for he "repeatedly uses the metaphor of life as a journey."[7] In fact, he would like to see a Church which is on a pilgrimage.

There are other aspects of Jesuit formation and Jesuit practices that exerted a lot of influence on this Jesuit Pope, but we shall not discuss them right now.

After two introductory chapters Chris Lowney discusses six foundational commitments of Pope Francis as leader. They are (1) Know yourself deeply, (2) but live to serve others (3) Immerse yourself in the world (4) but withdraw from the world daily; (5) Live in the present and revere tradition (6) but create the future.[8]

If you examine these foundational principles carefully, you will see something paradoxical. "Each pair verges on being contradictory. I must be immersed in the world yet withdraw from the world. I must stand for something, yet embrace change. I must invest in knowing myself only to transcend myself and serve others."[9]

1. Self–Knowledge and Self-Acceptance

The South African leader Nelson Mandela, who was kept in prison for more than two decades, once said: "My greatest enemy was not those who put me and kept me in prison. It was myself. I was afraid to be who I am."[10] It is difficult to believe this. He has always come across to us as a very self-confident leader.

A close acquaintance of Pope Francis once remarked: "That guy seems to be really comfortable in his own skin."[11] Pope Francis has a deep knowledge of himself and accepts himself fully. In an address from St Peter's Square he said. "Do not be afraid! We are frail and we know it, but he is stronger." Fr Hernan Parades, an Ecuadorean Jesuit, who was trained as a young Jesuit under Fr Bergoglio, has observed: "For him (Bergoglio) it was important that we love and accept ourselves the way we are". This was a powerful affirmation of Bergoglios conviction that leaders must find peaceful self-acceptance, the conviction that "they have a worthy contribution to make, their flaws withstanding."[12] As Lowney points out:

When you look into yourself, not everything you find will be pretty. Everyone is flawed: the demons of self-centredness, hunger for power, fear or lack of self-confidence are found in every leader. Leadership is, therefore, not only knowing yourself but also fighting your demons. If you have not courageously dealt with your weaknesses, and become the best version of yourself, how will you credibly challenge the rest of us to be better versions of ourselves.[13]

It is interesting to note that leadership literature over the past couple of decades has stressed the importance of these qualities: self-awareness, integrity, authenticity and character. "Self-awareness is the foundation of the others: I can be authentic, true to myself, only if I know myself, what I stand for, and what I ultimately think that humans are here for. And integrity is nothing more (or less) than understanding that I cannot honour such truths selectively: I must lead a "whole" life (the root meaning of integrity is "whole") not a split life."[14] Alejandro Gauffin, a Jesuit priest who studied under Fr Bergoglio watched the Pope's first few days and then observed:

Everything I see from the new pope now, everything I hear now…I saw then, and I heard then… It is like reliving our days together in the parish, when he taught me that gestures were worth much more than words.[15]

Commenting on Bergoglios personal creed Lowney says: "Anyone familiar with Jesuit spirituality would immediately perceive how Bergoglio came by this worldview because the opening week of the Spiritual Exercises reinforces exactly the same dynamic."[16]

Introspection may appear to be a burden. Would not one be a better leader if one is not aware of one's insufficiencies? This is not true. Introspective impulse will liberate and empower a leader. Ultimately it will bring the blessing of self-acceptance or the courage to be oneself.

On the other hand, those leaders who have never practised introspection will go on making decisions and performing actions blissfully unaware of their weaknesses and the harm they cause to their families or organizations by their wrong decisions.

2. Commitment to Serve

As a Jesuit Fr Bergoglio sought to follow Jesus. This was inculcated in him by the Spiritual Exercises of St Ignatius. Now Jesus gave a powerful, even dramatic, demonstration of his determination to serve others. When Jesus and his disciples came together for the Last Supper, Jesus shocked everyone by what he did. As the evangelist John describes it: "Jesus poured water into a basin and began to wash the disciples' feet." The disciple Peter protested: 'you will never wash my feet. He was quite embarrassed, and even outraged, that Jesus was doing something which at that time was performed only by slaves, in fact non-Jewish slaves, because such dirty work was thought to be beneath a Jewish slave's dignity. After Jesus had finished washing the feet of all his disciples present there he told them what he wanted them to do: "You call me Teacher and Lord – and you are right, for that is what I am. So if I, your Lord and Teacher, have washed your feet, you also ought to wash one another's feet" (Jn 13:13-14).

This shocking event is commemorated in Catholic churches all over world on Holy Thursday with selected men from the parish standing for the disciples and the parish priest for Jesus. The Pope does it at the Basilica of St John Lateran with select bishops or seminarians representing the apostles. By routinizing this gesture of Jesus the Church has made it a tame performance.

But Pope Francis recaptured some of the shock-value of feet-washing. On Holy Thursday in 2013 he did not go to St John Lateran. Instead he went to Casal del Marmo Juvenile detention center and washed, wiped and kissed the feet of Juvenile delinquents. Some of them were Catholics, others non-Catholics. One was a Moslem woman. The Pope explained his action: "This is a symbol, it is a sign… Washing the feet means 'I am at your service….' As a priest and a bishop, I must be at your service."[17]

The Pope was here challenging not only Church leaders. Addressing "all those who have positions of responsibility in economic, political and social life, and all men and women of good will", Pope Francis said: "Let us never forget that all authentic power is service."[18] As Chris Lowney points out: "Good leaders see farther. They feel called to transcend themselves and serve a greater mission than self-interest alone."[19]

It is obvious that when unchecked ambition, careerism and self-interest run amuck it can negatively impact a leader's primary task of serving the people. St Ignatius was clearly aware of this danger. Hence, he devised means to form Jesuits in service mentality. One of the chief means was the meditation on the two standards that he developed in the Spiritual Exercises. In this meditation he asked the Jesuits to imagine the world as a battlefield where the followers of Jesus are pitted against those of Lucifer. I shall now quote Ignatius' description of the main elements of this meditation:

Imagine you see the chief of all the enemy in the vast plain about Babylon, seated on a great throne of fire and smoke, his appearance inspiring horror and terror.

Consider how he summons innumerable demons, and scatters them, some to one city and some to another, throughout the whole world, so that no province, no place, no state of life, no individual is overlooked.

Consider the address he makes to them, how he goads them on to lay snares for men and bind them with chains. First they are to tempt them to covet riches (as Satan himself is accustomed to do in most cases) that they may the more easily attain the empty honours of this world, and then come to overweening pride.

The first step, then, will be riches, the second honor, the third pride. From these three steps the evil one leads to all other vices.

In a similar way, we are to picture to ourselves the sovereign and true Commander, Christ our Lord.

Consider Christ our Lord, standing in a lowly place in a great plain about the region of Jesrsalem, His appearance beautiful and attractive.

Consider how the Lord of all the world chooses so may persons, apostles, disciples, etc., and sends them throughout the whole world to spread His sacred doctrine among all men,no matter what their state or condition.

Consider the address which Christ our Lord makes to all His servants and friends whom He sends on this enterprise, recommending to them to seek to help all, first by attracting them to the highest spiritual poverty, and should it please the Divine Majesty, and should He deign to choose them for it, even to actual poverty. Secondly, they should lead them to a desire for insults an contempt, for from these springs humility.

Hence, there will be three steps: the first, poverty as opposed to riches; the second, insults or contempt as opposed to the honour of this world; the third, humility as opposed to pride. From these three steps, let them lead men to all other virtues.[20]

In spite of his Jesuit training, Pope Francis knows that he is not totally immune to the demons of honour and pride. That is why he wrote to the Argentinian bishops asking for prayers that "I do not grow pound and always know how to listen to what God wants and not what I want"[21]

He also believes that his fellow priests and church workers are not free from the allure of fame or riches. He sees the demons of clericalism and careerism at work in them. "These social climbers exist even in the Christian communities, no? Those people are looking out for themselves... They went glory for themselves."[22]

In a homily he preached on April 14, 2013, Pope Francis speaks of the idols in our life.

There are "many small or great idols that we have and in which we take refuge, on which we often seek to base our security. They are idols that we sometimes keep well hidden; they can be ambition, careerism, a taste for success, placing ourselves at the centre, the tendency to dominate others, the claim to be the sole masters of our lives, some sins to which we are bound, and many others... I would like a question to resound in the heart of each one of you, and I would like you to answer it honestly: Have I considered which idol lies hidden in my life....[23]

Addressing the Pontifical Ecclesiastical Academy which trains priest-diplomats, Pope Francis warned them not to let their prestigious work go to their heads. 'Careerism is leprosy; Leprosy," he pointed out. He insisted that priests had to labour only for the "cause of the Gospel and the fulfilment of the mission", and never for public recognition."[24]

3. Immerse Yourself in the World's Joys and Sufferings

After he finished his term as the provincial of the Argentinian Jesuits, Fr Bergoglio was assigned to oversee the training of young Jesuits at Collegio Maximo San Jose'. The Collegio Maximo had a farm, the produce of which helped to support the financially straightened Jesuit community. All the members of the community worked on the farm. Herman Paredes, who was a Jesuit in training at that time, observes: "Bergoglio worked. I have in mind an image, one afternoon when I was comingback from the Parish where I was helping, seeing him there in his plastic boots, feeding the pigs."[25]

Though he was the rector of the Collegio Maximo Fr Bergoglio did the laundry of the community. Fr. Thomas Bradley who was a Jesuit trainee remembers: "Already at 5.30 in the morning, Bergiglio would be placing clothes into those two industrial washing machines we had."[26] Apparently there were lots of clothes to wash, since there were more than a hundred of us living there".

Fr. Bergoglio "always insisted that the seminarians should go out at the weekends to offer (religious instruction) to the children. He said that someone who is able to make the catechism simple enough for a child to understand is a wise person."[27] And when the seminarians returned from the barrio, he "would look to see if they had dusty feet. If they come back with clean feet he took it as a sign that they had done nothing."[28]

Around that time the bishop of Burnos Aires decided to start a new parish near the Jesuit seminary and asked Fr. Bergoglio to serve as its first pastor. The new parish priest drew up a crude map of the neighbourhood, divided it into zones and assigned seminarian volunteers to each zone. This is what he told the seminarians: "Get into the neighbourhood and walk it; don't comb the sheep, meet all of them, visit the poor and take care of their needs."[29]

Bergoglio instructed the seminarians: "You are going to learn from the people before you teach them anything". A few days after his papal election, he preached at the Chrism Mass on Holy Thursday in St. Laterano. Hundreds of priests gathered there. He exhorted them to be shepherds, "so deeply inserted in the midst of their sheep that they were living with the smell of the sheep."[30]

In an address to the Brazilian bishops Pope Francis raised a question: "Unless we train ministers capable of warming people's hearts, of walking with them in the night, of dialoguing with their hopes and disappointments, of mending their brokenness, what hope can we have for our present and future journey?"[31]

The Pope is convinced that "a Church that does not go out of itself, sooner a later sickens from the stale air of closed doors."[32] He also maintains that "we understand reality better not from the centre, but from the outskirts."[33] He firmly believes that "we cannot be starched Christians, too polite, who speak theology over tea. We have to become courageous Christians and seek out those who need help most."[34]

It is from the *Spiritual Exercises* that Pope Francis learnt not to withdraw from the world but plunge into it. For the world is a very good place, because it was created by God. And whatever God made is unfailingly good. It is also a world that has been redeemed by Jesus Christ. Besides, this world is the dwelling place of God. In the *Spiritual Exercises'* crowning meditation, St. Ignatius asks us to "consider how God dwells in creatures… in the plants, giving them life; in the animals, giving them sensation" According to Ignatius, God "dwells also in myself, giving meexistence, life, sensation and intelligence; and even further, making me his temple…."[35]

This world-engaged attitude is the foundation of one of the great mantras of Ignatian Spirituality: "to find God in all things". It is interesting to note what one of his spiritual daughters, Soledad Albisu' said of Fr. Bergoglio:

> He took me outside where the community kept sheep and pigs. He told me that "this was a good place to pray and to remember that God is to be found in the lowliest things."[36]

4. Kneeling Alone: Withdraw to Find Perspective

On his first morning as Pope he knelt for fifteen minutes of solitary prayer at St Mary Major Basilica. Commenting on this Chris Lowney says: "The Pope was praying of course, but in the very act of praying he was recalling his sense of mission and the values he needs to keep and regaining perspective by acknowledging that the world is not ultimately under his control anyway."[37]

When he was in charge of Jesuit seminarians Fr. Bergoglio insisted on "a daily schedule of prayer, reading and reflection – and a commitment to sustaining and being punctual at it… in order to understand what is happening in one's life, and all the more so when one is going to be exposed to a very active life."[38]

As Lowney points out: "The pace, volume, complexity and volatility endemic to today's working life conspire to raise stress unimaginably, mire us in overwork, erode our decision – makingskills, distract our focus' and, as a result, threaten our very well-being."[39] In USA, the National Institute for Occupational Safety and Health believes that 40% of all workers feel overworked to the point of anxiety and depression.

Henry Mintzberg, a dean of modern leadership thinking, observes: "These days, what managers desperately need is to stop and think, to step back and reflect on their experiences."

Pope Francis has learnt from the Spiritual Exercises the practice of "examen of conscience". Jesuits practise it for fifteen minutes twice a day. During the examen "First You remind yourself why you are grateful as a human being; Second you lift your horizon for a moment by calling to mind your ultimate sense of purpose and values or some habitual failing you hope to address; And third, mentally review the past few hours to extract some insight that might help you in the next few hours. If you were irritable with colleagues or students or patients what might have been happening?" Jesuits also "reflect on how God was present to them in the encounters of the day thus far, make amends for their shortcomings and ask God's blessings on them during the next few hours."[40]

The practice of examen, which seems to be tailor-made to suit today's chaotic lifestyles, was in fact Ignatius of Loyola's ingenious solution to the dilemma presented by his highly active vision for Jesuit life. "Ignatius envisioned his Jesuits fully immersed in the world as teachers, pastoral counsellors or missionaries in far – flung, lands, getting their feet so dirty in the world's slums that they carried the smell of the sheep. That active lifestyle was incompatible with going to the chapel every few few hours for communal prayer – the periodic chanting of the Divine Office, the hallmark of monastic-style religious orders. So the examen, undertaken individually, whenever and wherever circumstances permitted, would keep Jesuits recollected and God-focused, despite their activist lifestyle."[41]

Great leaders delegate, and delegate wisely. They know that they are not omni-competent. "Common sense tells us that no executive will understand every legal issue better than a competent legal counsel, or every manufacturing question better than an production pro."[42]

While delegating keep the following in mind: Give that person a realistic goal and the resources for it, but trust him/her to figure out how to accomplish it. He/she may be more creative than you.

Best results follow when the readiness to delegate is married to the ability to trust. Already in the 16th century, St Ignatius was quite aware of this.

He sent Francis to Asia on a mission soon after the Society of Jesus founded in 1540. He relied completely on Francis' judgment to organize every aspect of Jesuit life and operations there.

Listen to Ignatius' words: "I leave everything to your judgement and I will consider best whatever you decide". Or again: "Whatever means you shall choose I fully approve... you are in closer touch with affairs where you are."[43]

This is a strong exercise of authority coupled with an equally bold delegation. Does Pope show as much skill in delegating as his spiritual father Ignatius. As Lowney reports: "The cardinal-overseer of a key Vatican department, needing to fill the slot of a second-in-charge, recounted in an interview that the pope has asked him, "Who do you want as your secretary [i.e., your number two]? Give me three names." "So I gave him three names," the cardinal recounted. "But [the pope] said, 'Of the three, which is the one you want? I said this one, Carballo. [The pope] said, 'Good, fine.' And he gave us Jose Carballo [Jose Rodriguez Carballo, OFM]."[44]

The cardinal's next comment aptly summarizes our discussion of trust and delegation: "It's a wonderful, simple way of doing things: I trust you, I trust Carballo, so that's it.... He [the pope] doesn't complicate it."[45]

5. Live in the Present and Reverence Tradition

Life is short. Don't fritter it away on what is not important to you. Don't do what you might regret later. Conversely, seize each day's precious opportunity; one like it may or may not come your way A coach tells the team: "Run like this is the last race you will run in your life."

Fr. Bergoglio first refused to hear the confession of a young man who looked quite disoriented, because he was in a hurry to catch a train. Then he changed his mind, heard the young man's confession and then prayed together with him.

There is a Jesuit mantra: *Age quod agis.* Do what you are doing. Dedicate yourself to what you are doing, and do it well. Fr. Bergoglio told the seminarians to strive for "excellence in their studies" and put in "demanding hours of daily study". He often said: 'We run the risk of scattering ourselves on too many directions."[46]

Jesuit Father Jean Pierre Caussade wrote a book: *Abandonment to Divine Providence* also known as the *Sacrament of the Present Moment*. In it he says: "There is not a moment in which God does not present himself under the cover of some pain to be endured, some consolation to be enjoyed or of some duty to be performed."[47] Fr. Bergoglio may have read this book.

Effective leaders commit themselves to the mysticism of the present moment. Yesterday's opportunity has passed, tomorrow's might not come, today's is waiting for me.

The present moment can never be divorced from the past. How I behave right now is an affirmation or rejection of what has been bequeathed to me by those who came before me: the values, culture, practices of my spiritual tradition, community or country.

Unfortunately, we sometimes imagine ourselves to be "Lords of history, nature and culture". It is not merely that we live in the present; it is as if what came before us never mattered. We free ourselves from the moral shackles of antiquated religious believes and outmoded customs of our grandparents. We insist on judging right and wrong by our own personal standards.

For Pope Francis "A Christian without memory is not a true Christian... he/she is a prisoner of circumstance, of the moment, a man or woman who has no history."

When that happens, we find ourselves going from one experience to another without thinking and following the fashions of the time. We are reduced by temporariness."[48]

Pope Francis, who is relentlessly committed to seizing every present opportunity, understands that no leader effectively engages the present without some set of orienting values to distinguish one opportunity as more meaningful and worthwhile, moral or just than another.

In the Ordination Rite of the Deacon, he is asked to believe, teach and practise what he reads in the Gospel.

Inspiring are the leaders who believe, teach and practise – that is, leaders who stand for something. A Jesuit teacher of the seminary said of Fr. Bergoglio who was the Superior of the seminary: "I wasn't always in agreement with the way he was doing things, but I looked up to him. He had a vision, and he was committed to it."[49] In other words, he stood for something.

Pope Francis says: "Precisely if one is faithful one changes. One does not remain faithful, like the traditionalists or the fundamentalists, to the letter. Fidelity is always a change, a blossoming, a growth. The Lord brings about change in those who are faithful. That is Catholic Doctrine."[50]

He also said: Memory of our roots, courage to face the unknown, capturing the reality of the moment.[51]

6. Create the Future: The Challenge of Leading through Change

In an address from St Peter's Square on 18 May 2013 Pope Francis asked: "What happens if we step outside of ourselves. The same as happens to anyone who comes out of the house and onto the street: an accident. But I tell you, I far prefer a Church that has had a few accidents than a Church that has fallen sick from being closed."[52]

Thomas Bradley was on summer duty in Collegio Maximo, a large seminary headed by Jorge Bergoglio. The Theology and Philosophy students had dispersed for summer. Bradley had studied agronomy. Yet he was assigned to do the Porter's duty, not to work in the farm. Why? Bradley gives two explanations: 1) Fr. Bergoglio "understood that we needed to develop an interior life in order to be effective in mission, in our work, and saw in the seminary's stillness an ideal school of the soul where an action-oriented young man could cultivate an increasingly rareskill: the ability to sit in solitude; 2) It is part of the spirituality of the Jesuits: one cannot always gravitate towards the work that one likes or what comes more easily; instead in order to live fully our Jesuit mission it is utterly essential that we learn to follow the path of detachment, of availability, of Ignatian indifference."[53]

Fr. Bergoglio told the young seminarians: "we have already made the hard decision (to become Jesuits). What for? We have to use that freedom."[54]

Bergoglio says: "Our orienting mission, goals, values and moral principles and the very sense of who we are as human beings often flow from traditioin. If we are free, those convictions pull us foreword and keep us properly oriented as a magnetic compass might."[55]

Fr. Bergoglio is ready to take risks. It is said that Bergoglio didn't have "shaky hands" in the face of tough choices. He made lots of them. He transferred to the care of trusted lay colleagues a Jesuit – run university in Buenos Aires and a school in Cordoba.

As Provincial Bergoglio sent some young Jesuits outside the country to shore up personnel-strapped Jesuit ministries in Ecuador – this at a time when Argentina was short of personnel. His explanation: "We Jesuits are not about guarding Jesuits (in our Province). We are about sending people in mission to wherever God's glory may be served, to wherever the need may be the greatest."[56]

It is not true that Fr. Bergoglio made every decision correctly. Leaders have to make judgements often amid uncertainties, under time pressure, and without a crystal ball for the future. The Pope confesses: "I have made mountains of mistakes."[57]

At the time of Cardinal Bergoglio's election as Pope, many Cardinals voiced discontent with the work of Vatican Headquarters. The German Cardinal Walter Kasper said: "The Curia must be revolutionized". What did Pope Francis do? He appointed a commission of eight Cardinals to advise him on Vatican reform. This was declared a revolution by a Vatican watcher Paulo Rodari.

It was certainly not a revolution for Pope Francis steeped in Ignatius' management vision. Jesuit rule book (the Constitutions) gave extraordinary decision – making authority to the Superior General and the Provincial Superiors.

Yet at the same time, the rule book stated "that leaders should have persons designated to give counsel, with whom they should consult on matters of importance which arise. When the system works well, the quality of the decision invariably improves. Leaders must articulate their rationale, say, for wanting to launch a new ministry or replace a key assistant. The consultors can probe for blind spots or derailing attachments that might be clouding the leader's judgement."[58]

By gathering smart advisors, the leader can mitigate his own weaknesses. In private comments that were later leaked to the press, the Pope revealed that such a motive had figured in his decision to convene the commission: "The reform of the Roman Curia is something that almost all cardinals asked for in the Congregations preceding the Conclave. I also asked for it. I cannot promote the reform myself, these are matters of administration…I am very disorganized, I have never been good at this. But the Cardinals of the Commission will move it forward…Pray for me…that I make the least possible mistakes."[59]

This is because the Pope has to make the final decision. Healthy leaders are secure enough to seek advice.

However, Pope Francis is not convinced that structural change alone will create a new Church. This is what he wrote in *Evangelii Gaudium*:

> There are ecclesial structures which can hamper efforts at evangelization, yet even good structures are only helpful when there is a life constantly driving, sustaining and assessing them. Without new life and an authentic evangelical spirit, without the Church's fidelity to her own calling, any new structure will soon prove ineffective.[60]

In his view a total commitment to mission and an earnest effort to fulfil it will transform the Church. In his own words, "I dream of a "missionary option", that is, a missionary impulse capable of transforming everything, so that the Church's customs, ways of doing things, times and schedules, language and structures can be suitably chanelled for the evangelization of today's world rather than for her self-preservation. The renewal of structures demanded by pastoral conversion can only be understood in this light: as part of an effort to make them more mission-oriented, to make ordinary pastoral activity on every level more inclusive and open, to inspire in pastoral workers a constant desire to go forth and in this way to elicit a positive response from all those whom Jesus summons to friendship with him. As John Paul II once said to the Bishops of Oceania: "All renewal in the Church must have mission as its goal if it is not to fall prey to a kind of ecclesial introversion."[61]

The Pope knows full well that an inward-looking Church will never change.

There are some clear indications that Pope Francis is going to change the Catholic Church. As Lowney points out:

Well known for his dedication to Catholic tradition, Pope Francis started dispensing with tradition within minutes of his election, refusing the traditional red cape (mozzetta), placing his own phone calls, and hopping onto a bus instead of into the papal limo.

Further, He washes the feet of juvenile delinquents, kneels for fifteen minutes of solitary prayer on his first morning as pope, wears plain black shoes instead of red ones, wades into a crowd of refugees on theisland of Lampedusa.

Besides, Pope Francis has chosen not to live in the papal palace. Instead he lives in a hostel..

Addressing young Catholics gathered in Rio de Janeiro for World Youth Day Pope Francis stated:

I want you to make yourselves heard in your dioceses, I want the noise to go out, I want the Church to go out onto the streets, I want us to resist everything to do with clericalism…. May the bishops and priests forgive me if some of you create a bit of confusion afterwards.[62]

Moreover, he challenged "lukewarm Christians" and "couch potato" Christians to engage much more energetically in spreading the Church's message, not to "take refuge….in a cozy life," but to get beyond our "comfort zones" and live with greater "apostolic fervour."[63]

He challenged his Church to be more forthrightly "poor, and for the poor."[64]

He warned Vatican diplomats–in-training that "careerism is leprosy."[65]

He challenged a global culture in which "money… for the mighty of this earth, is more important than people."[66]

He challenged his own fellow bishops to be "Men who love… poverty, simplicity and austerity of life."[67]

He asked Brazilian bishops bluntly, "Are we still a Church capable of warming hearts?[68] Cardinal Timothy Dolan of New York, reacting to the pope's challenges, told an interviewer, "I find myself examining my own conscience... on style, on simplicity, on lots of things."[69]

Endnotes

1 C. LOWNEY, *Pope Francis: Why He Leads the Way He Leads,* Mumbai: St Pauls, 2014

2 *Ibid.,* p. 23.

3 *Ibid.,* p. 19.

4 *Ibid.*

5 *Ibid.,* p 24

6 *Ibid.,* p 2

7 *Ibid.,* p 29

8 *Ibid.,* p. 21

9 *Ibid.,* p. 22

10 *Ibid.,* p. 43

11 *Ibid.,* p. 47

12 *Ibid.,* p. 48

13 *Ibid.,* p. 47

14 *Ibid.,* p. 49

15 *Ibid.*

16 *Ibid.,* p. 57

17 *Ibid.,* p. 68

18 *Ibid.*

19 *Ibid.,* p. 65

20 *The Spiritual Exercises of St. Ignatius* nos. 140-146

21 C. LOWNEY, *Pope Francis: Why He Leads the Way He Leads*, p. 79

22 *Ibid.,* pp. 78-79

23 *Ibid.,* p. 80

24 *Ibid.,* p. 87

25 *Ibid.,* p. 89

26 *Ibid.,* p. 94

27 *Ibid.,* p. 90

28 *Ibid.*

29 *Ibid.,* pp. 97-98

30 *Ibi*d., p. 100

31 *Ibid.,* p. 83

32 *Ibid.,* p. 100

33 *Ibid.*

34 *Ibid.*

35 *The Spiritual Exercise of St. Ignatius,* no. 235

36 LOWNEY *Pope Francis: Why He Leads the way He Leads*, p. 90

37   *Ibid.*, p. 122
38   *Ibid.*, p. 199
39   *Ibid.*, pp. 113-114
40   *Ibid.*, p. 123
41   *Ibid.*, pp. 124-125
42   *Ibid.*, p. 114
43   *Ibid.*, p. 117
44   *Ibid.*, pp. 117-118
45   *Ibid.*, p. 118
46   *Ibid.*, p. 140
47   *Ibid.*, p. 145
48   *Ibid.*, p. 148
49   *Ibid.*, p. 149
50   *Ibid.*, p. 158
51   *Ibid.*
52   *Ibid.*, p. 161
53   *Ibid.*, p. 163
54   *Ibid.*, p. 165
55   *Ibid.*
56   *Ibid.*, p. 168
57   *Ibid.*, p. 170
58   *Ibid.*, pp. 173-174
59   *Ibid.*, p. 174
60   Pope FRANCIS, *Evangelii Gaudium*, Rome, 2013, no. 26
61   *Ibid.*
62   *Ibid.*, p. 15
63   *Ibid.*, p. 17
64   *Ibid.*
65   *Ibid.*
66   *Ibid.*
67   *Ibid.*
68   *Ibid.*
69   *Ibid.*

Chapter 22

Pope Francis
Making of a New History of Church Leadership

Errol A. D'Lima SJ
Xavier Institute of Engineering, Mahim, Mumbai, Maharashtra

Introduction

When Vatican One (1869-1870) referred to the Catholic Church, the image it drew on was of a pope exercising universal and immediate jurisdiction over each baptized person. This image was influenced by the account of the Church given by St. Robert Bellarmine (1542-1621). He elaborated an ecclesiology that saw the Church in terms of a pyramid-structure with the power of the papacy supreme within the Church. Such an ecclesiology stressed the institutional structure of the Church where the pope was seen primarily as an administrator rather than one called to exercise the Petrine Ministry.[1] Peter's role was to strengthen his brother bishops by speaking in their name, overseeing the activities of the Church, preserving the apostolic faith and inspiring the Church through his words and actions. Bellarmine's ecclesiology supported a Church that was juridically structured, and where centralized authority was exercised less as service and more as power to command obedience. Bellarmine stressed the visible aspect of the church community by comparing it with a secular state. Just as the secular state needed offices/organs to perform its manifold functions, so too the Church needed its institutional and administrative structures to function in the world.

During the papacy of Pope Sixtus V (1585-1590), a reorganized Roman Curia continued its task of providing the papacy with secretarial functions.[2] As head of the Vatican State, the pope ordered the affairs of the Church through the Curia so that every diocese in the world would be well administered; there would be appointments made and directives given for the successful running of the Church. However, the papacy itself was enveloped in a history that had absorbed customs and practices which gave it a settled form. For instance, the pope was expected to live in the papal apartments in the Vatican, follow protocols in dress, travel and interaction with the laity, and present himself as a head of state to the nations of the world. Changes in the Church were seen as signs of instability and imperfection especially as the Church was considered a *societas perfecta* having within itself the necessary means to attain its goal.

The 16th century Reformation and the 18th century Enlightenment fostered a deep fear in the Church of responding to an evolving rather than a static world. This was seen very strikingly during the pontificate of Pope Pius IX that lasted 32 years.[3] The lifestyle of the popes was seen to be unchanging and their teaching and governance in a fast-changing world affected the common life of the Catholic marginally. The risk of change and new beginnings was avoided but the Catholic Church remained linked to a past age and became increasingly irrelevant to the present. And then Vatican II was announced by Pope John XXIII (1881-1963) a few months after he was elected pope. When Vatican II (1962-65) happened, it was a gift and a task: a gift of the Spirit that enabled the Church to have a new self-understanding, and the challenging task of updating itself in a changing world (*aggiornamento*).

1. A New Self-understanding of the Church and Pope Francis

The new self-understanding of the Church was spelt out in the sixteen documents promulgated by the council but especially in the four constitutions: *Sacrosanctum Concilium* suggested far-reaching changes in the celebration of the liturgy; *Lumen Gentium* spoke of the Church primarily as the People of God and not as hierarchy; *Dei Verbum* saw divine revelation as a continuing action of God in dialogue with humankind, and not merely a sum of truths making up the deposit of faith; and *Gaudium et Spes* envisaged the Church as sharing hope centred in Jesus Christ with the secular world. Much was expected in the aftermath of Vatican II. Some decades later, elected as the 266th Pope on March 13, 2013 Francis began his mission of recasting the role of the papacy and, in the process, the image of the Church.

The mind of Pope Francis in his effort to recast the Church is well reflected in the following:

a. How I would like a poor Church for the poor,
b. Mercy is the Lord's most powerful message,
c. Authentic power is service,
d. Tell priests they must be shepherds who 'smell of their sheep'.[4]

a. *How I Would Like a Poor Church for the Poor*

As pope, Francis enjoys being with people, especially the poor and neglected. He draws inspiration from them and he looks to learn from them in their life of faith. His contact with the poor led him to theologize from their concrete actions. He wrote the following in an article entitled *Criteria of Apostolic Action* in 1980:

Walking patiently and humbly with the poor, we shall learn how we can help them, after first having accepted that we receive from them. Without this slow walk with them, action in favour of the poor and oppressed would contradict our intentions and impede the poor from making their aspirations heard and acquiring for themselves the tools they need for an effective assumption of their personal and collective destiny.[5]

His compassion for the poor was very apparent already when he was the bishop of Buenos Aires, even though he retained his convictions about what he wanted to pursue. In his life as a Jesuit superior, novice master and provincial, Francis had encouraged those in his care to reach out to and spend time with people by responding to their needs. He harboured suspicions about Liberation Theology and when appointed provincial sought to enforce a conservative stance in living out religious life. He wanted liberation theology activists to cease their activities on behalf of the poor. His priorities were: mass, catechesis and the alleviation of poverty.[6] To some in the province, the future pope appeared authoritarian; consultation was not something that came to him easily. To others, he was doing the right thing. The result was a division among the members of the province.

In 1971 he had become Novice Master; in 1973 Provincial; and in 1979 the Rector of its ceremony [seminary]. From 1971 to 1986 he had been the most influential figure in the [Jesuit] religious order but by the end of that period Argentina's Jesuits were deeply riven between those who loved him and those who loathed him.[7]

A major change was in store for the future pope and it took place when he was sent to Cordoba. Before that, he had led the Jesuits in Argentina for fifteen years. Cordoba gave the future pope time for deep reflection, introspection and prayer. He could look at his past, assess it with searing honesty and experience the change that God's action made in him.

He took full responsibility for his actions which caused harm, especially those that injured his Jesuit brethren: "…I made hundreds of errors. Errors and sins. It would be wrong for me to say that these days I ask forgiveness for sins and offences that I might have committed. Today I ask forgiveness for the sins and offences that I did indeed commit."[8]

After he was elected pope, Francis gave his first interview to Fr. Antonio Spadaro where he spoke of the change that had been effected in him. The interlocutor began by asking Francis: Who is Jorge Mario Bergoglio?" and after a moment of silence, the answer came: "I am a sinner. This is the most accurate definition. It is not a figure of speech, a literary genre. I am a sinner."[9]

As pope, Francis lost no time in sharing the fruits of his newfound convictions. He made the Casa Santa Marta (a guest house) his residence; he kept on using his old black shoes, carried his own brief case and made people aware that they could phone him directly. He had already requested his friends in Argentina not to spend money to attend his inauguration as the 'Bishop of Rome'—that is how he continually referred himself in his new position—but to spend it on helping the poor. Pope Francis had assumed a new lifestyle and the universal Church began to follow suit! A series of concrete actions like washing the feet of women and the non-baptized, his meeting with and chatting with people during his outings, his refusal to leave the Vatican for summer holidays, etc., announced to the world that imitating the spirit of the man from Nazareth could rejuvenate the papacy and the Catholic Church. The head of the Roman Catholic Church found his inspiration for governing the Church from the very persons who formed the Church, the People of God.

At his first press conference after his election as pope, Francis announced the main idea that would guide the acts and events of his papacy: "How I would like a poor church for the poor," a refrain to which he would return often.

b. *Mercy is the Lord's Most Powerful Message*

In *Misericordiae vultus*, the Bull of Indiction of the Extraordinary Jubilee of Mercy, Pope Francis has spelt out some of his deepest convictions concerning the mercy of God.[10] In its second paragraph, there is a profound consideration: "Mercy: the bridge that connects God and man, opening our hearts to the hope of being loved forever despite our sinfulness." There must be a just order in the world and efforts to make justice available to all are necessary, but mercy is that which defines God best since it is unfathomable, unconditional and eternal. While returning from the World Youth Day in Brazil, Francis said the following in an impromptu press conference:

I believe this is the time for mercy. The Church…must go down the path of mercy. It must find mercy for everyone. When the Prodigal Son returned home, his father didn't say: "But you, listen, sit down. What did you do with the money?" No, he held a party. Then, maybe, when the son wanted to talk, he talked. The Church must do the same…I believe that is a *Kairos* of mercy.[11]

Just before the beginning of the conclave that elected Bergoglio pope, Cardinal Walter Kasper gave him a copy of his latest book *Mercy: The Essence of the Gospel and the Key to Christian Life*. Seeing the title, he exclaimed: "This is the name of our God."[12] Since the time of St. John Paul II, Kaspar had wanted the ban lifted on remarried Catholics receiving communion, even if their first marriage had not been annulled. Kasper was suggesting a change in pastoral practice, not a change in the Church's teaching on marriage. He was opposed by the then head of the Congregation for the Doctrine of the Faith (CDF), Joseph Ratzinger. The CDF's view prevailed.

Pope Francis' deep concern for mercy in the different and often difficult situations of marriage inspired him to promulgate *Amoris Laetitia*, Love in the Family.[13] To imitate God in showing mercy calls for an inclusive society according to Francis. Not only those who followed Church teaching on Christian Marriage, but also those in irregular unions, civil unions and even those cohabitating, were to be seen as part of the Church and deserved the Church's pastoral care unconditionally. Pope Francis questions applying a law to a situation without discerning the context in the light of mercy. He did not claim that what was wrong had now become right! Instead, he looked to find in each situation the merciful hand of God bringing out the positive that was present. Francis was basing himself on theological roots that had been part of authentic Catholic Tradition.[14] Hence he could justifiably assert:

For this reason, a pastor cannot feel that it is enough simply to apply moral laws to those living in "irregular" situations, as if they were stones to throw at people's lives. This would bespeak the closed heart of one used to hiding behind the Church's teachings, "sitting on the chair of Moses and judging at times with superiority and superficiality difficult cases and wounded families". Along these same lines, the International Theological Commission has noted that "natural law could not be presented as an already established set of rules that impose themselves a priori on the moral subject; rather, it is a source of objective inspiration for the deeply personal process of making decisions."[15]

Moral insight is not the result of rational logic alone but of admitting in the first place that human actions and decisions are the outcome of complex factors. Pastoral concern should be exercised while taking these complex factors into account. Canon law and magisterial diktats alone are insufficient to respond to problematic situations. Pope Francis was retrieving a holistic way of relating to persons and dealing with situations that are presumed "sinful". God's mercy is unconditional and has no limit. The Church, as the enduring, public witness to God's active presence in the world is called to celebrate this unconditional and limitless love of God when serving God's people. Discernment and accompaniment should be included in pastoral care.

c. *Authentic Power is Service*

Earlier in this article, Bellarmine's description of the Church stressed authority as the ability to command obedience. Usually it is the magisterium of the Church that makes known official teaching which includes the setting down of directions, policies and rules by which the People of God are to be governed. The dicasteries (Congregations) in Rome had overseen formulating and sending out directives to the different dioceses in the world. Whereas the dicasteries were meant to work as the secretarial agents of the pope, they were creating and fixing norms to guide the Church, tasks that clearly belong to the bishops, the teaching church, *Ecclesia docens*. This was already seen at the time of Vatican II. At the council, one of the charges made against the dicasteries was that they did not represent sufficiently the international character of the Church. Persons from other countries were inducted in the dicasteries in response to the charge. But the deeper malaise remained. The dicasteries were in effect overseeing the day to day running of the entire Church.

It is a moot point whether the issues taken up by the dicasteriesare issues that affect the whole Church or only part of it; perhaps they affected the European Churches. How does one justify their action of sending out instructions and rulings to be followed by the entire Church as though the languages, cultures and customs were the same for whole world? Many examples can be given of dicasteries sending communications to all the dioceses in the world without awareness of different contexts due to languages, cultures and customs. For instance, the dicastery in charge of divine worship decided that many abuses were being committed in the celebration of the Eucharist.[16] For the Latin Church, one of those abuses was the pouring of consecrated wine from one vessel into another at communion time; yet the same practice followed by the Syro-Malabar Church did not constitute an abuse! On September 16, 2016, the Conference of Catholic Bishops of India (CBCI) published *Directives for the Celebration of the Liturgy*.[17] Frequently, in the publication, the General Instructions of the Roman Missal (GIRM) are referred to as supply ingnorms to be followed. Should not there have been a greater effort to indicate norms for eucharistic celebration that considered cultures and customs and usage that flow from the way of life in India?

Pope Francis has put into effect the practice of consultation with his fellow bishops in mapping out policies and guidelines for the Church. This quasi-synodal mode of governing the Church does not mean that that Francis abdicates his own responsibility as the final authority in the Church; it means that an informed authority has greater credibility and that decisions from the centre are made in dialogue with the periphery.

Pope Francis has had to steer a path that questioned a merely doctrinal approach but he is also aware that crossing swords with the incumbents in the Vatican could produce unnecessary turmoil. In the case concerning the Leadership Conference of Women Religious (LCWR) in the United States, he waited for the 'right' moment to intervene. In April 2008, Cardinal William Levada was the CDF head. He told the nuns that the Vatican would conduct a doctrinal assessment. They were also told that some of their attitudes to women priests and homosexuality were contrary to those in the Vatican, and that they should articulate the classic Catholic position more clearly in matters of birth control and especially abortion. There seemed to be no common ground between the Vatican and the Sisters for dialogue. Worse still, Pope Francis supported the investigation against the Sisters. However, in 2014 when the final document was published, it contained the following:

Since the early days of the Catholic church in their country, women religious have courageously been in the forefront of her evangelizing mission, selflessly tending to the spiritual, moral, educational, physical and social needs of countless individuals, especially the poor and marginalized. Throughout the nation's history, the educational apostolate of women religious in Catholic schools has fostered the personal development and nourished the faith of countless young people and helped the Church community in the US to flourish.[18]

In this episode, Pope Francis allowed the dicastery in question to fulfil its given task but he also saw to it that the persons who presided over the dicastery were objectively well-disposed to what the LCWR stood for.

One can accept that the authority of the magisterium is constitutive of the Church—in so far as it indicates God's concrete providential care guiding the Church, but must the magisterium in its teaching role always appear as one commanding obedience? Teaching (*ecclesia docens*) can be communicated also by example, inspiration, emulation and evocation. When the magisterium is restricted to dealing with doctrine and its imposition on the faithful, is it really exercising itself in the spirit of the gospel? "…the Son of man came…to serve …" (Matt 20:28) Through his actions that are self-explanatory and answers that acknowledge the complexity of life, Francis suggests a pattern of living in the world that seeks to serve one's neighbour. His image of priests muddying their shoes while caring for their people aptly describes authentic power as service.

d. *"Tell Priests They Must be Shepherds Who 'Smell of Their Sheep'"*

Over the years, the efforts to distinguish the specific aspects of priestly life from those characterizing the lay Catholic has often resulted in the ordained minister becoming distant from the very persons he is called to serve. Worse still, the culture of clericalism made out that the ordained ministers belonged more properly to the Church than did the laity. In stressing the closeness of priests to the people, Francis is asking for a simpler life style, a humbler demeaner, an attitude of learning from the poor that should characterize the ministerial priest as envisaged by Vatican II. It was with this understanding that Francis spoke about the diseases that the Curia suffered from. One can be a true shepherd only if one walks with the flock under his care. To be a pastor one must bring solace to those who are needy and celebrate the saving presence of God among the poor and suffering.

After his council of 8 cardinals had been appointed to assist the pope in his ministry, the pope asked that the norms for the Roman Curia be written anew.[19] Cardinal Sean O'Malley, one of the eight, explained the pope's mind as follows:

The Curia [was] to be at the service of the universal Church and that means great efficiency, greater transparency, collaboration among the different departments, a great focus on collegiality and involvement with the bishops through the world and the local churches.[20]

To smell like the sheep includes first consulting the people one serves and cares for. Whether in sacramental celebration, counselling, rendering aid to others or building the flock more completely into the People of God, one should start not with doctrinaire reflection but from the praxis of a believing people who are centred on Jesus Christ.[21] In the spirit of *Gaudium et Spes*, the priest representing the Church must make "the joy and hope, the grief and anguish" (no. 1) of the people his own, thus establishing a deep solidarity with his flock.

2. A New History of Church Leadership

It is now time to put together the elements that contribute to a new history of Church leadership as symbolized by Pope Francis.

First, Francis has recognized that the history of the Catholic Church until the present is mostly the effect of a Top-Down movement. This movement used the deductive method where the truths of the faith contained in scripture and in the tradition of the Church (statements of Councils, papal proclamations and magisterial teaching) were the premises from which conclusions could be drawn. These conclusions were presented to the faithful as teachings of the Church. Francis has inserted dialogue into this method, dialogue with the People of God before the Church presents its teaching.

Second, contextual reflection means that a Catholic theology is constructed by conducting a dialogue between sacred scripture, Christian tradition and the context of the living community today. Each age must rethink its theology; if it does not, the Church will be repeating answers made in response to questions of an age gone by. Pope Francis has taken *aggiornamento* seriously especially since this was one of the reasons adduced by St. Pope John XXIII for calling Vatican II.

Third, "establishment theology" tends to suppose that most, if not all, important questions concerning living a Christian life have been answered. Pope Francis is willing to address questions that many persons ask today; he is willing to concede that the Church has still to find adequate responses to the issues of the modern age. This may call for a re-examination of Church doctrine and practice. He also knows that structures in the Church may need changing so that the witness to Jesus Christ may be preserved. Introspection by the official church as well as its members will be part of such a re-examination.

Finally, Pope Francis prefers to view the Church as inclusive since *Lumen Gentium* no. 1 sees the Church as sacramentally expressing the action of God in the world. For him, it is important to recognize what God has already done in every person. One builds up relationship on this premise. This understanding calls the Church to serve the world in a new way and build a world community.

Endnotes

1   Richard MCBRIEN (General Editor): *The HarperCollins Encyclopaedia of Catholicism*, New York, 1995. Jean-M. R. Tillard "Petrine Ministry", 995: to witness to the faith, to preserve it and hand it over with integrity, to assist fellow bishops in defending the content of faith, to

coordinate the activities of the local churches, to declare solemnly the true faith of the church when required.

2   The next reorganization of the Curia took place with Vatican II.

3   Calling himself "the prisoner of the Vatican" he refused to negotiate with the Italian nationalists who wanted to include the papal states in a future united Italy.

4   Paul VELLELY: *Pope Francis untying the Knots*, The Struggle for the Soul of Catholicism, Bloomsbury Continuum, Revised and expanded, London and New York, 2015, 434.

5   Paul VELLELY, 135.

6   Paul VELLELY, 40.

7   Paul VELLELY, 111.

8   VALLELY, 84.

9   VALLELY, 84.

10   April 11, 2015, given at St. Peter's, Rome.

11   VALLELY, 184.

12   VALLELY, 333.

13   St. Peter's, Rome, March 19, 2016.

14   That tradition includes discernment, the mystery of God, proportionality and *epikeia*.

15   *AmorisLaetitia*.

16   *Redemptionis Sacramentum* (Instruction from the offices of the Congregation for Divine Worship and the Discipline of the Sacraments, Rome, on the Solemnity of the Annunciation of the Lord, 25 March 2004).

17   Published by the Deputy Secretary General of the CBCI after being approved by the 28th Plenary Assembly of the CBCI on March 6, 2016.

18   VALLELY, 382.

19   VALLELY, 283.

20   VALLELY, 293.

21   This was clearly seen in the two sessions of the Family Synod where the pope wanted the understanding of lay persons concerning marriage to be heard.

Chapter 23

Relationality as the Paradigm of Pope Francis' Leadership

Joseph A. D'Mello SJ
*Coordinator, PG Diploma in Ignatian Spirituality,
Jnana-Deepa Vidyapeeth, Pune, Maharashtra*

On 22 February 2017, a 32-year-old Indian techie, Srinivas Kuchibhotla, was shot dead in a bar outside of Kansas City, US. Meanwhile, the alleged shooter yelled "Get out of my country".

On 11 July 2016 four Dalits were stripped and beaten up for skinning a cow in Gujarat.

On 28 September 2015, Mohammed Akhlaq was lynched for allegedly eating beef in Dadri, Uttar Pradesh.

The world in which we live today is replete with such incidents of hatred and hostility and it appears that they are in concurrence with the definition that the other is my enemy as expounded by French existentialist philosopher, Jean Paul Sartre.[1] The rise in religious fundamentalism, nationalism, ethnic rivalry, etc., is a sign that relationality is restricted to one's religion, caste, nation, race, state, sect, language, etc., leading to intolerance. Such a narrow worldview of relationality will always create a feeling of 'we - they, insiders - outsiders' and while the former (we, insiders) will live in security, the latter (they, outsiders) will live in fear and insecurity.

The words and deeds of Pope Francis clearly reveal that for him the human person is essentially a relational being. "Let us help each other, all together, to remember that the 'other' is not a statistic, or a number," says Holy Father Pope

Francis, "We all need each other."[2] Animosity and antipathy will ultimately erect walls, isolating oneself from the other whereas true relationality will build bridges leading to communion and meaning. The Church, as it is in its *Kairos* moment with the leadership of Pope Francis, invites us to recapture the spirit of relationality in our life and mission as human beings and Christians.

1. Relationality Leading to Encounter

The very term "encounter" signifies that one is open to the other. It is the encounter with somebody. For a Christian, it is the encounter, the *anubhava* with the Trinity. The Triune God is relational, outward looking and self-emptying. "For God so loved the world that he gave his only Son." (Jn 3:16) But, unfortunately, when we are caught up with ourselves, with our "own interests and concerns, there is no longer room for others, no place for the poor. God's voice is no longer heard, the quiet joy of his love is no longer felt, and the desire to do good fades." (*Evangelii Gaudium* 2) Therefore, every Christian is invited to be a person of encounter. (EG 3) "What I tell people is not to know God only by hearing. The living God is He that you may see with your eyes within your heart."[3] In this encounter one sees the face of God. Such encounters liberate one from one's narrowness and self-absorption. (EG 8) "When we put Christ at the centre of our life, we ourselves don't become the centre! The more that you unite yourself to Christ and he becomes the centre of your life, the more he leads you out of yourself, leads you from making yourself the centre and opens you to others."[4]

2. Relationality Leading to Seeing the Reality with the Eyes of Jesus

The first Pope from Latin America says that the name of God whom we encounter is Mercy.[5] This "mercy has become living and visible in Jesus of Nazareth." (*Misericordiae Vultus*1) In his first Angelus address on March 17, 2013 he reiterated and delineated that God is never tired of forgiving us.[6] As children of God, we share God's DNA.[7] The transforming experience brought about by encounter with Jesus makes us more and more altruistic, compassionate and merciful towards others. The eyes of Jesus are the eyes of mercy, compassion and hope. Even though there is dissension and discord in the world, the experience of encounter makes us to see the wounded world with optimism since we see the reality with the gaze of Jesus. "Let us see ourselves and the world with Christ's eyes."[8]

3. Relationality Leading to Respect

As we gaze at the world with Jesus, with the eyes of mercy and hope, we look at it with deep respect since every creature has come from the Creator. Globalization of indifference (EG 54) and technocratic paradigm (*Laudato Sí* 106) undermine the transcendental dimension of creation. Creation is God's gift for us and at the same time we have a task. But we forget that it is a gift and the human person thinks that "everything is the fruit of his [one's] labor and that there is no gift. It is what I call the Babel syndrome."[9]

Pope Francis sees a callous disregard for the ageing and elderly who are also becoming victims of disposable culture. In many urban areas where both spouses work, the care of the elderly is a major concern. It is not an issue of children who are busy with work but it is mere egoism.[10] The octogenarian Pope Francis questions such an attitude of children. "The elderly are not taken care of like they should be, but rather they are treated as discarded material. Sometimes they are deprived of medicine and ordinary care, and that is what is killing them."[11]

Relationality invites one to respect the God experience of the people of other religious traditions. Pope Francis is pained to see the world divided in the name of God. A believer from other religions is viewed as a threat than as a brother and sister. "God is patient, He waits, and God does not kill. It is man that wants to do so on God's behalf. To kill in the name of God is blasphemy."[12] "God is open to all people. He calls everyone. He moves everyone to seek Him and to discover Him through creation."[13] "No believer can limit the faith to himself, his clan, his family, or his city. A believer is essentially someone who goes into an encounter with other believers, or non-believers, to give them a hand."[14] During his visit to Egypt in April 2017 he decried that "violence is the negation of every authentic religious expression."[15] "*The courage to accept differences*, because those who are different, either culturally or religiously, should not be seen or treated as enemies, but rather welcomed as fellow-travellers, in the genuine conviction that the good of each resides in the good of all."[16]

4. Relationality Leading to Discernment

We follow Jesus in space and time in a particular historical context. Jon Sobrino, a renowned liberation theologian, while mentioning the presuppositions and foundation for spirituality, underlines that spirituality should begin with "an act of profound honesty about the real, the recognition of things as they actually are."[17] Relationality makes one to take the reality seriously.

Before discerning the spirit in the outside world, Pope Francis desires to bring reform within the Church by putting order in the Roman Curia, by reforming the governance structures.[18] While greeting the Roman Curia on the Nativity of our Lord on 22 December 2016, the Holy Father invited them to embrace the process of reform saying Christmas is "the feast of the loving humility of God, of the God who upsets our logical expectations, the established order."[19] In the course of his message, he highlighted the twelve guiding principles of the reform and one of them being 'Discernment.'[20]

It is also the priests who need this gift of discernment as they can be carried away by the values of materialism, consumerism and hedonism. Therefore, "today the Church needs to grow in discernment, in the ability to discern. And priests above all really need it for their ministry."[21] During his exhortation to the members of the Pontifical Ecclesiastical Academy, Pope Francis pointed out that careerism is so rampant among the priests. He used a stern language saying "Careerism is leprosy! Leprosy!"[22] He has also critiqued the culture of clericalism among the clergy considering themselves above the laity and refusing to be close to people.[23]

Meanwhile, the Argentina-born Pope is aware of the contemporary challenges of the world and called Christians to have an evangelical discernment which is nourished by the light and strength of the Holy Spirit. (EG 50) Vehemently denouncing the economy of exclusion and inequality, the Apostolic Exhortation, *The Joy of the Gospel* says "Just as the commandment 'Thou shalt not kill' sets a clear limit in order to safeguard the value of human life, today we also have to say 'thou shalt not' to an economy of exclusion and inequality. Such an economy kills."(EG 53) As a consequence "masses of people find themselves excluded and marginalized: without work, without possibilities, without any means of escape." (EG 53) We need to discern this reality, need to be alert by reading the signs of the times.

The Joy of the Gospel condemning the idolatry of money indicates "The current financial crisis can make us overlook the fact that it originated in a profound human crisis: the denial of the primacy of the human person! We have created new idols. The worship of the ancient golden calf (cf. Ex 32:1-35) has returned in a new and ruthless guise in the idolatry of money and the dictatorship of an impersonal economy lacking a truly human purpose. The worldwide crisis affecting finance and the economy lays bare their imbalances and, above all, their lack of real concern for human beings; man is reduced to one of his needs alone: consumption." (EG 55) Any financial system should be at the service of the people and not vice versa. Beneath this there is a rejection of ethics and God. (EG 57) "Money must serve, not rule! The Pope loves everyone, rich and poor alike, but he is obliged in the name of Christ to remind all that the rich must help, respect and promote the poor. I exhort you to generous solidarity and a return of economics and finance to an ethical approach which favours human beings." (EG 58)

5. Relationality Leading to Include the Excluded

The Pope who stands for and walks with the poor has made it clear that our faith in Christ, who became poor and was always close to the poor and the outcast[24] makes us include the excluded and not any ideology. Besides, relationality is at the core of the Church which is open to all. "The Church, which is holy, does not reject sinners; she does not reject us all; she does not reject because she calls everyone, welcomes them, is open even to those furthest from her."[25]

Following in the footsteps of Jesus, the people's Pope imbued with a strong social sense, continues the mission of including the excluded. His encyclical 'Laudato Sí' has called upon everyone to be sensitive to the cry of the Mother Earth and the cry of the poor. Today the Mother Earth and the poor should become the focus of the mission of the Church. He envisages a Church where the poor have a primary place. Therefore, often he has been categorical saying "How I would like a church that is poor and for the poor." (EG 198)[26]

Since Pope Francis is known for thinking outside the box, his pontificate has been one of surprises. Some of the surprising deeds are: Washing of the feet of women, refugees, disabled people and people of other religions on Maundy Thursday. During the Extraordinary Jubilee Year of Mercy, on "Fridays of Mercy", he made surprise visits to nursing homes, rehabilitation centres, SOS village, etc. Such prophetic deeds reveal that the Church embraces all without any distinction. It has a mother's heart that is compassionate and merciful. These poor and the marginalized are children of God who have inherent dignity. "Behind these statistics are people, each of them with a name, a face, a story, an inalienable dignity which is theirs as a child of God."[27]

Though the prophetic Pope has received withering criticism for some of his views and gestures on inclusiveness, he strongly believes that the Church should go to the periphery and we need to find God in the marginalized. Those who have experienced Christ should not be afraid of going to the outskirts. It is a call to move beyond our comfort zones. God is bigger than our little way of seeing things! He is not afraid of the outskirts. If we go to the outskirts, we will find him there.[28]

6. Relationality Leading to Conflicts

Discernment leads one to choose what God wants. This choice is made in communion with the Lord. Often this choice becomes counter-cultural. The words and deeds of Pope Francis have become counter cultural witness. His way of thinking and acting is not in sync with the value system of the world. Jesus paid the price for being counter-cultural and radical. Pope Francis, who is known as a radical Pope, has challenged the youth to be counter-cultural, to come out of their comfort zones. He called upon the youth of Argentina to create a mess in their Dioceses. "But I want a mess in the dioceses! I want people to go out! I want the Church to go out to the street! I want us to defend ourselves against everything that is worldliness, that is installation, that is comfortableness, that is clericalism, that is being shut-in in ourselves. The parishes, the schools, the institutions, exist to go out!"[29] The Pope from his life experience is aware that when the Church goes out, it will have to face turmoil and conflict. He is convinced that "like anyone else, in going out, the Church risks running into accidents. 'I prefer a thousand times over a Church of accidents than a sick Church.'"[30] It is a call to swim against the current, to rebel against the contemporary culture of materialism and such attitudes are bound to bring tension within and without the Church.

7. Relationality Leading to Proclamation of Life

As the world is torn by violence and strife, divided by divisive ideologies and politics, it needs living examples of persons who can show to the masses that another way of relating is possible founded on the person of Jesus Christ. Often we think of proclamation in terms of words, in terms of bringing out documents. But the need of the hour is proclamation and witness through life. The life of Pope Francis is louder than words and any document. His exemplary life has been a tangible expression of the love and mercy of God. "Less is more" (LS 222) has been his conviction when it comes to leading a simple life which sheds the VIP culture.

Pope Francis asked forgiveness for Rwandan genocide, for victims of clergy sex abuse, apologized for the Church's non-Christian attitude and behavior towards the Waldensians from the 12th to 17th Centuries. His attitude of mercy stretches out towards the homosexuals and divorcees. The litany of such extraordinary gestures is unending. Pope Francis walks the talk. He denounced a double life, a life of compromises with strong words *"I am very Catholic, I always go to Mass, I belong to this association and that one; but my life is not Christian, I don't pay my workers a just wage, I exploit people, I am dirty in my business, I launder money…' A double life. And so many Christians are like this, and these people scandalize others. How many times have we heard - all of us, around the neighbourhood and elsewhere – 'but to be a Catholic like that, it's better to be an atheist.'"*[31] The world of today is in need of life witness to the Gospel and Pope Francis wants every Christian to be a living witness of Christ's mercy and compassion.

Conclusion

As he is about to complete five years in the pontificate, one can opine that the paradigm of the leadership of Pope Francis has been relationality founded on the encounter with Jesus. Today, when many see religion as the cause of division and violence, Pope Francis is convinced that authentic religious expression can foster peace and harmony. The paradigm of relationality is an antidote for hatred and vengeance. If peace, harmony, brotherhood and sisterhood have to prevail, we need to carry forward the spirit of relationality. To conclude with the words of Pope Francis: "What is needed today are peacemakers, not fomenters of conflict; firefighters and not arsonists; preachers of reconciliation and not instigators of destruction."[32]

Endnotes

1　　J. P. SARTRE, *L'être et le néant*, 1949, p. 251 Cited by John D. Zizioulas, *Communion & Otherness. Further Studies in Personhood and the Church*, Ed. Paul McPartlan, (London: T&T Clark, 2009), 1.

2　　https://www.ted.com/talks/pope_francis_why_the_only_future_worth_building_includes_everyone?language=en (accessed May 10, 2017).

3　　Jorge Mario BERGOGLIO and Abraham SKORKA, *On Heaven and Earth: Pope Francis on Faith, Family and the Church in the 21st Century* (London: Bloomsbury, 2013), 3.

4　　Pope FRANCIS, *The Church of Mercy: His First Major Book: A Message of Hope for all People*, Ed. Giuliano Vigini (Bangalore: Asian Trading Corporation, 2014), 17-18.

5   Pope FRANCIS. *The Name of God is Mercy: A Conversation with Andrea Tornielli,* Tr. Oonagh Stransky, (London: Bluebird, 2016), 7.

6   http://www.catholicworldreport.com/Blog/2091/full_text_pope_francis_first_angelus_address.aspx (accessed April 5, 2017).

7   https://zenit.org/articles/popes-morning-homily-gods-given-us-the-dna-of-his-children/ (accessed April 5, 2017).

8   Pope Francis, General Audience, Feb 22, 2017. https://zenit.org/articles/general-audience-pope-let-us-see-ourselves-world-with-christs-eyes-2/ (accessed March 25, 2017).

9   Jorge Mario BERGOGLIO and Abraham SKORKA, *On Heaven and Earth,* 5.

10   Ibid., 98.

11   Ibid., 92.

12   Ibid., 19.

13   Ibid.

14   Ibid., 21.

15   Holy Father's Address to Participants of the International Peace Conference in Cairo, "No to Hatred in the Name of God," *L'Oseervatore Romano,* May 5, 2017, 8-9.

16   Ibid. (Italics as in the text)

17   Jon SOBRINO. *Spirituality of Liberation. Toward Political Holiness,* Tr. Robert R. Barr, (Maryknoll: Orbis Books, 1989), 15.

18   Thomas Reese, "Four Years of Pope Francis", *JIVAN: News and Views of Jesuits in India,* (April, 2017), 6: "The financial reforms are spreading through the various Vatican agencies, beginning with the Vatican Bank and moving through other entities. The Vatican budgetary process has been tightened up, and various offices have been consolidated."

19   http://biblefalseprophet.com/2016/12/22/francis-christmas-greetings-to-the-curia-gradualism-discernment/ (accessed April 5, 2017).

20   Ibid.

21   http://www.cyberteologia.it/2016/09/today-the-church-needs-to-grow-in-discernment-a-private-encounter-of-pope-francis-with-some-polish-jesuits/ (accessed March 25, 2017).

22   https://zenit.org/articles/pope-francis-to-pontifical-ecclesiastical-academy-careerism-is-a-leprosy/ (accessed April 5, 2017).

23   http://www.catholicnewsagency.com/news/in-stressing-error-of-clericalism-francis-calls-for-humble-priests-32780/ (accessed April 5, 2017).

24   Pope FRANCIS, *The Church of Mercy,* 24.

25   Ibid., 34.

26   https://www.ncronline.org/blogs/francis-chronicles/pope-francis-i-would-love-church-poor (accessed April 5, 2017).

27   "Refugees are God's Children, Pope says in Wake of Paris Attacks," http://www.catholicnewsagency.com/news/refugees-are-gods-children-pope-says-in-wake-of-paris-attacks-27455/ (accessed November 19, 2015).

28   Pope FRANCIS, *The Church of Mercy,* 20-21.

29   Pope's Address to Argentinian Youth, *Zenit,* July 26, 2013, https://zenit.org/articles/pope-s-address-to-argentinian-youth/ (accessed January 24, 2015).

30   "Pope: Mission, the Best Cure for the Church," http://en.radiovaticana.va/storico/2013/04/18/pope_mission,_the_best_cure_for_the_church/en1-683985 (accessed October 12, 2015).

31   http://en.radiovaticana.va/news/2017/02/23/pope_dont_put_off_conversion,_give_up_a_
      double_life/1294470 (accessed March 1, 2017).

32   "No to Hatred in the Name of God," *L'Oseervatore Romano,* May 5, 2017, 10.

Chapter 24

Pope Francis, the Game-Changer
From the Top-Down Tradition to Down-Up, Communitarian Approach

Job Kozhamthadam SJ
Director, IISR (Indian Institute of Science and Religion), Delhi

Introduction

The long history of the Catholic Church for over two millennia tells us that challenges and periods of tension were never strange. The secret of the success of the Church has been that it has been able to look upon these challenges and tensions not so much as oppositions to be suppressed, as opportunities to rethink and re-vision its self-understanding and current position, and make appropriate course-correction. Naturally, being a very large institution – in fact, the largest single institution in the world – this process has often been arduous and slow. History also tells us that the Catholic Church has been fortunate to have specially gifted persons from time to time, who could play the role of game-changers by initiating, or at least serving as catalysts, in this all important process. In fact, Christ himself was the super game-changer. True, his mission led him to the most humiliating death on the cross between two certified criminals, but the world in general, and humanity in particular, could never remain the same after his entry into human history. To mention a few others, Francis Assisi in the early part of the 13th century, St. Thomas Aquinas soon afterwards, and St. Ignatius of Loyola in the 16th century, were some of these great, rare persons who could read the needs of the times, intuitively identify the principal problem spots, and make appropriate course corrections. In our own times, it seems to me that the Pope John XXIII–Vatican II – Pope Francis combination is playing the all-important role of a game changer. I put these three together because I see in all three a commonness of purpose and a continuity of process. In this present paper, I focus mainly on the role of Pope Francis in this ongoing process.

There is no doubt that the Catholic Church in recent times has been at a crossroads. The Church is challenged by critically-minded scholars from both inside and outside, has been lost in the flood of unprecedented developments in science and technology (many of which question some of its fundamental beliefs), and embarrassed by scandals and other disturbing happenings. Although, some recent statistics show a marginal increase in the number of Catholics in the world, this is mostly because of the success of the missionary world in Africa and certain Asian nations. The disappointing news is that many western countries, particularly Europe, is showing a marked decline. This is also true of parts of the world which are economically better-off and educationally advanced. This is a matter of grave concern because Christ and the Church are for all humans at all times. Christ has an important message for the educated and the economically better-off also. Catholicism can and should respond responsibly and creatively to the legitimate aspirations of the educated, the scientifically-minded, the critically-minded, and the economically advanced persons also. Otherwise, Catholicism becomes hollow and meaningless; so, this situation needs careful study and creative responses. Some years ago, there was a move to respond to this situation under the garb of the "New Evangelization." To my knowledge that does not seem to have made any significant advance. My observation is that Pope John XXIII in his prophetic insight convened the Vatican II Ecumenical Council precisely to meet this crucial challenge. Both the documents and the spirit that animated Vatican II were moving in this direction, particularly under Pope Paul VI. However, in the course of time over the Post-Conciliar years that spirit seems to have weakened and a tendency to return to Pre-Conciliar days began to grow. In my view the principal contribution Pope Francis' is making today is to regain the momentum set by Vatican II, thereby responding to the challenges facing Catholicism in a responsible, creative and constructive way. This paper is an attempt to identify and analyse some of the most important challenges the Catholic Church is facing today and the role being played by Pope Francis' leadership in this momentous task. It is my humble submission that this critical situation requires a serious course-correction and a game-changer is the need of the hour. The spirit of Pope John XXIII and the message of Vatican II coupled with the new form of leadership offered by Pope Francis seems to be the best path to address this all-important mission.

1. Developments in Science and Consequent Changes in Human Attitude

1.1. Origin of Modern Science and a Positive Attitude towards the Material Universe

Modern science has historically had a reverent attitude towards the material universe. In fact, such an attitude was a precondition for the origin and development of science, since, if it had been otherwise, creative scientists who are unusually gifted with brilliant minds, and other outstanding talents, would not have ventured into this field. History also bears testimony to this fact. For example, Johannes Kepler, one of the founders of modern science and the father of modern astronomy, believed that the universe was the "sacred temple of God." Nicolas Copernicus, who is credited with the honour of laying the foundation for modern science, was often considered a "sun-worshipper" because of the God-like respect and regard he had for the sun, which he considered the centre of the universe. Sir Isaac Newton, undoubtedly one of the greatest scientists of all times, also had a very high regard for the material universe. For him the universe was the sure path through which one was led to the Creator.

On the other hand, Christianity, particularly in the Middle Ages and later, had a negative view of the material universe. One can cite much evidence to illustrate this unfortunate point. For instance, the universe was considered one of the principal enemies of humans along with the devil and the flesh (the body). The universe was a source of sin, and so the more one distanced oneself from it, the higher one grew in spirituality and holiness. It was depicted as "the vale of tears," where humans were "poor banished children of Eve." According to *The Imitation of Christ* by Thomas A Kempis, a masterpiece of spiritual literature from the Middle Ages, "Whenever a monk went out, he came back less a monk." No doubt, one can also show instances of a positive attitude by the Catholic Church towards the material universe. For instance, St. Irenaeus of Lyons, the well-known Church Father of the 2nd century, took a positive view of the universe as created by God. But the dominant historical view, particularly during the Middle Ages, has been negative. It should be noted that in recent times many Christian theologians have moved away from this view. However, some shadows of this negativity still lurk in many areas of Christianity. Thus, in many ways, the traditional Church and science have had very different attitudes towards the material universe and nature.

2. Paradigm Shift in the Nature and Role of Science

Of importance is the paradigm shift that science has undergone, particularly with regard to its nature and role in matters of human concern. I discuss a few of the most important ones, here.

2.1. Shift from the Age of Discovery of Nature to the Age of Mastery over Nature

In the past, scientists were satisfied with discovering the laws of nature. For instance, Kepler, Galileo, Newton, and others, were noted for their outstanding scientific discoveries that uncovered some of the secret laws of nature. Most scientists and science remained content and happy when and if this goal was attained. But today, science wants to have mastery over nature. It wants to have a hand in controlling nature and a say in determining the future course of nature. In fact, the discovery of unversal laws is but a crucial step on the path to gain mastery over nature. This shift in this goal has serious religious implications, because religion considers God to be the master of the universe; science is now trying to take over that role.

2.2. Paradigm Shift in the Role of Science

In the past science was looked upon as a provider of certain means and amenities to facilitate life. Science in this context touched humans from the outside, the world around humans. But today, thanks to developments in genetics, notably genetic engineering, cloning, stem cell research, and the like, science is capable of touching humans from within; from the inside. In the past science could determine what humans have and wish to have; today science, in some ways, is in the role to decide what humans are and wish to be.

2.3. Science Providing a Worldview

Furthermore, today science has grown to be capable of providing a worldview that plays a crucial role in forming the knowledge system, determining the value system, shaping themeaning system, deciding crucial criteria governing decisions, controlling the expectation level, etc.

These subtle, though slow, changes in the nature and role of science are enabling science to take over some of the functions traditionally relegated to religion. There seems to be a subtle, perhaps unconscious, move by science to replace religion in the life of contemporary humans.

3. Developments in Science and the Gradual "Eviction" of God and Religion

Many developments in science and technology, especially the revolutionary ones, have been having serious impact on traditional religion and belief in God. More specifically, they are posing serious questions to the traditional understanding of the nature of God and the role of God in the creation and running of the universe. It looks as though they are in some significant ways making God more and more dispensable in the universe, as far as God's traditional functions are concerned.

3.1. Dispensability of God and Religion in the Universe

a. Developments in Newtonian Mechanics and the Emergence of the Mechanical Philosophy of Nature

Some of the developments in Newtonian Mechanics, particularly in the context of the Mechanical Philosophy of Nature, led many scientists and thinkers to conclude that our universe was, in many ways, self-operational, and hence no external agency was needed for its maintenance and preservation. This obviously undermined the traditional belief in God as the conserver/preserver of the universe, thereby rendering God dispensable in this regard.

b. The No-Boundary Theory of Stephen Hawking and the Dispensability of the Creator-God

Newton's God was very much a "plumber God" since according to him, God had to make periodic visits to repair and set aright the universe to ensure smooth cosmic functioning. Laplace, later on showed that this kind of "maintenance work" was unnecessary since nature was capable of maintaining itself. This meant that God's role as the maintainer and preserver of the cosmos can be dispensed with; the only role God left was that of the Creator. However, in 1983 Stephen Hawking and James Hartle proposed the "No-Boundary Theory of the Universe" according to which the universe did not have a boundary, i.e., starting-point or end-point, and hence it did not need a starter/creator. Thus, God was left totally unemployed: What need then for a God?

c. Developments in the Biological Sciences, Especially the Darwinian Theory of Evolution

Darwin's theory of evolution, proposed in 1859, gave a more scientific and evidence-based theory concerning the origin and development of the different items in the universe. The belief in a God who is directly responsible for the creation of different beings was questioned. God seems to have become dispensable in the creation and development of different beings.

d. Genetic Revolution and Related Developments: Cloning, Genetic Engineering, Stem Cell Research, etc.

Reproductive cloning can, at least in principle, produce the exact duplicate of a living being. Human cloning, designer babies, etc., are no more scientific fiction, but will soon, if not already, be scientific facts. Therapeutic cloning can produce parts of bodies of living beings on demand. Cloning, coupled with genetic engineering, can produce designer babies of any description, at least in principle. It can change and modify different characteristics of humans, e.g., internal qualities like the level of intelligence, external qualities like the colour of the skin, shape of the body, etc. In the past, human talents like high intelligence, physical traits like beauty, etc., used to be God's free gratuitous gifts to the person, to which the person had no claim or control. Today science seems to be in a position to decide and determine what talents and traits a person can have. God seems to have become dispensable with regard to human talents and traits.

e. The Immortality Project and Human Search for Longevity and Immortality

High level research is afoot to prolong life and eventually achieve immortality, with some success, especially in prolonging life. The future of this project seems to be very bright because, according to the latest news, deep-pocketed multi-billionaires like Peter Thiel, Larry Page, Sergey Brin, Mark Zuckerberg, Larry Ellison, etc., have started funding this project generously.[1] In the past, whether a person will have long life or short life was considered completely in the hand of God. Today science seems to be in a position to have a say on the matter. God seems to have become dispensable in deciding many crucial matters concerning life.

f. Neurological Revolution and the Problem of the Human Soul and Spirituality

Christianity and many other religions still subscribe to the Platonic paradigm of the soul, which was developed in the 4rd century BCE, or some versions of it. This Platonic view is beset with many problems. In recent times, thanks to the developments in the neurological sciences and in Artificial Intelligence, new theories have been proposed on the nature and creation of the human soul. Today many scientists explain the origin, development and functioning of the soul in terms of the latest findings of the most active field of neurological sciences and related theories, particularly the phenomenon of emergence. As matter becomes more and more complex, it begins to have emergent properties. According to this theory, what we consider the soul is the collection or combined manifestation of these emergent properties. This theory questions the traditional understanding of the soul as well as the traditional belief in God's special intervention in the creation of the soul. Naturally, it also calls into question the whole realm of spirituality. True, this theory of the soul is somewhat in its initial stages and has serious problems. However, if further developed and scientifically established, it can render God dispensable in the creation of the human soul and as the foundation of spirituality.

4. Dispensability of God and Religion in the Life of Humans

Meeting the basic needs of food, shelter and clothing has always been a serious concern for humans. In the past they often had recourse to God and religion to meet these needs since the vagaries of nature made it unpredictable and unreliable. For instance, since agriculture depended heavily on seasonal rains, any failure in this regard meant poor crop, and consequently shortage of food. Drought, floods, volcanic eruption, etc., were all unpredictable calamities from which humans sought special protection from God. Epidemics and contagious as well as incurable diseases were another set of miseries on which humans had no control. In the past in all these situations, humans almost routinely sought assistance and protection from God and religion. But today, thanks to developments in science and technology, many of these natural phenomena are being brought under human control. In the medical field great strides have been achieved. Weather forecasting, flood control, etc., can claim partial success, and are making steady progress. Since in all these fields science and technology is making steady progress, many are optimistic about the future success of science in dealing with these matters effectively. All these developments are making humans less and less dependent on the vagaries of nature, and hence less reliant on the traditional God and religion. Given all these new developments, God and religion seem to have become dispensable with regard to the basic necessities of life.

5. Some Remarks

These developments pose a serious challenge to many traditional beliefs of Christianity. They can be ignored only at the peril of worsening the predicament of Christianity discussed in the beginning of this paper. At the same time, it has to be emphasized that these developments are also beset with many problems of their own, which need to be brought to the fore. For instance, scientific developments are exposing the limits and limitations of science itself. It is becoming more and more clear today that although science has successfully unravelled many past puzzles and problems, there are areas and issues on which science still remains clueless and helpless. Also, not everything science has achieved has resulted in the betterment of humans. The many negative impacts science has been having on humans need to be taken serious note of. The environmental degradation to which science has made its own contribution is well known. Consumerism and certain forms of commodification of humans, for which also scientific developments need to take partial responsibility, have led to dehumanization and serious undermining of human dignity.

The Catholic Church has been rendering invaluable service in countering some of these negative impacts. But much more needs to be done. Traditional philosophy and theology cannot carry out this challenging task, since they are inadequately equipped to deal with this formidable task. We need to take steps to evolve a new philosophy and a new theology, with the help of experts who are well trained and well informed in the sciences and who remain loyal to the fundamental tenets of the Christian faith. Catholic philosophers and theologians need to work in collaboration with these experts. This can be done. Some work is already going on along this line, e.g., the initiatives by the Vatican Observatory Group, IISR Delhi (Indian Institute of Science and Religion), JCSR Pune

(Jnana-Deepa Vidyapeeth Centre for Science and Religion), ISR Aluva (Institute of Science and Religion), Science-Religion Samgam, Goa, etc. In Europe and America also such initiatives are rendering invaluable service. But much more needs to be done, and with great urgency.

6. Some Developments in Scientific Cosmology and Their Impact
a. Shift from the Static Worldview to a Dynamic Worldview

The Catholic Church under the influence of Greek cosmology and philosophy subscribed to a static worldview. Although, some changes and modifications have been made, even today it has not been able to free itself from this influence. According to this perspective, the universe God created in the beginning was finite and perfect in the sense that right order prevailed and it had all that was needed, and no further modification was required. Hence, no major change that affected the whole universe was needed; in fact, change was considered a sign of imperfection and inferiority. However, humans through disobedience and selfishness changed radically the whole scenario, and the universe lost its perfection and right order. The principal role of Jesus the Saviour was to restore the universe back to its pristine form. The Catholic Church continues this redemptive mission of Jesus Christ.

This view, being a worldview, had many serious implications. The physical universe was ruled strictly by immutable laws of nature, and human life was strictly governed by immutable moral laws and official doctrinal dogmas. The principal duty of humans was to obey the law and live in accordance with the teaching of the dogmas, and thus preserve the right order in the world and attain the salvation and sanctification of their souls. Orthodoxy was of prime importance, and any form of dissent or disagreement was strictly dealt with. Human labour was expected to be difficult and arduous because it was imposed as part of the punishment of the disobedience by the first parents.

b. Shift from a Readymade, Finished Universe to an Evolutionary, Unfinished World

According to the traditional view, the universe itself and the different items in it came as finished-products – God created them all in his "workshop" and brought them out section by section each day. On the other hand, with the advent of modern science, particularly the theory of Evolution in the 19th century and the Big Bang theory in the 20th, a new view of the origin and development of the universe was presented, according to which God intentionally created an unfinished and imperfect but perfectible world. Creation was not a one-time event, it is continuous – it is a process and the universe is being created continuously in the sense that its vast potentialities are unfolding gradually and continuously. Teilhard de Chardin and other theistic evolutionists would argue that today this process is going on through human collaboration with the Creator, particularly through developments in science and technology. Thus, this view gives a greater and nobler status to humans since they are given the privilege of being collaborators or co-creators with the Creator. Human labour also takes on a new and sublime significance – work becomes a privilege rather than a punishment since it enables humans to become collaborators with the Creator.

This scientific view has serious epistemological implications. If the universe and beings in it are intrinsically imperfect and modifiable, human concepts, ideas, laws and theories also should share in this limitation. Our concepts and ideas, laws and theories also undergo change and modification for the better in the light of better data and information. Some theologians point out that this mutability may be valid in the realm of science and the physical world, but not in the case of religion and theology, since they belong to the celestial, spiritual world. However, modern critical-minded scholars have put these religious thinkers on the defensive since this kind of sharp distinction between the celestial/spiritual and terrestrial/secular is getting eroded in the light of some of the recent developments in science, e.g., the discovery of gravitational waves. Also well-informed critics point out historical failures and inconsistencies in defending some of the claims regarding the immunity of religious matters from immutability.[2]

c. Change as a Fundamental and Universal Phenomenon

From the discussion above it is clear that with the advent of modern science a completely new worldview began to appear. Change is considered a fundamental and universal characteristic of nature. Nothing is free from change, although the pace with which change takes place can vary from phenomenon to phenomenon. The universe was intrinsically dynamic and constantly changing. The earth itself was constantly moving, both diurnally around its own axis and annually around the central body of the sun. In fact, the dynamism and change, particularly in the form of motion, was necessary for the stability of the universe. For instance, if the earth and other planets stopped moving, the whole solar system would collapse and destroy itself. Change was normal and expected not only in the metaphysical world of terrestrial and celestial bodies, but also in the epistemological world of knowledge. Ideas and concepts, scientific laws and theories change in the light of new findings and data. Many philosophers of science point out that there are no permanent principles or laws, since every law has exception and can be modified when no data and information become available.

d. Cautious Absolutism and Responsible Relativism Advocated

Plato, Aristotle and their followers in ancient times, Newton and his followers in recent times subscribed to absolute principles, laws and principles. Absolute means applicable to all persons at all times and in all places. According to them, there have to be certain absolute principles which can serve as a foundation with respect to which other things are considered and judged. In the absence of such principles, objectivity will be impossible; anarchy and lawlessness will result. As Cardinal Ratzinger, in his homily just before his election as Pope Benedict XVI lamented, the present world was subjected to the tyranny of relativism, and hence called for emphasizing the need for absolute values and principles. However, modern science has challenged many of the principles which the Aristotelians considered absolute and has shown them to be untenable. For instance, dual nature of matter in quantum theory says that one and the same reality can have two natures, which went against Aristotle's absolute Principle of Identity. For the Newtonian system space, time and mass had to be absolute, but Einstein showed that they all were relative to the frame of reference. This relativity did not prevent Einstein from building up a solid system of science which was far more powerful and successful than the Newtonian system. At the same time, it may be noted that the need for certain absolutes cannot be denied. The most noteworthy example is Einstein's theory of relativity itself. Although he denied Newton's absolute space, time, mass, etc., he brought in a new absolute to serve as the foundation of his theory – velocity of light is an absolute and constant quantity in Einstein's theory of relativity. Not even Einstein could extricate himself from subscribing to some absolute.

At the same time, Feyerabendian type of relativism which leads to the chaotic state of "anything goes" also cannot be accepted. There is a middle position of responsible relativism. What many scientists advocate today is a carefully nuanced relativism, which I call responsible relativism. Here one accepts certain principles as reliable because of reliable evidence at a given time. It is possible that at a later time because of new and more reliable data, one may have to give up the former principle for a better one. This is a common experience in the world of science, as was evident from Newton's Law of Gravitation. In 1687 when Newton announced his law and showed how wonderfully it worked, all took it as a wonder of wonders and a permanent scientific truth. But in 1915 Albert Einstein showed the weakness and limitedness of this law and gave a new Law of Gravitation based on a completely different approach. History of science tells us that this kind of responsible relativism does not lead to any form of anarchy or lawlessness – it seems to be one of the ways the universe and humans operate.

e.   Gradual Blurring of Many Traditional Dichotomies and Clear-cut Distinctions

Past history of human thought, particularly science, is full of dichotomies and clear-cut distinctions. Plato already in 4th century BCE presented the dichotomy of the world of Ideas and of material beings. Plato, Aristotle and others made a sharp distinction between the celestial and the terrestrial world, the former being perfect, unchanging and superior, while the latter imperfect, changing and inferior. In the middle ages the distinction between the spiritual and the secular, supernatural and natural was very prominent. Today, in the light of scientific developments a unified view, which attempts to blur these distinctions is emerging. Differences are not ignored, but they are not being emphasized. On the other hand, there seems to be a move to look upon them in a positive way, more as complementing and enriching each other, rather than contradicting and eclipsing one another.

f. Uncertainty Principle and the Uncertain Cosmic Condition

One of the most unexpected and most controversial findings of quantum theory is the uncertainty principle of Werner Heisenberg in 1927, according to which there is a limit to the accuracy, certainty, objectivity, predictability, etc., attainable by science, at least in the quantum/nano world. In the light of this and other principles it is no pessimism to conclude that we humans live in an uncertain world among imperfect humans, governed by uncertain laws and uncertain principles. Religions had said this long ago, particularly in order to underline the need for having faith and hope in the Divine. Today science also has come to the same conclusion.

7. Some New Developments in the Socio-Cultural Field

7.1. Experience-Based Rather Than Abstract Principle/Dogma-Based Approach

The world of today seems to have a preference for an experience-based approach rather than an abstract ideal-based one. In a pragmatic, result-oriented world ideals seem to be remote and unattractive. Today people are more impressed and influenced by what they can see and experience, by concrete actions and lived-out examples. Politics and politicians have become suspicious and unattractive precisely because they score very low in this area. It is also clear that this fact of cosmic/human condition should guide also our dealings with fellow-humans; it should make us more realistic, more compassionate, tolerant and patient towards them. Later in this paper we will see that Pope has taken this point very seriously both in his thinking and action.

7.2. Emphasis on the Democratic Spirit and the Personal Dimension

Our age is the age of democracy. Even the Kingdom of Nepal which was often considered the last monarchic kingdom has now become a democratic nation. One of the trademarks of democracy is the emphasis on the personal dimension. Every person is important; every person matters; no one can be taken for granted. The top authority, be it the prime minister or the elected president, is accountable to the people. The administrative structure of the Catholic Church took shape mainly during the Middle Ages when monarchy was the rule of the day, and this tradition in some significant ways continues even today. Hence, one can expect occasional tension with regard to the authority structure in the Church, particularly with regard to the participation of the laity and women in the administration. This point is getting more and more serious these days because the laity and women are becoming better educated and well trained, in some cases even better than ecclesiastical leaders. Greater sensitivity in this area has become the need of the hour, especially because the number and quality of vocations – religious and diocesan – is showing a marked downward trend.

Another dimension of the democratic spirit is a new understanding of dissent and differences of opinion. In a monarchic world, dissent or deviation from the view of the top authority was frowned upon, often considered a punishable serious offence. But today, under the influence of the democratic spirit, this attitude is changing. Dissent or differences of opinion is expected, and can often lead to a wider understanding of the matter andwiser decision making.

7.3. Emphasis on Communitarian, Collaborative Approach

Another important characteristic of our age is the emphasis on the communitarian approach to serious decision-making process and in the execution of the matter. This is a very positive approach since it encourages co-responsibility and collaboration. In the Ignatian tradition this approach is very conducive to the discernment process employed successfully in major decision-making process.

7.4. New Understanding of Leadership

Our understanding and the actual practice of leadership have undergone revolutionary changes over the centuries. Perhaps Jesus Christ presented the most tradition-shattering understanding and practice of leadership when he defined leadership in terms of selfless service: "He who is the greatest among you should be the servant of all." He is not talking about service of a day labourer who serves for a material remuneration, rather Christ talks of service rendered out of love and in the spirit of generous giving; a sign of nobility and the spirit of a "mahatma." In our world today true leaders have become an endangered species. A leader today is called upon to find a harmonious blending of two mutually incompatible roles. On the one hand, he/she has to stand out among others as firm, strong, courageous, decisive and insightful; on the other hand, he/she has to identify him/herself with followers through humane understanding, empathy and compassion. Blending these two almost mutually exclusive set of requirements is a challenge indeed. This is particularly true of religious leaders – the higher one climbs the ladder of religious leadership, the harder the challenge. The real genius of leadership, it seems to me, is to turn these two incompatibles from being contradictory to complementary – a formidable task! There is no doubt that the Catholic Church, in fact, all religions, are finding it very difficult to respond effectively to this challenge. The example of Jesus Christ in this regard is paradigmatic. He could tell Peter, "Get behind me, Satan," on the other hand, he could also commission the same Peter, "Feed my sheep," even after Peter disowned him three times, despite prior warning!

7.5. Globalization and the Quest for National Identity

Another pair of incompatible phenomena is the process of globalization, which has been going on for quite some time, on the one hand, and the rising national spirit in various nations that seek definitive identity. Globalization ideally seeks universalization of humanity so that each one can claim to be a global citizen, while nationalism wants each cultural group to have its own definite identity with all of its implications. Balancing these two legitimate and noble aspirations is certainly a challenge before global religions like Catholicism.

I began this paper with the statement that the Catholic Church today is at a crossroads, struggling to identify and appropriate an effective strategy to deal with an almost impossible task. It seems to me that the Pope John XXIII-Vatican II-Pope Francis combination has in remarkable ways read signs of the time and has made a valiant attempt to respond to them effectively. Pope Francis' role is very much in the initial stages, and only time will tell how effective and successful his efforts will be. In the coming sections we will focus on his contribution in this all-important divine mission.

8. The New Form of Leadership of Pope Francis

a. Pope Francis, the Person

Controversy has been a constant companion of Cardinal Bergoglio in the past and of Pope Francis in the present. In some ways, one may say that he has been a "sign of contradiction:" "Some saw him as a reactionary, others as a revolutionary."[3] According to Poirier who knew him closely, "It is very hard to define him. He has held the bishops together through trying years, but both within the Jesuit community and within the Church of Argentina, he is either loved or hated – nothing in between."[4] Martha Zechmeister considers him "a complex and ambivalent personality."[5] Soon after he was elected pope, Cardinal Joachim Meiner of Cologne remarked: "He will surprise us all."[6] Later events have proven Cardiner Meiner a true prophet. Pope Francis refers to himself as a "man on the border." It has been pointed out in *Criterio*, a Catholic magazine, that "he was always a man on the brink ... keeping the same distance from liberation theology as from Opus Dei."[7] Even as the Pope today he refuses to be pigeonholed into any standard category.

On the other hand, there is no ambiguity with regard to his honesty and humility. Whenever I watch him speak on the television, I am touched by both his verbal and body language – his words seem to come straight from the heart, not so much from his head. This has been observed also by Fr. Oritz who knew him for years: "Bergoglio doesn't speak as he is speaking from some university chair; he speaks to you directly."[8] The much-publicized allegation of his having colluded with the Argentinian dictatorship, particularly in the case of two young Jesuits when he was the Provincial Superior, is too well known to need any discussion here. Although a number of people had pointed the finger at the Cardinal, many eminent leaders and scholars, even the well-known Brazilian liberation theologian Leonardo Boff, have spoken out in favour of him. Even after such solid support, and after addressing the charges against him point by point in *El Jesuita* and a magazine interview, he humbly said: "The truth is that I am a sinner, whom divine mercy has treated particularly well …. I have committed so many mistakes that I cannot count them."[9]

A down-to-earth wise man of wide experience, he was a person who walked the talk, one who emphasized orthopraxis (how we live our faith) more than orthodoxy (how we explain the faith). For instance, he believed that "the first words of evangelization must be about the compassion and mercy of God, rather than a list of dogmas and rules that must be accepted."[10] The way he goes about carrying out his plans and projects also have the same trait: he does not seem to have thought through every move he makes, as professional scholars are wont to do. In the words of Fr. Oritz, "He has a holistic view of things. He learns from what he sees; he puts things together. His ability to think in large terms, so to speak, has always impressed me. He is a great leader."[11] All these do not mean that he is a kind of foolhardy leader who takes uncalculated risks, rather he remains open to the spirit and is convinced that the same spirit moves in his heart and guides him. Fr. Antonio Spadaro, SJ, editor-in-chief of the Jesuit run journal *La Civilta Cattolica,* shares the same view: Pope Francis does not go about with a master-plan. "He decides what to do by looking at events and praying, which means he doesn't build big plans. He goes step by step."[12]

Pope Francis is an exceptionally popular Pope, as can be seen from the innumerable number of mementos, and large number of books and paraphernalia that are on display in the shops of Rome, particularly near and around the Vatican. That he is indeed a mass-attractor is obvious from the popular response he gets whenever and wherever he appears in public. It did not come to him for free; he earned it. All through his life and ministry he has been a highly people-centred person, particularly for the poor, the marginalized, and the disadvantaged. As he emphasized in his Apostolic Exhortation *Evangelii Gaudium*[13] (EG), the ecclesial vocation should become an "outgoing" movement to the outskirts of its own territories or towards a new socio-cultural setting (cf. EG 30). In his view, the focus of the Church should be the salvation of the world, and so the prime concern of the Church cannot be her self-preservation or the meticulous following of the past traditions and external rubrics. Rather it should be her self-giving in the order of Jesus Christ (Phil 2:5-9).[14] The poor have had a very special place in heart. The slums of Buenos Aires was a place he used to frequent so much that the people there called him "Padre Jorge." In fact, on hearing of his election as the Pope, the residents of these slums exclaimed: "Bergoglio is one of us; he often visited here."[15] As he said in an interview with *30 Days,* he wanted to put people at the centre of his thinking and planning.[16] It is well known today that as soon as it became clear that Bergoglio was going to be the next Pope, his friend Brazilian Cardinal

Caludio murmured to him a gentle reminder: "Do not forget the poor." This is where he was already as a Cardinal, and by taking the name 'Francis', sealed this concern as one of his life-principles.

b. Pope John XXIII, Vatican II and Pope Francis as Game-Changers of the Church

As we have seen, the Catholic Church is at a crossroads for various reasons, some of which were discussed in the early part of this paper. Popes John XXIII and Francis clearly read the signs of the times and came to the conclusion that the Church could not continue business as usual, if she is to carry out her Christ-given mission. Some important course correction has to be made. John XXIII expressed this point accurately in his inaugural talk for Vatican II: "Today the Church is witnessing a crisis under way within society. While humanity is on the edge of a new era, tasks of immense gravity and amplitude await the Church, as in the most tragic periods of its history. It is a question in fact of bringing the modern world into contact with the vivifying and perennial energies of the Gospel, a world which exalts itself with its conquest in the technical and scientific fields, but which brings also the consequences of a temporal order which some have wished to recognize excluding God. This is why society is earmarked by a great material progress to which there is not a corresponding advance in the moral field."[17] Vatican II was a genuine response to this challenge rightly explained by Pope John. Pope Francis gave a similar statement soon after his election in his speech delivered in Brazil where he was reflecting on the predicament of the disciples on their way to Emmaus (Lk 24:13-35): "We need a Church unafraid of going forth into their night. We need a Church capable of meeting them on their way. We need a Church capable of entering into their conversation. We need a Church able to dialogue with those disciples who, having left Jerusalem behind, are wandering aimlessly, along with their own disappointment, disillusioned by a Christianity now considered barren, fruitless soil, incapable of generating meaning."[18] Of course, he knew fully well that this can be accomplished only if we are ready to walk with Christ carrying the cross, and so he declared: "When we walk without the Cross, when we build without the Cross, when we profess Christ without the Cross... we aren't disciples of the Lord."[19] I discuss below, very briefly, some aspects of the game-plan of Pope Francis.

c. The Strategy

As mentioned already, Pope Francis usually does not proceed with a master-plan like an architect. At the same time, this does not mean that he jumps into a process aimlessly. Intuitively he has a plan, and with firm truest and hope in the Spirit, knows fully well that it will reach the right destination. His game-plan seems to be to take the Catholic Church in its spirit and ideology close to apostolic times, especially as exemplified in the Acts of the Apostles. That was the time when the Church was most alive, most vibrant and most successful, although she had hardly any material resources. He is also well aware that the Church is divine, living and dynamic and has grown and changed in many ways during its 2000 odd years of history; these great traditions are gifts of the Holy Spirit and so should be taken seriously. Thus the overall strategy, though not articulated in a highly systematic and scientific way, seems to be to recover the initial charism of New Testament days, while preserving the essential elements of the great traditions of the Church and the experience and wisdom she has received over the centuries. He wants to build a Catholic Church that is fully aware and appreciative ofcurrent developments and the rich resources those developments place at the service of humankind, particularly in science and technology. He wants to build a Church that is fully aware of the needs and aspirations of men and women of today, particularly the materially and spiritually poor; a Church that can respond to these challenges creatively and constructively, withoutcompromising the fundamental principles of her faith, under the constant guidance and power of the Holy Spirit. It is indeed a highly ambitious program, but it needs to be done and can be done with the grace and power of the Divine Source. It cannot be accomplished by one person or in one lifetime. However it is necessary that a leader should take the initial plunge and set the ball rolling. The Second Vatican Council under the leadership of Popes John XXIII and Paul VI has initiated it, and Pope Francis wants to give it a much-needed forward momentum.

Because an ambitious program of this type is vulnerable to the criticism that these "ultra-progressives" are on the way to making a new Church that compromises the fundamental tenets of Christ's Church, Popes John and Francis have time and again made clear that they in no way wishe(d) to be party to such misguided adventure. As Pope John made clear in his inaugural address of Vatican II, "The substance of the ancient doctrine of the deposit of faith is one thing, and the way in which it is presented is another. And it is the latter that must be taken into great consideration with patience if necessary, everything being measured in the forms and proportions of a magisterium which is predominantly pastoral in character."[20] Pope Francis also has made it abundantly clear that he was in full agreement with his illustrious predecessor.Below, I discuss a few steps that are already at work in this momentous task.

A Church That Is "Poor and for the Poor" – Emphasis on the Spiritual Kingdom

Only three days after his election as Pope, Francis shared his view of the Church with a large gathering of journalists in Rome: "How I would like a Church that is poor and for the poor."[21] Indeed, this can be said to be part of the very essence of Christianity. She has always had a special care and concern for the poor, the marginalized, and the underprivileged. We know that although Christ welcomed all – the poor as well as the rich – the vast majority of his followers were ordinary poor people. The messianic prophets had foretold this centuries before the messiah entered into human history. In fact, special care for the poor was one of the sure signs of the messianic age. By making this statement almost as the opening statement of his pontificate, Pope Francis made very clear his desire that the Catholic Church today should emphasize imbibition of the spirit of New Testament times. Historically, particularly in the Middle Ages, the Church has been accused of favouring the rich and the influential. Even now such accusations are raised time and again. The unfortunate case of Bishop Franz-Peter Tebartz-van Elst of Limburg, whose residential renovation bill came to a whopping $USD 43 million, is still fresh in the memory of many.

As many writers have pointed out, Pope Francis' best argument in this regard is his own personal life – the residence he chose, the dress he wears, and his mode of transportation, both in Buenos Aires and at the Vatican. All are too well known to merit special mention.

Move from a Static to a Dynamic Worldview – Openness to and Willingness for Appropriate Change and Adaptation in a Responsible Way

We have seen that more and more people, particularly among the educated, are realizing that ours is a gradually and continuously evolving world, where change is no more a sign of weakness or inferiority, but a mark of dynamism and inner richness. According to theistic evolutionists, God intentionally did not create a perfect and complete universe, but invested the initial creation with immense potentialities to develop and grow. This growth process is to continue until the universe reaches its final fulfillment (parusia) in Christ (Christ-Omega, as Teilhard de Chardin would say). Change is a fundamental aspect of nature, and when viewed in the right manner becomes a source of enrichment. The Church of Christ is always alive and active, vibrant and growing. Vatican II had shown its openness to a dynamic and evolutionary worldview, although it left the theme undeveloped. Today after more than half a century the landscape has changed, and even the official Catholic Church has given it its carefully qualified approval.[22]

The Pope reminds the Cardinals that the Church of Christ cannot stand still: "Our life is a path. When we stop walking, there is something that isn't right."[23] As O'Loughlin points out, according to Pope Francis, "Reform is first and foremost a sign of life, of a Church that advances on her pilgrim way."[24] He reminded the Vatican Curia: "Absence of reaction is a sign of death."[25] His frequent reference to the Church as a pilgrim also makes the same point, as he indicates in *Evanelii Gaudium*: "The Church, as an agent of evangelization, is more than an organic and hierarchical institution; she is first and foremost a people advancing on its pilgrim way towards God. She is certainly a mystery rooted in the Trinity, yet she exists concretely in history as a people of pilgrims and evangelizers, transcending any institutional expression, however necessary."[26] The metaphor of the pilgrim is most appropriate and relevant. A pilgrim is always on the move, without permanent residence on his/her pilgrim way. He/she has to adapt and adjust, without losing sight of his/her essential nature and final destination. This, then leads to a balance– no break from the roots, at the same time flexible and open to change to make him/herself more relevant and meaningful. His talk on "I Dream a Restless Church" also brings out this creatively dynamic aspect. According to him, the Church should distance herself from the condition of confinement within structures "which give us a false sense of security, within rules which make us harsh judges, within habits which make us feel safe."[27]

Mercy and Compassion as the Distinguishing Marks of the Church Today

It may not be an exaggeration to call Pope Francis the Pope of mercy and compassion. Although, all of the popes considered these two virtues central to Catholicism, none has emphasized it so forcefully in word and deed as has Pope Francis. *Misericordiae Vultus* was the Bull of Indiction of the Extraordinary Jubilee of Mercy. This special Jubilee was inaugurated on 8 December 2015, on the occasion of the 50th anniversary of the closing of Vatican II. In his view Jesus is the face and revelation of God the Father's mercy. He considers mercy the very foundation of the Church's life. Announcing God's mercy is the principal mission of the Church, and on it depends the credibility and greatness of the Church of Christ. The Church and every Christian is called upon to be an apostle of mercy not because the Church is afraid of confronting difficult situations, but because it is a sign of strength and inner confidence. The publication of *Amoris Laetitia,* the Post-synodal Apostolic Exhortation of Pope Francis, can be considered as an expression of some of his views on mercy and compassion in action. Since its publication, it has become a matter of heated controversy because it opens the door for those in "irregular situations," i.e., the divorced and remarried', to become part of the regular life of the Church. The conditions and procedures for implementing it are very carefully spelled out. Yet many, particularly those with a legalistic bent of mind, consider it unacceptable. The Pope's point is that "the confessional must not be a torture chamber, but rather an encounter with the Lord's mercy." In his view, the Eucharist is "not a prize for the perfect, but a powerful medicine and nourishment for the weak." Since the release of the document, theologians have expressed views both for and against;the jury is still out. As I have already indicated, Pope Francis is very much continuing the great game-changing process initiated by Pope John XXIII and Vatican II. In this context the close link is very obvious. While addressing the Council members at the inaugural session Pope John affirmed the special spirit and attitude animating the Council: "The Church has always opposed these errors. Frequently she has condemned them with the greatest severity. But at the present time, however, the Spouse of Christ prefers to make use of the medicine of mercy rather than of severity."[28] Taking an advocacy approach, "she considers that she meets the needs of the present day by demonstrating the validity of her teaching rather than by condemnation."[29] In a similar vein, Pope Francis' *Misericordiae Vultus* reminds us that "it is absolutely essential for the Church and for the credibility of her message that she herself live and testify to mercy."[30] We can give any number of instances of how an approach of mercy and compassion has transformed even the most hardened criminal. As Francis says, "A little bit of compassion makes the world less cold and more just."[31] Obviously this fresh approach is a game-changer for a Church dealing with dissent and erroneous teachings. For a person like me with a background in modern science, and who has spent more than half of his life searching for ways and means of bringing about a harmonious blending of authentic religion and genuine science, the view of Pope Francis is the way to go. Adequate precaution have been taken to avoid precarious slippery-slopes. If the Church of Jesus Christ who has asked us to forgive not just seven times, but seventy times seven times, who forgave and promised eternal life even to a certified criminal on the cross, is reluctant to give those in "irregular situations" another chance, her credibility will be in serious jeopardy, particularly among non-believers.

A Collaborative Approach – Collegiality and Synodality Emphasized

Although, the Catholic Church began in apostolic times firmly on the principles of collaborative mission and co-sharing of responsibilities, in time this great tradition began to erode. The Church became highly centralized with the Pope as the supreme head, somewhat like the large empires, particularly in Medieval Europe. In the early Church Peter was the undisputed leader of the apostolic school and everyone acknowledged it. However, the way Peter exercised his leadership was very different from the way Papal authority was understood and exercised in later times. In the Second Vatican Council there was a strong move to emphasize collegiality and synodality. "Collegiality refers to the Pope governing the Church in collaboration with the bishops of the local Churches, respecting their proper autonomy. Synodality is the practical expression of the participation of the local Church in the governance of the universal Church, through deliberative bodies."[32]

Vatican II had emphasized the need for collegiality and synodality. In fact, the practice of holding regular synods of the bishops was established soon after the Council. However, many critics point out that it failed to produce the expected results. Pope Francis wants the spirit and substance of Vatican II to be made an integral part of the Catholic Church today, as it was in the earliest periods of our Church. He made this point clear in his talk on the occasion of the Vatican ceremony commemorating 50 years of synods in the post-conciliar Church in 2015. He desires "consultation and dialogue to the norm in the Church." In his view, "synodality can guide the Church today."[33] Following the democratic mindset that is the trademark of our contemporary world, he believes that everyone has a role to play in the process of deciding what is best for today's Church. According to Archbishop Coleridge of Brisbane, Australia, "For Pope Francis, it's more that he is part of a great conversation that belongs to the whole of the Church."[34] Perhaps one of the clearest statements of Francis on this theme was made when he spoke to the Belgian Catholic newspaper *Tertio:* "Either there is a pyramidal Church, in which what Peter says is done, or there is a synodal Church, in which Peter is Peter, but he accompanies the Church, he lets her grow, he listen to her, he learns from this reality and goes about harmonizing it, discerning what comes from the Church and restoring it to her."[35] Thus in Francis' vision, the bishops as a collegiate body move forward, sharing with the people of God the responsibility to carry forward the mission of Christ in the world, with due respect to regional and local Churches that reside in their cultural context. At the same time, to dispel any misunderstanding or misinterpretation which can lead to degradation and denigration of legitimate authority, he clarified that although there would be movement and dialogue in the synodal Church, "the Pope would always be in Charge."[36]

Ripples of this emphasis on collegiality and synodality can be seen in the role of the laity in the Church. Francis believes that the hour of the laity has already come. Particularly memorable are his words in his talk "The Hour of the Laity Has Come:" "Looking to the People of God is to remember that we all made our entrance into the Church as lay people. The first sacrament is baptism."[37] As Joseph Xavier points out, in the post-conciliar period there was a concerted effort to sink the notion of the People of God. Francis wants to restore the emphasis on the Church as the People of God. This is indeed the right move, particularly when there is marked decline in the quantity and quality of vocations in virtually all parts of the world.

Bottom-Up Approach to Decision Making – A Process of Wide Consultation and Prayerful Discernment

The administration of the Catholic Church is often noted for its highly centralized character – the Pope as the supreme authority with the Vatican Curia and bureaucracy acting as his extension and supporting team. This top-down approach has often been a highly vulnerable target of critics. The tradition is quite understandable because the Catholic Church became a well-organized and well-run worldwide super-organization, largely in the European Middle Ages, when absolute monarchy claiming divine right privileges was the order of the day. Because the Popes at that time often wielded spiritual and temporal powers, the Church naturally adopted this system. In those days the level of education among the laity was low and most people were ordinary peasants. Consequently, this state of affairs was accepted as the norm. However, with the historic event of 1215 when King John of England signed the history-changing Magna Carta at Runnymede, a new era in the history of humankind was ushered in – a democracy was born wherein "government of the people, by the people and for the people" slowly began to erode the powers of absolute monarchy. Today, democracy is widespread and has serious consequences both for rulers and the ruled. The Catholic Church, to a great extent, continued in the old medieval tradition of authority and administration, largely because it embodies a more a spiritual dimension. It must be said also that not everything is right and advantageous with the democratic system, and so a hasty democratization of any vast organization may not be the most prudent and wise move. Still, because a majority of governments in the world have at least the appearance of democracy, many voices have raised concern regarding democratization of the Catholic Church. Many people, in particular well-informed and balanced scholars, are of the view that a happy and harmonious blending of democratic and monarchic systems may be the best way to proceed. It seems to me that Pope Francis subscribes to this view via the use of media in his own administration. He encourages open and uninhibited discussion on any matter of importance to the universal Church – "nothing is off the table," as he puts it – but also reminds us that the "Pope is in charge."

A participatory, collaborative, well-informed, interdisciplinary approach in an atmosphere of sincerity, openness, selflessness and prayerfulness with genuine sensitivity, prudent firmness, care and concern is the ideal Francis would like to have in the process of decision-making in the Church of Christ. It is of course, an aspirational ideal. As O'Loughlin puts it, "widespread consultation with the greatest number of people from the far reaches of the Church, is the key to understanding how Francis governs."[38] In more practical terms, "ask difficult questions, deliberate with as many minds as possible and make a decision. Take one more step along the journey. Pope Francis may not know where the process will take him or the Church, but he is confident that staying in one place is not an option."[39]

Discernment within the tradition of the *Spiritual Exercises* of St. Ignatius, the founder of the Jesuit Order, is central to Francis' process of decision-making. Discernment is not a subtle technique to get a consensus. Rather it is a process – often long and arduous – in which one, in an atmosphere of total openness, sincerity, selflessness and prayerfulness, places oneself at the disposal of God so that God's will becomes manifest and known to him/her. In such an atmosphere the participants develop such a disposition that they give up all personal ambitions and interests, and focus only on what God wants and wills. Perhaps, the paradigm for this mode of procedure is the process Mary followed when she said: "Behold the handmaid of the Lord, be it done unto me according to thy word." This is indeed a sacred, prayerful God-experience, and it works. Ordinarily we find it put into real practice in the context of the election of the new Pope in the Cardinal Conclave, and in the case of the General Congregation of the Jesuits when they are in the process of electing the new Superior General. Pope Francis uses this method whenever he has to make a major decision. The words of Cardinal Kasper are worth recalling: "Pope Francis is a Jesuit through and through. In the spirit of the founder of his Order he proceeds not from doctrine, but from the concrete situation. Naturally, he does not simply intend to accommodate himself to the situation; rather as is envisaged by the *Spiritual Exercises* of Ignatius, he attempts to evaluate the situation according to the rules of discernment of spirits. With the help of such spiritual discernment, he then comes to concrete, practical decision."[40] Francis put this discernment process into action, most conspicuously during his formation and writing of *Amoris Laetitia,* a post synodal apostolic exhortation on family, published in April 2016. Certainly, the process was long and tedious. Certainly, there were moments of serious tension, disagreement, misunderstanding and misinterpretation. It took two long sessions, the second one year after the first inconclusive session, when Francis wanted the delegates to relive the experience, and if needed, modify and change their views.

Pope Francis wants this method and attitude to pervade the Church at all levels of decision making. According to Fr. Antonio Spadaro, SJ, of *La Civilta Cattolica,* the Pope wants discernment inside the process of the Church. "He is trying to say to the pastors: your work is not just to apply norms as something like mathematics or theories. Your job is to look at the life of your people and to help them to discover God and to help them to grow in the Church without excluding, without separating anyone from the Gospel and the life of the Church."[41] Indeed, Pope Francis is clearly moving from a top-down to a responsible bottom-up approach – he is a game-changer.

Towards a New Understanding and Approach to Dissent and Disagreement

Dissent with a dominant authority of any kind – political, social, religious – has been a dark page in the history of humanity, arguably at all times, in all places and in all systems. Any form of open dissent or strong disagreement has been looked upon as an attack on the dominant authority, and dealt with harshly and often mercilessly. For self-righteous seats of power, history has often later proven these "protectors of the law and tradition" wrong. The Catholic Church as a powerful and vast worldwide institution has seen its share of embarrassment. Pope John Paul II showed a beautiful display of his true greatness when he publicly apologized for mistakes committed by the Catholic Church in the past.[42] There is also good evidence to believe that Pope Francis is breaking with the old tradition and is changing the way the "game is played."

Today it is well known that there is serious and even somewhat aggressive opposition to the Pope from a number of quarters, mostly from expected pockets and for predictable reasons. But, the Pope does not seem to be at all perturbed. In fact, it has been reported that he publicly told media persons he did not lose his sleep over the matter – he does get his usual 6-hour sleep every night! In October 2014 when he convened the synod attended by more than 200 bishops from all corners of the globe, he assured them that "nothing was off the table." In fact, he wanted them to speak openly and frankly without any inhibition because of the presence of the Supreme Pontiff. In fact, when I read this report, I was at once reminded of St. Peter listening to St. Paul and his followers at that heated debate described in Galatians 2:11-21 – another reason that persuades me that the strategy of Francis is to take our contemporary Church as close to the values of Apostolic times as possible. Of course, there were differences of views, debates, opposition, and expressions of disappointment. After the first session, Francis asked the Bishops to go home, think over the matter in a cool, unexcited, open-minded atmosphere, taking into account the existential state of their own people, and then return for a follow-up session, convened a year later. Six months after the second session, *Amoris Laetitia* saw the light of day, in which he had taken into account the different views expressed by the synodal members. O'Loughlin reports that the Pope, far from being disturbed or disappointed by the diversity of views and the clash of emotions, was "heartened that the bishops felt free to express themselves. Indeed, he would have been 'very worried and saddened' had the bishops chosen a 'false and quietist peace' over robust dialogue."[43] A "yes, sir" situation may lead to a smooth uniformity, but often at the expense of suppressing talent and crippling growth.

When we reflect on the world in which we live, and the circumstances surrounding us, it is very clear that today's dissent, expressed in good faith and purity of intention, should be taken as something positive. Our world has become highly complex and complicated – the knowledge produced is immense, the possibilities are innumerable, and people, especially the laity, are better educated; some decidedly more so than clergy. In many situations very often the differences expressed may not be opposition, but additional aspects of the multifarious subject matter, that leaders may have missed. Dissent in our world can be source of enrichment rather than an attempt to put the leader down. This constructive attitude and approach to differences of opinion can be a genuine game-changer in our complex world today.

Conclusion

God created humans and the universe imperfect and incomplete, but with immense powers and enormous potential. The human vocation is to uncover its vast resources and utilize them in the noble mission of collaborating with the Creator in the ongoing creation. Today, more than ever, humans have been giving a good account of themselves in pursuit of this noble process, especially through science and technology. Indeed, the world is changing, at an unprecedented pace, and along unchartered pathways. The flood waters of progress are strong and furious. Swimming against the current is foolhardy and futile; standing still will only lead to sure drowning and death. Humans have to flow with the current, but fortunately, thanks to genuine religion, they are blessed with sound values and solid principles. Wisely utilizing these, and with the assistance of the Maker of all things, we can make a long-needed contribution. It seems to me that this is the right path to follow. Pope John XXIII and Vatican II have initiated this move, and Pope Francis is today continuing it.

Endnotes

1   See *Sunday Times,* 8 October 2017.

2   For instance, in 1633 when Galileo was officially condemned, it was claimed by the official Catholic Church that the Bible should be understood literally even in the case of scientific matters since, although the subject matter is outside the purview of religion, the author of the text was free from any error or limitations. But today this emphasis on the literal interpretation of every word of the Bible is no more followed by the Catholic Church.

3   Stephen von KEMPIS and Philip F. LAWLER, *A Call to Serve: Pope Francis and the Catholic Future* (Bangalore: Claritian Publications, 2013), p. 100. Hereafter *Call to Serve.*

4   Idem.

5   *Call to Serve,* p. 94.

6   Ibid, p. 23.

7   Ibid, p. 94.

8   *Call to Serve,* p. 86.

9   Ibid, p. 92.

10   Thomas REES, SJ, "Four Years of Pope Francis," *Jivan,* April 2017, p. 5.

11   *Call to Serve,* p. 86.

12   Michael J. O'LOUGHLIN, "How Pope Francis is Changing the Church," https://www.america magazine.org/faith/2017/01/12/how-pope-francis-changing-catholic-church, accessed on 28.8.2017. Also in America, 12 January 2017. Hereafter Loughlin.

13   "Apostolic Exhortation of the Holy Father Francis," 24 November 2013. Available at https://www.google.co.in/search?dcr=0&source=hp&q=evangelii+gaudium&oq=Evangelii&gs_l=psy-ab.1.0.0l10.151, accessed on 13.10.2017. Hereafter EG.

14   See EG 27 and 95. See also Joseph XAVIER, SJ, "The Church *of* the People: Ecclesial Vision of Pope Francis," *Vidyajyoti Journal of Theological Reflection* 80 (2016), 599.

15   *Call to Serve,* p. 10.

16   See ibid, p. 104.

17   "Pope John Convenes the Council," Walter M. ABBOTT, SJ, General Editor, *The Documents of Vatican* II (London: Geoffrey Chapman, 1967), p. 704.

18   Pope FRANCIS, "A Church that Accompanies Man on the Journey Home," https://www.americamagazine.org/issue/213/they-know-suffering-christ 13.10.2017 *Romano,* 31 July 2013, 12 (The English Translation). See also Joseph Xavier, op.cit. p. 585.

19   *Call to Serve,* p. 113.

20   "Pope John's Opening Speech," Abt, p. 715.

21   Stephen J White, "Why We Need a Church That Is Poor and for the Poor," https://www.americamagazine.org/issue/213/they-know-suffering-christ , accessed on 13.10.2017.

22   The official Catholic position with regard to human evolution is that the body may have been a product of the evolutionary process, but the soul requires the special divine intervention, and so cannot come under the purview of evolution.

23   *Call to Serve,* p. 113.

24   LOUGHLIN, op.cit.

25   Ibid.

26   EG 111.

27   Joseph XAVIER, SJ, op.cit., p. 599.

28   Ibid., p. 716.

29   Ibid., p. 716.

30   *Misericordiae Vultus,* 12.

31   Pope FRANCIS, in the homily at St. Anne's Parish Church, on 17 March 2013.

32   Synodality, collegiality: two keys to the coming Francis reform, https://cvcomment. org/2013/08/28/synodality-collegiality-two-keys-to-the-coming-francis-reform/,   accessed on 14/10/17.

33   LOUGHLIN, op.cit.

34   Quoted in LOUGHLIN, op.cit.

35   LOUGHLIN, op.cit.

36   Idem.

37   "The Hour of the Laity Has Come," *L'Osservatore Romano,* Eng. ed., 29 April, 2016, 4.

38   LOUGHLIN, op.cit.

39   Idem.

40   KASPER, *Pope Francis' Revolution of Tenderness and Love,* 10-11, quoted in Joseph Xavier, SJ, op. cit., p. 608.

41   LOUGHLIN, op.cit.

42   See List of apologies made by Pope John Paul II, https://en.wikipedia.org/wiki/List_of_ apologies_made_by_Pope_John_Paul_II, accessed on 15.10.2017.

43   LOUGHLIN, op.cit.

VIII. ENDURING IMPACT

Chapter 25

Pope Francis
The 'How' and 'Why' of His Impact

Johnson J. Puthenpurackal OFM Cap
Former President, Associaton of Christian Philosophers of India
Eluru, Andhra Pradesh

Introduction

The present article is not an analytical study on a theme, but a reflective look at the person of Pope Francis, in whom is reflected the picture of being '*good, humble, kind* and *compassionate*';[1] these are the most commonly used words, when respondents were asked to describe in one word the person of Pope Francis. It is not that common to refer to a public person who decisively matters to one's religious and moral life in mostly and almost exclusively in positive terms! It is indicative of the great *impact* that he has made and continues to make within such a short span of his pontificate. Here a few questions pose themselves: *How* does Pope Francis create such an impact in the world? *Why* is the world touched by the mode and style of his life? The 'how' and the 'why' are not, in fact, two different questions, but two aspects of the single question of wonderment at his impact on the world: the *how* of his making an impact, and the *why* of the world being impacted.[2] The *impact* is the result of Pope Francis making, and the world receiving the impact.

Although the term 'impact' has primarily an empirical meaning of physical force or action of one object hitting another, — other synonyms being crashing into, colliding with, striking, meeting head-on, dashing against, etc — it is mostly used in its intentional or extended meaning, such as having a strong effect or influence on someone, creating a deep impression, making a powerful effect on a situation or person. Quite evidently we are using the term, impact, in the title and in the content of this paper in the intentional meaning of Pope Francis creating a great impression in the world. The impact is great because of its *depth* and *width*: *depth*, because his influence has gone deep into the people, so much so that even the religiously callous people have been 'touched' by the style and approach in his life and thought; *width*, because his influence embraces almost the whole of humanity and more especially the Catholic population. In delineating in this paper the 'how' and 'why' of Pope Francis' impact, we shall make a distinction between Pope Francis (1) *impacting* the world, and (2) the world being *impacted*.

1. The 'How' of the Impacting by Pope Francis

"Even in the darkest times we have the right to expect some illumination, and that such illumination may well come less from theories and concepts than from the uncertain, flickering, and often weak light that some men and women, in their lives and works, will kindle under almost all circumstances and shed over the time span that was given them on earth."[3] Although, these words of Hannah Arendt referred to Pope John XXIII, they can be equally applied to Pope Francis, whose kindling style of life has been gathering momentum during the past four years. How has it taken place? Does he employ a new methodology in his life as the Pope? We wouldn't say that he has developed a new technique or methodology in order to create an impact on the people; far from it; we would rather say that not having any preplanned 'way' is his way or method.

a. Spontaneity of Gestures, Actions and Responses

If there is no preplanned 'way' as the style of life for Pope Francis, then spontaneity characterizes his way. Within the short tenure as leader of the Catholic Church, he has demonstrated a keen understanding of the transformative power of spontaneous or unexpected gestures — shocking actions of humility and solidarity — to impact opinion and to bring hope to those who have felt the sting of rejection. Such gestures and actions emerged from his heart at the spur of the moment.

One of the surprising choices that he made was his choice of *Francis* as his name: a simple act with a profoundly symbolic meaning! In an interview Pope Francis explains that the name 'Francis' kept on coming to his mind as the papal voting was going on: "Francis is the man of peace. And so the name came to my heart: Francis of Assisi. For me he is the name of poverty, the man of peace, the man who loves and safeguards creation."[4] Hans Küng, a great theologian who has been considered a strong critic of papacy, sees Pope Francis in a totally different light. His choice of *Francis* as his name – the first Pope with the courage to take this name – is a loud statement on the *need to rebuild the church* in the way of poverty, humility and simplicity—*poverty*: not a church of pomp, wealth and financial scandal, but a church of modest frugality and financial transparency; *humility*: not a church of power and domination, bureaucracy and discrimination, repression and inquisition, but a church of humanity with an attitude of dialogue, of brotherhood & sisterhood, and of welcoming the non-conformists; *simplicity*: not a church of dogmatic immovability, moralistic censure, legal hedging, but of good news and of joy, a church that not only speaks and teaches, but listens and learns.[5] Thus, the new Pope clearly declared the *poverello* of Assisi as his new manifesto.[6] In the words of Pope Francis, 'Saint Francis brought to Christianity the idea of poverty against the luxury, pride, vanity of the civil and ecclesiastical powers of the time; he *changed* history.' But did he really change history? He did bring about a 'disturbance' in the church and in the world. In order to keep the church and the world constantly 'disturbed' in their slumber of pomp and luxury, occasional 're-presencing' of Francis is required; Pope Francis is, perhaps, such a 're-presencing'—a re-incarnation of the Gospel-values as preached by St. Francis in his life.[7] By taking the name of Francis, the Pope has taken up this challenging task.

It is with a spontaneous and touching gesture of asking the people to pray for God's blessings on him, Pope Francis made his first public appearance at the balcony of St. Peter's basilica. After giving a warm and simple greeting to the people, the Pope asked for prayers for Pope Benedict, and then for himself; he then led the people to pray the Our Father, Hail Mary and Glory Be—simple prayers that every Catholic knows...these are the prayers that unite us as a Catholic people in our life of faith and worship of God.[8] The Pope not only prays for and gives blessing to others, but asks for and receives prayers and blessings from others! It was an expression of humility and identification with the ordinary. He brought himself down from the 'pontifical' pedestal to the 'ordinariness' of life and style. The whole world took note of this humble gesture of bowing before people— something that no other Pope thought of doing; it was the beginning of the long series of 'surprises' from Pope Francis. Although he was standing physically 'above' the people, he was standing 'with' the people—identification with the ordinary. It is also evident from the daily homilies that he gives at the Eucharist: speaking in ordinary and simple language to communicate Christian messages of profound depth.[9]

Another unexpected gesture that shocked the Catholic traditionalists was his washing and kissing of the feet of prisoners, one of whom was a Muslim woman on his first Holy Thursday Mass. Although this gesture shocked, it was widely seen as a profound demonstration of humility and courage to think and act differently. For centuries the practice of the washing of the feet was carried out on twelve baptized men. A few months later, Pope Francis made his first trip out of Rome traveling to Lampedusa, the island refuge for Africans seeking entry into

Europe. It was his way of confronting the continent's growing anti-immigrant sentiment. His sensitivity to the poor and the suffering has been really inspiring.

In addition to these relatively planned gestures, there have been the more frequent unexpected papal acts that have made 'Francis-watching' a rewarding exercise; such spontaneous acts were on display during his three day visit to the Holy Land.[10] His unplanned stop for a moment of prayer at the Wall that cuts Bethlehem off from Jerusalem is a case in point. The photo of the pope resting his head against the Wall at a place where clearly written were the words "Free Palestine" and "Bethlehem looks like the Warsaw Ghetto" was on the front pages of newspapers world-wide. Then there was the unscheduled stop at Dheisheh refugee camp and the compassion he demonstrated during his conversations with families who had lost homes and land in the continuing conflict with Israel.

After the image of Pope Francis resting his head in prayer against the Wall, probably the most reported of the Pope's unscripted moves was his invitation to the Presidents of Palestine and Israel to meet with him in Rome. While Francis has said that he is merely inviting the leaders to join him at his home in prayer, with Pope Francis at the helm, one must always expect the unexpected.

b. Simplicity of Life

Pope Francis' mass-appeal is largely due to his simple style of life and demeanour. Almost everywhere we can hear the silent speaking among the people in the following or similar words: 'Wow, this guy looks a bit different; …there is something earthly about Jorge Bergoglio, … The papal attire is familiar enough, but the papal attitude is very different… here is someone who is one of us, who is like us, he is not standing off….he stands on the steps of a church inside the Vatican, greeting people as any parish priest does…' Pope Francis' simple authenticity is evident in his modest dress and easygoing demeanor, as different from a formal demeanor, luxurious life-style and glittering attire.

Through his humility, authenticity and charity he attracts attention; it is the Pope's ability to connect with everyday people that sustains the popularity of this papacy and gives him this opportunity to revitalize the Church.[11] Tweeting, for Pope Francis, helps to lift the shrouds of secrecy hanging over the interior world of the Vatican by making his intentions open and accessible, a goal he has sought out in other aspects of his papacy as well.

Pope Francis has been showing his predilection for the poor by being poor and moderate in his life as an Archbishop. Instead of living in a luxurious house, and being chauffeured about, he lived in a small apartment, cooked his own meals and took public transport.[12] The same pattern of simplicity is continued to be followed even after his becoming the Pope: his place of stay,[13] means of transportation,[14] doing away with all the paraphernalia of pomp and power,[15] dining with others, etc. Known for having a humble approach to the papacy, he chooses to reside in a modest apartment, instead of the Apostolic Palace used by his predecessors. He arrives for important meetings in a fuel-efficient Ford Focus.

Pope Francis, who is known for being an advocate for the poor by both words and deeds, maintains his reputation for humility and modesty. Much has been made of Pope Francis' decision to wear a simple white cassock instead of the red papal cape when he appeared on the balcony above St. Peter's Square immediately after being elected Pope, asking for prayers from those gathered below. The Pope prefers a look much plainer and more practical than of his predecessors, dispensing with any excess adornment and tending toward simple, lightweight fabrics. His sash, for instance, is not made of silk, and in a break from tradition, it does not bear his emblem. He has also stuck to the simple black footwear.

His simple style of life and demeanour has earned him the popular title, 'The People's Pope,' and it is getting reaffirmed by his simple and 'out-of-the-way' actions and gestures: carrying his own bag onto the plane for his trip to World Youth Day, paying his own hotel bill after becoming the leader of the Catholic Church, asking for forgiveness, in Bolivia, from the indigenous people of the Americas since 'many grave sins were committed against the native peoples of America in the name of God.'

His commitment to stand for the cause of the poor and the underprivileged, supported by his simple and credible lifestyle, has greatly contributed to the popularity and impact of Pope Francis.

2. The 'Why' of the World Being Impacted by Pope Francis

As mentioned in the introductory section of this paper, the distinction between the 'how' and the 'why' of the impact of Pope Francis is very minimal. In the phenomenological language, the 'impacting' by Pope Francis goes with the world being 'impacted.' We look at 'the world being impacted' in terms of the 'widening' of the Church and of the world—Church, a Home with open doors, and the world, our common Home. As the 'heart' Pope Francis is open, the Church and the world have become truly catholic—universal, all embracing and borderless.

a. 'Widening' of the Church: A Church with Open Doors

In re-building the church, unlike many of his predecessors, Pope Francis took an approach of openness. Instead of making the Church a fortified citadel with higher 'walls' and protected 'doors,' he wants to continue the shift of approach started by Pope John XXIII, who, while opening the Second Vatican Council indicated the shift in the understanding of the Church 'using medicine of mercy rather than arms of severity.'[16] Pope Paul VI sums up the model of the spirituality of the Council in terms of the parable of the Good Samaritan. With the Second Vatican Council the Church, perceiving the need to present God in a more accessible way, entered a new phase of history. The walls, which made the Church a strong fortress, were torn down, as the time has come to proclaim the Gospel in a new way.[17] In order to reiterate the shift in the attitude of the Church—a shift from 'depressing diagnoses' to 'encouraging remedies'—brought about by the Council, Pope Francis makes the Church a home with open doors.[18]

Church can become a home with open doors only insofar as it is open to the various sections and factions in the Church. The Pope is painfully aware of the neglected half of the members of the Church: the women.[19] In his words, 'it is necessary to make more room for a more incisive feminine presence in the Church.'[20] The qualities of gentleness, sensitivity and tenderness help women generate life not only in the family but also in society. "Without women there is no harmony in the world."[21] Hence, the Pope wholeheartedly proposes to promote the effective presence of women in the various areas of public sphere, including the Church. He describes the feminine dimension of the Church as a welcoming womb that regenerates life, as the women are better placed to incarnate the tender face of God.

Going against the two thousand years of Catholic doctrine, Pope Francis has opened the doors of the Catholic Church to people who have historically been excluded from the Church, including people who are divorced, unmarried couples and their children, and gay people.

A few months after his election Pope Francis stated that the church had grown 'obsessed' with abortion, gay marriage, and contraception, and that he chose not to focus on these issues, but instead wanted to create an inclusive church, a 'home for all.' He has repeatedly made it clear that he welcomes all people, even communities that have previously been harshly excluded from the Catholic Church. A much publicized statement of his was made soon after his election to the Papal office, "If someone is gay and he searches for the Lord and has good will, *who am I to judge?*" In his interview with Antonio Spadaro Pope Francis puts it in other terms. "A Person once asked me, as if to be provocative, if I approved of homosexuality. I replied with another question: 'Tell me: when God looks at a gay person, does he affectionately approve of this person's existence, or does he reject the person with condemnation?'"[22] Although the church doctrine is not changed, there is a great shift in the tone of the Catholic Church's outlook toward groups of people traditionally considered by the Church as 'sinners.'

The pastorally caring and tenderly sensitive heart of Pope Francis opens the doors of the Church to the so-called sinners in his post-synodal apostolic exhortation, *Amoris laetitia* (The Joy of Love).[23] The document focuses on several of the issues of contemporary morality and church practice that had proved contentious during the presentations and discussions at the synods.[24] The document urges compassion for all, and speaks the language of the ordinary people, and it acknowledges the reality of ordinary people's lives. All of us sinners—the Pope himself acknowledges that he too is a sinner—and then, how can we pose ourselves as righteous with a condemnatory look to others? This is the simple logic that motivates the Pope to open the doors of the Church to everyone.

Pope Francis is committed to bring about unity, not only of the Catholics, but also of the various Christian denominations and different religions. Even as a Cardinal, Pope Francis had a positive relationship with the Eastern Orthodox Churches; he had friendly meetings with Evangelical Protestants in Argentina; and he has long been recognized as a friend of the Jewish and Islamic communities. In his visit to the Holy Land, it was specially noted that the Pope was accompanied on his journey by two Argentine friends, a Rabbi and an Imam, and that, while in Jerusalem, he had a meeting with the Grand Mufti and Israel's Chief of Rabbis. These are real gestures of unity, and symbolic gestures of what Pope Francis is looking towards.

The Pope envisions the unity of the Church: "We must walk united with our differences. There is no other way to become one. This is the way of Jesus."[25] It is to be noted that the Pope acknowledges the need of learning from one another. Thus he looks forward to a Church that not only speaks and teaches, but also listens and learns.[26]

Pope Francis dreams of a church as a home—a home where we dwell together in peace and harmony: 'The picture of the Church should no more be a *Fortress with high walls*, but a *Home with open doors*.'[27] Thus, his re-sketching of the Church as a home for all—the so-called sinners and righteous—has greatly contributed towards the whole world being impacted by Pope Francis.

b. 'Widening' the World: Caring for Our Common Home

The 'widening' takes place when we break open the various borders, not around us, but within us![28] Pope Francis, with his open heart, has been opening the doors of the Church to everyone. The same process of opening is carried further extending it to the whole creation, humans and non-humans.

Pope Francis' attitude of welcoming all humans irrespective of their colour, caste or creed is an evident expression of his 'widening' the world. He has been very tender to the vulnerable people, especially to migrants, exiles and refugees. He exhorts that the Church should offer a shared response to the problem of migration, which could be 'to welcome, to protect, to promote and to integrate.' Along with the vulnerable people, he pleads to respect the indigenous (tribal) people as well.[29]

His concern for the larger home of the earth is given shape in his courageous and revolutionary encyclical, *Laudato Si: On Care for Our Common Home*,[30] in which he makes a pleading call to the whole humanity to protect our common home by seeking a sustainable and integral development. Taking inspiration from St. Francis of Assisi, Pope Francis calls the earth our 'common home,' or 'mother,' wherein everyone and everything are interrelated as brothers and sisters. But, laments the Pope, we are damaging this familial relationship and harming the environment. In so doing, we are damaging our relationship with other humans, particularly those least equipped to defend themselves: the poor and future generations. We are forgetting our interconnectedness with the earth and with those around and ahead of us who depend on our good stewardship of the gift of creation.

In this apparently 'silent' document is hidden the loud proclamation of powerful socio-politico-economic messages; the Pope links climate change with poverty and indigenous rights, transforming the environmental crisis into an issue of global social justice. During a visit to South America, Pope Francis appealed to the world, linking climate change to greed and financial interests: 'Let us say 'no' to an economy of exclusion and inequality, where money rules...That economy kills. That economy excludes. That economy destroys Mother Earth.'[31] Despite the inclination of the political machine to suit the interests of the wealthy by ignoring the needs of the poor, we can find that Pope Francis does not mince words in critiquing the wealthy nations and multinationals for their role in making the world what it is today. He is reported to have said: "If investments in the banks fail, 'Oh, it is a tragedy,'...but if people die of hunger or don't have food or health, nothing happens. This is our crisis today." The Encyclical specifically criticizes consumerism, irresponsible development, institutionalized greed, and fossil fuels. The Pope cites these as the causes of 'a relentless exploitation and destruction of the environment' and 'unprecedented destruction of ecosystems, with serious consequence for all of us.' The document speaks of how the poorer countries suffer at the hands of the rich, and the actions of the rich advance climate change. "The warming caused by huge consumption on the part of some rich countries has repercussions on the poorest areas of the world ... There is also the damage caused by the export of solid waste and toxic liquids to developing countries, and by the pollution caused by companies which operate in less developed countries in ways they ... would never do in developed countries or the so-called first world." The Pope's stance on technology is especially interesting. He says that the "dominant technological paradigm" is a key contributor to the environmental crisis and human suffering.[32]

Thus Pope Francis dreams of a world, not of inequality and injustice, exploitation and competitions, divisions and hierarchies, poverty and suffering, but of homely relations and mutual responsibility.

Conclusion

Our general reflection was on the *impact* of Pope Francis was made from the two complementary angles: the 'how' and the 'why.' The 'how' of his *impacting* was considered from his style of life and thought: spontaneous and simple. He expresses himself quite spontaneously as he does not believe in using calculative language and formal demeanour to manipulate the truth and to mask his life. He does not have to carefully conceal the inner being and conviction from the outer expressions. The simplicity of his life-style too flows from his conviction that he is expected to follow Jesus Christ whose life was stretched between the Crib and the Calvary. We elucidated the 'why' of the world being *impacted* in terms of his open approach that considers the Church, not as the protected sanctuary of the so-called righteous Catholics, but as the sacrament of salvation; he also finds the world not as the exclusive property of the economically and technologically powerful humans, but as the common home for humans and non-humans. As his approach of simplicity and openness continues to show itself with greater intensity, the *Francis Effect* continues to be more active.

In the year 2013—the year when Pope Francis was chosen to be the head of the catholic church—he was named by *Time* magazine as the 'Person of the Year.' *Time's* managing editor, Nancy Gibbs, wrote that Francis was selected 'for pulling the papacy out of the palace and into the streets, for committing the world's largest church to confronting its deepest needs and for balancing judgment with mercy.' In her words, Pope Francis has 'changed the tone, perception, and focus of one of the world's largest institutions in an extraordinary way.' Within months after his becoming the Pope, an internationally recognized secular institution could see ahead the *impact* of Pope Francis in the world; their assessment is being proved right.

The secret of Pope Francis' impact consists in doing the ordinary things in an extraordinary way; in fact, he is just ordinary; but his being ordinary is seen as *extraordinary*. Inheriting a feudal style of functioning, the Church has developed a 'myth' of papacy with no human and earthly touch. But here comes a humane Pope, whose heart pulsates with the pains of the exploited humans and non-humans; here is a Pope who does not believe in playing on the power of infallibility, but in commanding a power to change the way the papacy has been functioning: it is the 'how' and 'why' of his impact.

Endnotes

1   Several surveys were conducted in different parts of the world one year after Bergoglio became Pope Francis in 2013. The respondents were almost unanimous in their responses— only positive responses. Today, some conservative and orthodox type of people from the hierarchy and the laity express their dissatisfaction at the gradual 'loss' of the pomposity, glory and glamour that have been traditionally attached to 'Papacy.'

2   From a phenomenological point of view, these two are the *noetic* (subjective) and the *noematic* (objective) dimensions.

3   Hannah Arendt, in the preface to her essay collection *Men in Dark Times*, wrote it, referring primarily to Pope John XXIII.

4   Andrea Tornielli, Jorge Mario Bergoglio, *Francis: Pope of a New World* (Bangalore: ATC, and San Francisco: Ignatius Press, 2013), 67.

5   Hans Küng http://ncronline.org/authors/hans-kung; accessed on 21 May 2013.

6   On 16th March while talking to the journalists the new pope revealed the reason for the choice of name Francis. He started to say that as the voting went on his "dear, dear Friend Cardinal Caludio Hummes" who had comforted him very much during the conclave, hugging him

said, "Do not forget the poor." The Pope continued: "That word stuck here [tapping his forehead]; the poor, the poor. Then, immediately in relation to the poor I thought of Francis of Assisi. Then I thought of the wars, while voting continued, until all the votes [were cast]. And Francis is the man of peace. And so the name came to my heart: Francis of Assisi…" Andrea Tornielli, *Jorge Mario Bergoglio, Francis: Pope of a New World* (Bangalore: ATC, and San Francisco: Ignatius Press, 2013), 67.

7   Indian Capuchin Research Forum (ICRF) has brought out an edited book on the theme of St. Francis being re-presenced in different persons and movements. Cf., John Peter Vallabadoss, OFMCap, ed., *Journey of Re-Presencing St. Francis of Assisi: A Silent Stream* (Kottayam: Jeevan Books, 2017). Two articles are of special relevance: Johnson Puthenpurackal, "Francis as a Movement: Philosophical Plunge into the Silent Stream," (pp. 23-39; Scaria Kalloor, "Re-Presencing through Pope Francis: Hermeneutical Reading of Call to Renew the Church," (pp. 195-217).

8   Cardinal Sean O'Malley, OFMCap., "Foreword," in *Pope Francis: The Pope from the End of the Earth* by Thomas J. Craughwell (Bengaluru: ATC & Charlotte, NC 28241: St. Benedict Press, 2013), 18.

9   Pope Francis gives a short reflection at the Holy Eucharist that he celebrates in the private chapel in *Santa Martha*. The homily that he gives comes from his prayerful reflection, and not from theological books; before the Mass he spends almost an hour in meditation. There is some 'ordinariness' in his thought and in his use of words and phrases.

10   Pope Francis made his visit to the holy land on 24-26 May 2014.

11   Michael J. O'Loughlin, *The Tweetable Pope: A Spiritual Revolution in 140 Characters* (New York: Harper, 2015).

12   Hazel Sillver, "The Pope and St. Francis," *Faith Today:* Pope Francis Special Edition, (Ireland: Alive Publishing Graphic House, 2013), 70.

13   When the pope was elected, he went against Vatican tradition by choosing not to live in the apostolic apartments. Instead he lives in the Casa Santa Marta, a Vatican residence that houses visiting clergy and non-clergy members.

14   The pope has also made headlines for his mode of transportation, a 30-year old white Renault 4. Although he later purchased another vehicle, he has since raffled it off to raise funds for the poor.

15   It is evident from the simple cross that he wears, vestments that he uses, etc.; he avoids thus the atmosphere of the glory of the triumphalist church that is enrobed in gold and silver and diamond.

16   Pope Francis, *Misericordiae Vultus: The Face of Mercy,* No. 2.

17   Jerry Rosario, *Out of the Box: Extraordinary Jubilee of Mercy* (Chennai: New Leader Publications, 2nd Edition, 2016), 10.

18   The Jubilee Year of Mercy was declared by Pope Francis in order to highlight this aspect of the Church. All his exhortations and writings during the year of mercy were centred on the need of the Church and the Christians to be, not only more tolerant to others, but more open and loving towards others.

19   When we consider the participation and active presence in the Church activities, the women constitute, not just the half, but the majority of the Church-members.

20   Pope Francis with Antonio Spadaro, *My Door is Always Open: A Conversation on Faith, Hope and the Church in a Time of Change*, trans., Shaun Whiteside (London: Bloomsbury, 2014), 63.

21   From the Homily of Pope Francis at the Casa Santa Marta on 9th February 2017.

22 Pope Francis with Antonio Spadaro, *My Door is Always Open: A Conversation on Faith, Hope and the Church in a Time of Change*, 56-57.

23 This document, based on the Synods on the Family held in 2014 and 2015, was dated 19 March 2016, but it was released on 8 April 2016.

24 Controversy erupted after the document was published, and in July 2016, a group of Catholic scholars, prelates and clergy sent an appeal to the College of Cardinals asking that they petition Pope Francis to 'repudiate' what they see as 'erroneous propositions' contained in *Amoris Laetitia*. Four Cardinals took up the case with the Pope, pointing out the lack of clarity (*dubia*) on the teaching of the Church regarding some of the issues.

25 Pope Francis with Antonio Spadaro, *My Door is Always Open: A Conversation on Faith, Hope and the Church in a Time of Change*, 62.

26 Johnson Puthenpurackal, "Compassionate Love: Passionate Plea of Pope Francis for the ExtraOrdinary Jubilee of Mercy," in his (ed.) *Call to Be Merciful: In Religious Commitment and Pastoral Charity* (Bengaluru: Asian Trading Corporation, 2017), 10.

27 Ibid., 15.

28 Apparently the borders are around us; but in fact, they are within us. When we remove those borders within us, the world becomes wider and border-less. Cf., Johnson Puthenpurackal, *Human Existence as Home-Coming: An Approach in Reflective Phenomenology* (Bangalore: Asian Trading Corporation, 2015), 192.

29 As a sign of his love and respect for the indigenous people the Pope prayed the Lord's Prayer in Guarani, the language of the tribals in Paraguay, when he visited the country. More importantly, he apologized to the indigenous people of the Americas for the many 'grave sins' committed during colonization.

30 *Laudato Si* was his second encyclical, and it was published on 24th May 2015.

31 Pope Francis' thoughts on the close relation between ecology and economy are given in the compact book: Andrea Tornielli and Giacomo Galeazzi, *This Economy Kills: Pope Francis on Capitalism and Social Justice* (Collegeville: Liturgical Press: 2015).

32 https://www.pachamama.org/blog/pope-francis-changing-the-catholic-church-and-the-world, accessed on 16 July 2017.

Chapter 26

The New Pope
Analysing the Shift in the
Indian Media's Coverage of the Papacy

Ananya Dutta and Gayatri Mendanha
*Humanities and Social Sciences, Symbiosis School for Liberal Arts,
Symbiosis International (Deemed University), Pune, Maharashtra*

Introduction

In October 2014, senior journalist Vir Sanghvi took to Twitter, a social networking site, where he wrote: "Judging by his comments on accepting gay people Pope Francis may turn out to be the man who finally drags the church into the 21st Century." Sanghvi's optimism about Pope Francis' ability to "drag" the Catholic Church into the 21th Century stems from the pontiff's, "Who am I to Judge?" remark made to a group of reporters in July 2013, when asked to comment on reports of a "gay lobby in the Roman Curia" (Davies, 2013). The Pope's now famous remark is widely seen as a part of the more inclusive stance the Church has taken towards the LGBT community since he became its head. (Hale, 2015) While entrusting the task of modernising the Catholic Church to the present Pope, Sanghvi failed to take into account the fact that in 2010 when Argentina was on the verge of becoming the first country in Latin America to legalize gay marriage, Pope Francis (then Cardinal Jorge Bergoglio, the Archbishop of Buenos Aires) had led a massive campaign against gay marriage in Argentina. He decried the legislation as "a move by the father of lies to confuse and deceive the children of God" (Goñi, 2010).

Less than a decade ago, in a September 2006 editorial analysing Pope Francis' predecessor Pope Benedict XVI's controversial remarks about Islam at the University of Regensburg in Germany, Sanghvi had characterised the latter as "right-wing" and "reactionary" and had revisited Ratzinger's past as a member of Hitler Youth[1] (Sanghvi, 2006). Sanghvi's admiration for Pope Francis, which stands in sharp contrast to his scrutiny of Pope Benedict XVI, is congruous with a larger media trend.

The election of Cardinal Jorge Mario Bergoglio as the Pope in March 2013 marks a turning point in the conversation in the Indian Media's coverage of the papacy. From scandals dominating the media coverage of the Church in the last few years of Pope John Paul II's papacy and throughout Pope Benedict XVI's papacy, a shift has been witnessed wherein the personality of Pope Francis and eventually his ideas became the main talking points in the media. This research article documents this shift in the way the papacy has been covered in the Indian media and explores reasons for it.

Since the news media in India is highly diverse, both linguistically and across a range of media, for our research, we restricted ourselves to print media and within that category to English-language national dailies. We closely studied news reports and editorials published in five national dailies – *The Times of India, The Hindu, The Indian Express, The Telegraph* (the newspaper published in India, not UK) and *Hindustan Times* to document the coverage of the papacy. These include reports and editorials written by staffers at these newspapers, guest columns as well as reports from Indian and international agencies. Some of them were accessed from archives, other articles were sourced online. In order to capture the change in media perceptions, we did a comparative study of how the media covered both Pope Benedict XVI and Pope Francis during similar key moments, such as the day of the announcement of the papal election results. Comparing the content and tone of these coverages enabled us to draw certain conclusions. This was supplemented by existing research in the area.

1. Documenting the Media Shift

a. First Impressions

The shift in the coverage of the papacy is evident from Pope Francis' very first day in office, with the very first reports in the Indian media, about the new Pope. *The Times of India's* front-page headline marked the historic nature of the event: "Papacy leaves Europe after 1,300 years: Francis I's 1st S American, Jesuit pope" (Donadio, 2013). An infographic accompanying the story reiterated the fact that Pope Francis was the first Pope from outside of Europe since the 8th century and that he was the first Pope from the Jesuit order; there was an additional emphasis on his roots as the son of Italian migrants to Argentina and his reputation for simplicity and austerity. In contrast, when the results of Pope Benedict XVI's election had been announced, *The Times of India* front-page headline merely stated, "Ratzinger is Pope Benedict XVI." Moreover, the story's kicker[2] also emphasized his German nationality and described him as "John Paul II's Hard-line Defender of Church Doctrine" (Fisher & Goodstein, 2006). The 366-word story that followed made three references to Pope Benedict XVI as a hard-line conservative, giving little other information about him other than his place of birth, age and his close association to Pope John Paul II. From the reportage of other papers on these two days a trend immediately becomes clear – the papacy of Pope Benedict XVI was expected to be a continuation of the legacy of his predecessors, particularly Pope John Paul II, whereas the election of Pope Francis was hailed as an unprecedented event – the start of something refreshingly new.

The front-page story in *The Hindu* also stressed that Pope Francis was "the first pontiff from the Americas and the first from outside Europe in more than a millennium." The story went on describe the new Pope's humble demeanour "a stunned-looking Cardinal Bergoglio shyly waved to the crowd" and lifelong service, "76-year-old archbishop of Buenos Aires has spent nearly his entire career at home in Argentina, overseeing churches and shoe-leather priests." ("Argentina's Bergoglio elected", 2013) This story was followed by others in the inside pages that painted the portrait of a man of the people, describing his service in Argentina as: "The son of middle-class Italian immigrants, he denied himself the luxuries that previous cardinals in Buenos Aires enjoyed. He lived in a simple apartment, often rode the bus to work, cooked his own meals and regularly visited slums that ring Argentina's capital." ("Pope Francis prays", 2013) However, when Pope Benedict XVI's papacy had been announced, *The Hindu* carried only one story on the front-page. This story made a cursory reference to the mood at St Peter's square on the day before moving on to two key points – Benedict XVI's "uncompromising views on Church doctrine" and the fact that his election was likely to carry forward Pope John Paul II's legacy. It went so far as to say that his election was likely to be "a disappointment" to those expecting major changes in the policies and the manner in which work is conducted in the Church. (Naravane, 2005) There was no mention of Benedict XVI's scholarship and commendable work as a theologian.

b. Omissions

The manner in which the media perceived these two events is as evident in the stories that were left out as in the ones that were carried. In the coverage of many key International events, one of the most obvious angles for a story in the Indian media is to see if there is an Indian connection that can be made. For instance, in the event of any international disaster, separate stories are carried about Indian citizens affected by the tragedy. However, at the time of Pope Benedict XVI's election two Indian news agencies, the Press Trust of India (PTI) and the Indo-Asian News Service (IANS), released a story about his Indian connection. It drew from an interview of a priest from Kerala, who recalled how when the pontiff had been the Archbishop of Munich, he had responded to a plea for financial assistance in the construction of a church in Alappuzha. Most mainstream Indian papers ignored the story with the *Hindustan Times* being the only one to publish it. ("Pope Benedict XVI's Indian connection", 2005)

Further, while *The Times of India* had in 2005 published a list of Pope Benedict XVI's opinions and statements on controversial issues such as homosexuality, celibacy of priests and the role of women in the Church, no similar tally was put together after Pope Francis' election ("Benedict's view," 2005). For instance, there were no references to his caustic remarks on homosexuality when Argentina legalized same-sex marriages. These omissions help further the media narrative that the new Pope offers the promise of a clean slate for the Catholic Church.

c. Early Days

Another contrast that emerges from the media reportage is the characterization of Pope Benedict XVI as a hard-line conservative and Pope Francis as an austere man who had stayed away from the power centre of the Church at Vatican City. *The Telegraph,* which described Pope Benedict XVI as the "doctrinal watchdog at the Vatican since 1981," made several references to Pope Francis as a "humble and simple man." ("Vatican's combative defender," 2005; Biswas, 2013) The Media fascination with Pope Francis' election and humble ways continued in subsequent days. Emphasizing his Jesuit roots, *The Telegraph* ran a detailed story about Pope Francis' actions on the first day after his election such as paying the hotel bill of the lodge that he was now in charge of, declining a "throne-like chair" when meeting with the cardinals and refusing the papal limousine, instead choosing to commute by boarding a bus (Chatterjee 2013). Subsequently, reports about his decisions to not live in the Papal Palace appeared in many papers. His gesture of washing and kissing the feet of two women at a juvenile detention centre on Maundy Thursday caught the media pleasantly surprised with *The Times of India* declaring it "his most significant break with tradition yet." ("In a first, pope washes women's feet," 2013) The media celebrated the arrival of a Pope who would finally challenge centuries of Church orthodoxy. However, O'Leary (2013) reminds us, "Francis says Mass in prison and washes prisoners' feet; but Benedict said Mass in the same prison, championing prisoners' rights, at Christmas, and washed the feet of laymen, in his first years, on Holy Thursday" (p. 260). Yet, no one took notice and there was no celebration.

d. Changing the Image of a Scandal-Ridden Church

The overwhelmingly positive media coverage of Pope Francis' election came on the tails of reports of Pope Benedict XVI's surprise resignation on 28 February, 2013. The conversation in the media had been dominated by the crises of paedophilic priests, allegations of money laundering and other scandals that have come to be seen as the legacy of Pope Benedict XVI's papacy. The *Times of India* report on Pope Benedict XVI's resignation mentions in the third paragraph: "The Pope's leadership of 1.2 billion Catholics, since April 2005, has been beset by child sexual abuse crises, charges of money laundering, an address in which he upset Muslims, and a scandal over the leaking of his private papers by his personal butler" ("Benedict XVI, 85, becomes first Pope to quit in 600 yrs", 2013). The paper printed a separate story on the inside pages documenting the details. ("Benedict's legacy," 2013) The media exposé of large-scale child sex abuse in the Catholic Church occurred when Pope John Paul II was alive, but the taint of the scandal continued to haunt Pope Benedict XVI's papacy. For over a decade, the scandal had dominated the media coverage of the Catholic Church and any steps taken against the incriminated priests was seen as too little too late. Noonan (2011) cites Ed Koch, a former Jewish mayor of New York "'I believe that the continuing attacks by the media on the Roman Catholic Church and the Pope have become manifestations of anti-Catholicism…Many of those in the media who are pounding the Church and the Pope today clearly do it with delight and some with malice …" (344-345). Koch was referring to the media "attacks" on the Church and Pope Benedict XVI during the clerical sex abuse scandals.

While the scale of the abuse and attempts by the Church to keep it under wraps was undeniably an issue that deserved media attention, efforts taken by the Church to confront the scandal were downplayed in the media. For instance, *The Times of India* reports make no mention of the measures taken by Pope Benedict XVI to tackle the issue or the fact that during his papacy as many as 800 offending priests were defrocked. ("Pope quietly trims", 2017) Pope Benedict XVI's statement in Portugal: "the greatest persecution of the Church does not come from out-side enemies, but is born of sin within the Church" (Noonan, 2011, p. 344) was also downplayed. O'Leary (2013) reminds us that "Pope Benedict made the scandal of sexual abuse a central concern of his pontificate, and was scolded for not speaking of it often enough. Pope Francis did not speak of it immediately, and everyone seemed happy with that, as if wishing the topic would simply go away" (p. 260)

Given the media's preoccupation with the scandal, it is remarkable that within a month's time the conversation had entirely shifted to gushing accounts of the election of the simple, unassuming and affable new Pope. A 1336-word editorial published in *The Hindu* about the expectations from the world's first Jesuit Pope makes no mention of this scandal or any others that had made headlines throughout his predecessor's papacy. (Heredia, 2013) Details about Pope Francis' background, lifestyle and unconventional decisions made in his first few weeks in office gave sufficient grist to the media's mills so as to keep discussions of past scandals almost entirely out of the papers.

Ironically, when Pope Francis did speak of this issue, O'Leary (2013) reminds us, "in a statement to the Prefect of the Congregation for the Doctrine of the Faith, urging that the issue be pursued 'continuing along the lines set by Benedict XVI,' it was portrayed by the media as another stirring initiative…" (p. 260).

e. A Global Media Icon

Noonan (2011) writes that, "It makes evangelisation easier if Church leaders and media officials are friendly with newspaper editors and reporters" (p. 345). Ever since his election, Pope Francis has been perceived to be a global media icon. His statements and actions have been happily deconstructed by the media and are being read as symbolic of hope and change. Photographs and videos of the smiling, affable Pope saying and doing, all that is good and pleasing, see the media lapping it all up, presenting to the world the message of a new Pope who can do no wrong."Judging by the sheer volume of new books on Pope Francis, major publishing houses are persuaded that the world's fascination with the man and his papacy shows no signs of abating" (Ivereigh, 2015, p. 261). And, with it the papacy quickly sheds the ugly image of a dying beast, shackled by scandals and becomes an attractive Prince once again!

2. Reasons for the Shift

a. The Outsider

The resignation of Pope Benedict XVI left his successor with a number of daunting challenges and scandals that had to be dealt with. Gallagher (2013) highlights the bigger challenges, "the credibility of the church as a religious institution" (p. 666) and the recovery of "vitality within the institution of the church" (p. 667). And so, Flamini (2013) writes of how while, "Benedict was the quintessential insider, a long-time senior Curia prelate, a brilliant theologian... To clean up the mess, the cardinals elected Francis, a total outsider with no Curia experience" (p. 27). The non-European, Cardinal Bergoglio from Argentina, coming in as a "total outsider" would bring a different perspective into the papacy. "Francis impressed his fellow cardinals in the days before the conclave by saying that the Church must stop looking inward in a narcissistic way and instead go out to the poor and marginalised in society" (O'Leary, 2013, 263). The cardinals supported the idea of a Church that was not inward looking and self-referential but outward looking and people-centred. Instead of highlighting the refreshing choice made by the cardinals in their election of an "outsider" who was not an intellectual and did not have a doctorate in theology, the sole focus was on the refreshingly new Pope whom by very virtue of being an "outsider", had already won over the media. Later media stories highlight clashes between the new Pope and orthodox minded cardinals whose voices the Pope is supposed to have brushed aside. Further, Ivereigh (2015) writes of Vatican experts who write of "a popular revolutionary Pope facing down resistance from rigorists and vested interests both inside and outside the Church" (p. 261). The media focus on the Pope, his story, his origins, his personality, centres the conversation around him, rather than on other winds of change in Rome.

b. A Pastoral Approach

As the first Jesuit Pope and in the choice of 'Francis' as his new name, reminiscent of St. Francis of Assisi, a famous saint known for his simplicity, practice of poverty and care for the poor, the media could not but paint a picture of jubilant hope. Pope Francis' simplicity was demonstrated through his actions in the first few days of his papacy. This prince of the Church, chose Domus Sanctae Marthae, a guest house for clergy over the Apostolic Palace, his official residence and called to cancel his newspaper subscription in Argentina. Francis' first address as Pope from the balcony was in Italian, instead of the more traditional Latin, which Benedict XVI has used. In "breaking security protocol to shake hands with the people" (O'Leary, 2013, p. 261) the Pope came across as more human and humble. His actions and words demonstrated a pastoral heart for the people.

Benedict XVI's language and focus was more theological and scholarly which tended to create a communication gap which distanced him from the people. Benedict XVI's writings highlighted Christological issues at stake within the Church. These scholarly discussions seemed of little use to problems faced by the majority of Catholics. Francis' approach is pastoral, centered on understanding people and their problems. Gallagher (2013) writes that Francis believes:

Unless you meet people where they are (anthropology, in a sense) you will never lead them to Christ. And we meet people in very strange places and situations. We don't judge them, but seek to understand why they have come to this place in life, and how the light of Christ may heal them, especially through his mercy (p. 666).

Flamini (2013) cites Francis, "This is the first criterion: pastors close to the people. A great theologian, a great thinker, let him go to the university where he can do much good. What we need is pastors" (p. 30). Here he clearly defines the role and the place of the pastor versus the theologian, shifting the focus and discussion to people's lived experiences and everyday problems.

His approach to problems is not that of a detached scholar, sitting on a high throne, standing in judgement of the sinner, but that of a pastor reaching out in empathy, choosing to uphold the good in human nature. This genuine desire to understand, invites a culture of dialogue in and discussion that is relevant and useful. This shift was welcomed by the media, which celebrated this charismatic new Pope who warmed hearts and changed the conversation to problems faced by individuals within communities. In being inclusive and open and in calling for Holy Year of Mercy, his papacy demonstrates dialogue, acceptance and hope. However, there are those who hold that this reduces the Catholic Church to merely "some sort of global NGO" (Agnew, 2015, p. 281).

Further, O'Leary (2013) demonstrates that Francis' papacy and approach isn't radically new or different from his predecessors:

Francis has no taste for Benedict's splendid vestments; but that is merely a return to the simplicity of John Paul II and even of Paul VI...Francis has a warm relationship to crowds, kisses babies; but for this kind of populist appeal he is no match for John Paul II. Francis speaks of the fundamental role of women in the Church, perhaps more warmly then, but not really differently from his predecessors. Francis lives a simple, ascetic life; but so did they. (p. 260)

c. Pragmatism

While Francis comes across as an affable, smiling Pope, his "opponents should not underestimate his political sophistication and shrewdness" (Vallely, 2014, p. 11). He still has before him the daunting task of responding to issues regarding Church doctrine and responding to opposing factions within the Catholic Church regarding homosexuality, communion for the divorced etc. He has chosen a balanced, pragmatic approach. While demonstrating that he is open and inclusive, he hasn't made any change in Church doctrine. While he has changed the conversation and is seen to be a wind of change, he hasn't really said anything radically different. Sometimes, his nuanced statements sit on the boundary line of the doctrinal *lakshman rekha* inviting interpretation, discernment and wisdom. Sometimes, his statements just shift the perspective and change the language, allowing for a different viewing.

Through unexpected symbolic gestures and enigmatic statements, Pope Francis makes his point. Flamini (2014) writes:

His impromptu stop by the twenty-six-foot-high Israeli security wall that cuts through the West Bank, where he rested his forehead against the concrete and prayed silently while a child holding a Palestinian flag looked on, was a powerful image that angered some Israelis, but the fact that he made no statement defused the incident… (p. 26)

Agnew cites Pope Francis' famous response to the gay issue, 'If a person is gay and seeks the Lord and is of good will, then who am I to judge?' (Agnew, 2015, 282) The Pope also said that, homosexuals "should not be discriminated against. They should be respected, accompanied pastorally". (Udayakumar, 2016) This is in line with his pastoral approach which seeks to understand rather than judge.

However, Flamini (2013) writes that the Pope's position on the Vatican's "non-negotiable values," suggests "that any differences from John Paul II or Benedict are a question of style - that any real, major changes on doctrinal issues is unlikely" (p. 32). O'Leary (2013) writes:

Eamon Duffy noted that the reference to laws inscribed in our nature in the homily at the inaugural Mass is from the anti-gay-marriage lexicon; it seems that Francis associates gay marriage with environmental degradation just as Benedict did. In all probability Francis will seal the entrenched Catholic opposition to gay marriage. Generally speaking, the best hermeneutic for deciphering his views is to assume that they are the same as Benedict's. (p. 261)

As, Francis later explains, with his remark he was, "paraphrasing by heart the Catechism of the Catholic Church where it says that these people should be treated with delicacy and not be marginalized." (McElwee, 2016) The Catechism of the Catholic Church states that homosexuals, "must be accepted with respect, compassion, and sensitivity. Every sign of unjust discrimination in their regard should be avoided" (1993, n. 2358). It further states that, "the support of disinterested friendship, by prayer and sacramental grace, they can and should gradually and resolutely approach Christian perfection"(*Catechism of the Catholic Church,* 1993, n. 2359). With this, we see that Francis' much celebrated response, hasn't changed doctrine or said anything radical.

However, the *Catechism of the Catholic Church* also states that, "Sacred Scripture, which presents homosexual acts as acts of grave depravity, tradition has always declared that 'homosexual acts are intrinsically disordered.' They are contrary to the natural law" (1993, n. 2357). In his choice of which aspects of Church doctrine to highlight, he shifts the rhetoric drawing from the same text, yet changing the conversation. And so, the frenzied media paints pictures of great change, which carry within it seeds of radical reform, when in fact there has been no change in the doctrinal sense.

This proves pragmatic, since it saves the Pope from having to pass a ruling that could lead to a split in the Catholic Church breaking an already precarious unity. In neither affirming, nor denying, he is saved from being dragged into endless discussions and justifications regarding Church doctrine and can focus on crucial, troubling issues that he cares deeply about such as the "impact of migration, of war, of poverty, on families" (Agnew, 2015, p. 289). Agnew (2015) cites Antonio Gasparri in Zenit, a Catholic on-line news agency, "Obviously, there can be no change to the sacrament but there will be a radical change in pastoral approach..." (p. 291)

Pope Francis' nuanced language leaves his remarks open to interpretation. In responding to issues, through symbolic gestures and enigmatic remarks, he leaves judgement to the discerning, intuitive practitioner. Yet, it is the media that takes on the job of "interpretation". Since the media enters the homes and minds of people, the magnification of the Pope's personal style and statements has caused "occasional consternation among members of the Vatican Curia" (Flamini, 2013, p. 26). There are those that are sceptical about this new Pope, who in his lack of a doctorate in theology, will not be able to address "theological issues in all their complexity" (O'Leary, 2013, p. 262).

d. Taking a Stand on the Environment

Two years into Pope Francis' papacy, even as the novelty of the world's first Jesuit Pope and first non-European Pope in 1,300 years had begun to wear off, the pontiff wrote his encyclical titled "*Laudato Si* (Praise Be), On the Care of Our Common Home." The 184-page document, described by *The Telegraph* as "the most controversial papal pronouncement in nearly half a century," spurred tremendous media interest. ("On same side of Earth", 2015) As *The Telegraph* report points out, even though the document had been leaked a few days before it was formally made public, its release was a major media event because "this was the first time that a Pope had written an encyclical about environmental damage…" The encyclical not only mentioned climate change and the impact of human activity on global warming, but also commented on inequalities of wealth – issues that are important concerns for the media. The response from the media was overwhelmingly positive. An editorial published in *The Hindu* while acknowledging certain inadequacies in the document opined that "Pope Francis had gone well beyond any of his predecessors, and perhaps he will surprise us a few more times by progressive pronouncements along these lines." (Kothari, 2015)

Some analytical pieces such as an editorial in *The Indian Express* did point out that several of Pope Francis' predecessors had also commented on environmental issues and "the church's environmental message has been articulated for years…" but on the whole the encyclical that was released months before the 2015 United Nations Climate Change Conference at Paris, was depicted as a major game-changer in the climate change debate. ("Before Francis", 2015) Since then, the media's coverage of the Pope's message on climate change has continued and his support of the cause is cited even in reports that don't directly deal with these issues. For instance, it featured prominently in the coverage of US President Donald Trump's visit to the Vatican as one of the several issues that the two world leaders disagree on.

Conclusion

A study of Pope Francis with his past as a rigid and authoritarian provincial superior of the Society of Jesus in Argentina to the smiling, humble Pope in Rome, that he is today, uncovers a Pope of paradoxes - one that is a radical, but not a liberal. While the media dances in a drunken celebration, and prophesises liberating reform, we find ourselves in no hurry to paint grand pictures or draw certain conclusions. We realise that an institution as old and large as the Catholic Church will only crawl towards radical reform. Pope Francis' personal and political vision come from his own extensive experiences and deep inner transformation. It would take both discernment and political wiles to bring winds of change in Rome, and behind the smiling face, we believe that Pope Francis does both. With his pastoral approach and his invitation to dialogue, he encourages a reform in the minds and attitudes of people, which sometimes is as important a task as structural and organisational reforms. We hope that his wisdom will guide the Church into the uncertain future.

References

1   Argentina's Bergoglio elected Pope Francis. (2013, March 13). Retrieved August 26, 2017, from   http://www.thehindu.com/news/international/world/argentinas-bergoglio-elected-pope-francis/article4505801.ece

2   Before Francis, long line of Popes voiced environment alarm. (2015, June 11). Retrieved August 26, 2017, from http://indianexpress.com/article/world/climate-change/before-francis-long-line-of-popes-voiced-environment-alarm/

3   Benedict XVI, 85, becomes first Pope to quit in 600 yrs (2013, February 12) *The Times of India*, p. 1

4   Benedict's legacy: A papacy hounded by rows (2013, February 12) *The Times of India*, p. 18.

5   Benedict's View (2005, April 21). *The Times of India*, p. 12

6   Biswas, R. (2013, March 15). Humble and simple: Toppo. Retrieved August 26, 2017, from https://www.telegraphindia.com/1130315/jsp/frontpage/story_16674912.jsp

7   Catechism of the Catholic Church. (1993). Retrieved from http://www.vatican.va/archive/ccc_css/archive/catechism/p3s2c2a6.htm

8   Chatterjee, C. (2013, March 15). Wealthy Vatican tastes Jesuit way. Retrieved August 26, 2017, from https://www.telegraphindia.com/1130315/jsp/frontpage/story_16675603.jsp

9   Davies, L. (2013, July 29). Pope Francis signals openness towards gay priests. Retrieved August 26, 2017, from https://www.theguardian.com/world/2013/jul/29/pope-francis-openness-gay-priests

10 Donadio, R. (2013, March 14). Papacy leaves Europe after 1,300 years: Francis I's 1st S American, Jesuit Pope *The Times of India*, p. 3

11 Drury, Ronan. Pope Francis. *The Furrow, Volume 64.* (Issue 4). p 195.

12 Fisher I. & Goodstein L. (2005, April 20). Ratzinger is Pope Benedict XVI *The Times of India*, p. 1

13 Flamini, R. (2014). PETER AND CAESAR: Is Pope Francis Shifting the Vatican's Worldview? *World Affairs, 177(2),* 25-33.

14 Flamini, Roland. (2013). Ressurecting Catholicism's Image? *World Affairs, Volume 176.* (Issue 3). pp. 25 – 33.

15 Gallagher, Raphael. (2013). A Preliminary Portrait – Pope Francis: Untying the Knots. *The Furrow, Volume 64*(Issue 12). pp. 663 – 668.

16 Goñi, U. (2010, July 15). Defying Church, Argentina Legalizes Gay Marriage. Retrieved August 26, 2017, from http://content.time.com/time/world/article/0,8599,2004036,00.html

17 Hale, C. J. (2015, July 28). The Pope Francis Statement that Changed the Church on LGBT Issues. Retrieved August 26, 2017, from http://time.com/3975630/pope-francis-lgbt-issues/

18 Heredia, R. C. (2013, March 18). The significance of Pope Francis. Retrieved August 26, 2017, from http://www.thehindu.com/opinion/lead/the-significance-of-pope-francis/article4522751.ece

19 In a first, pope washes women's feet (2013, March 30) *The Times of India*, p. 22

20 Ivereigh, Austen. (2015). What We Still Don't Know About Jorge Mario Bergoglio. *Studies: An Irish Quarterly Review, Volume 104.* (Issue 415). pp. 261 – 272.

21   Kothari, A. (2015, July 11). A game-changer? Retrieved August 26, 2017, from http://www.thehindu.com/features/magazine/will-the-popes-encyclical-make-a-difference/article7407449.ece

22   McElwee, J. J. (2016, January 10). Francis explains 'who am I to judge?' Retrieved August 16, 2017, from https://www.ncronline.org/news/vatican/francis-explains-who-am-i-judge

23   Naravane, V. (2005, April 20). Ratzinger is new Pope. Retrieved August 26, 2017, from http://www.thehindu.com/2005/04/20/stories/2005042011070100.htm

24   Noonan, Patrick. (2011). Clerical Sex Abuse – The Issues Involved. *The Furrow, Volume 62*. (Issue 6). pp. 342 – 353.

25   O'Hanlon, Gerry. (2013). A Reflection. *Studies: An Irish Quarterly Review, Volume 102*. (Issue 407). pp. 279 – 282.

26   O'Leary, Joseph. (2013). New Pope, New Hope. *The Furrow, Volume 64*. (Issue 5). pp. 259 – 264.

27   On same side of Earth: faith and science. (2015, June 19). Retrieved August 26, 2017, from https://www.telegraphindia.com/1150619/jsp/frontpage/story_26614.jsp

28   Paddy Agnew. (2015). The Francis Process: Moving from a Minor to a Major Key? *Studies: An Irish Quarterly Review, Volume 104*. (Issue 415). pp. 281 – 291.

29   Pope Benedict XVI's Indian connection. (2005, April 20). Retrieved August 26, 2017, from http://www.hindustantimes.com/india/pope-benedict-xvi-s-indian-connection/story-kpZsDYFfgXc3dFVZ2q41jL.html

30   Pope Francis prays at Rome basilica. (2013, March 14). Retrieved August 26, 2017, from http://www.thehindu.com/news/international/world/pope-francis-prays-at-rome-basilica/article4508213.ece

31   Pope quietly trims sanctions for paedophile priests. (2017, February 25). Retrieved August 26, 2017, from http://www.thehindu.com/news/international/pope-quietly-trims-sanctions-for-paedophile-priests/article17369196.ece

32   Sanghvi, V. (2006, September 16). The Ratzinger Gospel. Retrieved August 26, 2017, from http://www.hindustantimes.com/india/the-ratzinger-gospel/story-8vuKIEGFqYo0qfVHvLW0hK.html

33   Sanghvi, V. (2014, October 15). Judging by his comments on accepting gay people Pope Francis may turn out to be the man who finally drags the church into the 21st Century. Retrieved August 26, 2017, from https://twitter.com/virsanghvi/status/522260816683212801

34   Spadaro, Antonio. Pope Francis. (2013). The Heart of a Jesuit Pope: Interview with Pope Francis. *Studies: An Irish Quarterly Review, Volume 102*. (Issue 407). pp. 255 – 278.

35   Udayakumar, G. K. (2016, June 27). Pope Francis, most liberal Catholic leader ever? - Times of India. Retrieved August 23, 2017, from http://timesofindia.indiatimes.com/world/europe/ Pope-Francis -most-liberal-Catholic-leader-ever/articleshow/52935067.cms

36   Vallely, Paul. (2014). The Audacity of a Pope. *The World Today, Volume 69*. (Issue 6). p. 11.

37   Vatican's combative defender of faith - Hardliner with steely intellect. (2005, April 20). Retrieved August 26, 2017, from https://www.telegraphindia.com/1050420/asp/foreign/story_4637730.asp

Endnotes

1 Joseph Ratzinger had joined the Hitler youth as a 14-year-old at a time when every male teenager in a Germany under the control of the Third Reich was expected to join the organization. In reality, he came from a family of anti-Nazis and didn't espouse anti-Semitic views.

2 A line of newspaper type set above a headline usually in a different typeface and intended to provoke interest in, editorialize about, or provide orientation for the article.

Chapter 27

"Guided by Prayer and Humility"
A Case Study on the Comments on a Provocative Article on Pope Francis

Kuruvilla Pandikattu SJ
Jnana-Deepa Vidyapeeth, Pune, Maharashtra

Introduction

How does Pope appear to the general public? What are the impressions ordinary people have of Pope Francis? In order to gauge the mood of the people on the Pope, I selected one provocative Op-Ed article, "Pope Francis' Next Act" published in *The New York Times* and tried to analyse both the article and the comments to it.[1]

The newspaper is a secular, liberal paper and the writer is a conservative catholic. The readers, especially the commenters, are educated. In the article, the writer criticises the liberal allies of Pope first and then insinuates that the Pope himself is a liberal, a position I do not agree with.

Then we catalogue the different comments and opinions of the readers into two broad categories: those unfavourable to the Pope and those favourable to him. I realise that obviously such a classification implies oversimplification.

Since it is a general newspaper, we cannot expect theological positions. Nor can we expect the reverential attitude that is normally assumed for a religious leader of Pope's stature. The informal views and impersonal nature of the comments are to be respected.

The aim of this article is to indicate where Pope Francis stands in the minds of ordinary educated people, not only limited to USA.

1. Pope Francis' Next Act?

Before analysing the article it will be good to introduce its author and the Newspaper in which it appeared.

a. *The Author: "Ross Douthat's Fantasy World"*

According to the journalist Oppenheimer we know that Ross Douthat (November 28, 1979) is "the devoutly Catholic, anti-porn, pro-abstinence, pro-life prodigy of punditry."

His path from agnosticism to Pentecostalism to Catholicism was rather an intellectual journey. "I was 17, a socially awkward teenager, and I was relieved to join a church where no one asked you to pray spontaneously," he told me. His reading had prepared him well: "You start reading C.S. Lewis, then you're reading G.K. Chesterton, then you're a Catholic. I knew a lot of people who did that in their 20s—I just did it earlier, and with a different incentive structure."

A certain kind of "cerebral Christian" will recognize the young Douthat's reading list, especially the prominence of English apologetic writers like Lewis, the mid-20th-century Anglican who penned *The Chronicles of Narnia*, and Chesterton, an English Catholic who, prior to his death in 1936, promoted an agrarian, anti-modern agenda and is now beloved by fantasy writers like Neil Gaiman. Douthat was also a huge fan of J.R.R. Tolkien, another anti-modern conservative Catholic.

He graduated from Harvard College in 2002 and spent some time as a researcher, editor, and blogger for *The Atlantic,* he joined The New York Times in 2009 at the young age of 30. He become the *youngest* regular op-ed *writer* in the history the New York *Times and* writes on "politics, religion, moral values and higher education." Mother Jones calls him The New York Times' wunderkind columnist "on a quest to save intellectual conservatism,"[2] who lives in his "fantasy world." Thus, Douthat comes across as a committed, convinced, conservative Catholic.

The New York Times (NYT), in which this article appears, is a liberal and secular American daily newspaper, it is founded and continuously published in New York City since September 18, 1851, by The New York Times Company. The New York Times has won 122 Pulitzer Prizes, more than any other newspaper. Nicknamed "The Gray Lady", *The New York Times* has long been regarded within the industry as a national "newspaper of record."[3] The paper's motto, "All the News That's Fit to Print", is instructive. People who read *BuzzFeed, Politico, The Washington Post* and *The New York Times* all tend to be liberal.

b. *The Article: The Ambition of the Pope and Anxiety of Allies*

The article begins by asserting that "By the standards of the Francis papacy, things were rather quiet in Rome for much of 2017." Some of the controversy of the previous years, including the debate over communion for the divorced and remarried, had entered a kind of stalemate, "with bishops the world over disagreeing and the pope himself keeping a deliberate silence."[4] The article assumes that one long era of the pontificate seemed finished. So the question raised by the author is natural: how much drama there is still to come? As part of the unfolding drama, the month of June 2017 brought in fresh incidents in rapid succession. He mentions the removal of four powerful cardinals as example.

The first, George Pell, was both in charge of the pope's financial reforms and a leading opponent of communion for the remarried. He had to return to Australia to face charges of sexual abuse — charges that either represent a culminating revelation in the church's grim stance on the issue, or else a "sign that the abuse scandal has become a license for prosecutorial witch hunts."

The second cardinal, Gerhard Mueller, was the head of the powerful Congregation for the Doctrine of the Faith, the office charged with safeguarding Catholic doctrine. Often sidelined by Francis, he had performed a careful walk on the pope's marriage document, *Amoris Laetitia,*[5] when he emphasizes that it did not alter church's teaching on remarriage and the sacraments while "downplaying the signals that the pope himself thought otherwise." After his first term was expired, he was shown the door "in a manner so brusque that the usually circumspect German publicly complained."

The third cardinal, Joachim Mein was a retired archbishop of Cologne and a longtime friend of Pope Benedict XVI. He was one of the signatories of the dubia — the public questions four cardinals posed last year to Francis about *Amoris Laetitia,* effectively questioning its orthodoxy.[6] He died in his sleep at 83 — shortly after Mueller, his fellow countryman, had called him to report the news that he himself has been removed from his office.

The fourth, Angelo Scola, was another confidant of Benedict XVI and a leading contender for the papacy at the last conclave. He retired as archbishop of Milan retired five days after Mueller's departure.

These four departures come from different backgrounds. But they have a combined effect, according to Douthat: "They weaken resistance to Francis in the highest reaches of the hierarchy." So the question facing the remainder of his pontificate: So the title of the article: "The Next Act of Pope!"

With the opposition thinned out and the vision of Pope John Paul II and Benedict in eclipse, how far does the pope intend to push?

It is clear enough that Francis has friends and allies "who want him to go forward in a hurry." They regard the ambiguous shift on divorce and remarriage as a proof-of-concept for how the church can change on a wider range of issues, where they have lately made forays and appeals: intercommunion Protestants, married priests, same-sex relationships, euthanasia, female deacons, artificial birth control, and more.

The author argues that in politics too the friends of Pope are making sweeping critique of all Catholic engagement with the political right in America, and especially the American Catholic alliance with evangelical Protestants.

In the liturgical issues also the Pope's friends are pushing forward. The interesting and convoluted argument runs thus: Pope has reached out to the Society of Saint Pius X, "the semi-schismatic group that celebrates the Latin Mass." This could first to this group's reintegration. The Pope will use this traditional group to quarantine all traditionalism and then the suppression of the pre-Vatican II liturgy for everyone else. A difficult argument to understand!

The author admits that the pope himself remains both more cautious than his friends. The new people he has appointed to succeed Mueller and Scola are moderate, not radical and "also perhaps more unpredictable."

His more liberal appointees can get ahead of him, as in the case of Charlie Gard, the dying English baby whose doctors and government won't let his parents pay for an unlikely-to-succeed treatment.[7] The pope's refashioned Pontifical Academy for Life, "which now accepts pro-choice and euthanasia-friendly members, issued a statement that seemed to support the government over the parents." The author notes that Pope Francis intervened personally supporting the parents' rights, "creating a somewhat defensive scramble by his allies."

Then the author makes a larger and somehow confusing remark: "We know that Francis is a liberal pope, but apart from the remarriage debate we don't know what priority he places on any given liberal-Catholic goal."

The author goes on criticize the friends of the Pope, who are liberals: "Among many liberals there is a palpable ambition, a sense that a sweeping opportunity to rout conservative Catholicism might finally be at hand. But there is also a palpable anxiety, since the church's long-term future is not obviously progressive — not with a growing African church and a shrinking European one, priesthood those younger ranks are often quite conservative, and little evidence that the Francis era has brought any sudden renewal."

So the article ends with another provoking question: "How much does Francis himself share either sentiment — the ambition, the anxiety? The next act of this papacy still tell."

I find it extremely sad that the article concludes using the catchwords ambition and anxiety. The ambition of the Pope? The anxiety of his allies? To caricature the three years of the Pope in these terms may be journalistically clever, but definitely not historically or theologically sound.

2. The Trends in General

Within eight hours of its publication, the article has received 229 comments. Of these 180 are recommended by other readers (reader's picks) and nine NYT's picks. Now the comments are closed. We highlight first the Newspaper's own picks and reproduce the first five verbatim, so that we gain an overall view of the responses from the readers.[8]

a. *NYT Picks*

Dan Welch from East Lymewrites:

Ross, your evaluation of Francis is misguided. You are bringing the secularized viewpoint of a political pundit (I guess you cannot help (yourself) on his papacy.

He is not president, he is a pastor. He is not simply the head of a government, he is someone seeking to bring consolation and hope to people. He is not preserving protecting and defending a constitution, he is seeking to live out a religiously motivated message.

PG Sydney is of the opinion:

Ross I agree with all of that but we can't ignore Frances' first shot across the conservative bow when he sacked Cardinal Raymond Burke from the Prefect of the Supreme Tribunal of the Apostolic Signatura, in 2014. Elevated from the Archdiocese of St. Louis by Ratzinger, Burke was the Vatican's leading conservative whose special hate was reserved for homosexuality. Not just marriage, its physical and emotional state. Given his distaste for rabid conservatives It was surprising that he elevated George Pell but his motive quickly became clear. Practicality. Pell was a Vatican outsider who had the management skills to detect and remove the financial corruption that was rife at the Vatican.

Greg from Savannah. gacomments:

Mr. Douthat's column is highly instructive but I think not in the way intended. This is a discussion of the politics of the Roman Church and what it will mean for the future of the Church. The loud take away from this column is that the politics matter more than the faith. This frightening trend seems ascendant in all of the major religions and points toward theocracy and zealotry

Nancy Fleming from Shaker Heights Ohio was pointed and precise:

What would Jesus Change? Signed an agnostic!

WMK York City perceives the empathy of Pope Francis for the poor and destitute. His comments:

Pope Francis has not made any sweeping changes to the Catholic Church and Will probably refrain from doing so. His views on traditional marriage and pro life will remain within the frame of Catholic teaching. They are still quite conservative and he feels a strong amity bond is important to the Church and society. He does not want to weaken the family structure which is often at odds with our liberal culture. The one area where Pope Francis has been very vocal is in helping the poor and destitute. Most Catholics are in full support of his views and feel we need to assist those who are living in poverty. Much is expected of those who have been given great wealth. There are areas of the world where people are starving and we need to assist them in alleviating their suffering and pain. This is what the Church has preached for centuries. This will never change nor should it. He shows great empathy for those less fortunate and is a wonderful role model for the world. We must all do our part and help those less fortunate then us. This is what Catholicism is all about.

b. *Reader's Picks*

Here we follow up the picks or recommendations of the comments by other readers. It may be noted that some of the comments may be sarcastic.

We can perceive sarcasm in Gemli's comments:

Heaven forbid! Mingling with Protestants, married priests, same-sex relationships, euthanasia, females breaking into the Church's male hierarchy and contraception! Man the lifeboats! The Church is sinking into the 21st century!

Pope Francis was put in power not by God, but by a Church that kicked out the complicit Ratzinger. The church was hemorrhaging believers in the wake of a scandal of pedophilia, which would have destroyed any other institution, and sent its participants and their apologists to jail. Ratzinger was a reminder of the abuse that had flourished under his hob' oversight, and for very earthly reasons that involved gold more than God, He was replaced by the kindly and forgiving Francis.

The self-flagellating crowd who are drawn to religion because of insecurity and a sense of unworthiness are furious. How can they enjoy the restrictions and the punishments that the Church once reliably doled out, keeping couples in loveless or abusive marriages, making unwanted children a consequence of sexual pleasure or ensuring that only men who had no interest in adult women were welcomed into the priesthood?

The connection between conservatism and religion is no coincidence. They revere hierarchy above human freedom. Pleasure is suspect, and must be controlled. There is no one so vulnerable that they will not be sacrificed on the altar of false piety.

Francis is popular because he's less religious. Catholic scolds are furious.

Meh, it's about time

KJ, Tennessee is highly impressed by Pope Francis.

I'm not a Catholic but I admire Pope Francis for his goodness, kindness, and willingness to accept and forgive normal human failings. The world is full of preachers, but his man leads by example.

Robert Steward from Chantilly, VA writes:

Douhthat, "We know that Francis is a liberal pope…."

Although you continue to portray Pope Francis as "liberal," I would argue that Francis is no more a liberal than Jesus, who took on the religious authorities of his time by asserting such "heresies" as "The Sabbath was made for man, not man for the Sabbath."

Francis, I would say, is in good company, i.e., in solidarity with the "founder of the firm," who taught that the purpose of rules and laws is something more than unquestioning observance of such. In this case, observance of the Sabbath was not abrogated, but properly interpreted in terms of how a law was intended to serve the human person—the human person is primary.

You obviously see "communion for the divorced and remarried" as a closed issue because there is a church rule that prohibits those in that group from ever having a "place at the table." Francis obviously is not in agreement with your understanding of religious legislation just as Jesus was in disagreement with his adversaries. The focus of Jesus, as is that of Francis, is on how does a religious rule serve the human person.

Because Francis understands the church in terms of a "field hospital" that is present to heal and care for wounded humanity, he does not, as you do, see "communion" simply as a "reward" for those not wounded.

Robert Stewart Chantilly furtherelaborates:

In his opening address at Second Vatican Council on October 11, 1962, Pope (Saint) John XXIII said: "The substance of the ancient doctrine of the deposit of faith is one thing, and the way in which it is presented is another... Frequently she (the church) has condemned them (errors) With the greatest severity. Nowadays, however, the Spouse of Christ prefers to make use of the medicine of mercy rather than that of severity." Like John XXIII, Pope Francis prefers the "medicine of mercy rather than that of severity," which is evident from his use of the image of the church as that of a "field hospital" and his insistence that the clergy need to be pastors with the 'smell of the sheep' on them.

Douthat, in this column and in prior ones, faults Pope Francis for his pastoral approach, an approach that applies the "medicine of mercy for addressing and healing the wounds and suffering of humanity. Ross apparently prefers the law enforcement (policeman) model of church leadership, a model of leadership intent on that enforcing rules and laws, rather than the model of the healer or the good shepherd.

Which model reflects a continuation of the ministry of the man who said he had been "anointed to bring good news to the poor.. .to proclaim release to the captives and recovery of sight to the blind, to let the oppressed go.

Christine McM from Massachusetts sees Pope Francis as a "groundbreaker:"

I'm not sure where you're going, Ross. Are you relieved the Pope really hasn't done that much (we know you're a conservative and a traditionalist) or are you're disappointed he hasn't done more to trigger an even bigger revolt from the chastened conservative wing?

And, why would the long-term future of progressive Catholicism be stymied by a growing African church? In Africa, there are clergy in high places given waivers from chastity if they already were found to have families, or needed to condone specific cultural and historical mores of their congregations, including, I believe, polygamy in remote areas.

I personally believe the impact of Francis has been far greater on issues that don't concern western obsessions such as communion for the divorced. This pontiff has raised grave concerns about the future of the planet, the rise of oligarchies, and lack of adherence to Jesus's admonitions to care for the vulnerable (feed the hungry, etc.)

I see Francis less as groundbreaker than as a most welcome "back to basics" Pope, focused more on how well people treat each other and the environment than on political smoke signals—who's in, who's out. Just as his creator taught him.

3. Taking an Unfavourable Stand

a. *Against Ross Douthat*

Expectedly, some of the comments are critical of the author. We start on a positive note. Hugo Furst comments:

Ross, thanks for your insightful article. You are a uniquely thoughtful and well-informed writer.

The other comments are not so favorable. For example from Windsor expresses his feelings thus:

So the Pope removed a prelate who rightly, or wrongly is accused of heinous behavior in a democratic society with a fair legal system.

He then didn't re-appoint a man who publicly disputed his position as stated in an encyclical, after which a man won agreed with the opposition died in his sleep at 83 years of age.

And finally another man retired for the Archbishopric at an age you 'forgot' to share.

My response….and then the sun rose in the east.

Aha you say but no it is all an evil plot to move on from the blind (but oh so satisfying) intolerance you seem to revel in, and embrace the lepers, love the sinner, emulate the good Samaritan, or move on to what Pat Robinson seems to think is the Tao of Jesus.

Tony Zitofrom Poughkeepsie. NY relates Pope to President Trump:

Of the many revolting aspects of Ross Douthat's writings here, the most revolting to me is his selective reverence for a Pope with conservative politics.

Pope Francis does not meet the test in that regard, and thus we have musings that a Cardinal may have been removed by the Pope as part of a "prosecutorial witch hunt" and rumblings about thinning of the political opposition. I would suggest that Douthat is engaged in the standard acts of right wing projection onto their antagonists - projection of the conservative proclivity to see everything in terms of winning and losing and nothing in terms of the actual progress of civilization. Indeed, any expression of faith in the latter is evidence in the eyes of cynics like Douthat that one is hiding his real agenda, which can only be to win something or other at all costs

That is, you can be devious like them or devious like yourself, but you can only be devious. There is something faithless about his treatment of issues of faith that only adds to the despair of Trumpian nihilism. Dare I say Heaven help.

NI Westchester is against Douthat and is favourable to the Pope:

Ross, ever since his inception as the Pope, you have never been a fan of pragmatic Papacy. I remember in your earlier op-eds you even denounced him because he was more human than dogmatic. You even had the temerity to understand catechism more than your Pope himself. George Pell - a felon, Gerhard Muller sitting on the wall, Joachim Meisner - died, Angelo Scola - old who was to retire anyway, who happened to be Pope Benedict XVI confidante.

Are you telling us that Pope Francis is playing dirty to get his agenda through? And Joachim Meisner died in his sleep! What are you implying here? I am no Catholic but I have great Faith in Pope Francis. He is what the Catholic Church needs - more humanity and compassion for the less fortunate.

Here it is not surprising that one of the comments goes against NYT itself. Martin Daly writes:

Surprise that such articles occur NY Times. I suppose this means that many of us had taken for granted not only the mainly secular identity of most readers but also that liberal Protestantism's victory had been so complete that the mere publication. In "the newspaper of record" of a regular op-ed writer's views on Catholic doctrine seemed oddly quaint: This realization - frankly of slight embarrassment - may resonate with more than one reader as more than an echo, like a sermon that doesn't begin with, "In today's Gospel we see...."

b. *Against Pope*

One knowledgeable reader called "MP" compares Pope Francis to President Trump and is particularly harsh on the Pope.

The pontificate of PF is not unlike the Presidency of Donald Trump. Unpredictable and often incoherent PE's early program to reform the Curia and update its operations and finances has stalled. He shows no inclination to press preferring, apparently, to advance progressive doctrinal and pastoral initiatives. These too have met with surprising-and notably Vatican ll-push back by orthodox bishops and lay leaders. PF demonstrates s personal harshness that was manifested in his treatment of Cardinal Burke and others, the 'hostile takeover" of the Order of Malta, and his rude walking out on Cardinal Mueller following PE's abrupt notice that his term would not extended. Progressives appear to adore him. despite his decidedly pre-Vatican ll and Argentinian autocratic leadership style. demonstrating that "it's about the agenda". PF conceded that he may cause a schism. It may already be happening as orthodox Catholics build intra-Church and para-church networks and linkages, amounting to a 'shadow Church" that will live in parallel with the institutional Vatican-sponsored Church, collaborating when possible with the official Church end silently attending to the preservation

Of the Catholic orthodoxy through prayer, fellowship, catechesis and liturgy. And yes, PF's eagerness to mend ties with the SSPX is s very obvious effort to blunt the continuing growth of the TLM, the Anglican Ordinariate, and other forms of traditional and liturgical orthodoxy.

c. *Against the Church: Its Hopeless Situation*

Some others lament the situation of the Church. One reader "John " comments thus:

> As a long term liberal Catholic in my 60s I still hope that Francis will accept divorced and remarried Catholics, married male and female priests, gay people, and birth control, and stronger laity control, but he does not seem to be doing much.

> My three adult children are not Catholics nor my 7 grandchildren, and my children raised in the Catholic faith have turned to other faiths or no faith.,

> Same is true with many of my parish friends adult children-something that means Catholicism will shrink greatly no matter what. I hold onto my faith but am realistic that the American church will shrink greatly and become more irrelevant even if Francis does the reforms mentioned above. The U.S. like most of the developed world has become a nation of non-church members.

ILL writes in a similar vain, (quoting the author John):

"Catholicism will shrink greatly, no matter what."

Yes, in the United States, but the world is bigger than the United States (something I think we In the United States forget, especially Trump). Catholicism is alive and growing in many parts of the world and it's growing more conservative.

And it's the conservative led faiths in the United States that are growing, not the mainstream liberal churches.

And that conservatism is what has allowed us, sadly to have a president named Trump.

4. Taking a Favorable Stand

a. *Beyond Labeling the Pope*

Many of the readers do not appreciate Pope Francis being labelled a liberal.

One "Teresa" comments:

> The continual, often inaccurate "labeling" being applied in today's world is reflective of the divisiveness and only continues to fuel division. Furthermore, pigeonholing human beings into liberal vs. conservative, republican vs. democrat is futile. To me, Francis continues to send a powerful message.

> Follow Christ's teachings and be like Christ. Jesus didn't label people, but included everyone. He didn't mention the "rules" of communion, which were man-made by the Catholic Church. He didn't mention abortion, homosexuality, marriage among priests (which was certainty allowed in the ears' Church), euthanasia, birth control, mass in latin vs. native language, etc. I am a proud

Catholic but I am far more about Jesus Christ than about the man-made rules of the Church. We are given free will by God. Follow Christ and that is all need to make good choices. Pope Francis exemplifies this but Ross and other doctrinal Catholics just don't seem to get it.

Another reader "Alex" from Atlanta adds on to this discussion.

Ross Douthat's discussions of "conservative" and "liberal" Catholicism will remain murky until he recognizes that the divisions within the Church are marked not only by differences on matters of the degree of sexual/procreational regulation but also by differences regarding the salience of Biblical literalism and Christian charity.

"Dominic from Minneapolis" emphatically claims Pope Francis is not a liberal Pope:

If we consider the actual teachings of Jesus at all seriously, our current Pope is the true conservative—he is trying his best to keep those teachings alive in the tumultuous present. You, Mr. Douthat, make clear in your writing that you are a liberal, or even more, a radical Christian. The Core teachings mean very little to you, it IS the organizational gloss on those teachings you seek to defend, beginning with those of St. Paul. As Will Durant so tersely put it, "Protestantism is the victory of Paul over Peter. Fundamentalism is the victory of Paul over Christ." You, sir, are no conservative when it comes to the teachings of Jesus Christ.

"Patriciafrom CO" agrees that the Pope is not liberal for different reasons.

What I recall from my 8 years of Catholic grade school is that God speaks through the pope. And I believe that is what God is doing - expressing his desire to get back to the basics-for the Church to bring all his children in, show compassion, mercy, forgiveness, charity. As said below by Hla 3542, getting closer to God and loving God and each other are more important than doctrine. Let's stop our bickering about whether or not divorced people can receive communion and let's listen to God and welcome people back.

And as others have said, Pope Francis is not that liberal; he seems pretty middle of the road to me. still waiting for women priests.

Another reader "Douglas" notes the radicality of the Gospel.

You label Pope Francis a "Liberal." The only people who can say that are those who have completely forgotten how radical the Gospel can be.

The bishops of Vatican II were not "liberals." But they listened and acted.

Archbishop Romero was profoundly conservative – but he was martyred or his defence of the poor. Francis has a history of conservatism

Maybe, Ross, you'll be liberal too, if you took your faith and founder seriously.

"Dan Styer" has clear and logical argument to show that Pope Francis is not liberal.

We know that Francis is a liberal pope" writes Douthat. Does Francis support the ordination of women? No. Does Francis support local control of church property? No. Does Francis support the marriage of priests? No.

And even if Francis did answer "yes" to any of these questions, that wouldn't make him liberal: Many conservative faiths have been able to answer "yes" to ALL THREE of these questions for centuries.

My conclusions: (1) Francis is not a liberal pope. (2) Douthat is not a trustworthy columnist.

The last comment on "liberal Pope" by Cheryl perceives the humility of Pope Francis. So four old men, resistant to change of any kind and deeply protective of their own, are gone.

Pope Francis, I always remind myself as a former Catholic, does believe in the basic tenets of Catholicism. "Liberal" applied to him has come to mean love for all of humanity, and an understanding of the difference between good and the impossible adherence to strictures set down by an isolated - not quite celibate - bunch of powerful men which set up large numbers of humanity as unacceptable in the eyes of God as they framed him.

The official Church has done so much damage over time - in the obvious ways - the unending sexual abuse in every corner of the world - and not quite so obvious - rejection of people for divorce and remarriage (oh, yes, but acceptance thru annulment for those with realty big bucks) or for who they are, in terms of sexual identity. He does seem more Christ-like in his humility and that is as radical as he can get.

b. *Personal Charisma*

Many of the readers admire the personal charism of Pope Francis, as are evident from the following comments. "Aftervirtue" writes:

Reinhold Niebuhr chose not to force integration on his Detroit congregation, not because he was a segregationist, but rather because he recognized integration at the time would cause a schism from which the church was not likely to recover. Francis likewise treads thoughtfully and like Niebuhr recognizes that seismic changes sometimes do more harm than good. The time may perhaps be right to ease away from certain orthodoxies which have lost relevance and not quite right to throw the baby out with the bath water, so to speak. I'm not even a little religious, but given the choice between Bill Maher's self-assured progressive fanaticism and the Pope's center left version of the Church, I'd eagerly choose the latter as the less scary.[9]

EEE, another reader has a simple message:

Francis' impact for most of us is motivated by His public persona, and that is a clear message; Love Your Neighbor. Ah.... the power of positive leadership. So refreshing . We need not see how sausage is made though,

Ross, I appreciate your insights and efforts.

But from our God it's enough to see the finished products.... the Stars, The Fishes, the Heavens.... without seeing the gore and the cataclysms of the 7 days.

"Frustrated Elite and Stupid," reader elaborates on the Jesuit mold of Pope Francis.

As s gay catholic in my 50s I have been attending a parish that recently was handed over by the Archbishop to the Jesuits. Before we had a very old Irishman pastor who was hardliner in the mold of B16. I personally didn't mind the old man's railing about abortion or his passing references to evil lifestyles, presumably mine as that is how he interpreted catholic doctrine.

Admittedly living in Georgia the old man had quite s financial following with the older parishioners. Now the Jesuits have filled the parish with numerous young people, young families and the sacramental life of the church is enriching our worship. Of course, the Jesuits, being in the mold of Francis, transformed the parish by actually instituting reforms of Vatican II, among other changes. We have lost our financial health because apparently the old folks who were big givers couldn't handle the Jesuits' changes. While we have many more people, young people understandably are not as generous. I am not sure why we have to politicize every aspect of our lives, Ross.

Furthermore, Francis as Vicar rightly should concerned shut the future of who will do the work of the Gospel. Western Catholicism been reeling and desperately needs a future flock. Somehow that future under JP2 and B16 was hardly bright nor robust and the clergy it was refashioned by Ratzinger was not healthy either. I think Francis is making needed reforms. It's not simple as the petty politics we practice in the USA.

A Jesuit priest, Joseph A. Brown SJ, holds that Pope Francis provokes only because he consistently tries to witness to "servant leadership." His comments:

Having been a Jesuit for just a few years short of Pope Francis, I must ask a very simple question, "Just what constitutes a 'liberal Pope?'" Some might the risk of confounding themselves in trying to apply a label that has never been all that adhesive to singular, prophetic witnesses to "servant leadership."

Some days he is; some days he isn't. And then on other days he is and isn't, all within hours. I marvel at the how consistent Pope Francis is, and how provocative that consistency seems to be for those who study him.

This comment was recommended by 98 readers!

c. *Compassion and Forgiveness*

Bill perceives the "compassion and forgiveness" that Pope Francis personifies:

The Pope seems to be a kindly man who speaks of compassion and forgiveness for mankind. However, he has not been constructive in changing the most egregious of the failings of the Church in current times.

Married priest, both male and female, would be a boon to a modern Catholic Church. I would allow an infusion of persons of intellect and compassion into a priesthood that is lacking in those qualities. Further, it would help prevent the situation that has come to light in the past 20 years that has caused such embarrassment and loss of many faithful. Recognize divorce as a common necessity. People make mistakes and people change. And end the complete and embarrassing sham of Annulment.

Most importantly, sanction the reality of artificial birth control. The vast majority of Catholics believe in it as do the majority of philosophers and theologians within the church. It would be the single most important step in helping rid the world of hunger and poverty and making abortion a rare event.

Finally, recognize that sexual orientation is not a choice. It is a human condition.

The Church needs to prove its relevance to the humans of the 21st century.

Another admirer of Pope Francis, Joseph C Bickford, comments succinctly:

As a non-Catholic I find it easy to admire Pope Francis. He has energy and good will and seems to believe in many of the things I believe in and hope for in a church I respect and admire. The church is the longest living complex organization on earth and its strength serves many human and social needs. Nonetheless for me the key is to make permanent changes to improve the church: more power to the laity, ordination of women, a more realistic attitude towards divorce, homosexuality, and abortion. So far it seems there is good feeling, good personnel moves, but not much which will last

"Hia 3452 from Tulsa" relates Pope Francis' healthy connection to politics in bringing "fresh air and clean water" to the people of the word.

Francis is not about politics, although he has a voice and opinion about them.

I believe he is about spirituality and faith, not about religious doctrine. I think he is trying to see what separates us from God and what brings us closer. If men or religion or politics separate us from the love of God and one another, then there is the evil, call it the devil or darkness or whatever. And he wants to bring light and fresh air, clean water and food and shelter to eliminate the shadows.

Many readers, including John McDonald from Vancouver, Washington perceives the humility of Pope Francis and are captivated by the mercy of God. His comments are perceptive:

Ross Douthat mistakenly routes Pope Francis' attempts to bring his Church closer to its people as a political effort rather than what it really is, the work of a person who believes that humility and mercy should characterize this institution of vast wealth, influence, and more than a billion congregants worldwide.

Attempts to create a liberal or progressive, or conservative political profile for Francis confuses his motives by attaching a political ideology to it and trivializes both his closeness to the needs of ordinary people and his desire to lift them up. It minimizes his single-minded effort to bring back to Catholic worship former congregants who frankly have been humiliated by the Church, or even Church sanctions, because they are divorced, or made a personal choice that does not comport with what some describe as arbitrary and capricious doctrine.

I agree as some have commented that he is today a genuinely kind and forgiving person whose foremost desire is to cast this institution in the ways and lessons of the founder, and his actions carry meaning. His motives may include the restoration of the Church's influence in making secular governments more attentive to the needs of the people they govern. Is this a bad thing? I think not. I would not allow myself to be fooled by the subtleties of his actions, either. Starting with changes made at the Vatican Bank, he has support from his caucus of cardinals, and more importantly, from the membership.

Finally, another reader "Tom J" puts it succinctly:

It seems not to occur to you that the Pope's actions are guided by prayer and humility rather than political maneuvering. Your belief is an example of the problem.

It may be noted that when "Tom j" speaks of "guided by prayer and humility," he is referring to discernment of the spirit, which Pope Francis has ardently been advocating.

5. The Analysis: "Guided by Prayer and Humility"

From the above select comments, it is obvious that the reaction to the article has been mixed. As indicated in the outline, there are some negative criticism against the author and even against the Newspaper for having published this piece. Furthermore, there are couple of comments hostile to the Pope and the Church.

But the general sense of the comments, as evident especially from the Reader's Picks and the Newspaper's picks, is positive. To highlight some of the comments:

The Pope cannot be judged as liberal or conservative. He is a moderate, with conservative and liberal tendencies.

There is praise for the Pope for his effort to bring in compassion in a spirit of humility and openness. "More humanity and compassion for the less fortunate."

There is high regard for going beyond the confines of the institutional Church and addressing the larger issues facing the world: poverty, nuclear disarmament and ecological concerns.

On the whole, roughly 85% of the comments are appreciative of the Pope, some even going to defend his position. They believe that the Pope is truly "guided by prayer and humility."

It may be noted most of the respondents are secular people who may not be Christians. As far as the designation of the commentators are concerned, there is only one comment by a Jesuit priest. What is interesting is that this motley group of people, who can criticise or correct the Pope, and who are not bound by Catholic loyalty, is on the whole highly appreciative of the Pope's words and actions.

Conclusion

In spite of some reservations and unfavourable views, the study on the article and on its comments find that the readers have a highly favourable opinion on the Pope. It is remarkable that more than 80% of 229 comments reflect a remarkably good impression of the Pope.

"Guided by prayer and humility" could be the catchword to describe Pope Francis' five years as a Pope, which necessarily demands continuous discernment.

Endnotes

1   Ross DOUTHAT. 2017. "Pope Francis' Next Act." *The New York Times.* July 15. https:// www.nytimes.com/2017/07/15/opinion/sunday/pope-francis-next-act.html. It may also be noted that I have not strictly followed the qualitative research methodology of social sciences, but have drawn valuable insights from this research methodology. I want to thank Dr. Dinesh Braganza for his helpful suggestions.

2   Mark OPPENHEIMER. 2010. "Ross Douthat's Fantasy World – Mother Jones." February.   http://www.motherjones.com/politics/2010/01/ross-douthat-new-york-times-conservatism/.

3   *The New York Times.* (2017, July 29). In *Wikipedia, The Free Encyclopedia.* Retrieved 23:26, July 29, 2017, from https://en.wikipedia.org/w/index.php?title=The_New_York_Times&oldid=792969085.

4   DOUTHAT. 2017. "Pope Francis' Next Act." *The New York Times.* July 15. https://www. nytimes.com/2017/07/15/opinion/sunday/pope-francis-next-act.html.

5   Catholic Church and Francis, Pope. *Amoris laetitia = The joy of love: on love in the family* - Post-synodal Apostolic exhortation. Vatican City: Vatican Press. 2016. Dated 19 March 2016, and released on 8 April 2016. See also Pentin, Edward. 2017. "Pope Francis Thanks Maltese Bishops for 'Amoris Laetitia' Guidelines | Ncregister.Com." April 6. http://www. ncregister.com/blog/edward-pentin/pope-francis-thanks-maltese-bishops-for-amoris-laetitia-guidelines.

6   For understanding the issues related to the dubia, please see Alt, Scott Eric. 2017. "The Incoherence of 'Just Clarify Amoris! Answer the Dubia!'" *Patheos.* April 24. http://www. patheos.com/blogs/scottericalt/incoherence-just-clarify-amoris-answer-dubia/.

7   For the tragic story of the child Charlie Gard, who is supported by both Pope Francis and President Trump, see Kevin RAWLINSON. 2017. "Charlie Gard: Pope and Trump Biggest Help in Keeping Him Alive, Says Mother | UK News | The Guardian." July 10. https:// www.theguardian.com/uk-news/2017/jul/10/charlie-gard-pope-and-trump-biggest-help-in-keeping-him-alive-says-mother.

8   It may be noted that as far as possible, I have not corrected the spelling mistakes or capitalisation, to respect the informal nature of the comments.

9   William (Bill) Maher is an American comedian, political commentator, and television host. For some of the controversies connected with this liberal political activist, see Itzkoff, Dave. 2017. "Bill Maher Apologizes for Use of Racial Slur on 'Real Time' - The New York Times." *The New York Times.* June 3. https://www.nytimes.com/2017/06/03/arts/television/bill-maher-n-word.html.

Our Contributors

A. Pushparajan was the Professor and the Head, of Interreligious Relations Dept., Madurai Kamaraj University, Coordinator of the School of Philosophy and Religions in the same University. He has authored 20 books, contributed over 350 articles in research journals, and presented over 400 papers in national and international seminars, symposia and conferences. He had been a Consulter to Pontifical Council for Faith and Culture and an Awardee of Charles Wallace Fellow in Dept. of Religions and Theology.

Ananya Dutta worked as a journalist for over six years with *The Hindu* and subsequently *The Times of India*. She got training as a journalist at the Asian College of Journalism. She is currently a Teaching Assistant at the Symbiosis School for Liberal Arts, Pune where she teaches courses in Media and Literature. Her areas of interest are women and media, freedom of the press and cinematic adaptation of literary texts.

Antony D'Cruz J.O. Praem, a prolific writer, did his doctorate in Theology from Gregorian University and is specialised in Indian Ecclesiology.

Errol A. D'Lima SJ taught Systematic Theology at the Faculty of Theology, Jnana-Deepa Vidyapeeth, Pune for three decades and at present he is emeritus at the same faculty. He was the President of Indian Theological Association and was the general editor of the Encyclopaedia of Christianity in India.

Francis Arackal did his PG Diploma in Media studies from Griffith College, Dublin, Ireland, and Licence and Doctorate in Social Sciences, specializing in media, from Gregorian and St. Thomas Universities in Rome. Licenciate in Philosophy from St. Thomas University, Rome. Taught Media, and Philosophy for 22 years at many Institutes and colleges. Has published five books. Presented papers in national and international conferences and seminars. Published scientific papers in reputed journals. He has a significant presence in online media with a personal website, blogs, and social networking pages. At present he is a Professor of Journalism and Mass Communication at Amity University, Gurgaon, Haryana.

Francis Gonsalves SJ, a Gujarat Jesuit, has taught at Vidyajyoti College, Delhi, for 18 years, being Principal for 4 years. He has authored 5 books, edited 6, and publishes regularly in India and abroad. Currently, he teaches Systematic Theology at Jnana-Deepa Vidyapeeth, Pune.

Gayatri Mendanha holds masters' degrees in both Philosophy and English. She is currently an Assistant Professor at the Symbiosis School for Liberal Arts, Pune where she teaches courses in Philosophy and Literature. She is a visiting faculty at Jnana-Deepa Vidyapeeth. Her areas of interest are religious literature, hermeneutics and modern drama.

George Therukaattil MCBS holds Doctorates in Philosophy and Theology from the Catholic University of Louvain. He was the Head of the Department of Christian Studies at the University of Mysore and Associate Professor at Jnana-Deepa Vidyapeeth, Pune. He has authored many books and articles including 3 Volumes of *Compassionate Love-Ethics*. Email: geotheroo@gmail.com

Gregory Mathew Malayil, a Catholic Priest and a member of the Carmelites of Mary Immaculate (CMI), is a lecturer in the Faculty of Philosophy, Dharmaram Vidya Kshetram, Bengaluru. He has two Masters' Degree (Physics and Philosophy) to his credit. He secured a Doctorate in Physics from Cochin University of Science and Technology. His areas of academic interest include Cosmology, Consciousness and Science-Religion interface.

Isaac Parackal OIC is a Professor of Philosophy at Jnana-Deepa Vidyapeeth, who has been specializing on Metaphysics and Cosmotheandric Vision of Raimun Panikkar. He was the coordinator of Master's Programme in Philosophy for many years at JDV. He has been publishing numerous academic articles.

J. Charles Davis is a Priest of the Catholic Diocese of Jammu-Srinagar. He has a Doctorate in Moral Theology for his remarkable research on ethics of human embryonic stem cell research: proposals for a legal framework for India from the Jesuit University of Sankt Georgen, Frankfurt. He was a teaching faculty of Philosophy, Theology, Bioethics and Social Ethics at Jnana-Deepa Vidyapeeth, the Pontifical Academy of Philosophy and Religion and Director of JDV Centre for Applied Ethics, Pune. Presently, he is doing a postdoctoral research on human digntiy for bioethics and biolaw at the University of Freiburg with the prestigious Humboldt Research Fellowship awarded by the Alexander von Humboldt Research Foundation of the Federal Republic of Germany.

Jacob Naluparayil MCBS holds a Doctorate in Biblical Theology from SBF (Studium Biblicum Franciscanum) Jerusalem. He is a Professor of New Testament at St. Joseph's Pontifical Institute of Philosophy and Theology, Aluva since 2000. He was the Chief Editor of *Karunikan* theological monthly and co-founder of the national monthly *Smart Companion*. He has authored three books on Pope Francis, one of them becoming a best seller.

Jacob Parappally MSFS holds a Doctorate in Theology from the University of Freiburg, Germany. He taught systematic theology at Jnana-Deepa Vidyapeeth, Pune and served as the dean of the faculty of theology. He was the President of the Indian Theological Association and the Rector of Tejas Vidya Peetha, Bangalore. At present, he is the Chief Editor of the *Journal of Indian Theology*.

Jery Njaliath is pursuing his Doctorate in Bioethics and is currently Associate Director, Lisie Hospital, Ernakulam, Kerala.

Job Kozhamthadam SJ has specialised on Kepler and is the pioneer of science-religion dialogue in India. He is the founder-director of Indian Institute of Science and Religion.

Johnson J. Puthenpurackal OFM Cap has specialised on Heidegger and is a well known philosopher, author and Heidegger specialist, based in Eluru, AP. He has been the President of Association of Christian Philospher's of India and has been the Editor of ACPI Encyclopedia of Philosophy.

John Peter Vallabadoss OFM Cap has his PhD in Philosophy from Satyanilayam, Chennai and resides currently at St. Joseph's Capuchin Philosophical College, The Friary, Kotagiri, Nilgiris, T.N.

Joseph A. D'Mello SJ has specialised in Ignatian Spirituality and is currently Coordinator, PG Diploma in Ignatian Spirituality, JDV, Pune.

Kurien Kunnumpuram SJ was Rector of Jnana-Deepa Vidyapeeth and Founder-editor of Jnanadeepa: Pune Journal of Religious Studies. Author of numerous books, he is a systematic theologian, having specialised in the ecclesiology of Vatican Council II.

Kuruvilla Pandikattu SJ is Dean, Faculty of Philosophy, Jnana-Deepa Vidaypeeth, Pune. He has been involved in science-religion dialogue. Areas of interest: transhumanism, artificial intelligence, philosophical anthropology.

Mariapushpam Paul Raj is a priest from the diocese of Sivagangai, Tamil Nadu, and currently teaches Biblical Theology at Jnana-Deepa Vidyapeeth, Pune. He has a doctorate in Biblical Studies from the University of Innsbruck, Austria. His area of specialization is Pauline Theology. He is engaged in the formation of candidates for priesthood at Papal Seminary, Pune

Mathew Chandrankunnel CMI, is a member of the Carmelites of Mary Immaculate Congregation, taught at Dharmaram Vidya Kshetram and holds a doctorate from the University of Leuven, Belgium in comparing two interpretations in Quantum Mechanics and a Post doc from the Smithsonian Centre for Astrophysics, Harvard University, Boston, USA on the Physics,

Philosophy and Religion of Galileo. He was awarded by the CTNS-Templeton Prize and Mgr Mathew Mankuzhikaray Atmavidya Award. Some of his books are *Philosophy of Quantum Mechanics, Ascent to Truth, Navajeevasadhana* and *Cosmosophy.* At present, he is the Director of the Ecumenical Christian Centre, Whitefield, Bangalore and General Secretary of ACISCA, Association of Christian Institutions for Social Concerns in Asia.

Paul Thelakat is the Editor of the popular Christian magazine, *Sathyadeepam,* in Kerala and was the spokesperson of Syro-Malabar Church.

Rajakumar Joseph SJ, teaches Theology at Vidyajyoti College, Delhi. He holds a Doctorate in Systematic Theology from Johannes Gutenberg University, Germany. He is currently the Director of Distance Education Programme and is involved in socio-pastoral ministry.

S. Stephen Jayard, belonging to the Diocese of Tiruchirapalli, Tamil Nadu, teaches at the Faculty of Philosophy, Jnana-Deepa Vidyapeeth, Pune and is a formator at Papal Seminary. Having a Doctoral Degree in Philosophy of Science, he lectures at several Institutes and presents papers at the national / international conferences.

Thomas Kalary MSFS holds a doctorate in Philosophy from the University of Freiburg Germany. He teaches Philosophy at Suvidya College, Bangalore, Jnana-Deepa Vidyapeeth, Pune and St Joseph's Pontifical Institute, Aluva. He is the Associate Editor of the international philosophical journal Heidegger Studies and together with Parvis Emad translated from German Heidegger's work Besinnung/ Mindfulness.

Thomas Padiyath is a priest of the Archeparchy of Changanacherry, holding a PhD in Philosophy and STL in Theology from the Katholieke Universiteit Leuven, Belgium. He was, resident Professor at Good Shepherd Major Seminary Kunnoth from 2006 to 2015. At present, he is a resident Professor and Dean of studies at Paurastya Vidyanikethan, Changanacherry, Kerala and a visiting faculty at various Major Seminaries and ecclesiastical Institutions in Kerala and outside.

Victor Ferrao has done his doctorate in science-religion dialogue from Jnana-Deepa Vidyapeeth and is Dean of Philosophy, Rachol Seminary, Goa.